ACCELERATING LEAN SIX SIGMA RESULTS

*How to Achieve
Improvement Excellence^{TM}
in the New Economy*

Terence T. Burton

J.ROSS
PUBLISHING

Copyright © 2011 by Terence T. Burton

ISBN: 978-1-60427-054-9

Printed and bound in the U.S.A. Printed on acid-free paper
10 9 8 7 6 5 4 3 2 1

Library of Congress Cataloging-in-Publication Data

Burton, Terence T., 1950-
Accelerating lean six sigma results : how to achieve improvement
excellence in the new economy / by Terence T. Burton.
    p. cm.
  Includes index.
  ISBN 978-1-60427-054-9 (hbk. : alk. paper)
  1. Total quality management. 2. Cost effectiveness. 3. Cost control. 4. Six sigma (Quality
control standard) I. Title.
  HD62.15.B8667 2011
  658.4'013—dc22

                                                              2010049163

Phone: (954) 727-9333
Fax: (561) 892-0700
Web: www.jrosspub.com

Contents

PART III: Next Generation Lean Six Sigma: The Intersection of Leadership, Innovation, and Enabling Technology

Chapter 14   Greatest Opportunities: Transactional Business Process Improvement..................................... 329

Preface

Today, most organizations are still emerging from the largest recession since the Great Depression. The recent meltdown has created a disturbing trend where leaders have their organizations stuck in short-term survival mode. Granted, many of these immediate survival tactics were necessary and well meant as the financial crisis unfolded before our eyes. However, too many executives are continuing to drive their businesses in this short-term, reactionary survival mode. These respective inconsistent leadership behaviors are a major contributor to recent benchmarking data indicating that over 80 percent of Lean, Six Sigma, and Lean Six Sigma deployments are now unsuccessful. When these improvement initiatives slide towards failure, it is not the fault of Lean Six Sigma, and these initiatives can be turned around into sustainable benchmark successes. Today, many organizations could add more to their top and bottom lines through successful improvement initiatives than they will add via their current scattered hot lists of daily actions. Organizations placed a freeze on improvement when they needed it the most. In all fairness to some executives, their Lean Six Sigma initiatives needed to be stopped because they were producing more waste than value. However, there is a serious flaw in this leadership thinking that has existed for over three decades: when things get tight, improvement is the first casualty. When things get better, improvement is also the first casualty. When organizations take their eye off the ball, the word *continuous* falls out of *continuous improvement*. It is obvious that the only way to become more competitive, more efficient, more customer focused, and more financially successful as a business and organization is to *continuously improve* the current state. If so, then why do leaders constantly make comments such as, "There's no money in the budget for improvement," or "The time is not quite right for improvement," or "We don't have time to improve," or "We had to cut back on improvement."

Executives do not always think through the ramifications of their communications and actions; they get caught up in the moment by short-term pressures and prettying up the financial statements. Consequently, organizations are once again on the verge of watching Lean Six Sigma (another solid improvement initiative) fail after investing millions in it—just as all the other fad programs for the past three decades have failed.

In the new economy, organizations cannot afford to brush off improvement as a non-essential element of strategy. However, a different improvement model is needed. Organizations need a more simplified, less overhead intense, sustainable, high-impact and high-ROI approach to improvement. The next challenge for organizations is not the latest repackaged improvement program and another *train-the-masses* effort: it is improving how they improve. Lean Six Sigma and other strategic improvement initiatives require new thinking and a new model— one that is a targeted and scalable approach, a lean and rapid deployment, a higher focus on core enterprise and extra-enterprise transactional processes, and that features rapid results with sustainable continuous improvement.

Accelerating Lean Six Sigma Results: How to Achieve Improvement Excellence^{TM} *in the New Economy* provides real-world direction on this new improvement agenda of rapid deployment and results. This book helps executives and leaders turn the tide from the recent meltdown, where 95 percent of their organization's time can be spent on getting and keeping things right, rather than on reacting to things that go wrong. Drawing on nearly four decades of business improvement experiences, the author provides proven guidance to executives and deployment leaders (who are responsible for strategic improvement) about how to lead and sustain improvement, transform culture, and achieve superior industry performance. The 15 chapters of the book center around five major themes, followed by practical, how-to-do discussions, case studies, and proven professional advice. The following provides an overview of these major themes.

1. *The importance of leadership strategy and vision, deployment planning, and execution infrastructure as the successful business architecture and improvement foundation (Chapter 1).* This is the underpinning of the core competency of Improvement Excellence^{TM}—the mastery of developing and implementing successful strategic and continuous business improvement initiatives, transforming culture, and enabling organizations to improve how they improve. This chapter provides guidance on the following areas:
    *   The true root causes of Lean Six Sigma and other improvement failures
    *   Developing the formal implementation architecture
    *   Understanding Improvement Excellence™

2. *Scalable Lean Six Sigma, a rapid deployment and rapid results model that aligns improvement to critical and selective strategic business needs (Chapter 2).* This accelerated improvement model addresses the realities of the new economy, with the primary focus on breakthrough performance and sustaining improvement instead of focusing on the traditional approaches of training the masses, certification, and belts. This rapid deployment, rapid results model demands that executives recognize and correct their cultural detractors to successful improvement initiatives. This chapter includes the following topics:
    *   Acceleration entrapment
    *   Improvement-dysfunctional organizations
    *   The separation disorder of improvement

- Scalable Lean Six Sigma™
- Rapid deployment, rapid and sustainable results
- Emergence of transactional enterprises
- The future of improvement

3. *The 10 Accelerators of Lean Six Sigma and other strategic improvement initiatives (Chapter 3, overview; Chapters 4–13, detailed discussion of each accelerator).* This is the full description of the strategic leadership and vision, deployment planning, and execution success infrastructure, with instructions on how to build this foundation for improvement success. Chapters 4–13 provide significant infrastructure details behind the Scalable Lean Six Sigma™ deployment model, and specifically how to use each of the 10 Accelerators to increase the velocity, magnitude, and sustainability of improvement initiatives, particularly within key business processes and other selected strategic activities. The accelerators are presented with practical applications and case studies based on several Lean Six Sigma benchmark deployments. In Chapters 3–13, readers will learn about the following topics:
   - Behavioral alignment and leadership best practices
   - Improvement strategy and vision
   - Planning, sponsoring, and chartering improvement initiatives
   - Defining, scoping, and assigning improvement-actionable projects
   - Customized education and talent development
   - Leadership of communication and change management
   - Building the best talent and learning organization
   - Leveraged mentoring best practices
   - Monitoring and measuring overall deployment success
   - Managing and integrating the accelerators, optimizing results
   - Control, validation, and sustaining improvement
   - Concurrent continuous deployment practices

4. *The future: improving the new network of interconnected transactional enterprises that are present within, and beyond the four walls of organizations (Chapter 14).* This chapter covers the need, thinking, and methodology to evolve Lean Six Sigma creatively and in a manner that enables a greater focus on transactional and knowledge process improvement. Topics in Chapter 14 include:
   - The migration to transactional enterprises
   - Challenges of complex, multistage transactional processes
   - Discussions of over 25 actual client transactional process improvement examples that have generated millions of dollars in savings, complete with specific process guidance and case studies

5. *The intersection of leadership, improvement, and technology (Chapter 15).*
   This chapter discusses the emergence of technology and how it is changing the business of strategic improvement. The author provides valuable
   information about how Lean Six Sigma and improvement in general
   must evolve so that it is readily applicable to current and emerging technology, which continues to replace the physical content of traditional improvement with digital organizations and cyber enterprises. This chapter
   covers the following topics:
   • Why IT matters in strategic improvement
   • Technology entrapment
   • Technology in the learning enterprise
   • Fusion roles of leadership, improvement, and technology
   • The new economy: fusion equals success

The purpose of this book is to provide a practical guide for strategic business improvement. Unlike most other books on Lean Six Sigma and other improvement
techniques, this book provides the proven leadership, business infrastructure, and
creative applications of Lean Six Sigma and other strategic improvement initiatives. Much of the knowledge, experiences, and the most critical infrastructure
success factors presented in this book have, at best, been superficially covered in
other improvement books. The book also includes many new applications areas
and case studies of Lean Six Sigma and strategic improvement in general. These
include larger-scale strategic transactional processes such as sales and marketing,
new product definition and development, supply chain management, outsourcing and supplier management, finance, strategic planning, customer service, acquisitions, advertising and promotions, field service and spares management, strategic maintenance management, information technology, utilities and facilities
management, and several other core transactional activities that represent millions of dollars in opportunity for most organizations. Much of this book is about
real-world strategic improvement and benchmark success, created and written
from actual client implementation experiences. Several case studies and guest
article contributions from various industry executives reinforce the reality and
results by following the book's demonstrated advice.

The new economy has created unlimited opportunities to grow revenue, implement industry best practices, and achieve superior global performance. Success or failure at these new opportunities is a matter of executive choice. Many
organizations have made the leadership shift from survival to strategic success
and are emerging in the post-recession environment with impressive operating
results. The most successful organizations stayed the course of strategic improvement before, during, and after the recession. The real challenge to every organization is keeping that key word *continuous* in continuous improvement. The limits
of improvement are the self-imposed mind limits that executives and organizations choose to place on it—unintentionally or otherwise. The core competency

of Improvement Excellence™, the Scalable Lean Six Sigma™ model, and the 10 Accelerators of Lean Six Sigma results provide this proven path to continuous and sustainable strategic improvement, and offer a great fit for the challenges of the new economy.

Terence T. Burton, President
The Center for Excellence in Operations (CEO)
Bedford, New Hampshire
www.ceobreakthrough.com

Acknowledgments

I have reached that pinnacle and reflection point in my career of continuous improvement, which has spanned nearly four decades. If I could mention the names of everyone who has influenced my ability to write this current book, the acknowledgement section would be larger than the book itself. *Accelerating Lean Six Sigma Results: How to Achieve Improvement Excellence™ in the new Economy*, is a compilation of several decades of learning, knowledge, and experiences implementing various successful strategic improvement initiatives in a wide variety of organizations and countries.

Believe me, I am proud to wear the scuffed knees and battle scars of these improvement initiatives: Time and Motion Studies, Scientific Inventory Management, MTM and Therbligs, MODAPTS, Short Interval Scheduling (SIS), Operations Research, Quality Circles, PDCA, Kepner-Tregoe (KT), Total Quality Management (TQM), Productivity, Human Factors and Ergonomics, Simulation Modeling, Little mrp, Distribution Requirements Planning (DRP), MRPII, ERP, Just-In-Time (JIT), OPT, APICS Certification, Statistical Process Control (SPC), Value Engineering (VE), EVOP and Optimization Studies, Boothroyd-Dewhurst DFMA, Total Preventive Maintenance (TPM), Single Minute Exchange of Die (SMED), Continuous Flow Manufacturing (CFM), Pipeline Inventory Management, Demand Flow Technology (DFT), Sales and Operations Planning (S&OP), the Toyota Production System (TPS), Business Process Reengineering (BPR), Theory of Constraints (TOC), Activity Based Costing (ABC), Benchmarking, Balanced Scorecard, Supply Chain Operations Reference Model or SCOR, Product and Cycle Time Excellence (PACE), TRIZ, Economic Value Added (EVA), Supplier Relationship Management (SRM), Supply Chain Management (SCM), Customer Relationship Management (CRM), Product Life Cycle Management (PLM), Value Stream Mapping (VSM), 5S, 6S, 7S, Lean, Six Sigma, Outside In (OI), Lean Six Sigma, and probably a few others that I have neglected to mention.

After all this effort and billions of dollars in investment, most organizations are still struggling to get continuous improvement right. The normal practice has been to jump on a fad improvement program, ride the bandwagon for a while, and then sweep it under the corporate rug and move on to the next one. Organizations eventually forget what happened with their last effort, but they are always in a hurry to repeat the same mistakes with the next improvement program. This strategy of improvement fails to understand the true root causes of improvement failures, and so organizations build their track record of unsustainable or failed continuous improvement initiatives. Most of it is due to wavering leadership, the implementation process (infrastructure and approach), and a zealous fixation on the tools themselves. Throughout my book, the ugly facts that surround these issues are not criticism—it is a simply a fact that leaders must deal with *head on* if they ever hope to achieve sustaining success with Lean Six Sigma and other strategic improvement initiatives. Most recently, I have been blessed by working with so many executives and organizations that have stepped up and embraced this different thinking, a different approach, and a different business model in response to the new economy; this is the essence of and the urgent need for my latest book.

At the top of my acknowledgment list are my family and friends who tolerated the lunatic dedication and passion that it takes to write a book. I sincerely tried to write as much as I could in hotel rooms, limo rides, and airline flights. However, the closet author thing just was not enough to create a book to my liking. I know this latest work consumed many weekends, holidays, vacation time, early mornings and late nights, and caused many delayed meals and missed personal and social events. The *process* of writing this book represents my ongoing commitment and personal signature to drive for excellence and superior performance, as I always advise clients and others around me to do. Writing a book also requires leadership, unwavering commitment, visionary thinking, planning, patience, discipline, structure, continuous effort, and delivering a useful and pleasurable customer experience. Unfortunately, this requires a significant investment in time and resources (but it takes a lot less time and resources doing the right things right the first time than it takes to do things over or to do 50 percent of the job and fail). I am blessed by the patience and understanding of my family and friends. Just as my family and friends close to my latest book project heard the message, you will hear this message loud and clear many times throughout the book.

Next, I wish to acknowledge the hundreds of client organizations and employers who provided the opportunity to develop our business improvement skills together. I have consciously decided not to attempt naming everyone, because it is inevitable that I would unintentionally fail to mention dozens and dozens of names. I am blessed by a career that has allowed me to work with over 300 corporations and thousands of executives around the globe on an unlimited spectrum of strategic improvement challenges. I used to have a fear of meeting a client that we could not help, but the right combination of external and internal expertise always creates the *big bang* of new improvement opportunities—most of the time at a level that we all thought originally to be impossible or unreachable. Of course, the individuals that really made things happen were the hundreds of thousands of employees in these organizations that worked elbow-to-elbow with us on many continuous improvement activities. I thank you for the experiences and realization of mutual success and the many lasting friendships that have resulted from our engagements. I cannot remember all of the names, but I enjoy thousands of positive flashbacks of working together and overcoming the challenges of improvement. Together we learned that strategic and sustaining improvement requires much more than a superficial striking up of the band and crashing the cymbals. The successes that we have shared are the best successes possible. First, it is success through multidirectional learning—learning and developing from each other's knowledge and expertise. Second, it is the kind of successes that positively affect people's careers, families, and lives in general. Personally, you have all helped me to grow an incredible knowledge base of implementation experiences, fun times, and lasting memories. Over the years, it has given me great pleasure and satisfaction to help and watch people integrate their improvement experiences and grow from an hourly or tier-1 salaried position to a competent and well-respected executive. For those of you who have worked directly with me, I am confident that you will smile and reminisce as you read this book because is all about the challenging journeys of our shared success, personal discovery, and fun.

A bit of literary trivia (true story): during one of our consulting assignments in the UK, I was wandering around London one late rainy Saturday afternoon and decided to visit the city's oldest pub, Ye Olde Cheshire Cheese, established in 1538. Upon entering this quaint little dim place with its own gloomy charm and coal fireplace, it was like stepping into another world; everything looked as if it had been there since 1538. It is a historical landmark and a hidden gem where one might meet anyone from a group of American Airlines flight attendants from Dallas, a few celebrities from Los Angeles, a politician from Greenwich, a vacationing couple from Calgary, a few soccer players from Italy, or some of the local regulars. I ordered my pint of the hand-pulled Sam Smiths lager, and then struck up a conversation with an elderly chap dressed in full tweeds, complete with the carved ivory handle cane and Sherlock Holmes cap. He proceeded to tell me about the pub's history as a place frequented by many famous literary figures such as Charles Dickens, Samuel Johnson, Edgar Allen Poe, Mark Twain, Oliver Goldsmith, Alfred Tennyson, and others. You could overhear everyone in the place giving more details about the pub's history. Then, I was encouraged to sit in a corner at the bench where Charles Dickens wrote *A Tale of Two Cities* (the pub is mentioned several times in the book). I was told that this particular bench was the seat of choice for several of these literary figures. Edgar Allen Poe supposedly passed out in this seat from a little overindulgence while working on his famous poem *The Raven* (based on the Tower of London just down the street, with its gory reputation for torture and its wing-clipped ravens perched at night throughout the fog-covered yards). The bench was actually worn as if it was carved for comfort. It was a seat where you could observe everything in the pub, but patrons might not notice your presence. During this bit of soak time (I was soaked from the rain) I was thinking about our client's Lean project and their early and impressive successes. Then, I began reflecting on why so many improvement initiatives have failed over the years. I also thought about all the fly-by-night improvement programs, the vanished experts, and all the textbooks that focused on tools, but missed the mark on the true critical success factors of successful improvement initiatives.

I reaffirmed within my own conscience that I could never write another book about my thoughts—it is too much time and effort, I am too busy working all over the place, there are already too many improvement books, and a few other excuses. I am not sure if it was the ambiance and the warm fireplace, the vibes from Dickens, Poe, Twain and others, or the pint of Sam Smiths at work. But this is where I began roughing out the original notes and sketches, and architecting the ideas and concept for this book. I felt an extremely strong need to share and give back the knowledge and experiences that I have gained about what really matters with successful improvement initiatives. So, I owe an honorable mention to the Ye Olde Cheshire Cheese for the magical inspiration or spiritual powers that may have been present that rainy afternoon.

Next, I want to thank the dozens of universities, professional societies, industry and trade associations and associated publications, various software user groups and sponsors of best practices summits, executive roundtable groups, Web sites, fellow authors and publishers, targeted seminar organizers, and many other enablers of learning and talent development that I have actively participated in as a student, author, instructor, facilitator, keynote speaker, webcast presenter, quoted executive, etc. I also thank the wide network of affiliates and industry partners that we have worked with for mutual advantage and mutual learning and development. We are all so fortunate to have access to this great learning and talent development infrastructure, and technology continues to make this access easier, broader, and more widespread. This book is my personal commitment to add to this great learning infrastructure and to give back and share the collected experiences and wisdom that has been bestowed upon me.

Finally, a special thanks to my publisher Drew Gierman and the staff at J. Ross Publishing. I enjoy working with this organization because they practice what I preach. They know how to put continuous improvement and technology into action. They have replaced the traditional stodgy publishing methods of the large publishers with lean, nimble, superior quality and velocity-conscious best practices. Although I may say, "This is it!" after writing every book, I look forward to working with Drew and J. Ross Publishing in the future.

About the Author

Terence T. Burton is President of The Center for Excellence in Operations, Inc. (CEO), a management consulting firm headquartered in Bedford, New Hampshire, with offices in Munich, Germany. Terry has over thirty-five years of experience in operations, quality, engineering, supply chain management, distribution and logistics, maintenance and repair, customer service, finance, and sales/marketing. He is best known for his "hands-on" approach to consulting and his executive leadership in transforming organizations.

Prior to his consulting career, Terry held several senior executive and line management positions at Wang Labs, Polaroid, and Atlantic Richfield, and practice leadership positions with two other international consulting firms—KPMG Peat Marwick, and Pittiglio, Rabin, Todd, & McGrath (PRTM). Terry has extensive and diversified business improvement experience with over 300 clients in North America and Europe, ranging from large diversified international Fortune 500 corporations to small and mid-sized companies.

Terry holds a B.S. and M.S. in Industrial Engineering from the University of New Haven, and an MBA from Boston University. He is a certified Six Sigma Black Belt and a former National LEAN SIG Chairman of APICS. He has held other national positions with AME, ASQ, and PDMA. Terry is a frequent speaker and webinar presenter for many industry and professional associations and he has written hundreds of articles on business process improvement for various trade publications. He is co-author of five books, including *The Lean Extended Enterprise: Moving Beyond the Four Walls to Value Stream Excellence* and *Six Sigma for Small and Mid-Sized Organizations: Success Through Scaleable Deployment* published by J. Ross Publishing, Inc.

Web
Added
Value™

This book has free material available for download from the
Web Added Value™ resource center at **www.jrosspub.com**

At J. Ross Publishing we are committed to providing today's professional with practical, hands-on tools that enhance the learning experience and give readers an opportunity to apply what they have learned. That is why we offer free ancillary materials available for download on this book and all participating Web Added Value™ publications. These online resources may include interactive versions of material that appears in the book or supplemental templates, worksheets, models, plans, case studies, proposals, spreadsheets and assessment tools, among other things. Whenever you see the WAV™ symbol in any of our publications, it means bonus materials accompany the book and are available from the Web Added Value Download Resource Center at www.jrosspub.com.

Downloads available for *Accelerating Lean Six Sigma Results: How to Achieve Improvement Excellence™ in the New Economy* include:

- Industry Week and SAP sponsored Improvement Excellence™ presentations, guest executive contributed articles and insights, real cases of Lean Six Sigma deployment experiences, and specific examples of transactional enterprise improvement
- Frameworks of the Center for Excellence in Operations Business Mastery, Improvement Excellence™, Scalable Lean Six Sigma™, and 10 Accelerators of Lean Six Sigma Results models
- Best practice models for leadership behavior, effective communication, leveraged mentoring, and deployment planning, and guidance for Macro Charter planning and project prioritization, skills assessment, resource deployment, and specific strategic project charters
- Templates, critical metrics and progress assessment tools for Lean Six Sigma and other strategic improvement initiatives
- A special report entitled *Improvement Excellence™ in the Federal Government: Addressing the Urgent Need to Reduce Waste and Deficit Spending, and Improve Service Delivery* which demonstrates how strategic leadership and vision, deployment planning, and execution infrastructure can transform the processes of government and eliminate significant waste.

PART I:
Accelerating Lean Six Sigma Results—The C-Level View

"The ancestor of every action is a thought"
Ralph Waldo Emerson

1

Improvement Excellence™: The Missing Factor

Lean Six Sigma 2010 and Beyond—The Jury Is Out

Lean Six Sigma . . . if your organization is not actively engaged in an initiative to significantly improve your business, you are the exception. You are also rapidly losing competitive ground in today's global economy. Only those who dwell in caves have not been privy to the publicity and widespread awareness and successes of Lean Six Sigma. We are living in exponential times, and great organizations recognize the need to continuously improve if they do not want to fall behind in this economy. More bad news: if your organization is actively engaged in Lean Six Sigma, the chances of a failed deployment exceed 80 percent! Yes, that is correct—80 percent or more—this is based on the consistent findings of many private and university benchmarking studies. Why would an executive lead their organization down a path with an 80 percent (or more) failure rate? The answer is simple: business improvement is not an option. Lean Six Sigma success or failure is a simple executive choice, the risk of failure is low with the right leadership and deployment infrastructure, and every organization needs to continuously improve their business to remain competitive. In addition, the failures are not the fault of Lean Six Sigma. There are some very impressive stories in the successful 20 percent segment, which also validates the power of Lean Six Sigma when deployed correctly.

This recent trend with Lean Six Sigma is not new. It is just the latest casualty of continuous improvement that has existed for three decades. To reverse this 30-year trend of failed improvement programs, it is time to challenge the elegant theories of Lean Six Sigma and strategic improvement in general with the ugly facts. If you are an executive, you will read many controversial points in this book about failed leadership, which has a significant impact on Lean Six Sigma or business improvement success in general. The purpose is not to slam

3

our executive friends, discredit the thousands of people giving it their all with continuous improvement, or self-promote Lean Six Sigma as the silver bullet or mystical cure-all for business challenges. However, the reality is that the recent economic meltdown and the responses of many executives to crawl out of it, has reduced the urgency for improvement and taken their organization's Lean Six Sigma initiatives off point. A successful Lean Six Sigma deployment has the highest ROI of almost everything else an organization can do in this uncertain warp-speed economy.

The Anatomy of Failed Improvement Programs, 2010 Edition

Unsuccessful Lean Six Sigma deployments follow one of the following three familiar lifecycles:

1. Organizations go it on their own, through what they believe to be the right actions such as widespread black belt education and development, identification of improvement projects, a perceived right level of executive support, and high visibility through numerous review meetings. These deployments may or may not produce early successes, the implementation and sustainment factors are downplayed, and eventually there are no measurable and lasting gains for all the costs and resources consumed on Lean Six Sigma. Commitment wavers and executives eventually abandon the effort and look for other improvement alternatives. Some organizations have terminated black belts, after having invested about $100,000 each for their development. Executives needed to cut back on visible financial statement costs such as improvement expenses in response to the meltdown to keep Wall Street happy. The same birth-death cycle of improvement has happened with previous improvement programs, and not surprisingly, it is happening again.

2. Organizations begin their deployments with a high level of excitement, enthusiasm, and commitment to success. An outside expert is usually engaged to help launch the deployment and provide black-belt training. Early progress reinforces the interest and commitment but over time, executive directions waver and motivation declines, and the organization slides backward to old habits and business as usual. This usually occurs after the outside expert leaves and the constructive irritant forces are removed, or as the organization shifts course and commitment shifts from improvement to other more pressing developments. People are left frustrated by this falloff of commitment and are not interested in being involved in other future improvement initiatives. Organizations also may go through several identical cycles with a variety of other improvement initiatives and gurus.

3. Organizations follow the herd with a disconnected approach focused on just one improvement label, such as: Lean, Kaizen, Six Sigma, 5S etc. There is a lack of understanding and commitment on behalf of the

leadership, and there are foregone conclusions about what needs to improve. The tool zealots and tool puppets begin by copying a perception of something they have learned about in a book, trade publication, seminar, or plant tour. Then, they run aimlessly around the organization with their foreign vocabulary of improvement terms trying to shoehorn in the Toyota Production System (TPS) or demonstrating application of the tools instead of solving strategic problems. Some of these tool heads spend more time in discussion forums on isixsigma.com or playing a name-that-tool game in a LinkedIn group than they spend implementing improvement. Improvement is set up for failure from the get-go. The effect lasts about as long as a bad stomachache and things slide back to business as usual. The people who understand how improvement could benefit the organization become very frustrated. Leadership is busy focusing on the next fire. The people who were not interested in improvement now have the opportunity to tout, "See I told you it wouldn't work here. We're different from any other organization you've worked with." That is for sure! Organizationally, improvement becomes a self-fulfilled prophecy of failure.

For decades, organizations have had the best of intentions when implementing improvement initiatives, but their actions have turned out to define the *laws of unintended consequences* with improvement. Executives who have been scuffing their knees with continuous improvement initiatives for several decades agree that the patterns of failure are similar and repetitive.

Maybe We Need a Lean Six Sigma Comeback

Back on September 10, 2009, *Business Week* published an article titled, "Six Sigma Makes a Comeback." This article included several large companies who have been involved in Six Sigma for years, and who have spent millions of dollars on training the masses and belts with little to show for it—that is, until the economy melted down and they were now becoming more serious about improvement. This article was both disturbing and confusing to many professionals, executives, and practitioners who have successfully leveraged the power of Lean Six Sigma and have achieved annualized improvement results exceeding 3 to 10 percent of their revenues! From the perspective of the glass is half full, a comeback is better than disappearing for good, particularly when the dramatic results are widely documented for successful deployments. This is the typical story in most organizations deploying Lean Six Sigma and many of their previous continuous improvement efforts. The *Business Week* article is symptomatic of poorly deployed Lean Six Sigma initiatives in these and so many other organizations. Why did they allow so much time, resources, and funds invested in training and certifying champions, master black, black, green, yellow, and white belts, and then do nothing? Where did Lean Six Sigma go since these organizations, and many others, began their deployments? What was everyone doing with Lean Six Sigma before this comeback? Why have so many organizations invested millions (and collectively, billions) of dollars in what has evolved to nothing more than another failed fad improvement program with nothing to show for it? These and many other organizations would be embarrassed to disclose how much has been spent on developing belts and how many of each level resided in their companies prior to the supposed Lean Six Sigma comeback of 2009. Here is the fundamental problem: Lean Six Sigma has become nothing more than another train-the-masses fiasco in many organizations. There is no correlation between *belts* and *results*, and the more important success factors are missing in organizations. If one looks at the history of improvement, organizations repeatedly buy into this aimless and hollow train-the-masses approach to no avail. Lean Six Sigma deployments have followed this same approach in many organizations, and the results are analogous to spreading fertilizer on the Sahara Desert hoping to realize a bravura crop harvest. In some organizations, Lean Six Sigma has been a fraudulent consulting effort delivered by opportunistic people who went through black-belt certification and are able to read a PowerPoint presentation to an audience, but have never changed anything! People have focused more on training and belts rather than on strategic vision, deployment planning, execution, and results. This is a leadership and deployment problem, not a Lean Six Sigma problem. Is education and training necessary? Sure, it is a brick in the foundation of a successful deployment, but only 5 to 10 percent of the real work. Organizations built a solid knowledge foundation and then stopped at the tough part: *execution and results*. The bottom line is that there is no need for a comeback if an organization deploys Lean Six Sigma correctly (and thus, successfully) the first time. In a Lean Six Sigma deployment, there are only two outcomes: breakthrough performance or excuses. Recognize that neither outcome is the fault of Lean Six Sigma.

But There Is No Budget for Improvement

In early 2009, we spent days over the course of several months working with a prospective client and helping the executive team understand how to implement Lean Six Sigma successfully. They actually started their initiative in 2008 when the CFO latched onto Six Sigma as a short-term cost-cutting activity for the board. After a few months, he decided that Six Sigma needed to become a human resource responsibility because of the extensive training requirements. Corporate HR took on the responsibility and assembled a million-dollar training budget. When the training budget was shot down, HR tossed Six Sigma to the vice president of operations. Responsibility now resided with a newly appointed well-thought-of executive as the deployment leader, with a directive to "make it happen organically" since the company was experiencing financial problems. This executive began educating himself via Google knowledge, articles, and Amazon books. On a positive note, he embraced the notion of integrating Lean and Six Sigma, or Lean Six Sigma. However, after 15 months they had nothing to show for their efforts except a 20-page PowerPoint presentation describing at 50,000 feet how they should implement Lean Six Sigma, highly influenced by their own "we're different" perceptions of themselves. The deployment leader presented this plan to hundreds of people in the organization, raising the excitement and interest bar and getting many people interested in moving forward. During this latter part of their Lean Six Sigma promotional period, the organization had two layoffs to cut costs. Coincidently or not, some employees became skeptical of the Lean Six Sigma message and wondered if it might lead to more downsizing.

The deployment leader decided to hire one recently anointed black belt with limited industry experience, who quickly became too sucked into the daily fires to add any value to a deployment. This deployment leader included others on his ad-hoc implementation committee, also with limited Lean Six Sigma "Google and Barnes & Noble" knowledge, who met occasionally, shared information, and visited other companies. The committee also held a wide dispersion of opinions about how to implement Lean Six Sigma successfully, and a few members had political motivations to create a large improvement organization and a new role for themselves. They were on that familiar big-bang, top-down, train-the-masses, 80 percent or more path to failure with a lot of talk and no action. People in the organization were frustrated at the lack of progress and were beginning to go off on their own tangents and look for their own Lean Six Sigma training options. Everyone was viewing Lean Six Sigma as a training and development *get-the-belts* initiative rather than a strategic business improvement initiative.

Leadership spent more time firefighting and moderating their multitude of business problems and pacifying their widespread customer dissatisfaction issues. On a positive note, they were a model Lean Six Sigma opportunity. We proposed our Scalable Lean Six Sigma™ deployment model and identified $15 to $25M in improvement opportunities that could be achieved within the next 12 to 24 months in this single division. We also identified the total upside potential to be $80 to $100M or more across the entire organization. We also counseled them on the importance of dealing candidly with the negative association between Lean Six Sigma and downsizing, and reintroducing Lean Six Sigma more positively to

"Don't even ask . . .
There's no money in the
budget for improvement!"

Performance

the organization. *All* of our references checked out, and *all* of our references have exceeded the initial improvement opportunities identified at the beginning of their deployments. The executive team concurred with our proposed approach and findings, but they were unwilling to sign on and collectively find the funds to conduct the project. They looked around the table and said to each other, "You fund it. I can't afford to and it's not in my objectives."

Another executive commented, "You know, even if we had the funding, I can't sign up for this on top of all the other things we're being asked to do right now."

The vice president of customer service said, "I don't need this in my area. . . . We know what's wrong and we're already good at solving problems every time they come up. . . . And I certainly don't want my people spending time on anything else but customer service."

The executive team reached a leadership impasse—the point of disagreement and stalemate, without hope for resolution and no hope for progress—the familiar short-term, self-interest behaviors that jeopardize the future. The deployment leader had about 2 percent of the required funding in his budget, and they asked if we could provide a few days of training because one department manager identified this desperate need for a minimum of seven green belts as a dependency to meet their performance objectives (there was no rational basis for this requirement). After several frustrating meetings and indecision on behalf of the organization, the deployment leader told us, "Look, there is a freeze on all discretionary spending and there is no money budgeted for Lean Six Sigma until 2010 or beyond. I'm not going to request additional funds because I will get my head handed to me. Besides, we could hire four or five black belts for the same price and do this ourselves."

However, they could not hire the black belts because there was a hiring freeze. Their lack of deployment performance during the first 15 months was a good indicator of their inability to implement a successful deployment internally. Hiring twenty black belts would not have made a difference in this organization. We expressed our disappointment, and I proposed the option of working with them for the next quarter on an expenses-only basis if they would agree to split the savings with us. To our amazement, the deployment leader replied, "Look, there is no money in the budget to pay you half of the savings either!"

He was not joking—another misdirected executive with an obstructed view of reality. This is a great example of how leadership drives their organizations with the wrong metrics, which drives the wrong cascading behaviors and achieves the wrong results. These executives were acting with a blind certitude that what they were doing is right and justified. On a personal note, sometimes it is frustrating for a globetrotting consultant to watch a group of grown executives debate foolishly about the need to improve, while grade school children in Japan are being taught the fundamentals of root-cause problem solving. Across-the-board freezes on all discretionary spending is common in a challenging economy, but these sweeping moratoriums destroy business-improvement initiatives and drive cultural gains backward. This is also a great example of a CEO misunderstanding Lean Six Sigma and underestimating what it takes to be successful. In a fairness, the deployment leader was set up for failure from day one. One minute he displayed confidence in going it alone, and in the next minute, he discussed in confidence his frustrations of an impossible role and his hopes for a new assignment soon. At the time of this writing, the deployment leader has jumped into a new assignment, and the executive deployment leader position has been open for months, waiting to be filled internally by another inexperienced candidate.

Imagine these executives anticipating a big year-end bonus for meeting their objectives while turning down the potential for $15 to $25M in improvement opportunities. Despite the belt tightening via layoffs, these executives all received their year-end bonuses for doing the wrong thing at an opportune time. This reinforced the wrong behaviors and separated the immediate needs from improvement. That savings opportunity is equivalent to $400 to $500 million in incremental sales revenue! How can the rest of the organization be successful when the executives in charge are turning a blind eye to these opportunities and misleading their people? At the time of this writing, the organization is in Lean Six Sigma limbo, and the executive team still doesn't get it. However, a few dozen people have received a few days of below-the-belt boilerplate Six Sigma training, and they have an updated plan to save about 1/100 of what they should be saving over the next 12 to 18 months. This is a multibillion dollar organization that has been in a Lean Six Sigma deployment for over two years with zilch for results, yet hopes to save a few million in the next 12 to 18 months. There should not be a nickel in the budget for this type of improvement or for executive bonuses! Over the years, I have lost count of the number of executives who have made the comment, "There's no money in the budget for improvement!" or "We need to improve but we don't have the time right now" or "The time isn't right for improvement."

Where have all the real leaders gone in this recent meltdown? Does no one realize that the only way to get better is to improve upon current conditions? Does no one else see that inattention to waste and nonvalue-added activity results in exponential growth in future waste and nonvalue-added activity? When it comes to financials, you can run but you cannot hide. Unfortunately, accounting practices allow organizations to postpone (hide) their waste by allowing the next executive to come in and sweep the problems of the previous regime under the rug of restructuring costs. Nevertheless, it still has a consequence to the organization and its people. My personal favorite quote of all time was by an executive who said, "We need Six Sigma because we finished our continuous improvement program years ago!" What are the executives in these organizations thinking?

Missing in Action—A Formal Implementation Architecture

Many organizations fail outright when it comes to defining, organizing, leading, mentoring, and implementing Lean Six Sigma initiatives or other strategic improvement initiatives. Organizations are missing the implementation infrastructure (i.e., strategy, structure, processes, people, technology, and linking metrics) to achieve long-term success. This infrastructure is missing in many Lean Six Sigma deployments today, just as it was missing in Just in Time (JIT), Total Quality Management (TQM), Reengineering, Lean, Six Sigma, and many other stand-alone improvement programs during the past three decades. Figure 1.1 provides an overview of strategic leadership and vision, deployment planning, and execution infrastructure in successful Lean Six Sigma deployments, and the remaining chapters in this book will shed more light on these topics.

It is a fact that organizations tend to skim over the tough process of building this strategic leadership and vision, deployment planning, and execution infrastructure and opt for education and a quick impact. For the most part, failed Lean Six Sigma deployments are the fault of leadership who sponsored the improvement initiative without the necessary patience, experience, commitment, knowledge, and interest to see it through successfully. Executive behaviors in the post-meltdown continue to contribute to improvement failures through a growing occurrence of conflicting priorities, political motivations, and a short-term performance focus. They are missing a very real set of core competencies in implementing and integrating strategic improvement initiatives throughout the enterprise and beyond to the total value stream—just as people outside your organization could be missing the core competencies to design and build products, generate software code, or maintain specialized production or laboratory equipment. Unfortunately, many consultants that organizations worked with turned out to be trainers and were also missing this core competency. Again, the objective of this book is not to bash leadership or deployment leaders or Lean Six Sigma consultants. Great leaders are great because they face reality with objectivity and candor; they know when to step back, evaluate, discover, and learn from the root causes of deployment failures. The executive behaviors cited as examples in this chapter are by no means intended to embarrass executives. Mistakes are part of the developmental and learning process for this magnitude of improvement initiatives. However, it always saves time, cost, and much pain to learn from the mistakes of other pioneers. Keep in mind that the ability to write this book comes from being blessed to work with, learn from, and together overcome these obstacles with thousands of executives and their organizations during the last twenty years.

We sincerely believe that every executive begins by being committed intellectually or in their heart, but their actions and behaviors are inconsistent with this commitment. Organizations have this fascination and tendency to dive into the Lean and Six Sigma methodologies and tools. Much of this is driven by consulting organizations that provide education on the stand-alone Lean and Six Sigma tools as if it were a commodity. People learn just enough to be dangerous and start running around the organization with a bag of improvement tools and a new acronym vocabulary, looking for a problem to solve. These individuals have the best of intentions because they are trying to act on what they perceive to be the executive direction: deploy Lean Six Sigma and make a quick impact

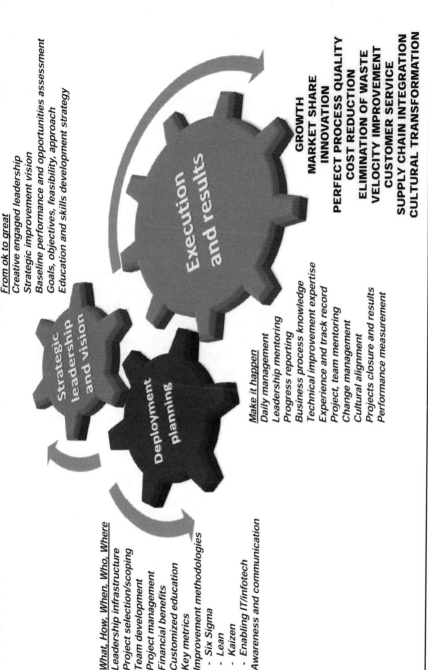

From ok to great
Creative engaged leadership
Strategic improvement vision
Baseline performance and opportunities assessment
Goals, objectives, feasibility, approach
Education and skills development strategy

Make it happen
Daily management
Leadership mentoring
Progress reporting
Business process knowledge
Technical improvement expertise
Experience and track record
Project, team mentoring
Change management
Cultural alignment
Projects closure and results
Performance measurement

What, How, When, Who, Where
Leadership infrastructure
Project selection/scoping
Team development
Project management
Financial benefits
Customized education
Key metrics
Improvement methodologies
 - Six Sigma
 - Lean
 - Kaizen
 - Enabling IT/infotech
Awareness and communication

GROWTH
MARKET SHARE
INNOVATION
PERFECT PROCESS QUALITY
COST REDUCTION
ELIMINATION OF WASTE
VELOCITY IMPROVEMENT
CUSTOMER SERVICE
SUPPLY CHAIN INTEGRATION
CULTURAL TRANSFORMATION

Strategic leadership and vision

Deployment planning

Execution and results

Figure 1.1   Lean Six Sigma success infrastructure.

Without the strategic leadership and vision, deployment planning, and execution infrastructure, these well-intended actions are usually self-driven rather than customer-driven, perception-driven instead of fact-driven, and not focused on gaps, root causes, and priorities of strategic performance. This approach may produce a few short-term benefits, but it never becomes a sustaining process. Soon, Lean Six Sigma takes on a life of its own and the original intent is replaced by the mechanics of the improvement process itself. Eventually, people begin to question the illusive benefits of Lean Six Sigma, and it rapidly falls down the priority list. For the employees of these organizations, the thought of another improvement program is about as popular as trying to contract the H1N1 virus. The last thing organizations need right now is another repackaged set of improvement tools or buzzword marketing. Many organizations have learned the painful and costly lesson that well-intended activities do not always translate into improvement. The good news is that the improvement opportunities are still out there, and the current improvement methodologies and tools available to organizations are the means of achieving these opportunities.

Success or failure lies within a well-designed and well-orchestrated implementation infrastructure: strategic leadership and vision, deployment planning, and execution infrastructure. These factors are the most critical success factors, but they are also the most difficult make-you-or-break-you factors. The root causes of failed deployments with Lean Six Sigma and every other improvement initiative are linked directly to poor performance in these areas. These factors are much tougher and less fun than training in some exotic location, and it requires a long-term level of attention, commitment, resources, and time from the CEO and the executive team—in fact, much more than is actually exhibited in the typical failed Lean Six Sigma deployments. These factors are either the most important deployment success factors, or root causes of Lean Six Sigma deployment failures and all other previous improvement initiatives in organizations.

Knock-Off, One-Size-Fits-All Lean Six Sigma

Another weakness with Lean Six Sigma has been the tendency for organizations to emulate the big-bang, top-down, train-the-masses, boilerplate, and one-size-fits-all deployment approaches of the initial successes of GE, Motorola, Honeywell, DuPont, Caterpillar, 3M, American Express, J. P. Morgan Chase, and many others. The large consulting firms packaged and marketed this approach as the best (and only) approach to Lean Six Sigma success. Why would organizations want to waver and choose a different course? It was successful for these organizations, so it must be the right approach for them, right? This is another shortfall of improvement. The advice, knowledge, and experiences of successful organizations are valuable data points in initiating a Lean Six Sigma deployment. However anxious or uninformed organizations make a mistake when they try to photo copy these deployments—the experiences of a particular executive are often a grossly inconsistent, ambiguous generalization of what it takes to be successful in your own environment with your own challenges and your own culture. Much of their generic knowledge and experiences are transferrable, but true success is dependent on how well organizations manage the course of their own specific strategic leadership and vision, deployment planning, and execution factors.

In the interest of time and getting things done (although improvement is never actually *done*) organizations have pursued these knock-off deployment approaches to Lean Six Sigma, hoping to achieve the same relative benefits of GE and others. Executives overlook the obvious success factors such as leadership commitment, improvement competencies, detailed deployment planning and mission-critical project selection, barriers to success, etc., and assume that the Lean Six Sigma deployment process itself will incorporate all the ingredients for success. One must not forget that GE's initiatives were led by Jack Welch and a strong leadership team (who used the term *lunatic fringe* to describe their leadership behavior regarding Lean Six Sigma). Everyone was amused by this descriptor, but Jack was right on the mark. GE has always had their own version of the strategic leadership and vision, deployment planning, and execution factors driving all their improvement initiatives. Success is a leadership choice, and a successful deployment is leadership controllable.

Lean Six Sigma does not have to cost millions of dollars and years of effort to implement, and it does not require a complicated hierarchy of champions, master black, black, green, yellow, or white belts to be successful. In our new economy, organizations do not have years and millions of dollars at their disposal to improve their businesses. Although the early Lean and Six Sigma pioneers achieved success with their traditional one-size-fits-all deployment, this approach is not the future of business improvement. A new way of thinking about how to implement Lean Six Sigma and business improvement is needed. A more rapid rollout, rapid results model is needed and is the new norm for jumpstarting the failed deployments, and for keeping new Lean Six Sigma deployments on an accelerated, breakthrough results path. Successful Lean Six Sigma has demonstrated that organizations can, and have, achieved savings rates in the range of 3 to 10 percent of their revenues within an 18 to 24 month period. This is not hoopla—these metrics are benchmarks from organizations that have achieved successful Lean Six Sigma deployments. One might be thinking that these organizations must have been more inefficient than your organization when they started off, but that is not the case.

Educate-Pontificate-Mortificate Deployments

After several years of involvement and experience with Lean Six Sigma, many deployments have focused too much on training and too little on execution and results. Part of the blame is leadership, who is ultimately responsible and accountable for making the right choices about how to implement the program successfully. However, a large part of the blame rests with the large Six Sigma training firms that have sold Lean Six Sigma as another massive, revenue-generating training program.

When an organization hires an external consulting firm, the executives expect that they are buying the depth of experience and expertise of many successful deployments. With Lean Six Sigma, these large firms were heavy on training expertise and weak on deployment and execution expertise. In retrospect, many of these experts were either strategists with intellectual solutions or individuals who spent most of their careers in quality organizations and developed their expertise on the statistical tools of Lean or Six Sigma. There is a fundamental problem with taking one of these individuals out of their prior element, having them teach statistical problem solving, certify people as black belts, and then expecting these black belts (many with limited business experiences) to improve every nook and cranny in the organization. There is another flaw in thinking that a black belt—any black belt—is capable of mentoring executives, a large-scale deployment, and individual projects in areas outside their backgrounds to a successful conclusion. Some of these consulting firms pumped up their fees by creating silly indices of how many black belts per million dollars of revenue were needed, or how many green belts per black belt, or several other ludicrous indices that, in retrospect, benefited the training firms much more than it did their clients.

Organizations took the bait and began training their people in droves. The interest and demand for Six Sigma spiked exponentially after the success stories of the early Lean and Six Sigma pioneers. These large consulting firms sold everyone another yellow-brick-road improvement initiative with their follow-the-herd black-belt certification programs, and disappeared when the tough work of implementation began. There was little to no focus on business needs and scant direction provided about strategic improvement issues. Training is easier and it requires little responsibility and accountability for results. Many organizations similar to those mentioned in the *Business Week* article blindly hired one of the large training firms and budgeted millions of dollars for education and the status of belts in their organizations. Others opted to attend some accelerated, low-quality certification course or sign their people up for Internet or self-study black-belt courses. Unfortunately, this *mad belt disease* is not the answer to breakthrough improvement. You cannot execute and change culture with a few weeks of training or over the Internet—at least not yet. Nevertheless, the primary focus of Lean Six Sigma has been on training and belts. A few years ago, we were invited into a large organization interested in Lean Six Sigma. We arrived and presented our firm's capabilities and case studies to about 25 people around a large conference room table. We then began discussing their interest and requirements. To our amazement, one individual commented, "Every one of us around this table has been certified as a black belt. We were given the funding to go through the certification program. Now we need help figuring out what to do next."

Most Lean and Six Sigma books are good at covering the mechanics of the tools, but little has been written about the strategic leadership and vision, deployment planning, and execution factors of success. Everyone wanted a black belt but unfortunately, Lean Six Sigma and the interest in improvement ceased for many after the graduation ceremony for their certification, or after they updated their resume with their newly acquired belt status. When one views all the Lean and Six Sigma websites or LinkedIn groups, it is obvious that there is more time being spent on how much everyone knows rather than on how much everyone is doing to improve their businesses. Knowing *how* to do something is a lot easier than *doing* it and being accountable for results. When everyone is running around saying, "I don't need help" because they already know *how* to change, usually not much is changing. Keep in mind that organizations have been churned through several cycles of this approach to improvement during the past few decades, and this is where mortification or slow death comes in. The organization is still alive, but deep down in the cultural fabric, employees are either dodging the current improvement initiative or are instantly turned off by the thought of participating in yet another improvement program.

Another weakness related to Lean Six Sigma (and most improvement programs) is in its presentation by many experts as an improvement initiative for the manufacturing area, and its presentation as a bag of disconnected improvement tools. Prior to the latest version of Lean Six Sigma, the underpinnings were presented as stand-alone improvement initiatives. Organizations were bombarded with Kaizen, Kaizen Blitz, and Gemba Kaizen focused on quick and obvious improvements. Industries have been bombarded by *tool head* consultants, trainers, and professional societies peddling their latest single point tool, DVD, or workshop, presenting improvement with the ease of making breakfast or playing games with blocks, marshmallows, grilling skewers, or other materials. Books presented improvement as implementing a series of tools in the right sequence. People were introduced to Lean and the TPS and an extensive vocabulary of Japanese terms

(that were unpronounceable by most) as a means of eliminating waste. The internal experts ran around talking about *gemba, heijunka, jidoka, kaikatsu, kaikaku, muda, poka-yoke,* or *shitsuke,* and wondered why people had a sheep-in-the-headlights response to improvement. There was a time in Detroit when this kind of language could get your automobile turned on its roof. Organizations were presented with Six Sigma as another initiative that promotes data-driven root-cause problem solving with statistics and other quantitative tools to reduce process variation. These decoupled and disconnected improvement approaches did little except confuse the organization. Some executives would make these off-the-wall comments such as, "We're very interested in Kaizen because it's faster and easier than Lean or Six Sigma" or "Lean must come before Six Sigma."

One day it was Kaizen, the next day it was Lean, and then it was Six Sigma. Executive directions bounce around until people are thinking, "What are we doing today? Is it Door 1, Door 2, or Door 3?"

Some were claiming to be implementing Lean, for example, but were focused on a single beautification exercise of Lean such as 5S or moving production equipment into cells, painting squares on the production floor, and hanging up signs. The strategic leadership and vision, deployment planning, and execution success factors were missing. People spent more time debating which tools were best rather than learning how to apply the right tools to the right improvement opportunities. Nobody could see the value of integrating all these improvement methodologies into a single powerhouse initiative.

Organizations waffled around with these initiatives and some even created and staffed their own separate Kaizen, Lean, and Six Sigma offices. One large aerospace company we visited a few years ago comes to mind. We had discussions with an executive prior to our trip, and had the impression that they were just getting started with Lean Six Sigma. When we arrived, we found an organization that began their journey two years earlier—fully staffed with over 100 black belts. Other than two million dollars in Improvement 101 savings, they had not accomplished much more than training. After the tour through their operations and after interviews with several people, the dynamics were obvious to an outsider. Whenever there was a problem, the process owner executive or manager would throw the problem over the wall and assign a black belt to look into it. Whenever these executives and managers were questioned about their issues, they would simply reply, "We have a black belt working on it."

The problem was in the black belt's court, and the process owner was waiting for the answer. Process owners had no ownership of the improvement—it was someone else's job. Functional managers bounced their problems over the fence to a black belt and moved on to the next fire. Another recurring comment was "They came up with recommendations but we didn't like them, so we still have them working on it" or "There was something wrong with their data."

We lost track of how many times we heard these remarks in our two-day visit. The black belts were frustrated about their arrangement of little support, little influence, and little motivation. They clearly lacked ownership of the improvement. Their disjointed approach to improvement was just another familiar organizational set-up where process owners were willing to listen to the black belts as long as it did not interfere with what they had already decided to do. Improvement was both functionally and realistically separated from the responsibilities and performance metrics of process owners. This was another *Field of Dreams* improvement initiative: if you train the black belts, the results will eventually come.

Educators and trainers have cleverly packaged and branded Lean Six Sigma as an enterprise-wide improvement initiative. However, the training materials, examples, and experiences of most educators have a production-floor focus and a leftover 1980s spin of TQM and other previous improvement programs. Lean Six Sigma is easier to grasp in terms of manufacturing. Production processes and parts are tangible things that we can touch, see, hear, smell, and feel. The input factors (e.g., speed, feed, raw material dimensions, labor skill, type of tool, etc.) and output factors (e.g., pieces per hour, yield, rework, finished product dimensions, surface quality, functional performance, etc.) are more tangible than soft transactional processes. For three decades we have beat the shop floor to death with improvement programs only to watch much of it move to another low-cost country. Why has this occurred? Because when one looks at manufacturing problems, the root causes of these problems lie outside manufacturing. They lie in areas such as design for manufacturing, supplier delivery and quality, sales forecasting and demand planning volatility, inventory management, engineering changes, warehousing and distribution, logistics and transportation, preventive maintenance and spare parts policies, order entry and fulfillment, bill of materials, and engineering drawings to name a few. Organizations still have a lot to learn and gain from true root-cause problem solving, particularly in these areas. A broad and creative focus of Lean Six Sigma is required to tap into these improvement opportunities. Nevertheless, organizations have the opportunity to learn several good lessons from their prior improvement experiences in manufacturing as a means of evolving forward.

Executives have this false expectation with Lean Six Sigma that a massive training effort or hiring black belts and then scattering them around the organization is going to make a difference. This is a totally unreasonable expectation. Dropping a few black belts into the middle of an improvement-dysfunctional organization is a waste of time and a disservice to individuals with the formal certification and the desire to make a difference. In fact, a hundred black belts are futile without the strategic leadership and vision, deployment planning, and execution factors in place. It takes years for an individual to not only master the Lean Six Sigma methodology and applications, but to develop the deployment strategy and planning skills, leadership, program management and project mentoring expertise, key business process knowledge, and interpersonal and communications skills needed to manage a deployment to a successful sustaining point (as opposed to a conclusion; continuous improvement is continuous). This is a point of having achieved real breakthrough results, making Lean Six Sigma fully self-sustainable internally, visually transforming culture to this autopilot problem-solving mode, and an improving-how-we-improve state.

Improvement Excellence™: The Competitive Differentiator

Over the years, the largest lesson learned from strategic improvement initiatives is that success has little to do with the improvement tools themselves. It all has to do with how Lean Six Sigma is deployed. The buck stops at the CEO and his or her executive team. There is a strong corollary between leadership and organizational behavior. Using the Six Sigma analogy, leadership has the largest *main effect* on organizational behavior and culture through strategy, directives, and communication. Leadership also produces large *interaction effects* on people and organizations as they individually and functionally interpret and act upon leadership expectations. Leadership controls the level of commitment and the rate, timing, and magnitude of Lean Six Sigma success by their actions and behaviors. This is not finger pointing; this is the reality of a successful program deployment. When one observes how many executives lead (or mislead) their organizations down the improvement road, it is no wonder that the *continuous* part of *continuous improvement* is missing in most organizations.

> *Improvement Excellence™—The mastery of developing and implementing successful strategic and continuous business improvement initiatives, transforming culture, and enabling organizations to improve how they improve.*

It is not the fault of the tools at all. The leadership sponsors the improvement initiative without the knowledge, patience, commitment, time, interest, and experience of what it takes to be successful. It is not the intentional fault of the executives in our organizations; they are missing the core competency of Improvement Excellence™. Failed deployments are also caused by the inexperienced individuals who try to implement and misapply Lean and Six Sigma after a brief introduction through a training-the-masses exercise. They, too, are missing this core competency of Improvement Excellence™. It is no one's fault—it is the process of how organizations choose to introduce and deploy improvement.

Figure 1.2 and the following discussion provide a few simple rules about Lean Six Sigma and business improvement in general:

1. *Improvement is always possible and necessary*—Improvement is universal and no organization or functional area is exempt from improvement. Improvement is not an option; it is a priority for creating competitive advantage and differentiation with customers. There are no free hallway passes when it comes to improvement. Every public and private company, financial services institution, advertising agency, law firm, healthcare provider (and particularly federal, state, and local governments) have staggering

waste in their business processes. These processes might be grouped into performance categories such as great, average, need improvement, and completely broken. No organization is great at everything or perfect at anything, and there are always unlimited improvement opportunities.

2. *There is no better time to improve than now*—Organizations can always find a variety of excuses for postponing Lean Six Sigma and other improvement initiatives. Being too busy doing all the wrong things, or not having a budget to implement improvements (improvements resulting in 20 to 50 times the necessary budget) are unacceptable excuses in a brutal economy with fierce global competition. Bad metrics are a primary cause for this, driving people to take asinine actions. Binary linear thinking about improvement is out (e.g., "If I do *A*, I can't do *B*; I don't have time to improve and still do my regular job"). It is both amusing and sad to watch organizations always find the time to do things over. We cannot rewind the economy to get back to the good times, we can only strive to take what we have and recreate the good times.

3. *Leadership and infrastructure make you or break you*—The success of any strategic improvement initiative is highly dependent on creative leadership driving the right strategy, structure, processes, people, technology, and dashboard metrics. The improvement tools themselves are the means,

Figure 1.2   Rules of strategic improvement success.

not the ends. Creative leadership is demonstrated by direct involvement and engagement—not verbal support. Direct involvement develops executive capabilities to lead by firsthand knowledge and experiences, instead of the typical intellectually-supportive-but-detached (token agreement) leadership mode. Experiences gained through engagement allow executives to modify their thinking and better influence and mentor culture change. Direct involvement and engagement sends a strong message of commitment to the organization (by demonstrating by their actions) expressing that the executives are not asking people to do something that they are unwilling to do themselves.

4. *It all begins with commitment and a different perspective*—A rigorous and committed effort is necessary on the front-end to establish strategic priorities, organization, deployment planning, and other infrastructure development elements to set a new course of improvement. A continuation of the same approaches and actions that landed the organization in its current state will not move the organization upward to a best-in-class state. What brought you here will not get you where you want to go. Failure to recognize this fact is called *insanity*: repetitiously doing more of the same things and expecting different results. Hyper-insanity is increasing the sense of urgency and throwing more effort toward repetitiously doing the same things and expecting different results. Improvement requires new injections of innovation and creativity and demands new ways of beyond-the-box thinking, new ways of leading, and new ways of problem solving. The phrase beyond-the-box thinking (vs. out-of-the-box thinking) recognizes that not everything in the organization's box is bad or needs to improve immediately. Beyond-the-box is targeted at the most critical strategic improvement needs.

5. *Strategic improvement is a scarce core competency*—The capability of successfully implementing strategic improvement initiatives is a legitimate core competency that can be either acquired through external expertise or organically grown over time. In reality, most organizations do not have the core competency to sustain improvement, and their experiences with improvement initiatives over the past three decades prove this point. The cost of external expertise may be viewed as prohibitive, but these cost are minuscule when compared to the upside velocity and magnitude for improvement that comes with proven expertise, or the organizational damage control and lost opportunities for a delayed, stalled, or failing deployment. Organizations that lack this core competency and are unwilling to engage the right expertise usually experience failure with Lean Six Sigma and other strategic improvement initiatives.

6. *The new economy has created new challenges that require new thinking*—In all strategic improvement initiatives, the same people plus the same

thinking, the same process, and the same information equals the same results. In order to change the outcome of this formula, we need to change one or more of the input factors. In order to change these input factors, organizations must think differently as a first step.

7. *Improvement must focus on root causes*—The outcome of the same results mentioned in the previous bullet point is a function of root causes. In essence, we are wasting time trying to improve outcomes such as delivery performance, inventory levels, or financial variances. These outcomes result from many factors or root causes. Outcomes are improved by diving deep into root causes, taking the right corrective actions, and continuously measuring the right performance to sustain or further improve the outcome. In the absence of data, facts, and a thorough understanding of root causes, organizations accomplish nothing but surface-level symptomatic problem solving, firefighting, and second-guessing the corrective actions. For easy improvements, this intuitive approach works well. For complex issues, failing to improve these outcomes via root-cause problem solving is a sure bet for repeatedly dealing with the same problems.

8. *Instant gratification kills improvement*—Most strategic improvement initiatives become derailed by the notion of *immediate reason*—the act of attempting to correct a situation with unreasonable actions based on opinions, perceptions, or direct orders from others who are missing the facts. Failure to peel back layers of the onion and conduct true root-cause problem solving results in short lived, reactive improvement and firefighting. These actions introduce more variation and waste and locks people into a mode where they are repeatedly fixing the same problems. Daily disruptions and reactive problem solving promotes more of a band-aid approach, while root-cause problem solving promotes elimination of the problem now and in the future. In reality, root-cause problem solving requires much less time than continuing to deal with the same problems. Sustainable improvement requires much more than sticking one's toes in the improvement water for a while. Success requires a strategic and structured approach to improvement, and staying the course.

9. *Strategy and planning is the foundation for improvement*—Organizations that refuse to make the *patience investment* fail miserably at Lean Six Sigma and all other improvement initiatives. This patience investment does not need to take years. However, it does require executives to exhibit visible unwavering commitment and staying the course with the right proven strategic leadership and vision, deployment planning, and execution success factors. Most executives these days act with the best of intentions, but their focus is on the next corner in the road rather than on the journey. Further, some of this lack of patience is justified because many improvement initiatives are headed down the wrong roads and fail

to deliver measurable results. In a Lean Six Sigma deployment, the entire organization pays close attention to executive signals and behaviors and acts accordingly. Changing the way an organization thinks and acts starts with the CEO and his or her executive team.

10. *Organizations get what they measure*—The success of business improvement must be linked to organizational and individual performance. Performance includes the cycle of measurement, feedback, interpretation, and corrective action. Business improvement incorporates provisions for recognizing and rewarding performance, as well as consequences for poor performance. The right performance metrics drive the right behaviors and achieve the right results. The opposite is also true.

Improvement Excellence™ Is a Legitimate Core Competency

There is a part of Improvement Excellence™—the mastery of developing and implementing successful strategic and continuous business improvement initiatives, transforming culture, and enabling organizations to improve how they improve—that cause many executives to go into denial. Improvement Excellence™ requires a continuous and flawless presence of the strategic leadership and vision, deployment planning, and execution success factors, and a broader, more creative and innovative application of improvement methodologies and tools. It also requires the fusion of all improvement methodologies into a uniform powerhouse initiative, and a broad scope that views and encompasses customers, all transactional and knowledge processes within the organization, and the supply chain as a translucent single enterprise model. The objective of Improvement Excellence™ is to search out, align, and pursue larger strategic breakthrough opportunities that either directly or indirectly benefit this single enterprise model. Breakthrough means either order of magnitude improvements or new improvements in critical-to-customer processes that create positive differentiation and strategic advantage in areas such as strategic product portfolio planning and management, engineering and new product development processes, sales and marketing processes, manufacturing and supply chain processes, and financial management processes. In short, it discourages improvements that may be good for a single function but bad for the whole organization, improvements that may benefit the organization at the expense of suppliers or customers, or improvements that do not aid customer satisfaction, growth, and financial performance. Executives and organizations think they already know how to do all of these things and either fail to recognize, grossly underestimate, or are in denial about the true core competencies of strategic improvement.

Improvement Excellence™ is a core competency missing in most organizations because quite honestly, improvement is not a person's only role and responsibility. Many executives and organizations do not possess this core competency, yet most believe that they and their organizations have it and are capable of it. Reading books about the tools and education is the easy part. These activities give many organizations a false sense of direction as it pertains to Lean Six Sigma. Confident but wrong about the strategic leadership and vision, deployment planning, and execution success factors equals a road to failure for Lean Six Sigma and any other improvement initiatives. Improvement Excellence™ is developed through years of the appropriate improvement experiences, successes and executive behaviors that cultivate many eureka moments in the organization and develop internal improvement *senseis*. (Sensei is the Japanese word for teacher and means someone who walks ahead. When you are walking on a path and you see someone in front of you, that person is not really teaching you anything as much as he or she is showing you the way.)

Lean Six Sigma and most other improvement initiatives have their roots in the formal discipline of industrial engineering. The Institute of Industrial Engineering defines this profession as:

> *The engineering discipline concerned with the development, improvement, implementation and evaluation of integrated systems of people, money, knowledge, information, equipment, energy, material and process. It also deals with designing new prototypes to help save money and make the prototype better. Industrial engineering draws upon the principles and methods of engineering analysis and synthesis, as well as mathematical, physical and social sciences together with the principles and methods of engineering analysis and design to specify, predict and evaluate the results to be obtained from such systems.*

The word *industrial* in *industrial engineering* can be misleading. While the term originally applied to manufacturing in the 1920s and earned nicknames such as head-choppers, time-study people, and axe swingers, it has grown to encompass virtually all other functions, industries, and services as well. Within the typical industrial engineering curriculum is a wide variety of courses on topics such as methods analysis and process improvement, management science, statistical engineering, financial engineering, supply chain management, human factors and ergonomics, team-based problem solving, value engineering, quality engineering, etc. The details and body of knowledge presented in these courses are almost identical to what has been packaged in the various improvement programs of the past three decades. Industrial engineering is the foundation for most of the analytical and human factors content of Lean Six Sigma. The fact that many elements of process improvement fall under the umbrella of an engineering discipline is a clue that improvement is not always as easy as it looks on the surface. However, most engineers and others have had it wrong for the last three decades. The aspect that makes improvement most difficult is the strategic leadership and vision, deployment planning, and execution—not the specific tools themselves. The purpose of this book is to take these mystical, theoretical leadership factors down from the 50,000-foot level and discuss them in a practical and workable framework.

During the post-World War II era, Japan became interested in these improvement topics. Dr. Deming and his expertise on statistical quality improvement, and Taichi Ohno with his visionary thinking from Toyota took center stage in business improvement. Some level of complacency set in for America after winning the war. Rather than listening to the wisdom of Deming, America sent him off to Japan where they were facing post-war reconstruction issues related to manufacturing. At Toyota, for example, there was a concern with quality and inventory levels, and the costs and space consumption associated with each. This was essentially unaffordable. As the story has it, Ohno visited an American supermarket and realized his vision of pull production. This became codified as an essential element of what was to become known as the TPS. Much of the TPS is Taichi Ohno's professional background and evolution of basic industrial engineering improvements aimed at the unique inventory, quality, space, and natural resource limitations in post-war Japan. Development and implementation of the TPS was a lot of work—relentless, never-ending work—work that turned out to go unnoticed by the Western World until it revolutionized global manufacturing by 1980. Several others such as Masaaki Imai, the father of Kaizen, also became internationally renowned for the continuous improvement work at Toyota and many other Japanese companies. American executives and educators began visiting these Japanese organizations and brought back what they observed. Somehow in the translation, these observations were packaged into a discrete series of improvement initiatives followed by their own vocabulary of acronyms and books on the topics. In retrospect, it has been a confusing ride for people unfamiliar with many of these topics. Replication of these improvements have focused largely on the improvement tools themselves, and have failed to recognize the relentless leadership that made companies such as Toyota successful. For the past thirty years, executives have faced (and continue to face) a major challenge to introduce and implement continuous lasting improvement initiatives such as Lean Six Sigma in their organizations. Toyota is great at continuous improvement because it has been actively implementing continuous improvement for over sixty years.

The desire for quick results and minimum commitment combined with the ever-changing shifts in priorities make improvement initiatives the first casualty. Wrapping up continuous improvement is a fallacy. These executive challenges result in an oversimplification of effort, time, resources, current workloads, and confusing performance expectations. Some executives delegate improvement to a functional area where it takes on a primary spin of the particular function such as human resources, quality, or manufacturing. Others are committed to Lean Six Sigma except in the fourth week of every month or the end of the quarter. Lean Six Sigma deployments are logical and straightforward when the right strategic leadership and vision, deployment planning, and execution success factors are integrated into the deployment process. In the absence of these success factors, Lean Six Sigma becomes another hollow, short-lived improvement initiative with no results. Step back and take a hard look at how many organizations have chosen to deploy Lean Six Sigma. First, improvement is not recognized as a formal professional discipline (if it were, there would be a vice president of business improvement or business excellence in every organization). Everyone thinks that he or she knows how to improve processes or the business. As we mentioned, reading about Lean Six Sigma and intuitively knowing *how* to do something is much different and much easier than *doing* it with success. More often than not, improvement initiatives have been delegated from the CEO or executive team to a lower functional level in the organization. They gather 10–20 people and tell them they are going off to become black belts. They assign them with a project—one that may or may not matter—so that participants can show up at their first training class with an assigned project. They take these people through four weeks of training and then ask them to apply what they have learned to their assigned project. Upon successful completion of the training and their project, they are awarded their black belts. Then they are sent back into the organization where there is no improvement infrastructure to further develop their new skills, and expect them become instantly disciplined, problem-solving superheroes while fighting with others who are fire-fighting and winging it with their leadership's blessing. Organizations have placed too much faith on belts alone as the improvement cure-all and end-all. Would you send someone off for four weeks of training and then expect them to be your vice president of sales or engineering? Then why do we treat improvement initiatives in this manner? Business improvement needs to be treated with the importance and organizational status of a vice presidential function. Many successful Lean Six Sigma organizations have this function in place. Another position that is beginning to emerge in organizations is an equivalent chief-of-staff position who assists the CEO in important strategic matters such as growth, cost reduction, and business improvement initiatives.

Implementation Architecture Matters

For many improvement-dysfunctional organizations, it is time to put on the crash-test dummy face and take a hard look at your improvement efforts and approach versus your results. When one removes the hype and the buzzwords of Lean Six Sigma, this is what improvement is supposed to accomplish:

- Define gaps between business strategy and mission-critical business processes, and set stretch improvement goals
- Establish an infrastructure (e.g., organization, project selection, resource management, skills development, metrics, people development, etc.) to continuously identify and improve these mission-critical processes

- Build a true, root-cause problem solving organization that can quickly sense, analyze, and overcome any business challenge
- Transform culture and make improvement a part of, rather than in addition to, everyone's responsibilities every day
- Continuously innovate improvement

Organizations have not done so well in the past 30 years. Sure, organizations have achieved some successes, but the good times bring along with it a permission to back off on improvement and backslide into old habits. Although your organization may have lost a few battles with business improvement, the war on global competitiveness is still on, and the opportunities for improvement are out there and within reach. At the time of this writing, Toyota has been in the news recently for its faulty brakes and other quality issues. This issue points out two important lessons: first, the best root-cause problem-solving organization in the world can fail when they lose focus; second, if these issues can happen in the most experienced root-cause problem-solving organization, the odds of quality and customer satisfaction issues are much higher in less experienced organizations. At this time, it is unknown how Toyota will recover, learn, and improve from its mistakes, but one thing is for certain: it will!

Success or failure with Lean Six Sigma or any other strategic improvement initiative lies within a well-designed and well-orchestrated implementation infrastructure. These factors are the most critical success factors, but they are also the most difficult make-you-or-break-you factors. Depending on how one looks at it these factors are unquestionably the most important deployment success factors or root causes of Lean Six Sigma deployment failures and all other previous improvement initiatives in organizations.

Improvement Excellence™ requires a flawless presence of the strategic leadership and vision, deployment planning, and execution success factors, and a broader, more creative and innovative application of improvement methodologies and tools. Improvement Excellence™ also requires the fusion of all improvement methodologies into a uniform powerhouse initiative, and a broad scope that views and encompasses customers, all transactional and knowledge processes within the organization, and the supply chain as a translucent single enterprise model. Improvement Excellence™ is a core competency missing in most organizations because quite honestly, improvement is not 100 percent of people's role and responsibilities. Many executives and organizations do not possess this core competency. However, most believe that they and their organizations have it and are capable of it. Confident but wrong about the strategic leadership and vision deployment planning, and execution success factors equals a road to failure for Lean Six Sigma and any other improvement initiatives. Many executives refuse to accept this fact, even though there is a demonstrated track record of over 80 percent failure rate with Lean Six Sigma deployments. We will cover how to accomplish this successful evolution and integration of Lean Six Sigma in more detail in subsequent chapters.

Figure 1.3 provides a simplified financial analysis of our Scalable Lean Six Sigma™ model (discussed in detail in Chapter 3) from actual deployment experiences. The chart highlights the accelerated results through a process called Concurrent Continuous Deployment, which is discussed in detail in Chapter 13. This process borrows concepts from concurrent engineering and lean thinking to significantly improve upon the traditional batch, discrete waves, and train-the-masses deployments. There has also been a considerable amount of confusion about Kaizen versus Lean versus Six Sigma, or the costs and resources required for success. This confusion has debilitated many deployments during the past decade. Lean Six Sigma does not have to cost millions of dollars and years of effort to implement, and it does not require a complicated hierarchy of champions, master black, black, green, yellow, or white belts for success. Yet many organizations have replaced their original improvement objectives with a complicated and overhead-intense process of Lean Six Sigma. Using the accelerated Scalable Lean Six Sigma™ model, several deployments can and have generated savings rates in the range of 3 to 10 percent of many organizations' revenues within an 18 to 24 month period. These metrics are benchmarks from organizations that have achieved a successful Lean Six Sigma deployment. Success is a leadership choice, and a successful deployment is leadership controllable. The big-bang, top-down, resource-intense, train-the-masses approach is not the right approach because organizations do not have years to make an impact on improvement challenges. A more rapid deployment, rapid-results alternative such as Scalable Lean Six Sigma™ is needed. Organizations must now build the long-term capability of improving how they improve—quickly, and with a significantly positive impact.

Lean Six Sigma and any other strategic improvement initiative requires the leadership and intensity of individuals with two operating modes: sleeping and tearing into red meat. In all seriousness, this new economy will present organizations with problems a year from now that they have no idea about and are not prepared to solve. Technology and the Internet are evolving new processes and capabilities faster than most organizations can deal with them. It has been estimated that organizations will invest billions of dollars in InfoTech improvements. This will introduce a full spectrum of non steady-state processes with the potential for improvement, but also the potential for more variation, waste, and tricky root-cause factors than ever before. The largest enablers of Improvement Excellence™ are the strategic leadership and vision, deployment planning, and execution success factors, not the current improvement tools by themselves.

The improvement tools are a means, not an end. Kaizen, Lean, Six Sigma, enabling IT, and all other improvement methodologies can and should be integrated into a unified powerhouse improvement initiative in organizations. By themselves, improvement tools are stand-alone enablers of particular types of improvement. The more an organization chooses to integrate these enablers, the higher the benefits and rate of improvement. No single-point improvement initiative or improvement tool by itself is all-inclusive and all encompassing. One is not better than the other—it becomes a matter of what improvement tools fit best with the improvement opportunities at hand. Organizations will never become best-in-class and

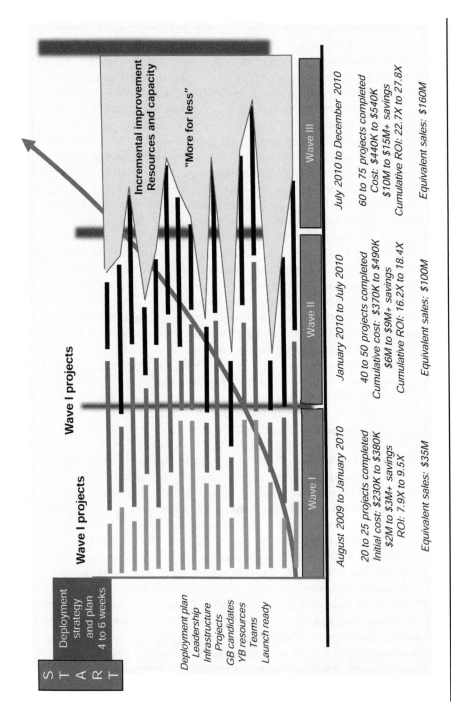

Figure 1.3 Scalable Lean Six Sigma™ simplified financial analysis.

stay there with just Factory Physics®[1], Lean, Six Sigma, or any other single-point improvement approach. The time has come to stop the futile debates about the tools and use the effort to improve how to improve. The best strategy is a continuous evolution and blending of the right methodologies, and deployment of the right improvement tools to the highest impact opportunities. We spend way too much time debating which tool is best, while others continue to move manufacturing and other core competencies to more efficient countries. The best results are derived by deployment of the right tools to the highest impact business opportunities. Many of our clients have chosen to use *business improvement* or *business excellence* for their Lean Six Sigma initiative so people are not confused or limited by the names of the specific improvement tools.

Finally, one must keep in mind that even the most publicized Lean Six Sigma successes such as GE, Motorola, Honeywell, DuPont, Caterpillar, 3M, J. P. Morgan Chase, American Express, and others have their pockets of failure or lack of buy in, and less successful deployment activities. There was so much positive and successful activity and momentum within each of their business units, divisions, and functional areas to cover up their laggards of improvement, and the results of the consolidated organization have been impressive. These organizations are still striving to improve after 15 years, and they continue to evolve Lean Six Sigma as a powerful enabler of competitive success. If you are a small or mid-sized organization, you do not have the luxuries of time, resources, and sheer investment that these larger companies have to get Lean Six Sigma right. There is only one shot at it with two possible outcomes: success or excuses for failure. One shot at success is all that is necessary for organizations that are intelligent enough to steer away from the familiar Lean Six Sigma deployment detractors.

The Good, the Bad, and the Ugly

The question then becomes, "How do you turn around a bad (stalled or failing) Lean Six Sigma deployment and make it a good (successful) Lean Six Sigma deployment in an ugly economy?" Using a military analogy, the *acceptable losses* from waste and inefficiency are no longer tolerated in this economy. Close enough is no longer good enough. Back in the 1980s, Deming discussed variation as a disease that threatened American business and we are still looking for the magic vaccine today. The message in this chapter is merely an update on Deming's philosophy from the 1980s. The buck stops at the executive suite. Leadership provides the structure, processes, and direction that defines business capability, organizational behaviors, and ultimately competitive success. Businesses face challenges and opportunities just as they did 30 years ago. The difference in the new economy is the competitive pressures, speed, magnitude, and sense of urgency for change.

The new economy is full of new opportunities and new problems that have not yet been solved. These opportunities require an investment in talented

---

Factory Physics® is a registered trademark of Factory Physics, Inc. All rights reserved.

people who can read, discern, analyze, and solve problems. Yet organizations have cut back substantially on costs in response to the recent meltdown. Worse yet, executives have pursued short-term actions and have moved these problems to other third world countries. Many of these responses were slash-and-burn actions to satisfy temporary Wall Street pressures, rather than to realize permanent productivity improvements to infrastructure. Executive actions during the past decade have been creating this lost and underclassed workforce that will be difficult to rebuild. Strategic improvement is the answer to this downward spiral. As the economy improves, the financials of organizations may appear stronger than they were before the meltdown. However, it will be a short-term mirage because organizations will struggle unless they add back some necessary talent infrastructure and make a more serious commitment to longer-term strategic improvement. Organizations must develop people who can create value, or they will increasingly become followers or victims of other global competitive forces.

Lean Six Sigma is not a business strategy, nor is it a replacement. However, Lean Six Sigma is a powerful enabler of business strategy and response to the new economy. Chapter 1 has provided the initial insights and the remainder of this book will provide additional details on the accelerators of Lean Six Sigma and how to achieve impressive and lasting results. Regardless of the label, the objective is the same: continuous improvement by different means to fit different improvement opportunities. Success or failure lies within leadership and infrastructure, not in the tools themselves. If the experiences and deployment detractors presented in this chapter have hit home, then it is time to replace the law of unintended consequences with strategic leadership and vision, deployment planning, and execution infrastructure. It is not that difficult to get strategic improvement right, and executives cannot assign a due date to, or wrap up continuous improvement. With the right leadership and infrastructure in place, a Lean Six Sigma deployment is straightforward, but requires a lot of unwavering commitment and unrelenting work. Eventually, this hard work becomes much more personally and professionally rewarding than dealing with the never-ending frustrations of inefficiencies and waste. However, the real payoffs are growth, profitability, happier customers, and loyal trusting and empowered employees. If the experiences and deployment detractors presented in this chapter could never happen in a million years in your organization, then congratulations, you may be on your way to a successful Lean Six Sigma deployment with successful, lasting results.

References

Blanchard, K., Miller, M. 2009. *The Secret: What Great Leaders Know and Do*. Berrett-Koehler Publications, San Francisco, CA.

Collins, J. 2001. *Good to Great: Why Some Companies Make the Leap . . . And Others Don't*. Harper-Collins Publishing, New York, NY.

Iacocca, L. 2008. *Where Have All the Leaders Gone*. Scribner Publications, a Division of Simon and Schuster, Inc., New York, NY.
Roberto, M. A., Levesque, L. C. 2005. *The Art of Making Change Stick*. MIT Sloan Management Review, Winter, Cambridge, MA.

Chapter 1 Take Aways

If your organization is actively engaged in Lean Six Sigma, the chances of a failed deployment exceed 80 percent! Why would an executive lead their organization down a path with an 80 percent or more failure rate? The answer is simple: business improvement is not an option. Lean Six Sigma success or failure is a simple executive choice, the risk of failure is low with the right leadership and deployment infrastructure, and every organization needs to continuously improve their business to remain competitive.

- Organizations fail at Lean Six Sigma because they are missing the implementation infrastructure (i.e., strategy, structure, processes, people, technology, and linking metrics) to achieve long-term success. In the Scalable Lean Six Sigma™ deployment model, these infrastructure components are strategic leadership and vision, deployment planning, and execution.
- A large weakness with Lean Six Sigma has been the tendency for organizations to emulate the big-bang, top-down, train-the-masses, boilerplate, one-size-fits-all deployment approaches of the initial successes of GE, Motorola, Honeywell, DuPont, Caterpillar, 3M, American Express, J. P. Morgan Chase, and others.
- Many organizations have focused more on training and belts rather than on deployment planning, execution, and results. This is a leadership and deployment problem, not a Lean Six Sigma problem. Education is a brick in the foundation of a successful deployment, but only 5 to 10 percent of the real work. Organizations built a solid knowledge foundation with their belts and then stopped at the tough part: execution and results.
- Most strategic improvement initiatives become derailed by the notion of *immediate reason*—the act of attempting to correct a situation at hand with unreasonable actions based on opinions, perceptions, or direct orders from others who are missing the facts. There is a failure to peel back the layers of the onion and conduct true root-cause problem-solving results in short-lived, reactive improvement and firefighting.
- Lean Six Sigma success has very little to do with the improvement tools themselves. It all has to do with how Lean Six Sigma is deployed. The buck stops at the CEO and his or her executive team. There is a strong corollary between leadership and organizational behavior. Using the Six Sigma analogy, leadership has the largest *main effect* on organizational behavior and culture. Leadership also produces large *interaction effects* on people and organizations. Leadership controls the level of commitment and the rate, timing,

and magnitude of Lean Six Sigma success by their actions and behaviors. This is not finger pointing. This is the reality of a successful Lean Six Sigma deployment.

- Improvement Excellence™ is the mastery of developing and implementing successful strategic and continuous business improvement initiatives, transforming culture, and enabling organizations to improve how they improve. Improvement Excellence™ requires a continuous and flawless presence of the strategic leadership and vision, deployment planning, and execution success factors, and a broader, more creative and innovative application of improvement methodologies and tools. It also requires the fusion of all improvement methodologies into a uniform powerhouse initiative, and a broad scope that views and encompasses customers, all transactional and knowledge processes within the organization, and the supply chain as a translucent single enterprise model.

- Improvement Excellence™ is a core competency missing in most organizations because quite honestly, improvement is not 100 percent of people's roles and responsibilities. Many executives and organizations do not possess this core competency. However, most believe that they and their organizations have it and are capable of it. Reading books about the tools and education is the easy part. These activities give many organizations a false sense of where they are going with Lean Six Sigma. False confidence in the strategic leadership and vision, deployment planning, and execution success factors equals a road to failure for Lean Six Sigma and any other improvement initiatives.

- Lean Six Sigma and most other improvement initiatives have their roots in the formal discipline of industrial engineering. Within the typical industrial engineering curriculum is a wide variety of courses on topics such as methods analysis and process improvement, management science, statistical engineering, financial engineering, supply chain management, human factors and ergonomics, team-based problem solving, value engineering, quality engineering, etc. The details and body of knowledge presented in these courses are almost identical to what has been packaged in the various improvement programs of the past three decades. Industrial engineering is the foundation for most of the analytical and human factors content of Lean Six Sigma.

- The challenge at hand becomes, "How do you turn around a bad (stalled or failing) Lean Six Sigma deployment and make it a good (successful) Lean Six Sigma deployment in an ugly economy?" Using a military analogy, the *acceptable losses* from waste and inefficiency are no longer tolerated in this economy. Close enough is no longer good enough.

- The message in this chapter is merely an update on Deming's philosophy from the 1980s. The buck stops at the executive suite. Leadership provides the structure, processes, and direction that define business capability, organizational behaviors, and ultimately competitive success. Businesses face challenges and opportunities just as they did 30 years ago. The difference in the new economy is the competitive pressure, speed, magnitude, and the sense of urgency for change.

2

Scalable Improvement 2010 and Beyond: Rapid Deployment and Rapid Results

The Fallacy of Improvement: Acceleration Entrapment

Many organizations are already in what they believe to be an acceleration mode. Without a doubt, the economic meltdown has propagated a variety of financial survival strategies within most organizations. Executives rapidly change directions and increase the level of activities and performance expectations, shortening completion times to *now*. This leadership strategy appears to work brilliantly—for a while—because the perception is that many fires are being extinguished. What starts as an intended burst of improvement activities becomes a continuous one-way saga of perpetually overloading people without communication and reason, with dire consequences for nonperformance. Executives try to make this chaotic execution process the norm in their organizations. Instead, it becomes leadership by interference.

This is a good time for a reminder that there is a big difference between *change* and *improvement*. Leadership may ask their organizations to make both value-adding and nonvalue-adding changes that do not necessarily end in improvement. They follow up with directive after directive that undermines process, reinforces firefighting, and shuns root-cause problem solving. In fact, many of these hip-shooting directives produce more waste and confusion than benefits. This agitation style of leadership direction becomes the familiar *Whack-A-Mole* game. As one problem appears to be resolved, two others pop up and the original problem pops up again, and so on. When things begin to break down, executives oversimplify the *whys* and attempt to deal with the symptoms instead of the root causes. They blame the failures on the lack of motivation, loyalty, and commitment, the quiet undermining of orders, or incompetence. Then they respond by adding more directives and increasing pressures, making matters worse. These frenzied cycles scatter the organization's focus and destroy trust, credibility, and teamwork. The symptoms are visible in the form of defeatist attitudes, hollow commitment, fear, insecurity, continuous complaints about lack of time, and long hours of presence without value.

For the past 18 months, the most asinine direction of organizations has been focusing on the present while failing to recognize that improving the present is what successfully takes them to the future. Leadership has been changing culture—now there is a deadline every nanosecond, which does not give people time enough to think through their actions. This speedy approach grows the waste and nonvalue-added activity in an organization. These leadership directives have driven some organizations and cultures backward while prettying up the financial statements. This is the worst culture to deal with when attempting to change anything because everyone is running around looking for convenient excuses not to improve, or do anything else that is additional work, when they need to improve the most.

First, this is not leadership in the long term. If continued, it will be a futile attempt at gathering the herd. Second, this is not acceleration, but *acceleration entrapment* and a false sense of productivity and success. Third, this leadership style might have made the difference between survival and Chapter 11 bankruptcy in many organizations during the past 18 to 24 months. However, executives must now take a critical look at their organizations, and question their meltdown leadership behaviors and cultural effects. Right or wrong, the leadership behaviors in this meltdown have driven a huge wedge between immediate needs and improvement to a point where many people again view the two as separate entities. History is exactly what it is, and we cannot rewind it. Nevertheless, it is now time for organizations to move from survival to success with the same urgency and immediacy as their executives demonstrated in response to the meltdown. This must also be a two-way process. Executives need to take a deep breath and listen to the voice of their organizations, and employees must possess the motivation to speak up and proactively participate in leading change and be comfortable enough to collaborate about acceptable options. Leadership must come from all directions: top down, bottom up, outside in, and inside out. However, it is the responsibility of the CEO and the official leaders to break the cycle. The only way to break this acceleration entrapment is for executives to recognize the need to shift from *survival* to *success* mode, and for employees to participate proactively in change instead of complaining about change.

Breaking this acceleration entrapment is a necessary step in moving forward successfully with any organizational initiative. Organizations have successfully used the following steps to reset direction and priorities:

1. *Stop, look, listen, and reflect*—Today is a good time for executives, organizations, and their people to look at all that they have accomplished

through the meltdown. These accomplishments may have come at the expense of negative effects on culture. Now it is time to set some new priorities for the new challenges ahead—new challenges that require new thinking, new talent and skills, and new actions for success. Continually adding new assignments and requirements is not the way out of survival mode and on to success. There are activities in the pile that are no longer essential or relevant. Executives need this time to pause and look for the visible symptoms of an acceleration-entrapped organization.

2. *Reset and realign priorities*—This requires a quick sanity check of the business strategy and performance to date. Then it is time to separate the wheat from the chaff in terms of organizational activities. This step involves recruiting help by listening to the voice of the organization. One effective approach is to ask key people throughout the organization to make a list with three columns:

   a. Activities that are essential (value adding) to fulfilling customer requirements and meeting business objectives

   b. Activities that are clearly disruptive and non-value adding to both of the above

   c. Activities that need to be either cancelled or postponed due to lack of realistic bandwidth

3. *Take out the trash*—Many organizations execute this step poorly. It is time to move aside the emotions and deal with the true value-adding facts. The CEO and the executive team should be able to translate the organization's inputs into actions that visually demonstrate a resetting of the course. This is the quick house cleaning and resetting of priorities identified in the above step. Over time, people receive so many directives that add to their roles that they cannot be effective at anything. Directives keep coming, yet nothing is ever removed from people's plates. Instead, it is managed by superficial statements such as, "Make it happen" and "Just do it." In reality, there is a lot of trash on people's plates—nonvalue-adding duties that are not needed for broader organizational success. This step should reduce total commitments so that people can do a better job on the remaining priorities or new initiatives such as Lean Six Sigma.

4. *Acknowledge and communicate*—Many organizations are loaded with employees who come to work every day with their eyes glazed over from change. Much of this change has been necessary, but is not communicated clearly. Acknowledge the successes through the meltdown, but also recognize the limitations of a narrowly focused and reactive leadership. People have been through so much change in the past 18 months—many have thrown up their hands in frustration, waiting to find out what they should change next or worrying about their jobs being outsourced to another low-cost country. The CEO and his or her team must lead the organization out of survival mode and into success mode. Organizations need to hear, understand, see, and believe in the resetting of priorities from

survival to success mode. This must be visible both in executive behaviors and in how their work environment is improving every day.

5. *Stay out of the traps*—This is simply avoiding acceleration entrapment in the first place. Executives must follow steps 1, 2, and 3, routinely keeping the most important organizational activities in the forefront and aligned to customer and business success. This also includes a regulated and disciplined process for prioritizing and adding new requirements into the organization. The other part of this routine is continuously weeding out the nonessential and irrelevant activities that seem to find their way into all organizations, intentionally or unintentionally. It is wishful thinking to expect success when loading organizations to 80 or 90 percent of bandwidth and providing additional capacity to deal with the surprises and unknowns in this new economy. Not only is it wishful thinking, it is also an impractical sell. The next best option is to stay out of the acceleration trap by routinely practicing the aforementioned guidelines. Executives need to become more sensitized to the real capacity limitations of their people, and proactively manage nonvalue-added activities that organically creep into their organizations. These deliberate leadership actions will improve how the organization senses and responds correctly to change, realigns priorities, and stays focused on value-adding activities.

The need for improvement and change is more prevalent than ever in every organization, business unit, function, location, country, etc. Acceleration entrapment needs to be prevented or it will continue to be a destructive force to culture.

Even the best performers eventually become ineffective at executing everything correctly, and some get frustrated and burn out. Organizations need to change, but they also need to retain their best talent in the process. When an organization is stuck in this acceleration entrapment, leadership needs to recognize, stop, and change it. We have all been through the most devastating economic cycle of our time. It is time to put the meltdown and the acceleration entrapment behaviors behind us and shift from *change and survival* mode to long-term *improvement and success* mode. Serious strategic improvement initiatives, such as a successful Lean Six Sigma deployment, are the largest enablers of this shift.

The Improvement-Dysfunctional Organization

Acceleration entrapment in the post-meltdown economy has led to the creation of improvement-dysfunctional organizations. This occurs because of two primary reasons:

1. *When acceleration entrapment lasts long enough to become the accepted norm*—This has been particularly prevalent in this economic meltdown. In these organizations, daily firefighting for survival is so entrenched that they cannot see the negative impact and inefficiencies of their actions. Organizations that remain in this mode long enough make these short-sighted practices the norms of their organization—norms that will not lead to success. This establishes a culture that runs counter to strategic improvement initiatives such as Lean Six Sigma. Although executives are working in good faith, it is with bad behaviors. Some of the practices that tend to stick in these organizations include:

   - One-way, dictatorial leadership that views discussions, negotiation, and disagreement as insubordination and incompetence. There is an unwillingness to provide direction on priorities because executives view and communicate that *everything* is important and expect employees to figure out how to make it all happen.
   - Launching a significant number of activities (more than the organization is physically able to complete) that produces a perception of progress but is totally disconnected and questionable in terms of immediate or ultimate benefit to the organization.
   - Survival politics and agendas that seem to fall in with the program on the surface, but stifle the loyalty, commitment, thinking, creativity, and morale of individuals in the organization. People know they cannot do everything, so they prioritize workloads according to what will cause them the least amount of overall trouble.
   - Inefficient use of key resources due to the severe overloading and underutilization of people and skill sets, fragmentation of organizational efforts, and other insensitive shut-up-and-just-do-it practices, eventu-

ally creating an environment of permanent hopelessness, frustration, and disrespect.

- Acceptance of mediocrity, waste, disconnected processes, band-aid fixes, excuses, and the appearance and perception of getting things done.
- Too much talk, too many versions of the facts, blame-gaming, destructive contagious behaviors, and too much time wasted in meetings that do not resolve issues or make anything better.
- A false sense of organizational cohesion, when there is actually a silent lack of consensus on strategy and conflicting views of what and how to change. This is blind obedience where people choose to remain silent and keep their jobs, rather than openly discuss the merits and options for a particular directive.

2. *When organizations underestimate, oversimplify, and lack the patience and leadership to implement successful strategies and processes to permanently change financial performance and culture*—They are clearly missing the core competency of Improvement Excellence™ and fail to recognize that it is a legitimate core competency. Executives put their organizations through the mechanics and process of change, but there is usually more sizzle than substance. This also establishes a culture that runs counter to strategic improvement initiatives such as Lean Six Sigma because people become tired of another program. Executives are working in good faith, but with bad information and bad behaviors. Some of the practices that tend to stick in these organizations include:

- A myopic view of their world where improvement is viewed as an in-addition-to, nice-to-have, we-do-not-need-now, or do-not-have-time effort. It is not viewed as a must-do effort. Executives openly condone and condemn improvement by their actions with phrases such as: "This is what is wrong. Now stop wasting time and do it."; "We don't have time to improve. Forget the analysis, I need an answer."; or "The time isn't right to improve." Their views are copouts for real leadership. Executives in these organizations are lacking a clear vision of change and are missing the courage to step up and move their organization forward correctly. This is further exacerbated by the stress of short-term performance clouding their minds.
- A subtle level of cultural arrogance of knowing how to do everything and an unwillingness to learn from other credible sources. Much of this is driven by executives who send clear messages similar to, "We're okay because we hire only the best people," or "If I need to hire someone from the outside then I must have the wrong people inside."
- Organizations that are stuck in the same-thinking, same-people, same-processes, same-results syndrome. They continue to stay on the same basic course, pumping in more effort without seeing any difference in

the results. Then they redouble their efforts and continue to see the same results.

- A false sense of confidence due to their belief that going through the motions and copying other organizations will improve organizational performance. Their idea of improvement includes training-the-masses, boilerplate-bandwagon improvement programs, or the recent black-belt certification approaches. They are now disillusioned about why the dropping in of dozens of black belts has not improved performance. The "banners-and-slogans" executives in these organizations are uninformed about the importance of infrastructure and drift unsuccessfully from one initiative to the next. One organization comes to mind whose lobby is full of continuous improvement plaques but is now facing Chapter 11 bankruptcy.

- "We-are-different" and "we-do-not-need-to" cultures in which executives are unwilling to acknowledge the effort and make the proper investment in planning, resources, time, and processes to move their organizations forward. They want the magic bullet and fail to recognize the complexities and time it took to get into their situations. They think about improvement in a series of superficial, oversimplified, and lightweight phrases such as: "How fast can we finish improvement?"; "Wrap up improvement."; or "Just give me the answers." Other phrases include: "We already know the problems."; "Just do it."; or "We don't have time to improve." These organizations view improvement infrastructure and planning as overhead and are interested only in action—usually the wrong action. Improvement is definitely an in-addition-to initiative, and the focus always tends to be on the results that offer instant gratification. These leadership behaviors undermine any chances for a successful strategic improvement initiative.

The net effect of the above is usually poor continued business performance, loss of customer and stakeholder confidence, lack of a clear path to a successful future, and a defeatist culture. No matter how much effort is expended, people are ineffective at trying to make sense out of this failing organizational infrastructure. Trying to overlay a serious strategic improvement initiative such as Lean Six Sigma on these organizations is like trying to squeeze fifty pounds of sugar into a ten-pound bag. Trying to accommodate these organizations with a courtesy level of Lean Six Sigma (e.g., a pinch of education, a dash of the tools) is also a worthless proposition. Within weeks, the daily pressures will erase improvement efforts as if they never existed. No matter how much certain members of these organizations pontificate about the tools or grandstand with PowerPoint presentations and the supercilious haughty spreading of buzzwords, successful and sustaining strategic improvement is not happening! Period! End of story!

A few years back we visited one such $100M organization that grew rapidly but had become unprofitable and in the red for 18 months. Everyone was in high gear and barely had time to talk with us, but the organization was literally oozing with improvement opportunities. We proposed an organization-wide improvement initiative focused on key business processes and critical strategic needs such as product development, field quality and reliability, customer relationship management, and visible quick-strike improvement. The proposal was structured more as a turnaround project using improvement, rather than an improvement project per se. We also identified over $5M in benefits that were achievable within the next 12 to 18 months. The CEO's response was, "This all sounds great, but we don't have time to stop what we're doing right now. Besides, I am comfortable continuing with our present course and confident that things will turn around." They were at the beginning of their financial sled ride and refused to look reality in the face.

At the time, that project would have made them a profitable and strategically focused organization again. However, they were too busy being inwardly focused, doing all the things that were not working, and hoping for things to turn around. Insanity got the best of this organization, and they are no longer in business today. A sad reality is that there are many organizations currently in this identical situation, and the new economy is going to become the nails in their coffin if they do not lead, think, behave, and act differently.

Turning an improvement-dysfunctional organization around is a challenging and difficult proposition; it is like spinning the Queen Mary around in Boston Harbor. However, this is a fact of organizational and cultural life that organizations must deal with if they are sincerely committed to change and strategic improvements. First, it requires the CEO to recognize and acknowledge that the organization is broken, and in a sense, admit to failure whether it was or was not on his watch. Then, the CEO needs to emerge from the ashes as the new visionary leader. It takes a serious commitment and level of effort to heal the wounds, repair broken communications, and rebuild trust and collaboration. Most CEOs and their executive teams benefit from external expertise in their ascent to break the treadmill of inefficiency. Improvement-dysfunctional organizations lack the infrastructure to change or to support a successful improvement initiative. These organizations usually need a new external executive or a strong internal executive to rise to the occasion and stop the insanity. The best way to turn around an improvement-dysfunctional organization is to lead them through the formal strategic leadership and vision, deployment planning, and execution infrastructure-building process. This identifies new suitable opportunities and a new course away from survival mode and toward success mode. Executives who are successful at transforming themselves through this process achieve the status of becoming the new admired leaders of great organizations.

The Separation Disorder of Improvement

There is a fundamental problem with improvement—a problem that has existed for decades. Today, there is a widespread acceptance of improvement in concept only. However, improvement has always been presented as a disconnected body of knowledge and only an option for business challenges. Improvement has never been built into the core curricula in business or engineering schools, with the exception of industrial engineering. Improvement is not viewed as part of the standard formal roles and responsibilities. General accounting courses make no mention of how to reduce defects, streamline the monthly close process, or reduce invoicing errors and obsolete inventory. Electronic circuit design courses make no mention of source selection guidelines or reducing the cost of design validation or effective teaming practices. Customer service courses make no mention of how to analyze and reduce warranty and returns or field-service spare parts shortages. Sales or marketing courses make no mention about how to improve the selling process or manage product proliferation. Hence, this is a basis for the continuing battle around improvement, and the perception of improvement as an effort that is in addition to the individual's normal duties. This dilemma is further complicated by business strategy, executive behaviors, performance management, and the growing demands of the new economy. We cannot wait for academia to catch up because even if it did, the knowledge may well be obsolete in two months or two quarters. The need for improvement is evolving faster than the capability of most organizations to improve, and to improve how they improve. One thing is for certain—a new model of improvement is definitely necessary for success in the future.

While there has been widespread acceptance of improvement in concept, there has been a reluctance to commit to improvement as a recognized business function. During the past three decades, the baton for improvement has been passed around in organizations between manufacturing, quality, IT, human resources, strategic planning, supply chain, engineering, and finance. Commitment to improvement has been more of a series of token agreements. Organizations have developed this recurring pattern of the separation disorder of improvement; when push comes to shove, improvement initiatives are the first casualty. Coincidently, another trend has existed for the past three decades: when times are bad, improvement is the first casualty. Conversely, when times are good, improvement is the first casualty. Continuous improvement becomes impossible to achieve with this separation disorder. Strategic improvement is every bit as important as sales and marketing, new product and services development, financial management, customer service, and other key business processes. Only recently have a small number of organizations recognized this and committed to it by creating a vice president position (e.g., VP business excellence, VP business improvement, VP Lean Six Sigma, etc.). Today, the majority of organizations is more interested in micromanaging overhead expenses and fails to see the strategic importance and benefits of improvement as a recognized role and responsibility center in their organizations. Every executive will openly admit that their organization needs to improve, but their behaviors and actions are often contradictory and undermining to improvement. This is why organizations have not been able to keep the *continuous* in continuous improvement. This reluctance to recognize the need for improvement and commit to it for the long haul has resulted in intermittent improvement instead of continuous improvement. The problem with *intermittent* improvement is obvious: the combination of competitive market forces, technology developments, emerging customer requirements, and competitor's improvements quickly wipe away any progress from intermittent improvement. *Catch up* is not a successful business strategy, particularly in the new economy.

Scalable Lean Six Sigma™: An Accelerated Improvement Model

In 2001, The Center for Excellence in Operations developed Scalable Lean Six Sigma™, a rapid-deployment and rapid-results approach (see Figure 2.1). This model was inspired by a eureka moment meeting with a CEO from a $100 million company. During this meeting, we presented our executive overview of Six Sigma and how to deploy the methodology for success. The CEO, an ex-automotive industry executive and engineer, commented, "I understand what large organizations must do to make Six Sigma stick—I used to work for one and it takes a tsunami to get anything off the ground. Our business is much simpler and our company can't afford this traditional approach. There's no question that we can benefit from Six Sigma. Further, I believe that we can achieve Six Sigma successes without all the overhead and start-up investment. Would you be willing to pursue a more entrepreneurial approach that fits our requirements?"

Being familiar with the realities and constraints of smaller and mid-sized organizations, I could not agree more with his comment, and it turned our lights on. The real question was, "Can an organization achieve significant benefits from Six Sigma with an alternative deployment model—one that does not require spending millions of dollars up front, a questionable payback period, education of the masses, and going through the traditional top-down black-belt approach?"

This innovative discussion unanimously confirmed that Six Sigma is not about belts at all. It is all about business improvement and whatever strategy, structure, and action it takes to make that happen. This executive made us Lean Six Sigma ourselves. We shook hands and went to work collaborating and experimenting with an alternative implementation model for Six Sigma. For nine months, their deployment was an entrepreneurial adventure and an opportunity to differentiate ourselves from the large pack of Six Sigma training firms. Their deployment was a raving success, catching the attention of several of their large customers pursuing Six Sigma who were astonished at how their $100 million supplier achieved a magnitude of success so quickly. During a visit, one Fortune 500 customer asked, "How many years have you been at this? We're going into our fourth year and your performance is better than ours."

Customers became even more astonished when their supplier began helping them solve their own design, process, and field service or repair issues. This experience spring-boarded the evolution of our rapid-deployment, rapid-results Scalable Lean Six Sigma™ model for us, and a great foundation for continuous success for our client.

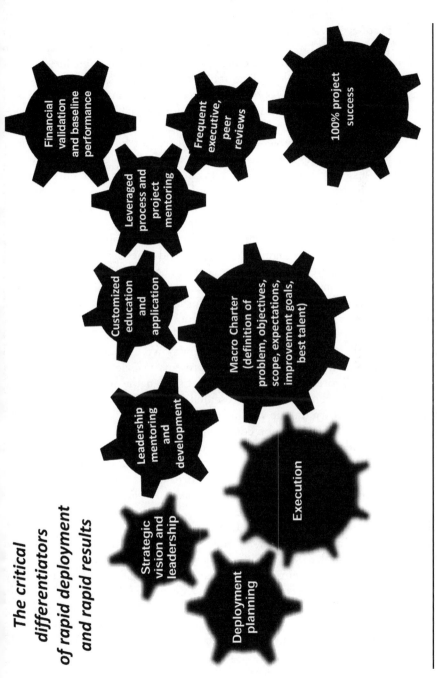

Figure 2.1 Scalable Lean Six Sigma™ model characteristics.

As a by-product, we reorganized our own consulting practice from a fragmented set of stand-alone offerings (e.g., Kaizen, Lean, Six Sigma, Supply Chain, and New Product Development, Change Management, Education, etc.) into an integrated powerhouse improvement effort for these organizations. It made so much sense to integrate the methodologies, since all problems in business are not just Six Sigma or Lean problems. The tools were the means, not the ends. The success of our deployments was directly linked to the strategic leadership and vision, deployment planning, and execution factors. Scalable Lean Six Sigma™ scaled down the Lean Six Sigma fluff and overhead of traditional deployments without compromising effectiveness. Ask any black belt how much of the four weeks of training content they use and, 80 percent of the time, the answer is 25 percent or less. Organizations can achieve significant improvements with the basic blocking and tackling tools of Lean Six Sigma. In addition, this model is also scalable upward with more rapid modularized certification and portability to other divisions with leveraged improvement opportunities. It is documented that we were either the first—or certainly one of a few—consulting firms that was delivering Kaizen, Lean, Six Sigma, Enabling IT, and other services in 2001 as an integrated improvement solution for our clients. The DMAIC (Define-Measure-Analyze-Improve-Control) methodology became our standardized structure, discipline, and common universal language for all improvement methodologies. It took years for large organizations to catch on to this fusion of improvement methodologies as terms such as Six Sigma-Lean, Six Sigma +, Lean Sigma, and Lean Six Sigma became more widespread. Today we encourage our clients to shy away from buzzwords or a name that represents a single-point improvement approach with a limited improvement toolset. When the words Kaizen, Lean, or Six Sigma are disconnected and presented as stand-alone improvement approaches with their own unique vocabularies and occasionally their own deployment organizations, it tends to be confusing. It also tends to make people view them as independent improvement methodologies and wonder such things as which methodology is best or what management's preferred improvement methodology is today. Instead, we encourage clients to use terminology such as *business improvement, business excellence*, or *improvement excellence*, which serves as an all-encompassing umbrella of improvement.

By the way, our sandbox Scalable Lean Six Sigma™ client has grown significantly in revenues and profitability. Several customers have transferred work from China and Mexico to their U.S. facility, reducing their total cost of ownership and capitalizing on their problem-solving capabilities. The CEO and his executive team all became black belt certified and today, Lean Six Sigma has evolved from an improvement initiative to a living and breathing improvement—autopilot improvement or improving how we improve. Since 2001, we have replicated and achieved several benchmark Lean Six Sigma deployment successes in many client organizations.

Originally developed for our small- and mid-market clients, it became increasingly apparent that the Scalable Lean Six Sigma™ model was applicable to all organizations large or small, domestic or multinational, public or private, who were interested in a rapid-deployment, rapid-results improvement model. The differentiating characteristics of Scalable Lean Six Sigma™ include:

- *One size does not fit all*—Every Lean Six Sigma deployment is tailored to the specific requirements of the organization. The Scalable Lean Six Sigma™ model integrates the existing skill sets and education with what is needed to reach the next level of improvement. For example, if an organization has been engaged in bits and pieces of Lean, we do not want to send the message that we are no longer interested in Lean. Lean is one of the valid improvement toolsets. Instead, the model integrates current capabilities with future needs and focuses less on the specific tools and acronyms and more on the message of improvement with a different, more robust deployment approach. Deployments strive to align improvement activities with key resources (e.g., improve what people are doing with a new approach and new improvement tools). This begins to build the expectation of improvement as a part of, rather than in addition to normal responsibilities. Scalable Lean Six Sigma™ is more of a middle-out, build-in approach, rather than the typical top-down, hierarchical deployment approach.
- *Leadership mentoring and education*—This involves educating leadership on the basics of Lean Six Sigma and the importance of the strategic leadership and vision, deployment planning, and execution factors. Executives develop subject matter skills up front, and they are encouraged to become directly involved in the deployment (e.g., beyond leadership support to leading a team through a successful improvement project and learn firsthand about Lean Six Sigma). The idea behind this is that leadership by personal discovery moments is much more powerful than intellectual leadership. It also sends a strong message of commitment to the rest of the organization. Several working sessions are held to openly discuss, clarify, and agree upon improvement strategy and vision, commitment and expectations, defining the deployment leader and implementation core team, uniform awareness and communication, deployment process metrics, executive sponsor accountability, and executive reviews.
- *Extensive focus on the strategic leadership and vision, deployment planning, and execution factors up front*—This activity sets the deployment up for success by selecting, scoping out, and aligning the most important, mission-critical projects (e.g., problem statement, objectives, scope, individual project metrics, baseline performance, improvement goal, benefits, and expected deliverables). It ensures that organizations launch Lean Six Sigma with the *best* in mind: best project opportunities, best deployment leader, best people and teams, best deployment approach, best use of limited resources, time, and workload capacity. The Scalable Lean Six Sigma™ model is a customer-centric, targeted approach to improvement.
- *Practical, customized education in parallel with individual projects*—Lean Six Sigma education is built around the specific needs of every

deployment. Education is practical with relevant participative exercises and focuses on the most likely methodologies and tools required in a particular organization's environment. It integrates improvement methodologies and tools with business process knowledge to the extent possible, including examples using client data and other information. Education is also modularized to inject additional skills as the need arises. Scalable Lean Six Sigma™ leverages the basic blocking and tackling tools in Lean Six Sigma and discourages overuse of theory and advanced, rarely used statistical techniques of a traditional black-belt certification course. The names of the traditional belt categories still remain, but the content has been changed to beef up the practical areas and downplay the theory or infrequently used statistical tools. Education begins with green belts (project leaders) and yellow belts (team members) who work on the initial improvement teams (usually 20 to 25 projects). There is no education and certification for the black belt initially; we serve as the external deployment champion and black-belt resources to the teams. Later, there is a modularized approach for upgrading skills such as transforming selected green belts into black belts and yellow belts into green belts, developing train-the-trainer capabilities, and what we refer to as basic improvement skills. The last is geared to individual contributor salary and hourly employees, and promotes improvement via the DMAIC thoughtware and basic improvement tools in their own immediate areas; these are more Kaizen or quick-strike improvements.

- *Leveraged mentoring of all projects to a successful conclusion; failure is not an option*—Mentoring is the most important, most difficult and most time and resource consuming in a Lean Six Sigma deployment. In many traditional Lean Six Sigma deployments, teams go through the education with an instructor who has never worked outside the quality department. Then candidates are expected to be successful without any infrastructure or processes where there is little familiarity, and with an objective (improvement) that is new to them. To complicate matters, they assign inexperienced black belts to mentor these teams. Many black belts—especially the newly anointed—may be strong in technical statistical tools knowledge but weak in deep business process experience or leadership, interpersonal, and facilitation skills. As mentioned earlier, one black belt project or passing a test does not make someone an expert. In the Scalable Lean Six Sigma™ model, we act as the external deployment champion or black belts and mentor each team to a successful project conclusion. This combines the strengths of daily executive leadership, Lean Six Sigma knowledge, business process expertise, multiple industry experiences through thousands of improvement projects, and best practices awareness. This leveraged mentoring approach is a major factor in accelerating project success because it allows teams to avoid wasting time and stay focused on the critical path of their projects. Projects become easier to visualize, accelerate, and lead to a successful conclusion when one has the benefit and experiences of completing the same or similar projects dozens of times in many different client settings. We are also big promoters of *on-demand mentoring*—not allowing teams to flounder with their assigned projects. In many cases, our firm is on the forefront and directly involved in achieving best practices with our clients.

- *Close the loop with metrics and corrective actions*—This involves discussions with each team to learn what is and is not working, and where they need help. Sometimes this is technical help; most of the time it is human-drama and barrier-busting help. Common issues might include team members skipping meetings, not making good on team assignments, political motivations, waiting for IT to provide data, or sometimes running into barriers external to the team such as lack of executive sponsor support or being railroaded or undermined by some other person in the organization. A successful deployment prevents these issues and alters its course through strong and swift corrective actions. These activities also involve weekly status meetings with the deployment leader and core team, frequent CEO and executive team reviews, running interference for executive project sponsors, or ad-hoc meetings with an executive or team leader as necessary. Deployment metrics and team status reviews provide information on the status, effectiveness, and success rate of the deployment. There is always uncharted ground, and there is always a need for constant corrective actions in a successful Lean Six Sigma deployment.

Figure 2.2 displays an example of the Scalable Lean Six Sigma™ model for a typical $500M business unit, including the rapid deployment details and rapid results. This is the accelerated, low overhead improvement model of the future.

Emergence of Transactional Enterprises

The business world is transforming itself into interdependent transactional enterprises. Technology is also enabling organizations to do more than they thought was possible a decade ago. This transformation is creating the greatest opportunities for organizations to improve, leapfrog competitors, and dominate global markets in the new economy. To be successful, organizations will need to become more committed to and aggressive about improvement—long term. They will need to build organizations that proactively seek out and act on every improvement moment.

The future of improvement will focus on the softer knowledge and transactional processes. Many of these soft processes are untouched territory and ripe for improvement with the right evolution of improvement approaches, and

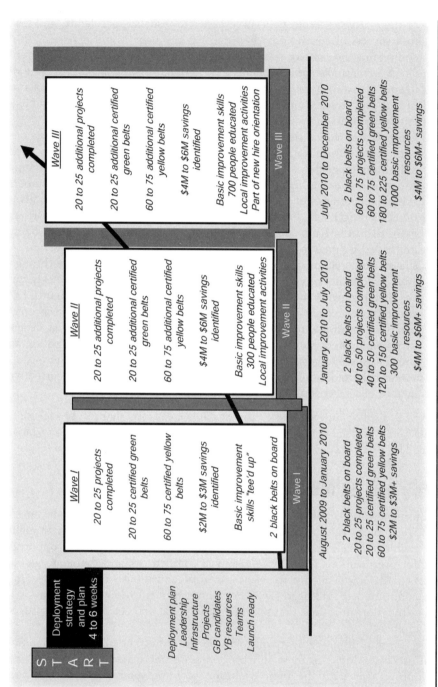

Figure 2.2 Scalable Lean Six Sigma™ implementation, accelerated goals, and timelines.

organizations can make rapid, dramatic improvements. Furthermore, the root causes of performance in transactional processes are often misunderstood. Opportunities in areas such as product and market strategy, product management, warranty and returns, invoicing and billing errors, excess or obsolete inventory, requests for quotations, customer service, global sourcing and outsourcing, sales and operations planning, supply chain planning and logistics, supplier development, selling and advertising processes and policies, new product development, and human resource processes are in the range of millions of dollars. The real challenge at seizing these opportunities rests on the ability to understand, retrofit, evolve, and apply the underpinnings of Lean Six Sigma. In the majority of cases, the basic blocking and tackling tools of Lean Six Sigma are all that is required to make a large impact on transactional processes. Successful organizations have capitalized on these opportunities by looking beyond the acronyms and statistical tools of Lean Six Sigma, and have recognized and learned the inherent power of well-structured, fact-based, root-cause decision making. Lean Six Sigma is well suited to this step-function change in scope and target. This requires the know-how of expanding the scope of Lean Six Sigma from a limited set of process improvement tools, to a creative and innovative way of thinking about strategic improvement opportunities that impact the entire organization and beyond. Any executive exposed to previous improvement initiatives might instinctively think of business improvement in terms of operations or manufacturing improvement and cost reduction, but this perspective is completely results-limiting with Lean Six Sigma. Organizations with the most successful Lean Six Sigma deployments have learned how to improve and innovate in all areas of their businesses—their key business processes, their products and services, their target markets, and even fundamental reengineering of their business models. These organizations have significantly improved business performance while establishing cultures with an inherent inclination toward continuous improvement and innovation.

The Future of Improvement

Organizations must be bold enough to recognize that the new economy has brought along with it new rules for success and the need to develop new models for improvement. We have discussed the big-bang, top-down, and train-the-masses approach to Lean Six Sigma followed by most organizations. These deployments have promoted the notion of scattered mass improvement through hundreds of individual projects across the entire organization. Many organizations have achieved several short-term successes with this approach. In hindsight, this is a great opportunity to take a deep breath, reflect and learn from these experiences, and discover how to take improvement to new levels of competitive success.

The last thing organizations need is more improvement tools and buzz-words, since many of these things are merely rehashed and repackaged improvement techniques that have existed for decades. Organizations must realize that innovation combined with a more formalized improvement infrastructure is needed in the form of three major components: strategic leadership and vision, deployment planning, and execution. A familiar question that many of our clients in the prospect stage will ask is: "With which company have you implemented your most impressive Lean Six Sigma deployment?" Although we have not contracted with them on a project at this point, our standard reply is "Yours" followed by a logical explanation.

Serious improvement professionals who are in it for the long haul leverage off their experiences and improve the value propositions of their own service offerings (or at least this is what they should be doing). These people hate doing the same things repeatedly because that is not improvement by nature, and enjoy pushing the envelope and discovering new improvement opportunities or applications. The consulting opportunists do not mind flipping their clients through the same boilerplate slides, giving the same generic advice, or charging exorbitant fees based on what happened at GE, Toyota, and other places. The truth will emerge with illusionary or quickly fading results. Professionals who have deep experiences in strategic improvement agree that the most impressive improvements are those that we do not know about yet—we just need the perseverance to discover them. These individuals also have the perseverance to mix improvement and innovation and discover new levels of breakthrough performance. The most rewarding aspect of improvement is discovery and having clients proudly boast about having blown away all the original aggressive improvement goals and savings estimates—especially to our new consulting prospects. Discovery leads to growth, higher rewards, better times, and opportunities for even more improvement, which fuels even more growth, rewards, and better times. These experiences and the thousands of personal discovery moments that accompany them are what improvement success, competitiveness, and culture change is all about. The road to these positive experiences is through the combined forces of innovation and improvement with robust implementation architecture as the foundation.

At the time of writing this book, the economy is still barely limping back, and organizations do not want to risk millions on an improvement initiative with questionable returns and questionable timing. Many organizations openly acknowledge the benefits of Lean Six Sigma but are still unwilling to invest until the prospects for the future become brighter. The need and nature of improvement continues to evolve, and the ability to improve requires injections of innovation and new skills. Just like equipment, the capabilities of people wear out or fade away with new directions and leadership, and organizations need to make the investment in human capital just as they do in other capital expenditures or the workplace begins to fall apart. Postponing improvement is the equivalent of postponing true success.

The future of improvement must become more strategic, and more targeted and precise to fewer critical areas. Strategic leadership and vision, deployment planning, and execution must be *continuous*. The returns on improvements must be higher and more rapid. This is the essence of the Scalable Lean Six Sigma™ deployment model. Rather than launch waves of activity via waves of mass training, organizations will do much better with a more restrained, but not constrained, approach to improvement. What this really means is focusing on a major strategic improvement theme (e.g., improve new product development, outsourcing performance, supply chain response, etc.) and then pursue less clearly defined, but more rapid and hard-hitting improvement activities in these areas. Executives will need to become more precise in identifying strategic improvement initiatives that will really move their organizations forward in the marketplace. The other aspect of this new model is education and skills development matched to more immediate needs. The focus is on continuing to develop the right improvement skills for the targeted improvement initiatives, and a less-but-right-is-more education strategy. This is a departure from developing small armies of master black, black, green, yellow, and white belts in organizations. The primary objective is on rapid deployment and sustainable results. However, there is nothing wrong with continuing with the longer term achievement of the traditional belt status as a secondary professional development objective. The future of improvement still requires a disciplined approach of DMAIC—the structured methodology and industry-accepted universal language of improvement. Improvement—particularly in the transactional and knowledge process areas—requires more of the basic improvement tools and common sense than the horsepower of advanced statistical engineering techniques. There might be a few exceptions such as dealing with specific contractor equipment issues or evaluating regional market effectiveness. Education may be phased across a longer horizon for certification requirements, but there is nothing like the just-in-time, learn-apply-develop-win mode of education. Putting the right people through a Motorola equivalent black belt certification is a great professional development activity. However, over 50 percent of the black belt content is irrelevant in day-to-day improvement. Organizations that modify their business improvement strategy to a more selective, less-is-more model will achieve quicker and higher returns on their investment and effort.

References

Burton, T. T., Moran, J. T. 1995. *The Future Focused Organization*. Prentice-Hall Publications, Upper Saddle River, NJ.

Burton, T. T., Sams, J. 2005. *Six Sigma for Small and Mid-Sized Organizations*. J. Ross Publishing, Ft. Lauderdale, FL.

Chapter 2 Take Aways

- Acceleration entrapment occurs when executives rapidly change directions and increase the level of activities and performance expectations, while shortening completion times to *now*. For a while, this leadership strategy appears to work brilliantly because there is the perception that a lot of fires are being extinguished. What starts as an intended burst of improvement activities becomes a continuing one-way saga of perpetually overloading people without communication and reason, and with dire consequences for nonperformance. Executives try to make this chaotic execution process the norm in their organizations, but instead it becomes leadership by interference.

- When acceleration entrapment becomes the cultural norm, it creates an *improvement-dysfunctional* organization. Trying to overlay a serious strategic improvement initiative such as Lean Six Sigma on these organizations is like trying to squeeze fifty pounds of sugar into a ten-pound bag. Turning around an improvement-dysfunctional organization is a challenging and difficult proposition—like spinning around the Queen Mary in Boston Harbor. However, this is a fact of organizational and cultural life that must be dealt with if organizations are sincerely committed to change and strategic improvement.

- There is a fundamental problem with improvement, a problem that has existed for decades. There is widespread acceptance of improvement in concept only that comes and goes and never permanently becomes built into daily practices. Improvement has always been presented as a disconnected body of knowledge and an option for business challenges. Hence, this is a basis for the continuing battle for improvement, and the perception of improvement as an effort that is in addition to the individual's normal duties.

- Scalable Lean Six Sigma™ is a rapid deployment, rapid results model that addresses the urgency of the new economy. Strategic leadership and vision, deployment planning, and execution infrastructure are the foundation of this model. Unlike the traditional big-bang, top-down, train-the-masses, get-the-belts approach, a deployment is customized around actual business needs, and highly targeted on the largest strategic improvement opportunities. The benefit of this scalable model is the rate of improvement in terms of velocity and magnitude of results.

- The business world is transforming itself into interdependent transactional enterprises. This transformation is creating the greatest opportunities ever for organizations to improve, leapfrog competitors, and dominate global markets in the new economy. To be successful, organizations will need to become more committed and aggressive about improvement—long term. They will need to build organizations that proactively seek out and act on every improvement moment.

- The future of improvement will focus on the softer knowledge and transactional processes. Many of these soft processes are untouched territory and ripe for improvement with the right evolution of improvement approaches, and organizations can make dramatic improvements rapidly. Furthermore, the root causes of performance in transactional processes are often misunderstood. Opportunities in areas such as product and market strategy, product management, warranty and returns, invoicing and billing errors, excess and obsolete inventory, requests for quotations, customer service, global sourcing and outsourcing, sales and operations planning, supply chain planning and logistics, supplier development, selling and advertising processes and policies, new product development, and human resource processes are in the range of millions of dollars. The real challenge at seizing these opportunities rests on the ability to understand, retrofit, evolve, and apply the underpinnings of Lean Six Sigma.

3

Lean Six Sigma Accelerators

This chapter provides an overview of the proven accelerators of successful Lean Six Sigma deployments. So much of business improvement has focused on the tools and acronyms themselves. The real, what-really-matters factors have been downplayed in most textbooks and education, and by many who have claimed to be the experts of Lean Six Sigma and other previous improvement initiatives. In all fairness, many of these self-proclaimed experts are great educators, but they are poor implementers (and poorer leadership mentors and change-management agents). Years of involvement in successful improvement initiatives enables one to learn invaluable lessons and experiences from the associated human drama alignment and cultural transformation that takes place.

These lessons are often complex and difficult to package into an illusively perceived recipe such as the stand-alone improvement tools. As we have previously mentioned, the devil of a successful Lean Six Sigma deployment is in the details of the strategic leadership and vision, deployment planning, and execution phases. Yet one of the dangers for those reading this book is the perceived simplicity of the details and requirements underlying these success factors. Chapter 3 will introduce the reader to the 10 Accelerators of Lean Six Sigma results, and the remainder of the book will provide those valuable details and requirements in a how-to format.

Lean Six Sigma Has Stalled

To better understand the dilemma of stalled or failed improvement initiatives, one needs to look no further than the deployment process. For the past three-plus decades, organizations have approached their improvement initiatives with a sort of *improvement imperialism*. Most recently, this is clear in the Lean Six Sigma imperialist approach of following the Motorola and GE models, because they were successful (and therefore must be right). Most consultants and educators have promoted this standardized one-size-fits-all approach to improvement, with a fanatical focus on the improvement tools themselves, and the downplaying of the deployment process that considers the specific realities and needs of a particular organization. This improvement imperialism is the root cause of failure in Lean, Just In Time (JIT), Reengineering, Total Quality Management (TQM), and other improvement initiatives of the past. Organizations move forward in great faith, following perfectly the advice of their experts. This advice has been either too conceptual or too buried in the details of the tools. In addition, the advice has been too much of a canned recipe approach and too focused on the training aspect. The majority of these programs begin with the momentum of Niagara Falls and silver bullet promises, but end with the numbing silence of failure and a drifting away from improvement initiatives.

In our experiences, no two successful Lean Six Sigma deployments have followed identical strategic leadership and vision, deployment planning, and execution paths. There are undoubtedly more similarities than differences from organization to organization and from industry to industry. However, the differences exist—differences in leadership styles, accepted industry practices, culture, business practices and processes, strategic improvement priorities, regulatory requirements, and the like. Success is always derived from leveraging the similarities, busting through the perceived differences, and actively addressing the real differences with a customized deployment. Picture a health club with its diverse exercise equipment, fitness information, 24-hour operations, specialized classes, and personal trainers. These are the improvement tools. It takes commitment, a good understanding of where you are and where you need to be, a personalized plan for getting fit, a lifestyle change, and an unwavering direction. These are the criteria for success, not the free weights, treadmills, or elliptical machines. The same holds true with Lean Six Sigma or any other strategic improvement initiative. The vitality of an organization's Lean Six Sigma initiatives is not in the genius of the tools, but in the mastery of their unique deployment process.

Improvement Excellence™ is not a simply acquired skill set of a few improvement tools. It is a legitimate core competency—period. End of story. Many executives refuse to accept this fact, even though a failure rate of over 80 percent has been demonstrated with Lean Six Sigma deployments. Historical benchmarking studies have confirmed this consistent failure rate for other previous strategic initiatives such as TQM in the 1980s, Enterprise Resource Planning (ERP) in the 1990s and Y2K, and Business Process Reengineering (BPR) between 1995 and 2000. Why does this happen repeatedly with improvement initiatives? It does not happen intentionally by the leaders of our organizations. If we walk ourselves through *why, why, why?* reasoning, the conclusions become obvious. The following explanations are not the all-inclusive list, but they hit the tall poles of the root-cause analysis:

- Executive and leadership behaviors are in a state of flux and confusion in this economy and beyond. Through the experiences and discussions with many executives, this is a heated but recognized topic. Over their careers the same leadership behaviors and actions that have allowed people to rise to the executive suite run counterproductive to strategic improvement and the future success of their business. These behaviors have evolved from successfully dealing with fuzzy, conflicting and ever-changing priorities to getting things done, and are perceived to be the very behaviors for continued success. It is a natural phenomenon for people to stick to the reasoning and actions that made them successful. It is a humbling experience for anyone to recognize that what brought you to this point will not get you where you need to go. Lean Six Sigma success requires a different way of thinking and acting about leadership behaviors. New leadership challenges include finding the delicate balance between: patience as opposed to the need for immediate results; commanding instead of mentoring people on how to make changes; meddling in details instead of trusting and developing resources; giving all the answers instead of asking the right questions; and leading by intuition and perception instead of by facts.

- The higher you go in organizations, the less people seem to understand the realities of business improvement. Lean Six Sigma appears much more simplified to the people who do not have to do the tough day-to-day work of implementation. Executives oversimplify and underestimate the commitment to success, and their organizations respectfully underdeliver results. Executives and managers do not do these things intentionally, but one thinks about how Lean Six Sigma has been packaged and marketed, it all sounds so logical and doable. It also seems easy, but it clearly is not!

- Beyond the exposure to improvement, many organizations lack the depth of knowledge, experience, and bench strength to implement Lean Six Sigma successfully or rapidly on their own. Organizations can spend years trying to put the puzzle of a successful deployment together. Improvement Excellence™ is every bit a core competency as is designing and developing new products or services.

- Another dilemma is that organizations expend time and resources on one improvement initiative and demonstrate progress, and then some of the improvement masters retire and new people are brought on board—and maybe become involved in another improvement initiative. Prior to the economic meltdown of 2008–2009, the first thing many black belts did with their certification was to look for a job in another organization, sometimes at twice their compensation or more! The perceived value of these people was blown way out of proportion by the hype of Six Sigma. Global competitiveness is driving organizations to improve beyond their capacity and capability to improve. Organizations are failing miserably at the velocity and evolution of improvement. For one of our clients, over $2 million in their recent Lean Six Sigma savings was instantly wiped out by a single-source supplier's price increase. You cannot stop improving in today's business world or you will die.

- There has certainly been a lack of Deming's constancy of purpose and a solid extension strategy for Lean Six Sigma and business improvement in general. Anger, aggravation, or looking the other way does not fix this continual succession, nor does it fix failed improvement initiatives. Global competitiveness is unforgiving to those who sit around and make believe that bad performance is good performance, or who tolerate a close-enough-is-good-enough mindset in their organizations. Success requires a different way of thinking and acting in regards to improvement. The right strategic leadership and vision, deployment planning, and execution actions can turn this situation around.

A major factor in successful Lean Six Sigma deployments is behavior. The collective thinking, communication, and actions of leadership have significant leverage on the course of Lean Six Sigma deployments. Whether your organization succeeds or fails is not due to Lean Six Sigma. It all comes down to the process and behaviors of how organizations choose to deploy Lean Six Sigma. The remainder of this chapter will explain these behavioral alignments and the best practice accelerators for the deployment process itself.

Behavioral Alignment Is Critical

Before we move jump into the accelerators, we should reflect on the economic meltdown of 2008–2009 and envision the next decade. In this uncertain economy, how have we led the charge of business improvement? Because many executives perceived and treated Lean Six Sigma as training rather than as an improvement, they chose to cut back on it. Many executives downsized and placed a freeze on business improvement resources when they were needed the most, subliminally placing a hammerlock on their organizations' improvement initiatives by their actions. In essence, many of these executive behaviors have communicated a strong message that improvement is not a priority. Were they justified by their actions? Absolutely not! A closer look reveals that these executive actions are the final steps in a self-fulfilling prophesy. The executives have approached Lean Six Sigma casually and without the correct level of understanding and commitment. The organization failed to build the strategic leadership and vision, deployment, and execution infrastructure up front. Instead, they provided significant funding for education, but little funding for implementation—the most important part. Their initiatives began to fizzle without the implementation expertise and support, and began to waver in commitment and direction. The value of the Lean Six Sigma deployment became questionable based on the comparison of costs and benefits. Thus, executives dismantled their Lean Six Sigma effort and laid off their black belts. They failed to recognize that improvement failure is not Lean Six Sigma's fault. There are many examples of these self-fulfilling executive behaviors:

- A manager in one organization explained their disappointing experiences with Lean Six Sigma during the past three years. The discussions about why this happened all point back to weaknesses in their strategic leadership and vision, deployment planning, and execution efforts (or lack thereof). During this conversation the manager commented, "We were told that we could no longer afford to support Lean and Six Sigma. The latest consultants convinced management to move on to a simpler, web-based improvement process. Although it sounded good initially, it has turned all of us into glorified web clerks filling in forms and report templates on mandated slash-and-burn cost reductions for the executives." Web-enabling a broken improvement initiative does not achieve much beyond being a political hammer for leadership. This approach has actually reinforced obstructive firefighting, masking the facts, and reactionary problem solving.

- A Fortune 1000 company contracted with our firm to help them implement Lean Six Sigma. After a few days on site with their relatively new executive team, we learned that their organization had extensive (bad) experiences with Six Sigma dating back to the late 1990s. We were told repeatedly by folks in finance, engineering, manufacturing, and other functional areas that, "Your project is going to fail because we already tried Lean and Six Sigma and it does not work in our complex environment."

The real party line was that their previous executive team decreed Six Sigma and spent a fortune training everyone in the company. Then they forced everyone to visibly use Six Sigma regardless of the situation. People openly admitted that they wastefully overused Six Sigma on everything because it was the new condition for success on their performance reviews. They told stories about how people would fabricate and report millions of dollars in funny money savings that went unchecked. Eventually, everyone became tired of the games and Six Sigma was pronounced *not applicable*. Convincing this organization that their failures were not the fault of Lean Six Sigma was an insurmountable task. Nevertheless, we all chipped away, communicated, demonstrated results with a different approach, and finally created the groundswell for participation and success. Within two years, this organization has achieved a benchmark Lean Six Sigma deployment.

- An executive (Dr. Z) in a high technology company rose from the ranks of engineering. He was (and is) most notably known as the most brilliant design engineer and technology person in the organization and in his industry. This CEO enjoys getting into the details of design, engineering, marketing, and sales, and he certainly believes in management by roaming around. As he makes his rounds and casually talks with people, he has a well-intentioned style of listening to what his employees are doing, and then interrupts them saying, "I don't want you to do it that way. I want you to do it this way. Why did you do that? Get rid of this. We don't need that, now we need this instead. Change this feature, I don't like it, I know we agreed on this but take it out of here."

His technical knowledge is over the top. This executive is one of the nicest people you could ever meet and he really cares about the company's success and his people's futures. However, his leadership style was not developing bench strength within his organization. In fact, he created a culture where people sit around and wait for Dr. Z to roam around and tell them what to do next. People were reluctant to step up because they knew that Dr. Z would change it the next time he walked through their area. They had their cutesy nicknames for Dr. Z's leadership: *drive-by engineering* and *new product interference*. This company continuously struggled with getting new products to market on time and on budget and that were reproducible in manufacturing, worked after release, and were still in demand by customers. Dr. Z never realized the impact of his leadership style but he was brilliant enough to recognize his unintentional style and shift gears, creating a benchmark product development capability.

- A team presented the status of their project to executives. This team made incredible progress in just two months and were already implementing changes that would save the company over two million dollars annually. The team leader mentioned with excitement that the Lean Six Sigma process has helped to uncover a problem that is much larger than everyone thought, and that his team was only 25 percent of where he thought they could be with the $6 million in improvements. The CEO commented, "Good job team, I don't want to downplay your progress." Then he looked around the table and said, "But, there is nothing earth shattering here. Why haven't the rest of you told me about these problems? You should have been working on these things long before this team! You guys (the team) need to hurry up with this project because you are still costing the company over $300,000 a month!"

This executive wanted to stress the importance of their project, but his actions and words demotivated and undermined the great efforts of the team and extended team participants with his use of one word—*you. How* executives say things matters much more than *what* they say.

Does the Name Pavlov Ring a Bell?

Ivan Petrovich Pavlov (1849–1936) was the famous Russian psychologist who is widely known for first describing the phenomenon of *classical conditioning*. The typical procedure for inducing classical conditioning involves presentations of a neutral stimulus along with a stimulus of some significance. The neutral stimulus could be any event that does not result in an overt behavioral response from the organism under investigation. Pavlov referred to this as a *conditioned stimulus* (CS). Conversely, presentation of the significant stimulus necessarily evokes an innate, often reflexive, response. Pavlov called these the *unconditioned stimulus* (US) and *unconditioned response* (UR), respectively. If the CS and the US are repeatedly paired, eventually the two stimuli become associated and the organism begins to produce a behavioral response to the CS. Pavlov called this the *conditioned response* (CR). One of Pavlov's most famous experiments was when he trained and conditioned a group of dogs to expect the occurrence of food by ringing a bell. Pavlov's experiment proved that animals could be trained or conditioned to expect a consequence on the results of previous experience.[1]

Leadership is the Pavlov's bell of strategic improvement and change. The accelerators—strategic leadership and vision, deployment planning, and execution—establish the appropriate CR to strategic improvement. Conceptually, there is not much difference between "It's time to eat" and "It's time to improve," except the improvement bell must ring continuously. Before an organization jumps into the accelerators of a successful Lean Six Sigma deployment, executives must put their behaviors in check and think about how these behaviors are either promoters or inhibitors of success. This is nothing personal—these are unintentional, good-faith behaviors in the strife for leading the organization down a successful path. But these behaviors are real and set the pace for the organization because people are observing these behaviors closely and acting accordingly. In this uncertain economy, many executives have been sitting tight, holding on to the purse strings, playing games with short-term results, watching their people dealing with the same recurring customer issues, tolerating the inefficiencies and waste growing around them, hoping that the economy will return to 2005 standards. People are too busy with short-term firefighting and doing more of the wrong things every day. Since 2008, many executives have their organizations ping-ponging around with short attention spans and total confusion about what they should do next. In a challenging economy, the behaviors of many executives suppress creativity and innovation and resurrect old habits of mind. Behaviors such as across-the-board spending moratoriums and belt tightening; wavering or sending mixed signals on direction and commitments; openly expressing despair, uncertainty, and panic; imposing conflicting rules, directives, and edicts; going back to the well—these behaviors create huge barriers to business improvement. Their effects transmit themselves swiftly and bamboozle the entire organization. Everyone knows that this is unintentional, but organizations act in direct proportion to the perceived directions of their leaders and executives.

Now the good news: all of leadership's blunders cited in this chapter have been turned around into benchmark Lean Six Sigma deployments. These executives have taken away many lessons from their Lean Six Sigma deployments and have grown into greater leaders in all their other roles and responsibilities. About nine months into one of these deployments, the CEO and I were meeting and reflecting on the early successes and the discussion will always be a special memory. His comments went something like this:

> You know, my staff and I had a few meetings early on about stopping this deployment and throwing your firm out. It made us very uncomfortable as your people and this process exposed serious issues that we had no idea about, and that made me and my staff very uncomfortable and angry, especially about things we all should have known about and were working

---

on. Here we are working our tails off and this process made us look like we were focused on all the wrong things. At times, the process made me feel like I was being exposed for not doing my job as the CEO. You lead and mentored us in a very professional and unintimidating manner, based on the facts, to new levels of improvement and performance that we could not have achieved on our own. I appreciate what you were doing now and it would have been a big mistake to stop this project. We did not know enough about how to lead this large effort and pull everything together on our own. It is a bit embarrassing to think that before this process, we talked a lot about some of these issues, and we were running this business with a lot of opinions, a lot of data, no analysis, and several versions of the facts. I cannot believe how much we have changed in this short period. We all appreciate your keeping us on the right track, and I hope you are not offended by your nickname of constructive irritant because it is well meant.

This is a realistic example of the anatomy of change and where it must begin. Leadership-driven behavioral alignment is an important and powerful prerequisite before, during, and after a Lean Six Sigma deployment.

The Drivers of Acceleration

Executive behaviors are important, because many are held over and are now becoming the norm in their organizations. Although this may be the exact opposite behavior that is needed based on our previous experiences with Lean Six Sigma, the new economy is creating an urgent need to shift the traditional deployment model to a more rapid-fire one. Many executive behaviors are symptomatic of the new global challenges they are facing coming out of the 2008–2009 meltdown. Like it or not, these challenges are not temporary—these are the new norms of business and life in general for the next decade and beyond. The real challenge at hand is displayed in Figure 3.1.

How do we achieve that delicate balance between leadership-behavioral alignment, creating an accelerated improvement and corrective-action process, while maintaining and even enhancing the logical, fact-based, root-cause thinking inherent within Lean Six Sigma and enduring and increasing the rate of improvement? This is not as simple as many make it out to be. All of these improvement issues require creativity and innovation. Successful rapid continuous improvement is now needed more than ever if organizations plan on remaining globally competitive. This means before, during, and after a recession or the good times with every employee and stakeholder naturally living and breathing improvement every minute of every day. Taichi Ohno's improvement evolution within Toyota created a new industrial revolution and redefined the rules of global competitiveness with Toyota in the lead. The time has come for the next evolution in improvement thinking and actions, just as Taichi Ohno created within Toyota sixty years ago, which is still alive and well today.

So what can we expect in the future? The global economic environment will continue to pressure organizations to become faster, better, and to add more

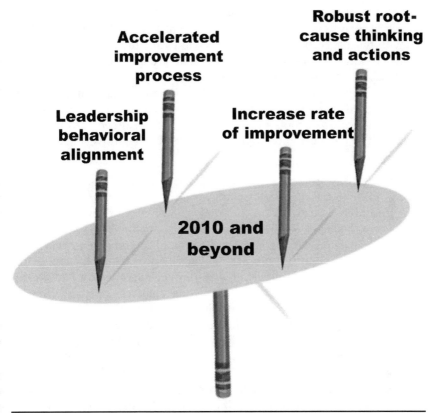

Figure 3.1   The delicate balance of improvement challenges.

value and services beyond products themselves. Creativity, innovation, and improvement will continue to become key components of a successful business strategy for many organizations.

Pointless Intuition Is Out, Fact-Based Root-Cause Problem Solving Is In

Much has been written about how intuition can work well, especially after years of experience. Intuition works well with poker players, firefighters, and medical professionals, and every executive can point to a good intuitive decision they made in the past. There are several limitations with intuitive or perception-based decision making:

- It takes a lot of time and experience to develop intuitive skills. For example, only an experienced firefighter can predict the type of fire and how it will most likely spread through a structure.

- Intuition requires reliable cause-and-effect feedback. A general practitioner can easily speculate whether a patient has a potential heart problem with reliable accuracy by a few procedures and tests.
- Intuition works best in more steady-state processes with limited and predictable outcomes; intuition is inconsistent and nonrepeatable in highly complex environments with unlimited variables and unlimited possibilities—particularly in this new economy.
- Intuition allows people to more quickly make bad decisions in this economy. The bad decisions are more costly and competitively damaging than they used to be.

Lean Six Sigma has promoted the notion of replacing opinions, perceptions, and intuitions with facts. Figure 3.2 displays a slide used in our *champion* education training to get the executive team to compare and contrast their current thinking and actions to the fact-based decision making of Lean Six Sigma.

Many organizations suffer from the dilemma of too much intuition and perception-based leadership and problem solving. This condition is perpetuated at the executive level and waterfalls its way through the organization, creating a culture that manages itself through conflicting opinions, emergency meetings, and several versions of the facts. A Lean Six Sigma deployment is a powerful enabler of changing this cultural norm because it replaces perceptions and opinions with facts and root-cause problem solving. In many cases, what people believe to be the drivers of a particular problem are not the drivers at all. Root-cause problem solving and data-driven conclusions usually reveal the drivers to be factors that were unknown or not considered in the past. Failure to discover and deal with root causes is exactly why organizations find themselves repeatedly dealing

"Without data, you are just another person with an *opinion.*"

- **Unless you are placed at a level at which your opinion becomes data and facts.**

- **If you are fortunate enough to be at this level and you lead your organization this way, you and your people make many incorrect decisions without data and facts.**

- **You will experience this "first hand" through your project involvement and certification process.**

- **"You don't know what you don't know." You will say this in your sleep!**

Figure 3.2   The Lean Six Sigma philosophy.

with the same issues. They lead and manage by opinion and do not take the time to discover and eliminate root causes. Some organizations claim that they do not have time to do root-cause problem solving, yet they always find the time to repeatedly deal with the same issues. This only sharpens the organization's mediocrity and firefighting skills.

The way most organizations have deployed Lean Six Sigma gives it the intense look and feel of costs, resources, and time to gain any legitimate payback, and this is due to the choices they have made in the deployment process. However, for executives observing other organization's activities, it is no wonder why they might choose to shy away from this commitment, especially in this warp-speed economy. Velocity of decision making does not need to occur at the expense of robust, data- and fact-based root-cause problem solving. These attributes of improvement are not a matter of choice: fast but wrong, or slow but too late, right data-wrong conclusions, or 70 percent right, being right about the wrong issues, or being slow but wrong anyway are unacceptable outcomes in the new economy. Intuition is not going away, and intuition over complex analytics is the right approach with obvious problems. *Obvious* refers to obvious not by intuition, but *visually* obvious. There is a huge opportunity to either supplement or improve decisions through more robust root-cause problem solving. The responses to the new economy have downplayed the importance of root-cause problem solving over reactionary management and firefighting. Going forward, organizations must add data-driven and fact-based root-cause problem solving into their mix of common practices and behaviors. Organizations also need to innovate their way to this new-and-improved plane of leadership and decision making—improving how they improve.

As organizations evolve globally and technologically, so do their complexities and inefficiencies. Organizations will spend billions of dollars this year alone through the introduction of more IT and InfoTech content into their business processes. This investment demands more discipline on process but also more quickly creates the inefficiencies (and on a larger scale) in cross-functional, transactional knowledge processes. This was certainly evident in the emergence of the dot-com industry, but unfortunately, it did not last long. Dot-comers were growing at rates of 30 percent per month. The industry was filled with brilliant technology people who, in the heyday of this unique industry setting, could not figure out how to define and process customer order requirements, plan and purchase hardware, develop customer-specified software applications, or invoice their customers. In a somewhat different way, organizations are facing improvement challenges today that they never had to deal with before. Forget about the production floor. How do you improve a web-based global product development process with people, research and development labs, manufacturing, and distribution scattered around the world? How do you improve the web-based sales process that serves as the channel for 95 percent of your revenues? How do you define, develop, and deliver more customer-centric profitable products to end customers in a global marketplace? How do you release a new product, including availability, spares, and multilingual literature in a dozen different markets around the world? Why do we have $50 million in returns? Where did the $64 million in excess and obsolete inventory come from? How do you improve global supply chain flexibility and responsiveness? How do you improve the hiring process now that you have 10 million electronic resumes on Monster.com? Where do we get the biggest returns on our advertising dollars? Are there less costly options to remain Sarbanes-Oxley compliant?

Organizations are working on challenges that they never had to deal with in the past. What is next? We have entered a future where we will all need to solve business problems at warp speed that we do not know about yet. We refer to this as Improvement Excellence™ or *improving how we improve*—evolving Lean Six Sigma and other improvement initiatives to discover and improve upon these new challenges. Gurus have been promoting strategic partnerships and relationships for years, but now it is a must for survival. Global and technological evolution is shrinking internal core competencies in organizations as they increasingly rely on outsourced activities for design, advertising, IT, manufacturing, distribution, and many other areas. It is impossible to be great at everything we have to deal with globally, so organizations need to embrace partnerships and strategic relationships who can *plug and play* their core competencies into the virtual value creation network. Going forward, organizations must focus on synergistic relationships, cooperating and collaborating for holistic success and tailoring superior, solution-based offerings to customer and market needs. The same holds true for strategic continuous improvement, which is demonstrated by the 80 percent or more failure rate of Lean Six Sigma and all other improvement initiatives over the past thirty years. Organizations should be accelerating their rate of improvement instead of cutting back on it, and the upside of hooking your wagon to another partner with stronger, proven core competencies is far superior to the downside of failing miserably at Lean Six Sigma and other improvement initiatives in the interest of saving a few bucks or making individual budgets appear okay. There is so much waste and hidden costs behind financial reports, usually in the vicinity of 10 to 20 percent of an organization's total revenues. Organizations should be building this foundation to seek out these hidden costs and capitalize on exponential change, rather than hanging around and becoming victims of a competitor's good sense to change.

The 10 Accelerators of Lean Six Sigma

Success or failure lies within a well-designed and well-orchestrated implementation infrastructure: the strategic leadership and vision, deployment planning, and execution success factors. These are the most critical success factors, but they are also the most overlooked, underestimated, and difficult make-you-or-break-you factors. The root causes of failed deployments with Lean Six Sigma and every other improvement initiative are traceable to poor performance in these areas. These factors are much tougher and a lot less fun than training in some exotic location, and it requires a long-term level of attention, commitment, resources, and time from the CEO and the executive team.

Improvement Excellence™—the mastery of developing and implementing successful strategic and continuous business improvement initiatives, transforming culture, and enabling organizations to improve how they improve—is only achieved through a flawless presence of the strategic leadership and vision, deployment planning, execution success factors, and a broader, more creative and innovative application of improvement methodologies and tools. Improvement Excellence™ also requires the fusion of all improvement methodologies into a uniform powerhouse initiative, and a broad scope that views and encompasses customers, all transactional and knowledge processes within the organization, and the supply chain as a translucent single enterprise model. Successful change is never easy and it often requires patience, commitment, and devotion levels far beyond initial expectations. Strategic leadership and vision, deployment planning, and execution begin this destination of Lean Six Sigma success by driving a huge wedge into the norms of organizations, and creating the proven path toward Improvement Excellence™.

The 10 Accelerators of Lean Six Sigma are the basic building blocks found with the strategic leadership and vision, deployment planning, and execution phases. These accelerators collectively create the rapid deployment, rapid enduring results of our Scalable Lean Six Sigma™ model (see Figure 3.3).

The following paragraphs provide the overview and objectives of the 10 Accelerators of Lean Six Sigma and any other major improvement initiative. Organizations should not limit their practice to Lean Six Sigma—much can be gained by applying this infrastructure and root-cause thinking to areas such as outsourcing decisions, acquisitions, IT, and InfoTech decisions, new product planning and development, and supply chain infrastructure development.

Strategic Leadership and Vision

1. *Reset deployment leadership, strategy, and vision*—This accelerator helps executives rationalize business strategy, understand gaps between current and desired performance, and aligns Lean Six Sigma improvement activities with business strategy. Executives must prevent Lean Six Sigma from becoming another fad or an improvement-for-improvement's-sake program with illusionary results. Interest and enthusiasm alone, without substance, allow these initiatives to roll out of the gate on a wrong course. This accelerator includes the following objectives:
   - Establish stakeholder engagement and commitment
   - Build a leadership deployment infrastructure
   - Assign a formal executive leadership team and a balanced deployment core team
   - Identify executive sponsors
   - Create a shared sense of executive knowledge via champion-level Lean Six Sigma education, and executive coaching and mentoring

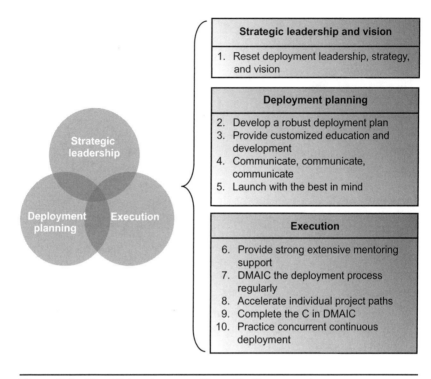

Figure 3.3   The 10 Accelerators of Lean Six Sigma results.

- Establish high-level strategic improvement needs
- Begin to build stakeholder commitment and engagement

Deployment Planning

2. *Develop a robust deployment plan*—This accelerator identifies the major themes of improvement required to meet or exceed the business plan. It also involves a formal process for stepping down the major improvement themes into specific project opportunities. In our deployments, we have developed several templates to guide our clients through this process. Although these will be covered in greater detail, we will introduce you to them now:
   - *Macro Charter*—A template used to collect and identify potential project information such as problem, probable root causes, cost of quality or waste, proposed project name, objectives, improvement goals, benefits, and deliverables.
   - *Project selection*—This template allows executives to evaluate projects against each other relative to their business plan contribution. Projects are scored and ranked against attributes such as cost reduction, growth, level of resources, time, availability of data, and capital investment. The

object is to remove subjectivity or executive preference, and to focus on the organization's most high impact projects with the least effort and resources possible.

- *Project and resource alignment*—This simple template evaluates potential participant resources against a variety of required skill sets and direct experiences, facilitates in the identification and selection of team leaders and team participants, and helps to align people to projects with a level of objectivity.
- *Team assignment*—Another objective within deployment planning is to spread and develop critical mass as much as possible. In our deployments, we exercise the one-resource-one-team rule, which forces a deeper development of bench strength. When everything needs the involvement of a handful of people in the organization, something is definitely wrong.
- *Project charters*—This is the team's reference document for their specific project. Project charters define a specific team leader and team, executive sponsor, and the project title. Project charters also include a crisp problem statement, probable root causes (clue data), project objectives, scope, boundaries, performance metrics, current baseline performance and cost of poor quality data, improvement goals, quantified benefits, expected deliverables, and a rough timetable for the project.

3. *Provide customized education and development*—The objective of this accelerator is to shy away from the traditional boilerplate education structure and develop the custom-tailored curriculum and module content that delivers the specific skill-set needs of a particular client with a specific set of challenges and projects. Scalable Lean Six Sigma™ discourages education on rarely used topics and theory, and instead focuses on a more targeted approach with the practical and most widely used improvement tools. In addition, this customized education includes skill-set development on the soft non-tools side of improvement such as project management, performance measurement design, teaming and team dynamics, change management, and other improvement leadership topics.

4. *Communicate, communicate, communicate*—There is no such thing as too much communication, as long as the message is consistent and value adding. The most important part of communication is to establish the recognition of the need to change, and to recognize why the organization must embrace change. The *why* of change is often inadequately explained or explained with emotional reasons. Well-executed and frequent communication builds commitment and trust, reduces confusion, sets expectations, builds continuity and interest, removes fear of change, provides a medium for publicizing success and recognizing people, and builds momentum for larger successes.

5. *Launch with the best in mind*—This accelerator means simply putting the best of everything into the deployment: projects, leadership, team leader, team members, innovative approach, implementation plans, use of limited resources, use of time and capacity, implementation path, and results. Although some organizations have attempted it, improvement is not something to be assigned to less desirable people with time on their hands. We want to pull in these people and develop their expertise at some point, but not at the front end of the deployment. Sports teams do not begin with their third string—they go with their best players. The same holds true with Lean Six Sigma and improvement in general.

Execution

6. *Provide strong extensive mentoring support*—These activities are the most important in a Lean Six Sigma deployment. There is a significant opportunity to reduce project completion cycle times and results, while still developing people in the improvement methodologies and tools. This requires project leadership and mentoring by experienced professionals with a thorough understanding of key business processes, deep knowledge in leading and implementing large-scale business improvement, and several previous experiences with the same or similar projects.

7. *DMAIC the deployment process regularly*—Variation exists in all processes, including the Lean Six Sigma deployment process. There is no magic mantra for success; the series of events that happen during a deployment are unpredictable and therefore subject to course corrections. Things such as project delays, a team pulled and assigned to an important customer issue, the departure of an executive or team member from the organization, misunderstandings in project objectives, shifting in priorities, and thousands of other events introduce variation and disruptions to the implementation process. Successful Lean Six Sigma deployments require the leadership, DMAIC thinking, and know-how to recognize these detractors and take the right swift actions to reset the course. More information is provided on the specific best practices and deployment performance templates in Chapter 10.

8. *Accelerate individual project paths*—This is the evolution of Accelerators 2 and 5. One of the largest challenges for teams is refining and targeting the true scope of their projects. Even a good job on defining and scoping out projects in Accelerator 2 results in a funneling down in direction once the onion layers are peeled back and data drives the team to the true, prioritized root causes. The objective here is to guide teams and projects down the 80/20 path—where 80 percent of the problem can be improved by focusing efforts on the 20 percent of the root causes. As we have previously mentioned in Accelerator 5, implementation know-how and experiences count more than self-proclaimed knowledge of individual improvement tools.

9. *Complete the C in DMAIC*—In the Define-Measure-Analyze-Improve-Control (DMAIC) cycle, C is the most important step. This is the actual point of implementation and process owner handoff. There are several important activities that must take place to ensure a smooth transition from a team project to the improved process norm, and these will be discussed in detail in Chapter 12.

10. *Practice concurrent continuous deployment*—The traditional rollout of a Lean Six Sigma deployment occurs in waves, similar to groups of soldiers completing basic training and military boot camp. The term *wave* refers to a sequential process for developing people and completing projects. There is a defined start and end time to a wave, and a deadline for certification. Waves tend to stretch out the smaller content projects and compromise the larger content projects in the interest of everyone marching to the same certification deadline and scheduled graduation day. Between the so-called waves, a lot of progress and momentum can be lost. In contrast, concurrent deployment is the development of people and constant completion of improvement projects, and is based on current critical needs. Although a deployment may begin with teams and projects leaving the same starting gate, improvement activities do not end at the same time. Some projects end earlier or later than others do. Concurrent deployment embraces projects, priorities, and resources that are always ready to go, opportunities are continuously targeted and prioritized, individual project launches are staggered based on resource availability, and improvement capacity is managed. The deployment process is concurrent and continuous.

Collectively, the 10 Accelerators of Lean Six Sigma results provide a proven implementation architecture for a successful deployment, and lasting sustainable strategic improvement. The accelerators provide a level of leadership, discipline, structure, and accountability that has been missing in improvement initiatives for the past thirty years. These accelerators are not limited to Lean Six Sigma; many of the accelerator concepts are directly transportable to other strategic initiatives whether it is evaluating, purchasing, and integrating a new acquisition, building a new factory in China, rationalizing global manufacturing or the global supply chain, or restructuring and consolidating global sales and distribution operations.

More Challenges—The Voice of X

Improvement initiatives of the past three decades have promoted the notion of listening to the voice of the customer. The new economy has complicated matters by adding more voices to the mix. It is no longer good enough to listen to some conceptual *voice of the customer* idea. For the most part, voice of the customer has been defined as attribute data based on opinions and perceptions. Organizations now must *define, listen to,* and *satisfy* multiple specific voices that drive the success of their businesses. These multiple voices often have conflicting objectives, which require more focused leadership and a delicate balancing act to achieve success. We refer to these multiple inputs as *voice of X* (see Figure 3.4).

Every initiative—be it Lean Six Sigma, a new acquisition, a new product, a compliance requirement, financial reporting, pricing and delivery terms, and every other activity in organizations—must be driven by the voice of *X* (and the correct voice of *X*). A list of voice of *X* inputs includes (but may not be limited to) the following inputs:

- *Voice of the market and market opportunities*—How well does the organization mine, develop, and create new market opportunities and total solutions with existing customers and prospects?
- *Voice of specific customers and customer segments*—What are the specific definable requirements of specific customers and customer segments that if met or exceeded, creates customer loyalty and growth in each of these specific segments?
- *Voice of the business*—How well does the organization develop and manage the higher level strategy and structural elements of the business such as strategic planning, organizational structure and design, constancy in leadership, alignment and linkages, balanced scorecard metrics, awareness and communication, a positive culture and work environment, etc.?
- *Voice of key business processes*—How well does the organization execute or voice of *X* inputs such as marketing and product management, sales and operations planning, new product development, supply chain management, advertising and promotions, customer service, financial controls, etc.?
- *Voice of compliance*—How well does the organization perform at preventing regulatory or compliance issues and meeting requirements such

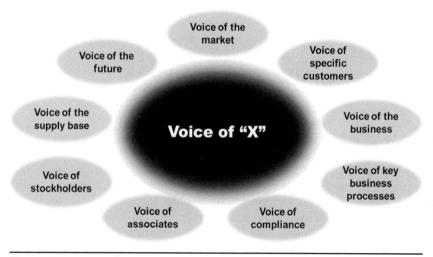

Figure 3.4   Voice of "X".

as Sarbanes-Oxley, FDA, IRS, state and local reporting requirements, environmental, etc.?

- *Voice of associates*—What formal practices are in place to listen to the issues of employees relative to working conditions and issues, safety, medical and dental benefits, day care needs, career development, uncooperative peers, political issues, departmental conflicts, improvement opportunities, etc.?

- *Voice of the stockholders*—How can the organization strike a better balance between short-term financial statement attractiveness and long-term profitability and growth?

- *Voice of the supply base*—How is the organization collaborating with external suppliers and contractors in the areas of product development, quick response delivery terms, digital communication and information exchange, quality and design issues, etc., for mutual gain?

- *Voice of the future*—How is the organization planning for future needs through organizational development, professional development and education, talent development and retention, building a flexible, multiskilled workforce, career development and exposure, etc.?

As we mentioned previously, organizations may define additional Xs or define their Xs differently for their specific enterprises. The real point here is that organizations can no longer treat voice of the customer as motherhood and apple pie. Organizations must define their specific voice-of-X model and align their organizations to respond successfully to it in a quantifiable and measurable way.

Learn from the Past, Accelerate the Future

The recent economic meltdown has driven many organizations to downsize as a means for survival. Organizations have reduced their resources to the bone, and in some cases, they have removed the bone. Today many organizations are in the largest firefighting mode of all times, trying to make sense of and address the challenges of the new economy. There is this reverse-prioritization happening where people are deciding the things on their plates that they can allow to fail or blow off, and there is not enough time and resources to perform the remaining tasks effectively. There are individuals in key positions who are extremely limited and linear in their thinking processes, who prefer shortsighted actions, brute force methods, and intimidation rather than creativity, innovation, and improvement. They are driving their employees in many different directions with many short-term demands. Some survivors of the meltdown are now spread so thin that they have difficulty doing anything effectively. These people dodge the addition of any other demands on their plates, including improvement. Some are feeling as if their positions will eventually be outsourced anyway, so they struggle to find a reason to go beyond the call. Many organizations are in this death spiral resulting in demoralization, lack of trust, and little loyalty. Executives have a real challenge in this recessionary thaw to sort out this organizational reality from fiction, and to create a new game plan for the future. If your organization exhibits these characteristics, you are in the majority of organizations satisfied with short-term compromises over long-term wins. There are only three options to change this lose-lose modus operandi:

1. Organizations can go out and rehire resources and reduce the daily workloads and pressure-cooker jobs of the present organization (this is not going to happen). It is a foolish strategy to staff business processes at an adequate level when these processes are no longer adequate to serve the marketplace. "If we only had more people" or "If we only had more materials" are poor responses to the new economy. This is a new time of improving how organizations do more with less, because these costs are prohibitive in the new economy.

2. Step back and recognize that the best way to succeed in the new economy is to reinvent themselves through strategic improvement initiatives (this is the best option). Regardless of what an organization chooses to call it, strategic improvement is the most intelligent path to future success. The new challenge lies in how much and how fast organizations can improve and own new market opportunities.

3. Acknowledge that there may be gaps between present organizational skills and capabilities, and the evolving requirements of the new economy (this is an excellent parallel option with Option 2). Every organization has this mismatch between current skills and future needs, and this process worsens in the absence of a formal talent management or human capital management program.

Too many organizations are continuing to operate in a nervous reactionary mode and are waiting for things to turn around before pursuing a formal improvement initiative. The new economy is flat lined; organizations risk their own demise if they continue to react in desperation without clear direction and fail to recognize that the only way out is to improve the current conditions. It is time to get off the survival trail and onto the success trail.

Some executives know intuitively that current practices are helping to meet revenue and profitability goals, but major change is needed for future success. Before an organization jumps into the accelerators of a successful Lean Six Sigma deployment, executives must first take a hard look at organizational behaviors and root causes. This challenging economy has driven many organizations to a dead stop or even backward relative to business improvement. People are too busy with short-term firefighting and doing more of the wrong things every day. The signs are loud and clear in people's comments. Figure 3.5 includes a list of firefighting comments heard in organizations.

In a world where over 80 percent of Lean Six Sigma deployments are failures relative to their potential, organizations can no longer afford to approach their improvement initiatives with a bandwagon mindset. Yet many organizations are

- *"The biggest problem we have is sales. Everything is fine when sales are up."*
- *"We don't have the time and bandwidth to improve and do our regular jobs."*
- *"These problems are caused by unreasonable customer expectations."*
- *"How do I know? I know because I know."*
- *"If I had more people and time I would have found a simpler way."*
- *"I'd like to sit down and talk to you about something I can't really show you."*
- *"I don't need data . . . I know because I've been here for 16 years."*
- *"No, I don't have any data. But I know there's something wrong with your data."*
- *"We've already been doing Lean and Six Sigma, we just don't call it that."*
- *"There's no money in the budget for improvement."*
- *"The time is not right for Lean Six Sigma because we have too many other problems."*
- *"We don't need work instructions because only certain people can do certain things."*
- *"I've watched many of these improvement programs fail with my previous employers."*
- *"We improved it by paying more attention to it."*
- *"I think . . . In my opinion . . . My perception is."*
- *"We don't need Lean Six Sigma because we don't have processes . . . it's all creative."*
- *"We've already fixed that problem dozens of times."*
- *"We don't have time for all that analysis. . . . We have real problems to solve."*
- *"You don't understand . . . this is unique, it's different here."*
- *"This is not like any organization you have ever worked in before."*
- *"We have variation, but it's acceptable because it's all a craft."*
- *"This is not a problem? It's just part of the cost of being in this business."*
- *"We don't really measure what we do, but we know when things are good and when they're bad."*
- *"We tried that one already. . . . It worked for a while but then it stopped working."*
- *"I know because I feel it. Some of this stuff you just need to get a feel for."*
- *"You can't measure it. You just know when it's right."*
- *"I don't care about (Department X's) problems, these are my objectives."*
- *"We never have the time to do things right, but we always seem to find the time to do things over."*
- *"I did nothing because I don't have the time. Now I still don't have time to continue to do nothing."*

Figure 3.5   Typical firefighting comments.

failing miserably at building the strategic leadership and vision, deployment, and execution infrastructure up front, and face a high risk of Lean Six Sigma failure. It is no wonder that the value of a Lean Six Sigma deployment becomes very questionable based on the comparison of quantified costs and benefits, but the root causes of failure have nothing to do with Lean Six Sigma. Even some of the better Lean Six Sigma deployments initially began with the absence of these success factors. However, soon after the initial experiences and familiarity with Lean Six Sigma, these organizations recognized the importance of formalized infrastructure to transform Lean Six Sigma from another improvement program to the organization's enduring and lasting cultural improvement mindset.

Globalization has brought with it a myriad of business challenges, sociopolitical problems, and an unending list of other uncertainties that require us to be much more conscious of what is happening and run in fast-forward mode. We are all on this treadmill of survival. If you are not improving your business every day, then some other competitor is and your organization is falling behind. Like it or not, this is the world in which we live. Business improvement through such strategic initiatives as Kaizen, Lean, and Six Sigma are now needed more than ever before. Even if your organization is currently involved in these initiatives, it is time to take a closer look at efforts and corresponding results. In this economy organizations cannot afford political improvement debacles and fad improvement activities with questionable benefits. Only enhanced creativity and innovation in our improvement efforts will relieve the pain points in our businesses.

Some organizations use the challenging times as their creative times. Great opportunities emerge in challenging times because it forces us to rethink and try things we might have never dreamed possible. It forces us to push the limits of our thinking and achieve successes beyond what we thought were possible. Enhancing value during a down cycle enables warp speed once the economy begins to accelerate on the backside. Organizations that do this successfully will become the emerging industry leaders at the other end of this turbulent economy.

Whether your organization is just beginning a Lean Six Sigma deployment or interested in kick-starting a faltering deployment, the game of improvement is on. The 10 Accelerators of Lean Six Sigma results are proven best practices in many benchmark deployments. Many organizations think that they have already incorporated these factors into their deployments, but their performance and financial results demonstrate something different. If you are not seeing annualized benefits from your Lean Six Sigma investment in the 3 to 10 percent of revenue range, recognize that you are missing the mark. Today is the best time to take an objective look at your organization's deployment progress and evaluate its activities against the proven best practices of strategic leadership and vision, deployment planning, and execution.

The 10 Accelerators of Lean Six Sigma results are true accelerators of organizations and culture change. They must be implemented with the commitment, constant attention, and precision of a Cirque Du Soleil show. Anyone who has experienced one of these unbelievable shows observes that actors appear out of nowhere riding bicycles in a circle or swinging from entangled sheers and dozens of other amazing intersecting and traversing scenes, all happening at varying degrees of speed. Actors are literally coming and going from all directions and in perfect creative unison. Every activity is a stretch of the imagination and sheer physical abilities, leaving viewers with the feeling of witnessing something that they cannot believe, and wondering how it was possible. Before one can think about it, another activity makes viewers repeat these emotions. These unbelievable activities are tight processes perfected by each performer. The acts and the music tell a visual story of perfection in execution. Individual actors are paying meticulous attention to their own roles and the other details around them. The performers are a cohesive team. There is real-time communication and information exchange. Every movement is an example of perfection with tight margins for error. Every motion of every act is in perfect harmony via quick response and instantaneous adjustment. Timing and delivery are precise. Commitment is obvious because the performers have an emotional connection to the consequences of failure (personal injury). Whether it is Boston, Orlando, Montreal, or Las Vegas, or whether it is Quidam, La Nouba, Mystere, Alegria, Zunamity, Kooza, or Banana Shpeel with different actors, the process is perfect. The customers are always astonished and thunderstruck by the experience of seeing and being a part of one of these shows.

References

McAfee, A. 2009. "The Future of Decision Making: Less Intuition, More Evidence." *Harvard Business Review*, Cambridge, MA. January 2009.

Rigby, D., Bilodeau, B. 2009. *Bain Management Tools and Trends*. Bain and Company, Boston, MA.

Rodes, D. T. 2002. *Pavlov's Physiology Factory: Experiment, Interpretation, Laboratory Enterprise*. Massachusetts Medical Society. All rights reserved. *The New England Journal of Medicine* is a registered trademark of the MMS.

Taylor, F. W. 1911. *The Principles of Scientific Management*. A monograph.

Chapter 3 Take Aways

- To better understand the dilemma of stalled or failed improvement initiatives, one needs to look no further than the deployment process. For the past three-plus decades, organizations have approached their improvement initiatives with a sort of *improvement imperialism*. Most recently, this is clear in the Lean Six Sigma imperialist approach of following GE because they were successful and therefore it must be right. Most consultants and educators have promoted this imperialism by their standardized one-size-fits-all approach to improvement, the fanatical focus on the improvement tools themselves, and the downplaying of the deployment process that considers the specific realities and needs of a particular organization.

- A major factor in successful Lean Six Sigma deployments is behavior. The collective thinking, communication, and actions of leadership have significant leverage on the course of Lean Six Sigma deployments. Whether your organization succeeds or fails is not due to Lean Six Sigma. It all comes down to the process and behaviors of how organizations choose to deploy Lean Six Sigma. Before an organization jumps into the accelerators of a successful Lean Six Sigma deployment, executives must put their behaviors in check and think about how these behaviors are either promoters or inhibitors of success.
- Success or failure lies within a well-designed and well-orchestrated implementation infrastructure: strategic leadership and vision, deployment planning, and execution success factors. These are the most critical success factors, but they are also the most overlooked, underestimated, and difficult make-you-or-break-you factors. The root causes of failed deployments with Lean Six Sigma and every other improvement initiative are traceable to poor performance in these areas. These factors are much tougher and less fun than training in some exotic location, and it requires a long-term level of attention, commitment, resources, and time from the CEO and the executive team.
- The 10 Accelerators of Lean Six Sigma are the basic building blocks found with the strategic leadership and vision, deployment planning, and execution phases of a deployment. These accelerators collectively create the rapid deployment, rapid enduring results of our Scalable Lean Six Sigma™ model. The 10 Accelerators of Six Sigma are:

Strategic Leadership and Vision

1. Reset deployment leadership, strategy, and vision

Deployment Planning

2. Develop a robust deployment plan
3. Provide customized education and development
4. Communicate, communicate, communicate
5. Launch with the best in mind

Execution

6. Provide strong extensive mentoring support
7. DMAIC the deployment process regularly
8. Accelerate individual project paths
9. Complete the C in DMAIC
10. Practice concurrent continuous deployment

- Whether your organization is just beginning a Lean Six Sigma deployment or interested in kick-starting a faltering deployment, the game of improvement is on. The 10 Accelerators of Lean Six Sigma results are proven best practices in many benchmark deployments. Many organizations think that they have already incorporated these factors into their deployments, but their performance and financial results demonstrate something different. If you are not seeing annualized benefits from your Lean Six Sigma investment in the 3 to 10 percent of revenues range, recognize that you are missing the mark.

- The best time to improve is now. Today is the best time to take an objective look at your organization's deployment progress, and evaluate your organization's activities against the proven best practices of strategic leadership and vision, deployment planning, and execution.

Case Study—Endicott Interconnect Technologies

Mr. K. Bradley Van Brunt, Jr. is the vice president of business excellence and quality at Endicott Interconnect Technologies, located within the original campus of IBM in Endicott, NY. Brad is one of the best executive deployment champions that the author has ever had the opportunity to work with. This case presents an overwhelming, real-world challenge of deploying Lean Six Sigma successfully, and demonstrates the importance of strategic leadership and vision, deployment planning, and execution infrastructure.

Business Excellence at Endicott Interconnect Technologies

Background

Endicott Interconnect Technologies (EI) is a leading supplier of complex, high-performance electronic packaging solutions utilizing a vertically integrated approach. EI was founded in 2002 as a spinoff of IBM's microelectronics division. EI's highly complex products and services include:

- *Printed circuit boards (PCBs)*—EI designs and manufactures leading edge, high-density-fabrication PCBs. This business includes unique high-speed boards with high-performance cores, precision layer-to-layer registration, extreme quality and reliability performance, and quick turn capability.
- *Semiconductor packaging*—This is EI's advanced flip chip and wire bond substrate technology. Characteristics of this technology include lightweight organic substrates, high-frequency applications, thin low profiles that are easily designed into tight board-to-board spaces, and full strip line structures with low coupled noise. These products deliver outstanding thermal and electrical performance, high reliability (2 to 10 times ceramic), and superior system-in-package and miniaturization solutions.

- *Complex assembly*—Complex, mission-critical assemblies that include everything from mission-critical module assemblies to full hybrid assembly, backplane, chassis and system builds using state-of-the-art fabrication and assembly processes. The scope of this technology may include product concept to launch, extensive test capabilities, full supply chain management, and managing large military and government contracts as a prime contractor.

Outstanding quality, service, and delivery performance are a minimum requirement for EI's business because their state-of-the-art products are used in many advanced, wide deployment military and commercial applications.

Mr. K. Bradley ("Brad") Van Brunt Jr., vice president of quality at EI, was given the charge to look into Lean and Six Sigma and how these methodologies could be adopted to their highly complex and different business segments. Previously as an IBM division, they had several experiences with almost every improvement initiative for the previous decade, including Lean and Six Sigma. Many of these programs were initiated by training the masses, followed by strong directives that the tools must be used in everyone's daily work. Like many other organizations, they had several failed attempts at various improvement programs including Six Sigma. Many of EI's employees are ex-IBMers brought over with the spinoff, so there was a high level of skepticism and a huge cultural barrier to overcome. This is typical in organizations with a history of failed fad improvement programs. Brad Van Brunt summed up his initial challenge:

> *"We believed in the methodologies and tools of Lean Six Sigma, and we knew that Lean Six Sigma could make a huge difference in our business performance. But we were determined not to go down the same big-hype, train-the-masses approach of other large organizations. First, EI could not afford the investment and the time to go through the highly publicized approaches of a GE, Allied Signal, Kodak, 3M, and other large companies. As IBM, we could have invested in large infrastructure corporate improvement programs, but EI is now a lean, privately owned, mid-sized manufacturer. Second, our business consists of programs with defined lifecycles that range from a single run to several years. Most of these programs require that EI invent the proprietary technology, so initial yields might be well under 50 percent. We needed an approach that would allow us to make focused high-impact improvements early in the lifecycle to gain maximum benefits. Seventy percent of our employees are ex-IBMers, many of whom are the most brilliant and industry-recognized people for their technological expertise. Our people participated in many fad improvement programs (including Six Sigma) that failed during our previous experiences. Launching a Lean Six Sigma initiative with the look and feel of the previous IBM program would fail because it is too costly, too slow, and would be rejected culturally. We needed to be successful, and at the same time, turn around our people's perceptions about improvement changes.*

EI began searching for outside help and met with several Lean Six Sigma service providers ranging from local universities, large Six Sigma consulting firms, public certification courses, and a wide variety of Internet offerings. Brad Van Brunt learned about a Scalable Lean Six Sigma™ model for small and mid-sized organizations offered by The Center for Excellence in Operations (CEO) and requested additional information about this different approach. After several meetings with Brad and the entire executive committee, EI selected CEO as their Lean Six Sigma consulting firm. A summary of EI's decision is provided by Van Brunt:

> We liked the structure of the Scalable Lean Six Sigma™ approach. CEO's model was a practical approach that focused on the most mission-critical improvement opportunities across the entire business. Their offerings included a custom tailored, turnkey approach that incorporated executive leadership development, improvement strategy and vision, deployment planning, awareness and communication, program and project management skills, leading and mentoring teams, deployment reporting and feedback, and successful results on every improvement initiative. We especially liked the fact that the Scalable Lean Six Sigma™ model was results focused and overhead light and not structured so much just on producing belts and certification. It was designed for rapid deployment and high-impact results—a critical requirement for our company.
>
> Changing the improvement culture at EI required us to recognize what our culture was and our business posture. We were a midsized high-technology company with a history of fad improvement efforts that have not been able to take hold. To make improvement a core competence, EI needed to start at the top. We focused the efforts first on the leadership behaviors and expectations, identifying the most critical challenges and opportunities, selecting the best leaders, and giving them the most beneficial tools and training (the critical 20 percent that would get them the 80 percent benefit). We really wanted a small-company model for deployment. The Scalable Six Sigma™ strategy was flexible and practical enough so that we could adopt their model and improvement methodologies to our extremely unique and complex technology environment. The model and the expertise behind it was a good fit for what we were looking to do.

EI began their improvement journey in April of 2007 with a solid improvement strategy, vision, and deployment plan, and strong unified support from the entire executive team. They established their formal executive steering team with Van Brunt as the executive deployment champion, and senior executives representing the entire business. The EI executive team also invested a good deal of thought around how to introduce this initiative to the organization, since there were already rumors and some resistance about the return of Six Sigma. Rather than introduce Lean Six Sigma as another improvement initiative, they acknowledged their previous initiatives and discussed how to modify the deployment approach so it was accepted by the organization. "Many of these programs came and went, but we did have positive experiences with improvement programs of the past," said Van Brunt. "Instead of introducing improvement as something new, we decided to position Lean Six Sigma as a major initiative to improve how we improve."

Because of EI's previous experiences as an IBM division, the executive steering team decided to call their initiative *business excellence*, a neutral label that was more representative of their total business strategic objectives.

Introducing Business Excellence

Business excellence was introduced as an initiative for improving how EI improves; in everything they do as an organization. *Business excellence* was further defined with the following objectives:

- Create a solid improvement foundation and business or leadership process for managing improvement initiatives
- Deploy and integrate more robust improvement tools for solving the wide spectrum of our critical business problems and challenges:
  - Six Sigma
  - Lean
  - Kaizen (Quick Strike)
  - More effective use of information technology
  - Future improvement methodologies integrated into a single initiative
- Use the structured and disciplined methodology (DMAIC) as EI's common language of improvement
- Build a culture that strives for total employee involvement, increased competitiveness, growth, and profitability
- Invest in the future of EI's most valued resource: our people

Business Excellence Strategy and Planning

EI began their deployment with a detailed, *outside in* analysis of their business. Within a four- to-five-week period, CEO talked to approximately 135 of our employees across the organization to understand their specific challenges, operating problems, symptomatic activities, and political or interpersonal issues. During these interviews, several reports and other performance data were collected and analyzed to further define specific issues and to dig deeper into respective root causes. This process also included a review of external information including interviews with a few key accounts, and a recently completed customer satisfaction survey. In parallel, the executive steering team was using this fact-based information to assemble a list of potential high-impact improvement projects, define objectives and scope, set improvement goals and benefits, and prioritize activities in their Macro Charter. This independent diagnostic process provided EI with the much needed direction, definition, focus, and alignment to start out on the right course.

The Macro Charter identified approximately 35 separate opportunities and served as their hopper of improvement projects. The initial diagnostic identified an upside potential of $35–$40 million in savings opportunities. EI began their journey by selecting 20 of the highest priority improvement projects across the business. The CEO, executive steering team, and the executive team were able to launch *business excellence* with great success: the improvement opportunities were defined with widespread organizational input and facts, so the improvement initiatives and teaming participants were received positively. Because these projects were tightly aligned to EI's business plan, teams achieved noticeable and measurable results. "At the start, the executive team was skeptical about this initial process because we thought we knew enough to make the necessary improvements," said Van Brunt. "It would have been a big mistake to jump into Lean Six Sigma without this solid and well-defined improvement foundation, and ongoing business and leadership process."

Business Excellence Results

Business excellence was not without its challenges. In the beginning, several employees felt that they had been there and done that, and that Lean Six Sigma would not work in their environment. The executive steering team proactively reached out and communicated to the organization about *business excellence*, listened to the organization's questions and concerns, and continuously brought it into focus with a comfortable level of acceptance.

Within the first two years of *business excellence*, EI achieved benefits of $18 million annually. During this period, EI also rolled out improvement to the grassroots level of the organization. All associates (e.g., first-line supervisors, hourly employees, salaried managers, and individual contributor employees) who were not directly involved in the major strategic improvement initiatives received Basic Improvement Skills™ education, followed by supervisor-mentored Quick Strike improvements in their immediate areas. The formal business or leadership process (e.g., leadership strategy and vision, deployment planning, execution) has enabled EI to continue mining, identifying, and prioritizing new opportunities, and to measure cumulative savings of major projects, talent development progress by area, and Quick Strike activities and savings by area and individual. *Business excellence* projects and Quick Strikes are communicated and showcased throughout the organization. *Business excellence* has become built into the new-hire orientation process, and their internal people conduct occasional continuing education on specific topics and areas of interest. Many of the executives have participated in (and continue to participate in) their *business excellence* initiatives, and several executives and directors have achieved green belt certification. Over 100 major improvement initiatives and hundreds of Quick Strike improvements have been implemented since 2007. *Business excellence* has also been integrated into performance reviews.

Beyond the savings is real cultural transformation. In the beginning, there were several brilliant but skeptical employees who were strongly opposed to Lean Six Sigma, and for good reason—they had a bad experience in the past. This is a very real issue in many organizations. What won them over? First, it was the opportunity for people to experience the leadership commitment and empowerment to work crossfunctionally on improvements that were extremely important to the success of their daily roles. Second, it was the opportunity for people to experience their own personal victories with *business excellence* and be recognized for it. Many of these same people have become the biggest proponents of *business excellence* and endorse it as a required cultural standard. These people demand and expect fact-based and data-driven decision making, and become irritated with others who are running by opinion. In a short time, EI's initiative is and continues to be a model deployment for others to follow. It is alive and well today with widespread acceptance as a cultural norm. EI continues down the Improvement Excellence™ journey and is continuously discovering how it can improve how it improves. Van Brunt finishes, "We have a strong inertia with *business excellence* throughout EI. We are continuing to reinforce behavior awareness and root-cause thinking at the executive, management, and leadership level because that's what keeps it as our gold standard for improvement. *Business excellence* is always right there, reminding our people about data-driven, root-cause thinking and reinforcing expected behaviors and improvement that leads to real business results."

PART II: How to Achieve Rapid Results with the 10 Lean Six Sigma Accelerators

"Strategy without tactics is the slowest route to victory. Tactics without strategy is the noise before defeat."
General Sun TZU, circa 500 BC

4

Lean Six Sigma Accelerator #1: Strategic Leadership and Vision

This accelerator helps executives rationalize business strategy, understand gaps between current and desired performance, and align Lean Six Sigma improvement activities with business strategy. Executives must prevent Lean Six Sigma from becoming another fad, or an improvement-for-improvement's-sake program with illusionary results. Interest and enthusiasm without substance allow these initiatives to roll out of the gate on a wrong course. This accelerator includes the following objectives:

- Establish stakeholder engagement and commitment
- Build a leadership deployment infrastructure
- Assign a formal executive leadership team and a balanced deployment core team
- Identify executive sponsors
- Create a shared sense of executive knowledge via champion-level Lean Six Sigma education and executive coaching and mentoring
- Establish high-level strategic improvement needs
- Begin to build stakeholder commitment and engagement

Leadership and improvement are practices that everyone embraces at an intellectual level. Executives know how to lead, managers *should* be improving the areas they manage, and most people in organizations know how to improve at some level. However, knowing *how* to do something, or knowing that you *should* be doing something is much different from actually *doing* it, especially within the daily norms of culture. Before we discuss how to reset leadership, strategy, and vision in a Lean Six Sigma deployment, it is important to stop and reflect, acknowledge our previous actions, and learn from the past. Most executives and managers have been through tons of improvement programs and problem-solving techniques. Most executives have landed in their positions because they are great at solving problems and getting things done. It is a cascading, self-perpetuating process: Executives reinforce and reward their organization for the same short-term behaviors. As people move around in organizations, their roles change but their behaviors do not. These roles represent a different problem to solve: setting up Lean Six Sigma and everything else for the success of others. Improvement Excellence™ is the new problem for leadership. It is time for true leaders to push away their platters of 50 problems that really belong to others in the organization and solve this challenge. Improvement Excellence™ is a best practice that needs to be embraced by an organization's actions to remain competitive in the future. It is a state where leaders no longer need to meddle in or second-guess the roles and responsibilities of others because people have developed the competencies to execute (with excellence) their own roles and responsibilities. One of the fundamental reasons for this book is that there has been a severe shortage of formal education, development, and shared knowledge of leadership roles in strategic improvement.

Organizations must break the same-thinking, same-people, same-process, same-results cycle—long term. Improvement is always possible and always necessary in this new economy. Executives and their organizations can no longer embrace improvement conceptually or on a part-time basis and then act in ways that are totally casual, symbolic, uncommitted, or even obstructive toward improvement. We have said multiple times that these actions and behaviors are not intentional—much of it is the response to this unpredictable global economy. Nevertheless, organizations must learn how to deal with improvement within these new (no) rules, rather than sit around passively waiting for the next buzzword improvement program.

The executives and organizations of successful Lean Six Sigma deployments do not hold a monopoly on these improvement best practices. They understand, acknowledge, and commit to everything it takes to deploy Lean Six Sigma successfully by their actions and direct involvement. In the process, these organizations have grown and achieved the *Great Gatsby syndrome*. This is where executives and their entire organization have risen out of improvement obscurity to become exactly what they should be: great organizations with great people and personalities, with great vision, great followership, great mutual trust, and great stakeholder results. For a bit of trivia, these words are a twenty-first century version of a similar paragraph in Frederick Taylor's 1911 monograph on *The Scientific Principles of Management* where he described the purpose of leadership and organizations.

The Omni Pattern

After nearly four decades in the improvement business, I have witnessed a variety of improvement programs (and their respective gurus) come and go and get cleverly repackaged, rebranded, and reintroduced under a different name in organizations. For a young mate in the high-tech industry, it was a mixed bag of fun and frustration as I worked with many of these so-called experts. They would march through with their improvement programs, borrow people's watches to tell the time, and then present the same recommendations to our leadership that our own employees recommended prior to the consultants. Looking back, these experts oversimplified the process of continuous improvement by reducing it to a recipe, a few catch phrases, and the latest tools and buzzwords. During their engagements some would say things like, "How do you know about Japanese manufacturing techniques? You should be a consultant!" or "Do you mind if I have a copy of your presentation?"

It was even more amusing as I switched companies and read *their* consultants' identical boilerplate reports (except for the front cover with the current company's name on it). In more serious retrospect, many of these improvement programs were released as splintered improvement initiatives, all claiming to be the magic bullet for success. The reality is that there is not much new in business improvement when you peel back the layers of an onion. We refer to this as the *same-box-with-a-different-ribbon syndrome*. The name of the box changes, but the contents of the box remain pretty much the same. If you go back and read some of the early twentieth-century writings of Henry Ford, Frederick Taylor, or Frank and Lillian Gilbreth, they were right on the mark of what we were still trying to get right 100 years later. Regardless of the *ribbon du jour*, business improvement is more leadership and common sense than it is rocket science and tools.

Thirty years ago, America became painfully aware of the importance of quality improvement and executives were scratching their heads as they watched the 1980 NBC documentary, *If Japan Can, Why Can't We?* This was a mammoth wake-up call for business improvement. We watched their industry success at reducing set-ups, defects, cycle times, and inventories based on improvement techniques introduced by Taylor and Gilbreth in the early 1900s. Suddenly there was a high degree of interest in improvement, but the United States still had a poor track record of implementing and sustaining continuous improvement. Back then, Deming talked about constancy of purpose and unfortunately, we still have not found it yet with business improvement. Many of today's executives may have been involved at some point in their careers with the following:

- Statistical Process Control (SPC)
- Scientific Inventory Management
- Short Interval Scheduling (SIS)
- Zero Base Budgeting (ZBB)
- Quality Control Circles (QCC)
- Total Quality Management (TQM)
- Deming's Plan-Do-Check-Act (PDCA) Cycle
- Material Requirements Planning (MRP) & MRPII
- Enterprise Resource Planning (ERP)
- Hoshin Kanri and Policy Deployment

- Theory of Constraints (TOC)
- Business Process Reengineering (BPR)
- Just In Time (JIT)
- Kaizen
- Gemba Kaizen
- Cycle Time Reduction
- Product and Cycle-time Excellence (PACE)
- The Supply Chain Operations Reference Model (SCORE)
- Customer Relationship Management (CRM)
- Lean
- Demand Flow Technology (DFT)
- Factory Physics®[1]
- 8D
- Simulation Modeling
- Toyota Production System (TPS)
- Six Sigma
- DMAIC
- Lean and Green
- Outside In (OI)
- Lean Six Sigma

Within each of these improvement initiatives is their own vocabulary of acronyms, buzzwords, and methodologies that often have confused the business-improvement playing field even more. The experts promoted their own wares while discrediting the offerings of other competitors. For decades, organizations have been grasping at and bouncing between the improvement tools themselves, and missing the mark of how to deploy strategic improvement successfully. Unfortunately, the banners and slogans were, and continue to be, a short-term replacement for the tough work of implementing, benefiting from, and continuing onward with business improvement. We walked into a new client a few years ago and one employee commented to us, "I know why you are here: Mr. X (the CEO) must have read another book!"

In retrospect, organizations have been on a random walk down Continuous Improvement Street during the past few decades. Improvement initiatives have been no more than throw-it-at-the-ceiling-and-see-if-it-sticks activities with a follow-the-herd implementation strategy. As Lean Six Sigma deployments have either stalled or derailed, the new economy is full of people trying to extend their positions by introducing another new buzzword tool. This is the last thing that organizations need.

The latest evolution of Lean Six Sigma has incorporated many elements that were missing in previous improvements such as fact-based, root-cause problem solving, leadership involvement, enterprise and supply chain scope, a well-structured

---

[1]Factory Physics® is a registered trademark of Factory Physics, Inc. All rights reserved.

improvement methodology, replication and validation of results, and the recognition of different improvement tools for different improvement opportunities. There is no need to wait for the next buzzword program because Lean Six Sigma is the most robust and all-encompassing improvement methodology in existence. The DMAIC methodology within Lean Six Sigma provides an effective structure, discipline, and standard for business problem solving. The DMAIC methodology also provides a common, universal language of improvement throughout the organization. Yet many elements of Lean Six Sigma are decades old and are derived from the discipline of industrial engineering. Reading the 1911 book *The Principles of Scientific Management* by Frederick Taylor makes one realize that much of Lean Six Sigma today is Taylorism improvement on steroids.

In the 1995 book *The Future Focused Organization*, the Omni Pattern was presented (see Figure 4.1). This model described how the incorrect leadership behaviors in times of challenge and change could actually drive the organization backward, and 15 years later, this model is still relevant today. For decades, executives have carefully guided their organizations through several cycles of the Omni Pattern. Each cycle has seen the death of one improvement program and the birth of the next.

The Omni Pattern model consists of four phases:

1. *Omni potent*—This phase is characterized by an organization's growth and success in spite of themselves. Executives believe that they have found the Midas touch; customers and employees are happy, the organization experiences double-digit growth and unparalleled success, and mediocrity and inefficiencies are overlooked because costs are not a concern on the break-even chart. Organizations develop this eternal *we-are-great-and-can-do-no-wrong* attitude. The higher the growth, the more the inefficiencies grow under the radar, and everyone is too busy to improve. Intelligent organizations use this opportunity to build infrastructure to support their success because there is adequate time and resources to change. For these organizations, improvement is viewed as a process capability strategy to meet growth and revenue demands. For some it is no longer viewed as a necessary element of success.

2. *Omni competent*—This phase is characterized by a slowing of growth and success, and more organization and controls are put in place. Waste and inefficiencies are beginning to expose themselves, but there is still a low urgency for improvement. There are enough funds, however, for sticking its toes into improvement initiatives via education, training, and development. This phase is the fat-dumb-and-happy, things-will-turn-around phase. Improvement is viewed as a casual strategy that the organization may want to consider to turn around these short-term performance blips.

3. *Omni complacent*—In this phase there is a clear loss of customer focus and reactionary responses to customer problems. There are the across-the-board mandates and freezes on discretionary spending combined with downsizing and wage concessions. It is clear that the double-digit

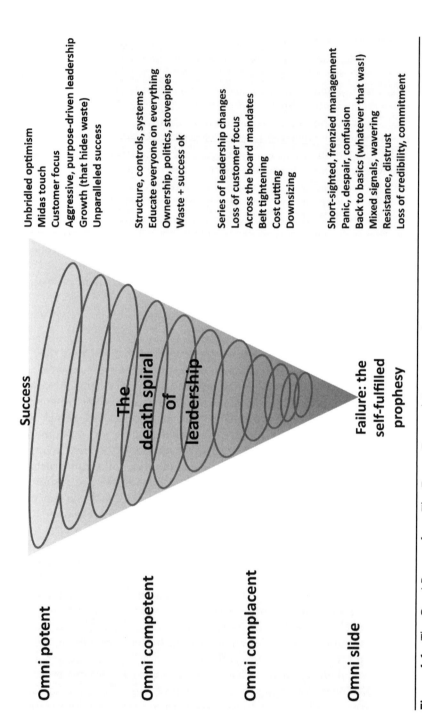

Figure 4.1 The Omni Pattern from *The Future Focused Organization* by Burton and Moran, 1995.

success has turned around and executives are challenged to do more with less in order to meet financial plans. Then there are the usual organizational changes that leave people scratching their heads. People have their heads down in the reeds; too busy doing anything and everything (usually the wrong things). This phase promotes the behaviors of avoiding all risks, doing only what you need to do to stay out of trouble, and keeping out of sight. Improvement is viewed as a temporarily unaffordable element of business strategy due to financial and resource constraints.

4. *Omni slide*—This phase is characterized by panic, despair, confusion, wavering in direction, and mixed signals about expectations for success. There is a significant loss in credibility, trust, and commitment because people may be wondering if they will still have a job next month. There are more organizational changes, a clear recognition of the need to change, and a strong sense of urgency to turn things around. In this phase, improvement is viewed as a survival strategy, but it is now a heated Catch-22—organizations are lacking the know-how to implement change and the funding to acquire outside help. The need for rapid and radical change is not an option; the sooner organizations recognize this, the better off they are at turning things around.

Over time all organizations go through several iterations of the Omni Pattern, like the stretching and compression of a spring. In a spring these actions introduce stresses and strains that change with the direction and force, much like the elements of culture, commitment, interest levels, and other emotions change in organizations. A constant oscillation of the spring creates multiple directions of stresses and strains, and excess stretching or compression may fracture or stretch the spring beyond its intended design. Extremes will cause the spring to yield before failure. This is analogous to diverting leadership commitment with Lean Six Sigma to some other priority. In the absence of the leadership, deployment, and execution success factors, the initiative shifts into limbo, and eventually fails permanently. Like the spring, it becomes much more difficult to piece together the spring or resurrect a failed improvement initiative than it would have if things had gone right in the first place. It is that old adage that organizations cannot find the time to improve, but they can always find the time to do things over.

The Omni Pattern impact on improvement displays the organic degradation of improvement over time (see Figure 4.2). As organizations cycle through the phases in the Omni Pattern, the momentum for, and rate of improvement fluctuates, but the direction is downward. The big question is this: how can we expect to transform culture when we keep restarting, reteaching, relearning, rebuzz-wording, and re-churning improvement initiatives to address the same recurring problems? Our workforces become frustrated with our recurring hyperbolic leadership behaviors and the parade of buzzword improvement programs that lack teeth and results. Organizations lose interest in future improvement initiatives. Executives cannot expect to transform culture with a constant wavering in direction and level of support. It drives organizational culture backward, it

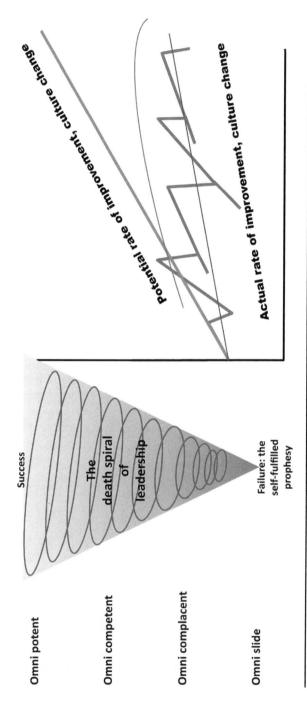

Figure 4.2   The Omni Pattern impact on improvement and cultural transformation.

reduces commitment and trust, it decouples people from participating in improvement initiatives, and it negatively impacts culture—for everyone.

Business Diagnostic: The Fact-based Foundation

One of the most valuable efforts an organization can invest in is an objective *business diagnostic*. An experienced business improvement professional knows how to test an organization's processes against industry best practices, and knows where to look for strategic improvement opportunities.

An objective business diagnostic is the foundation of a successful Lean Six Sigma deployment or any other strategic improvement initiative. The diagnostic provides the compass and working roadmap for the deployment because it provides the up-front, deep-core drilling to the organization's key strategic, business, and operations issues. At a high level, the business diagnostic includes:

- Reviewing the business strategy and operating plan.
  - o What are the organization's goals and expectations?
  - o What are the plans for new products and services?
  - o How does current performance align with the business plan?
  - o How is the organization performing against the plan?
  - o Where are the voids and risks of lower performance?

- Conducting a structured business assessment to understand current performance
  - o How are the current processes and practices working?
  - o Which key processes are working well, which are just okay, and which are severely broken?
  - o What is the current performance in all areas of the business?
  - o Is current performance characterized with data and facts?
  - o What are the key sales and marketing issues?
  - o What are the key operations issues?
  - o What are the key supply chain issues?
  - o What are the key engineering or new product development issues?
  - o What are the key financial issues?
  - o What are the key customer service issues?
  - o What are the current legal or regulatory issues?
  - o What improvements have been made?
  - o What have been the experiences of prior improvement initiatives?
  - o Where are the significant pain points, or detractors to success?
  - o How are leaders and managers performing to expectations?
  - o Who are the organization's champions of the future?

- Benchmarking best-in-class performance.
  - o Is the organization aware of industry benchmarks and competitor performances in key strategic areas?

○ How does the organization's performance and key business processes stand up to industry best practices? What are these specific gaps and strategic improvement opportunities?

○ What are the accepted industry practices, and how could the organization differentiate industry performance from competitors? (Benchmarking is a single data point, and is sometimes either outdated or irrelevant to the mission.)

- Defining gaps between current and desired performance.
  ○ How is the organization performing vis-à-vis the strongest industry competitors in the areas of product and services availability, profitability, cost, delivery, flexibility, responsiveness, innovation, new products, financial ratios, inventory performance, quality and reliability, productivity, customer intimacy, leadership, stakeholder development, or other key performance areas?

- Developing a Lean Six Sigma strategy and implementation approach.
  ○ What are the specific components in the Lean Six Sigma improvement strategy?
  ○ What are the focal points, priorities, and plans for improvement?
  ○ What deployment scope and magnitude is best for the organization?
  ○ What level of deployment will achieve results and rates of improvement compatible with the business plan?
  ○ What is the right implementation infrastructure for success?
  ○ What is the top-level plan for moving forward with the deployment?
  ○ How will the organization align the customer with the improvement activities?

- Defining improvement goals, benefits, and consequences of failure (failure is not an option!).
  ○ What are the strategic opportunities by key process area?
  ○ What are the reasonable but stretch performance objectives?
  ○ What can the organization expect to achieve and by when?

- Surfacing leadership, political, cultural, administrative, or other barriers to success.
  ○ What needs to happen around the executive conference table to set the deployment on a successful course?
  ○ Who are the organization's champions, spectators, resistors, and showstoppers to improvement?
  ○ What is the plan for dealing with the incongruity of leadership commitment, reconciliation of goals and performance expectations, and other immediate leadership barriers to strategic improvement?
  ○ How will the organization improve and take care of the day-to-day activities?
  ○ Does the organization have all the right skill sets internally?

- Establishing the clear need for improvement.
  - How will the organization provide a shared vision of change?
  - How will the organization communicate and reinforce the need to improve?
  - What communication media is best for various organizational segments?

The business diagnostic is the engine that drives a successful Lean Six Sigma deployment. No engine, no go. Figure 4.3 displays the relationship of the business diagnostic to other elements of this phase. The business diagnostic does not answer all the questions, but it sets organizations on the right deployment course. More details are developed in the deployment planning and execution phases. Developing this well-structured, fact-based, results-driven Lean Six Sigma strategy up front may not seem like such a big deal. But, the details of a business diagnostic are either missing or incorrect in the majority of organizations we visit who are pursuing Six Sigma, Lean, Kaizen, Supply Chain, ERP, New Product Development, and other strategic improvement initiatives. In successful Lean Six Sigma deployments, there is a huge difference between motion and progress, and between activity and results. Organizations that wish to achieve tangible progress, measurable results, and permanent cultural improvement with Lean Six Sigma may want to think about re-pointing their efforts via an objective business diagnostic. The business diagnostic is not a one-shot proposition. It should also become a living document and updated as new issues emerge.

One final thought about the business diagnostic: notice that the business diagnostic has not mentioned education or specific improvement tools. In our Scalable Lean Six Sigma™ deployment model, these things are driven by the specific project details defined in the deployment planning phase. As we have stressed repeatedly, education and the specific improvement tools are usually the initial interests of organizations. This chapter will provide additional details about *leadership strategy*, and *vision*. The chapters following this one will continue to provide more how-to details about deployment and execution success factors.

Kano Analysis: Aligning Customer Needs

A critical factor in a Lean Six Sigma deployment is making sure that the initiative is customer-driven and customer-aligned. The term *customer* refers to external customers, internal customers, and internal or external stakeholders. One formal process used to achieve this linkage and alignment is called Kano analysis—a methodology used to prioritize customer requirements based on their impact on customer satisfaction. Kano analysis allows organizations to identify, classify, and prioritize customer requirements—not all of which may be of equal importance from customer to customer. This is useful because customers have different needs with different distributions of importance, and maybe different needs for different

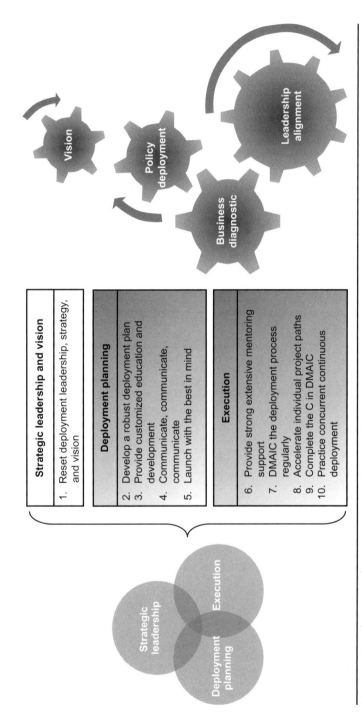

Figure 4.3   Elements of strategic leadership and vision.

market segments. Briefly, Kano (a Japanese researcher), stated that there are five types of customer needs or reactions to product characteristics and attributes:

1. *Attractive or surprise and delight factors*—Features that make a product stand out from the others, but do not dissuade a customer if not present (e.g., a supercomputing laptop and projector combo).
2. *More value is better*—Factors that result in an increase in customer satisfaction when value-adding marketing promises are fulfilled, and a decrease in customer satisfaction when value-adding marketing promises are unmet (e.g., low-cost upgradable memory and screen resolution that is far beyond the competition, or actually receiving the $50 product rebate in the mail).
3. *Must-be factors*—Things that must exist in order to sell the product (e.g., a supercomputing laptop or projector must also meet UL approval) but do not result in increased customer satisfaction when present (e.g., a cup lid that snaps on correctly does not generate increased customer satisfaction and will not generate positive feedback from a customer, but a faulty lid will cause dissatisfaction).
4. *Indifference factors*—Product and service attributes that have neutral value to the customer; they are neither good nor bad, and the existence of these factors do not result in either customer satisfaction or customer dissatisfaction.
5. *The dissatisfiers*—Reasons your customers to dislike your product (e.g., a heavy and bulky supercomputing laptop or projector, high failure and repair rates, high cost of using and maintaining product).

In practice, customer requirements are difficult to prioritize because most available data is perception-based. Trying to zero in on requirements usually creates emotional resistance with sales organizations who are dedicated to giving customers whatever they want. There is always an interest in adding products and features, but there is resistance to rationalizing and discontinuing unprofitable products and services. Sales has the responsibility and ownership for the revenue, and the rest of the organization bears the burden for non value-added costs. In the absence of formal methodologies such as Kano analysis and policy deployment, many wrong product decisions are committed to for the product's entire lifecycle.

Defining the Lean Six Sigma strategy and vision for the organization requires patience, time, intelligence, and a structured data-driven methodology to remove the emotions and perceptions of improvement.

Patience

The new economy is not always an environment that allows for patience. There are too many forces today demanding people to do something now. As history shows, a successful Lean Six Sigma deployment requires much more than training black belts and then cutting them loose. Organizations need to find the patience to walk through the logical business diagnostic and policy deployment steps if they want to discover their right vector for success.

Time

No organization has enough time, and yet everyone has the same amount of it. How is it, then, that some Lean Six Sigma deployments are failures while others are successes? Those who complain about not having enough time to improve and still do their regular job always find the time to do things over. The puzzle about time is figuring out how best to use it with limited resources. Organizations that invest time into this puzzle achieve more in dividends than they ever thought was possible.

Intelligence

If organizations had all the answers, they would not have any improvement opportunities. The need for improvement moves faster than the natural ability to keep up with it. Intelligent organizations actually recognize what they know and what they do not know. It comes back to the old adage, "You don't know what you don't know. If you don't know, you cannot act correctly. If you cannot act correctly, you cannot improve." It is true that the answers to most of an organization's problems lie within the minds of the people who make up the organization. That is half of the story; it is also true that the organization's current thinking brought about the current problems, and therefore may need help to solve them.

Structured, Data-driven Methodologies

Policy deployment provides a process for prioritizing and aligning customer-driven improvement activities. This methodology helps to minimize the wavering in directions and priorities by locking down the most critical requirements in a systematic way. By now, it is apparent that executives are the pinnacles of the organization and that a small amount of action at this level translates into a large amount of activity, interpretation, and speculation in the rest of the organization. Executives who continue to shift directions and priorities may be acting with the best of intentions, but they are keeping their organizations in a state of chaos.

These complexities must be dealt with outside of the normal boundaries of Lean Six Sigma. Lean Six Sigma is not a strategy itself—it is a key enabler to achieve strategic improvement initiatives. Organizations need to point their Lean Six Sigma efforts at the right target opportunities. One of the ways we balance conflicting directions and priorities is through a process called policy deployment that is discussed later in this chapter.

Executive Education and Development

This effort is usually conducted in parallel with the business diagnostic. The objective of this effort is to build awareness and knowledge about Lean Six Sigma and the broader success factors. This is best accomplished through the following means:

- *Educational working sessions (8 to 16 hours)*—This allows executives to become familiarized with Lean Six Sigma fundamentals, the DMAIC methodology, leadership and change management best practices, and several *real* case-study examples demonstrating how to improve various business processes.
- *External peer visits and communication*—Unlike pure Lean Manufacturing, it is difficult to walk into another organization and see the before-and-after results of transactional process improvements. At this point, the specific details of how a team in another organization deployed the Lean Six Sigma tools would not be understood well anyway. The most important objective here is to bring executives together to share the leadership process of how Lean Six Sigma was deployed. Listening to another organization's *why, what, where, how,* and *when* questions is much more informative than learning how a specific improvement tool works. These peer visits allow the executive team to *imagineer*[2] their own Lean Six Sigma deployments.
- *Direct involvement in the business diagnostic and policy deployment*—During these activities there is a wealth of information sharing and discussions about *why, what, where, how,* and *when* of various improvement opportunities. These discussions are at a high level at this point. More specific details, priorities, and improvement project details are filled in via policy deployment in this chapter, and a methodology called the *Macro/Micro Chartering* in Chapter 5. The point here is that direct executive involvement in these activities expands the shared knowledge of improvement requirements in the organization.

One of the largest mistakes that executives make is the public commitment of Lean Six Sigma without knowing the details and then delegating the ownership to a lower, powerless individual or group in the organization.

Walt Disney Imagineering is the master planning, creative development, design, engineering, production, project management, and research and development arm of The Walt Disney Company and its affiliates. Representing more than 150 disciplines, its talented corps of Imagineers are responsible for the creation of Disney resorts, theme parks and attractions, hotels, water parks, real estate developments, regional entertainment venues, cruise ships, and new media technology projects.

Policy Deployment: Defining and Prioritizing Target Opportunities

Most organizations have a well-defined strategy that is intended to align the actions of all individuals, teams, and business units to achieve corporate goals. But when it comes to execution, the process breaks down—especially during times of significant business change. The reasons for this gap vary by organization, but typically include the following:

- There may be insufficient executive sponsorship for the strategies and associated change initiatives, or there may be an organizational culture that does not embrace execution, accountability, and measurement leading to insufficient performance monitoring and measurement systems.
- Strategy is a cerebral story at fifty thousand feet and lacks the substance of addressing the tough *who, why, what, where, how,* and *when* questions of implementation. Deployment planning and execution are undefined. Therefore, it is unclear who is accountable for ensuring execution of initiatives, projects, and tasks.
- Strategy is not communicated in a way that employees understand and connect to. Consequently, they do not see how the strategy affects them, exactly what actions must be taken and when, and how their actions impact others in the organization.
- Reward and incentive systems are disconnected from strategy, so individual goals are not aligned with the company's goals. Expectations, rewards, and consequences are not defined well enough to influence the right actions and participative behaviors.

To close the gap between strategy and execution, companies need to build strategic alignment across all levels of the business. This is the heart of policy deployment.

The sheer market velocity of today's global economy is rendering obsolete the traditional annual strategic planning processes. Strategic planning, as we have known it, is quickly being modified to reflect these new conditions. In an annual process, the relevance of the plan and organizational alignment declines quickly over the yearly horizon. Many organizations have adopted quarterly or monthly updates to their annual strategic plan, and some have been dreaming about the near future that holds more real-time strategic planning processes. Organizations have a difficult time maintaining alignment with an annual process: if they move to multiple planning cycles within the year, a different methodology is needed to make the necessary organizational alignment adjustments and streamline the process.

One methodology that has gained popularity is called *policy deployment*. This is also called *Hoshin Planning* or *Hoshin Kanri*. Policy deployment is used in strategic planning and in managing complex projects or initiatives with many components, each of which require alignment, execution, measurement, and feedback for the plan. Hoshin Kanri emerged in the WWII postwar era in Japan, under the teachings of Peter Drucker. This methodology was adopted by companies such as Toyota, Komatsu, and Bridgestone Tire as a way to improve quality, cost, delivery, and inventory.

Policy deployment is a cascading *step-down* planning and execution process (see Figure 4.4) that helps in developing and organizing the strategic plan, midpoint plans, and the annual operating plan. Policy deployment is a useful methodology to translate findings from the business diagnostic into a simplified view of the Lean Six Sigma deployment strategy. Policy deployment also links improvement initiatives and all other business activities to the top-level plans, and it incorporates features that provide early warnings about the status and alignment of specific projects and actions. This is accomplished through a series of linked plans called *X matrices* (see Figure 4.5), a document the size of a sheet of A3 paper. Communication and status of all activities up and down the policy deployment process via remaining documents called A3s. The name stands for the format (A3-size paper, or two 8½" × 11" sheets) originally used by Toyota and other Japanese organizations. Obviously, these documents can be either manual or automated. These A3 documents include different formats depending on the intended planning component. This may include a specific project charter, a status report, a problem or corrective action report, or a project status report (see Figure 4.6). The components of policy deployment forces everyone involved in the planning process or specific projects to think crisply. Policy deployment discourages lengthy PowerPoint presentations and Word documents, which often confuse rather than communicate crisply the status of business activities. Rather, policy deployment drives people to know their audience and flow their stories concisely and logically on a single sheet of A3-size paper. This A3 format promotes highly visual and portable planning, and promotes management by walking around. Policy deployment also provides visibility to performance, which is designed to drive the right behaviors and achieve the right results.

We have standardized on the DMAIC thoughtware in conjunction with policy deployment, Lean, Six Sigma, Kaizen, and any other improvement initiative. Originally, the foundation of Hoshin Kanri was based on Deming's PDCA (Plan-Do-Check-Act) cycle. The DMAIC methodology provides a comprehensive, uniform, and structured problem-solving approach for all improvement initiatives. When DMAIC becomes the common language of improvement, it eliminates the confusion caused by feeding people six different versions of an improvement process.

Policy deployment is possible without using the specific *X* matrices and A3 forms. Hoshin Kanri is a packaged solution for policy deployment. Policy deployment can be achieved with spreadsheet logic and storyboards, as long as the objectives of resource alignment, communication, status checks, and corrective actions are in place. The bottom line is that policy deployment enables resource alignment—vertically, horizontally, and laterally—throughout the organization's

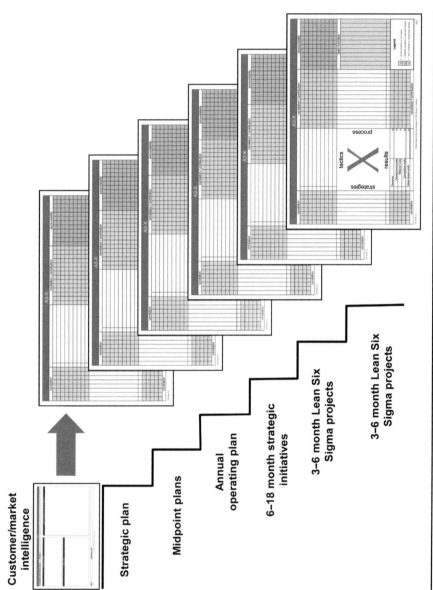

Figure 4.4 Policy deployment (Hoshin Kanri).

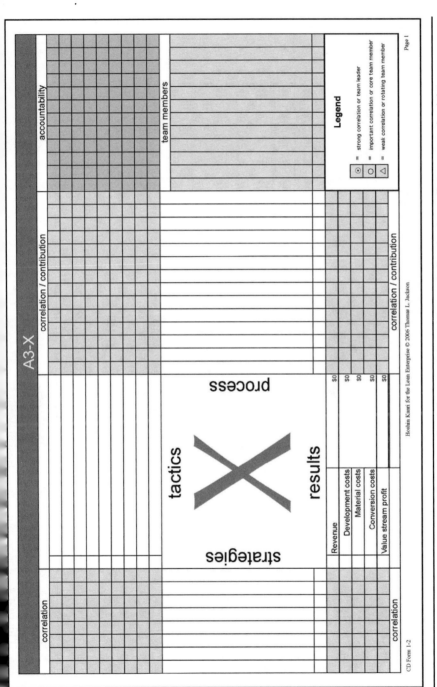

Figure 4.5 Policy Deployment is a formal methodology and should be capitalized universally in text and exhibits.

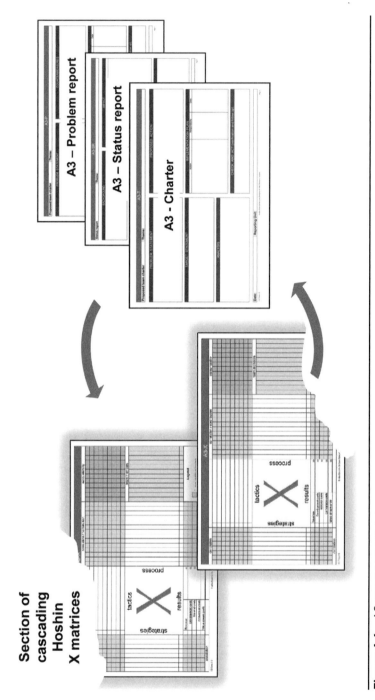

Figure 4.6   A3 management process.

mprovement initiatives. Most organizations deploying Lean Six Sigma are missng this succinct and robust planning and deployment process wrapped around heir efforts. Instead, most organizations jump right into the education and tools y developing black belts, scattering them throughout the organization, assigning ong lists of projects, and then moving on to the next priority. It is no wonder why heir Lean Six Sigma deployments fail—garbage in, garbage out (GIGO). Some xecutives have argued that they are already leading their organizations through olicy deployment intuitively, without all the fancy Japanese terms and forms. ntuitively setting and resetting priorities every day is much different than policy leployment. The problem with intuition is that it is a lot like inspecting the quality of products and services. Statistically, the odds of success are somewhere etween 60 and 85 percent, depending on the inspection criteria. Those misses n the range of 15 to 40 percent equate to millions of dollars in waste and hidden osts for many organizations. Organizations who think this way or underestimate he importance of policy deployment will realize only an illusion of improvenent or some limited results, but they will never see the annual 3 to 10 percent f revenues from their improvements or the complete cultural transformations of he best-in-class Lean Six Sigma deployments.

Building the Improvement Vision

The business diagnostic and policy deployment activities enable organizations to reate a fact-based and data-driven vision that is both realistic and compelling. This is a good time to update the organization on the results of the business diagnostic and the improvement vision. The improvement vision communicates the ompelling need to change as well as the consequences of doing nothing. The improvement vision is the formal protocol to communicate the strategy of improvenent at a high level, including the drivers of improvement, the consequences f inaction, and next steps. During its delivery, executives should also make the ommitment to provide additional details in the next two to four weeks. A comnon mistake that executives make is telling the organization *where* it needs to go vithout doing justice to the *why, what, how,* and *when* of the vision. *Why* is the nost important question of strategic change. If people do not understand *why* here is a need to change, the vision will not accomplish the momentum of drawng the organization together around a common theme. The same holds true for he *what, how,* and *when* questions. When executives gloss over these activities, he result is the same old analogy—you can dress up a fad improvement program nd you can put lipstick and cologne on a fad improvement program—in the end, t is still a fad improvement program.

The business diagnostic and policy deployment activities drive the CEO and he executive team to do their homework about strategic improvement. During his process, there may be several good discussions about issues and priorities that build shared learning and commitment among executives. A Lean Six Sigma vision statement usually includes the following elements:

- An image for change (why)
- A strategy for change (how)
- Bold and broad improvement goals (what)
- Narrower objectives (what—more detail)
- Specific improvement actions (what—even more detail)
- Accountability (who)
- Deployment timeline and expectations (when)
- The deployment monitoring system (formal deployment management process)
- Measurement and feedback (business improvement progress)

The vision becomes powerful and compelling when (and only when) executives can communicate these questions to their organizations with a uniform story based on knowledge and facts. When a vision is presented to the organization with information about all the elements outlined above, it begins to create urgency, understanding, knowledge, and commitment to Lean Six Sigma.

The objective of the vision is to:

- *Establish an unquestionable recognition of the need to improve*—This is accomplished by describing the current status of the organization, sharing customer and competitor information, and pointing out the gaps between current and desired performance. This objective includes the packaging and communication of critical business challenges (sometimes referred to as *burning platforms*), and the consequences of not moving forward with the changes.
- *Create a bold and compelling image of the future*—The vision activates the organization's conscience and creates a renewed sense of purpose, direction, urgency, and reason. Reason is accomplished by being prepared to answer the questions above. A fact-based image of where the organization needs to be to remain competitive appeals to people's emotions positively and builds cohesion, trust, and critical mass.
- *Build executive cohesion and commitment*—In the process of going through the business diagnostic, policy deployment, and vision creation, executives end up with a shared sense of direction, priorities, and specific details about the *why, what, where, how,* and *when* questions. Answering these questions results in the superglue of holding together the executive team in unity of purpose and with a consistent message of improvement. Although it is often underestimated, there is power to improve when executives can agree on and communicate a universal story of improvement.
- *Build stakeholder engagement and commitment*—A fact-based and data-driven vision is effective in setting uniform direction, expectations, and performance contracts with executives and managers about Lean Six Sigma or any other strategic initiative. This objective lays down the

gauntlet about Lean Six Sigma as the enabler of success, but promotes execution through a proactive and creative deployment. A strong sense of executive and stakeholder engagement or commitment is what makes successful deployments successful.

- *Act as the strategic reference point*—A vision should be constantly communicated to and referenced by the organization. This reference point serves to reinforce the message about improvement and how Lean Six Sigma is the enabler to success. The vision is also used as a benchmark to measure consistency of purpose against constancy of progress. The vision is just that—a vision. The details of how the vision is executed and achieved must remain creative and flexible in this new economy.

One of the greatest leadership challenges is keeping executives and the entire organization focused on their improvement mission. The vision is the media that enables organizations to continually resonate the unwavering improvement mission. Some organizations have postponed their Lean Six Sigma initiatives, hoping that the new economy will take care of things. Others have opted to skip strategic leadership and vision outright because they perceive that it will take too much time (or they can figure out these details as they move forward). Without saying it, they are destined to a journey of learning from their mistakes—mistakes that could have been avoided with more listening and less action. For these organizations, change will always be a reactive event rather than a proactive living mission unless they modify the same-people, same-thinking, same-process, same-results formula.

Sometimes executives begin a strategic initiative such as Lean Six Sigma without a well-thought-out vision. Their real vision is a me-too vision. For many executives, it is difficult to look reality in the face, and the first reaction is failure followed by a string of denial thoughts and opinions, or blaming suppliers, customers, or someone else. Another common occurrence is the continued procrastination and debates about what needs to be done in the absence of data and facts, which perpetuates more confusion and conflicting directions about improvement and change. The fact is, no matter where your current performance lies, it simply is not good enough beyond today. Stated another way, the best time to improve is now. Everyone knows this at an intellectual level. However, it is unfortunate that business improvement often requires a catastrophic event to prime the organizational pump for change. It is much easier to create urgency with catastrophe rather than leadership, but it often makes organizations late for the competitive party. Catastrophe-driven improvement is also intermittent. Without a solid recognition of the need to change, improvement programs are typically reactionary and short-lived, and the results are disappointing.

A solid vision exerts significant power and influence with organizations implementing Lean Six Sigma and other improvement initiatives. The vision provides the right consistent message of improvement and acts as a scale for aligning organizational actions to the vision. On the flip side, proceeding without a solid vision is a sure prescription for another failed fad improvement program.

Stakeholder Engagement and Commitment

Stakeholder engagement and commitment is the most important objective of the vision and high-level improvement strategy. A well-constructed and orchestrated vision is not only informative, it shakes and wakes the emotions of the organization and aligns people's emotional intelligence to the vision. Stakeholder engagement and commitment includes:

- *Stakeholder analysis and mapping*—Identifying the concerns, issues, and problems of various stakeholders; prioritizing stakeholders and problems; understanding various levels of commitment or resistance; and developing a turnaround plan.
- *Stakeholder awareness and communication*—Identifying the message, media, and formats; defining how to communicate initially and continuously with different stakeholder groups.
- *Stakeholder engagement*—Involving stakeholders in initial assessments, planning, and direct involvement in strategic leadership and vision. The business diagnostic facilitates this process by soliciting input from a wide variety of people in the organization. During this process, people with various roles within the organization are provided with a preview of their potential roles, responsibilities, and expectations in the Lean Six Sigma deployment.
- *Stakeholder assessment and feedback*—Constantly applying the DMAIC thinking to the vision and stakeholdering process, making necessary adjustments to increase awareness and commitment. Stakeholder awareness and commitment wavers over time if it is lacking continuous reinforcement and feedback of successes, or if it fails to recognize individual and team contributions.

Figure 4.7 provides an overview of stakeholder engagement and commitment This diagram includes the following spaces:

- *Inactive stakeholder engagement*—In this space, organizations are disconnected from customer and stakeholder requirements. Organizations that launch a Lean Six Sigma initiative in this quadrant are usually the me-too organizations. Acting with limited superficial knowledge, executives launch a train-the-masses, scatter-the-black-belts deployment strategy, and then go on to more important issues. They overlook the importance of the strategic leadership and vision, deployment planning, and execution factors of successful deployments. Stakeholder engagement becomes more selfish as people become more interested in earning the belt status than in applying these new skills to continuous improvement. Lean Six Sigma is a misunderstood, misdirected, disconnected, and voluntary approach to improvement Lean Six Sigma and other improvement initiatives are kept alive by a select few committed individuals who eventually hit the wall and lose interest as the rest of the organization continues to pocket veto their improvement

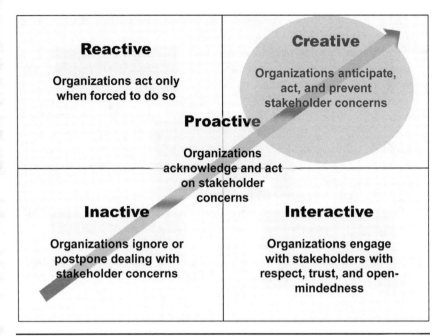

Figure 4.7   Stakeholder engagement.

activities. Individuals who were not involved are the first to comment that the organization tried Lean Six Sigma but was unsuccessful.

- *Reactive stakeholdering*—In this space, organizations postpone Lean Six Sigma and other improvement initiatives in favor of milking current conditions and firefighting. Catastrophic events usually push these organizations over the edge and into a Lean Six Sigma deployment. They do this with all the right intentions, but the actions resemble a mad rush to do all of the right things as soon as possible but without the right skills, knowledge, and facts. Some of these deployments are what we call the showboat-we're-working-on-it deployments. These organizations also overlook the importance of the strategic leadership and vision, deployment planning, and execution factors of successful deployments. Continuous improvement to these organizations is keeping the fires down for the next few months.

- *Interactive stakeholdering*—Organizations in this space make a concerted effort to deploy Lean Six Sigma correctly. They may go through several elements of strategic leadership and vision and make an honest effort at strategic project definition and a vision. These organizations may initially miss the mark on a few major elements and send their Lean Six Sigma deployment down a path with too many unknowns. These organizations are serious about being successful, but they view Lean Six Sigma as an oversimplified recipe of the right actions. They reach points of frustration and either figure out a renewed path or lose momentum. Results are good but suboptimized.

- *Proactive stakeholdering*—Organizations in this space continuously learn, apply, develop new knowledge and skills, and proactively respond to stakeholder issues and concerns. Improvement is finally viewed as part of, rather than in addition to, people's responsibilities. Knowledge through Lean Six Sigma involvement is spilling over into day-to-day activities, and people are holding each other accountable for fact-based, data-driven decision making. Comments like "How do you know that? Where is your data?" are commonly heard in meetings. This is the beginning of good to great Lean Six Sigma deployments.

- *Creative stakeholdering*—This is the autopilot mode of Lean Six Sigma where people are living and breathing improvement. They are constantly challenging themselves and others around them to improve how they improve in an effort to anticipate, act, and prevent stakeholder concerns. Stakeholdering is continuously aligning needs and actions inside the organization (vertical, horizontal, lateral alignment) and externally to customers and other external stakeholders.

Cultural transformation and the stakeholder spaces above are not steady state. The best Lean Six Sigma deployments follow a series of saw-tooth curves characterized by successes, mistakes, breakthroughs, many smaller gains, backslides, and recoveries. The rate of improvement changes for many logical reasons, and organizations should not be disappointed about this fact of life. It is only a disappointment when organizations watch all of these things happening around them and then choose to do nothing about it. A successful Lean Six Sigma deployment requires hard work, patience, and intellectual flexibility to achieve success. Transforming Lean Six Sigma into the cultural fabric and maintaining the same rate of improvement is even tougher. Successful organizations make their improvement philosophy their business philosophy and live it every minute of every day. They make a conscious and continuous effort to reinforce this business philosophy and expect the same in others. They also have a low tolerance level for those who are winging it. These organizations never let go of the *continuous* in continuous improvement.

Leadership Implementation Infrastructure

Another key element of strategic leadership and vision is building what we refer to as the *leadership implementation infrastructure*. This involves defining the organization and reporting structure, feedback and review processes, corrective action processes, and critical metrics for the Lean Six Sigma deployment. This also includes the clarification of roles and responsibilities of the CEO and executive team, the executive deployment champion, the executive sponsors, leadership champions, process owners, team leaders, team participants, and on-demand project resources.

In Scalable Lean Six Sigma™ deployments, the implementation infrastructures share many common elements. The specific participants may change depending upon availability and balance with other mission-critical activities. A good leadership implementation infrastructure manages the deployment through all the typical barriers of success. At a minimum, Lean Six Sigma deployments require the following infrastructure requirements:

- Lean Six Sigma deployments require direct involvement and engagement of the CEO and executive team through frequent reviews of deployment progress, issues, and corrective action plans. The CEO and executive team are also encouraged to participate in the formal scheduled peer project reviews, and by walking around and reinforcing the need and formal structured process of change.

- A day-to-day implementation team is required that is led by a designated executive deployment champion. This is called the Lean Six Sigma executive core team or steering team. Sometimes it may be called something more generic such as the business improvement core team or business excellence steering team. The executive deployment champion is a highly regarded leader by the organization just as it says—a *champion*. This individual acts as the 360-degree celebrant of the whole deployment. If this person is not a champion in the eyes of the organization, they need to be replaced by a true champion. The executive core team is responsible for identifying, prioritizing, scoping, assigning, and managing improvement project activities.

- Cross-leadership and mentoring is necessary through executive sponsors and process owners who are assigned to each improvement project. The improvement team, executive sponsor, and process owner are all accountable for performance and positive results.

- Improvement teams who are empowered to deploy the right improvement methodologies to an assigned improvement opportunity are critical. A team leader serves as the project leader and mentor to the participants of the team. Team participants are also selected cross-functionally and based on skill and process knowledge requirements. The executive core team manages project priorities, resourcing, and the birth-death process of teams.

- Mentors are necessary to serve as deployment experts for leadership, the overall deployment process, key business process knowledge, and expertise on successfully deploying the right improvement tools and achieving demonstrated results.

- Measurement and feedback practices are required that allow executives and the executive core team to monitor the status of the deployment and specific improvement actions, and focus limited resources on resetting all activities of the deployment. The combined rate and magnitude of improvement (validated by the finance organization for each improvement project or activity) are good metrics to track for the overall deployment.

Leadership implementation infrastructure is clearly defined in the front end of a Lean Six Sigma deployment. The structure and implementation architecture is molded and agreed upon, and the specific roles and responsibilities of each component are clearly defined. As you will learn in Chapter 5, the executive deployment champion and the Lean Six Sigma executive core team are actively involved throughout the deployment from strategy to ownership of individual improvement projects. This provides a formal and well-defined management system for the deployment, and eliminates any confusion about executive roles and expectations. Organizations that gloss over this requirement end up with an uncontrollable amount of improvement activities and questionable results.

Chartering Roles and Responsibilities

Hopefully, the need for leadership is evident for a successful Lean Six Sigma deployment. The remainder of this section will briefly highlight the roles and responsibilities of leadership by key infrastructure area.

CEO *and Executive Team*

- Actively participate in the business diagnostic, improvement vision, and strategy or policy deployment activities
- Develop improvement goals, strategy, boundaries, and focus of Lean Six Sigma
- Communicate the improvement vision and detailed implementation plan to the organization
- Update the organization on Lean Six Sigma progress and future improvement plans
- Provide commitment through the availability of necessary resources, skill set improvement, and funding
- Conduct structured reviews of progress with the executive core team, and keep the deployment synchronized to evolving corporate improvement needs
- Define recognition and reward criteria
- Leading by active engagement, asking the right questions, reinforcing the strategic importance of individual projects

Executive Deployment Champion

- Serve as the active internal leader of the executive core team
- Organize and hold frequent deployment status meetings with the executive core team and necessary extended members (e.g., executive sponsors, process owners, etc.)
- Ensure that the organization is following the proven strategic leadership and vision, deployment planning, and execution success factors
- Facilitate in activities such as the Macro Charter, identification of resources, selection and prioritization of projects, and managing barriers to success

- Maintain the Macro Charter (project hopper) and Lean Six Sigma shared directory on the network
- Lead the formal executive, project, and peer reviews
- Communicate purpose and formal status of individual projects and other improvement activities
- Verify valid completion of all required DMAIC activities for all projects
- Approve project closure
- Discuss progress as an agenda item in periodic one-on-one CEO meetings
- Make sure a spot is reserved on the executive team agenda to discuss Lean Six Sigma progress and issues
- Become the objective open-door godfather for individuals involved in all aspects of the deployment
- Maintain an accessible knowledge repository for completed improvement projects
- Maintain metrics on project completions, individual and cumulative savings by category, business unit, rate of improvement, etc.

Lean Six Sigma Executive Core Team

- Participate in activities such as the Macro Charter, identification of resources, selection and prioritization of projects, and managing barriers to success
- Provide updates to the Macro Charter (project hopper) and Lean Six Sigma shared directory on the network
- Escalate and work through any technical, educational, political, performance, or human drama issues that arise during the deployment
- Participate in the formal executive, project, and peer reviews
- Verify valid completion of all required DMAIC activities for all projects
- Approve project closure

Executive Sponsors

- Provide weekly mentoring and project leadership to the team
- Communicate a consistent message of Lean Six Sigma purpose, vision, updates, and expectations to their own organizations
- Solicit improvement ideas for consideration from their organizations
- Inquire about team issues and barriers, and provide instant resolution if it is within bounds; or work with other executives, process owners, or the executive core team to clear the path to team success
- Participate in activities such as the Macro Charter, identification of resources, selection and prioritization of projects, and managing barriers to success
- Escalate and work through any technical, educational, political, performance, or human drama issues that arise during the deployment
- Participate in the formal executive, project, and peer reviews

- Verify valid completion of all required DMAIC activities for all projects
- Approve project closure

Process Owners

- Participate in mentoring and weekly team reviews with the executive sponsor
- Assist the team in gaining process knowledge and coming up to speed on their project
- Provide the team with available information, endorsement, and local resources as needed
- Communicate a consistent message of Lean Six Sigma purpose, vision, updates, and expectations to their own organizations
- Solicit improvement ideas for consideration from their organizations
- Participate in conflicts and resolution of team barriers and issues

Financial Validation—Before, During, and After

Another important factor in a successful deployment is the integration of the financial organization throughout all planned and executed improvement activities. Finance plays a key role in:

- *Strategic leadership and vision*—Participating in the business diagnostic, improvement vision, and policy deployment efforts, providing financial and operational information, validating all findings, conclusions, assumptions, and improvement opportunities.
- *Deployment planning*—Participating in the Macro Charter development particularly in individual project baseline performance, and improvement goal assumptions and benefits. Occasionally a perceived issue identified during the business diagnostic is either smaller or larger than what was anticipated due to informal and less-visible improvement efforts.
- *Execution*—Assisting individual teams with improvement and savings assumptions, classification of savings, providing standard rates for savings calculations, prevention of double counting savings, and validation of claimed savings achievements. A financial representative should be a member or extended resource for every improvement project.

Some organizations look too hard at financial impact and attempt to limit Lean Six Sigma efforts only to projects that directly affect visible profit and losses. Successful Lean Six Sigma deployments recognize and dig out the hidden costs and associated waste in their business (cost of poor quality or COPQ). There is a difference between improving financial performance and improving financial statements. As we are all well aware, the latter promotes short-term thinking and band-aid improvements, while the former promotes root-cause problem solving, creativity, and innovative improvement. The real purpose of finance is to provide a consistent and standardized approach to identifying, evaluating, and calculating project savings whether they are visible or hidden. Visible costs such as labor, scrap, premium freight, returns and allowances, operating supplies, and many others are straightforward in terms of baselining current performance, calculating savings, and pegging the savings to a particular account in the income statement, cash flow statement, or balance sheet. These are the typical *main-effects* cost and operating income improvements. Costs such as excess or obsolete inventory, sales and operations plan (S&OP) accuracy, product development process inefficiencies, inventory shrinkage, customer service responsiveness, or advertising effectiveness are more complex in terms of isolating root causes of waste, defining value-added and non value-added costs, estimating improvement opportunities, and pegging savings to a particular chart of accounts. These are the *interaction effects* improvements such as growth, cash flow, variance reduction, cost avoidance, and restructuring of priorities that are difficult but not impossible to quantify. However, these savings are real savings and should not be overlooked or excluded in a deployment. To the extent possible, we are fanatical advocates of tying everything back to financial performance as much as possible. Successful Lean Six Sigma deployments begin and end with financial performance, one project at a time. Keep in mind that financial performance improves directly and indirectly with the right actions.

Improvement Best Practice Leadership Behaviors

Everything that has been previously discussed in this chapter is only achievable through the right leadership behaviors and actions. These behaviors are more widely known than they are practiced. As we have stated previously, diversions from these behaviors are not intentional; they are diversions driven by the new global economy and the availability of technology. Just when organizations are feeling as if they are unable to go any faster, the global economy has shifted the world into a new high gear. The technology of e-mails, the Internet and intranet, and Blackberries has promoted some behaviors that run counter to traditional improvement. Technology is not going away because these evolving capabilities are great—great enough to make one wonder how they got along without it. Leadership's new role is to figure out how to connect emerging technology and economic challenges to the desired behaviors for Lean Six Sigma success (and success in everything else in the organization).

There is nothing new about leadership behaviors that enable Lean Six Sigma success. The purpose of this section is to remind (not teach) the reader of these behaviors, and to increase awareness concerning executive behaviors and how they influence a Lean Six Sigma deployment. The following discussion does not follow any particular leadership guru's model, but is developed based on years of actual observations and lessons learned from successful strategic improvement initiatives. This model reflects the enabling executive behaviors of CEOs, executive deployment champions, executive sponsors, and other members of the executive team. This may not be an all-inclusive list. However, it certainly represents the leadership behaviors we have observed and experienced in Lean Six Sigma benchmark deployments. Best practice leadership behaviors can be grouped into five major categories:

1. Vision
2. Knowledge
3. Passion
4. Discipline
5. Conscience

Figure 4.8 provides a graphical summary and overview of these best practice leadership behaviors. Within each of these categories is a set of behaviors that contribute positively to Lean Six Sigma success, and in fact, personal leadership success. The remaining discussion provides additional details about these best practice behaviors as they relate to a successful Lean Six Sigma deployment. Keep in mind that these behaviors are transportable to any strategic leadership challenge.

Vision

Vision is the ability to see beyond current challenges and define a new direction for improvement. Vision is only attainable for individuals willing to pick their head out of the reeds, take a time out, stop the insanity, and dream a bit about how the business can and will improve. Vision is a reverse process beginning at a more fuzzy utopian state of improvement (e.g., zero inventory) and working backward to a more realistic state (e.g., reduce supply chain inventory by 20 percent)—one that is a believable but doable step-function improvement over current conditions and one that requires the collaboration and cooperation of many improvement activities to eliminate dependencies. The supporting best practice leadership behaviors include:

- *Courage*—The ability to confront fear, pain points, risk or danger, uncertainty, or internal and external intimidation.
- *Conviction*—The art of convincing oneself and others about reality, risks, and the consequences of not improving.
- *Charisma*—The magnetism, communications skills, and personal being to persuade and convince others about improvement.
- *Creativity*—The ability to imagineer (see footnote on page 103), think beyond the box, and think and act divergently.
- *Curiosity*—The desire and inquisitive interest to learn from others.
- *Strategic thinking*—Thinking beyond next quarter, and thinking big.
- *Guiding beacon*—Behaviors followed by actions that attract others.
- *Goals-oriented*—Setting the bar of expectations high, but achievable. Also raising the bar of expectations above current performance to encourage continuous improvement.

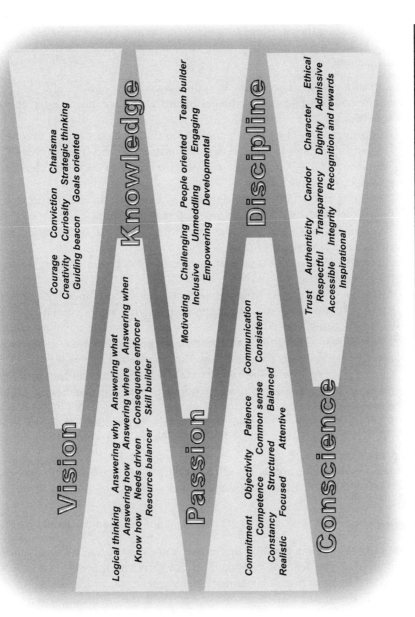

Figure 4.8   Best practice leadership behaviors.

Knowledge

Knowledge is the ability to act based on facts and data. Knowledge is self-education and self-awareness that enables one to understand how the vision may be possible. This includes taking the time and patience to understand what really matters in a successful Lean Six Sigma deployment. The supporting best practice leadership behaviors include:

- *Logical thinking*—The ability to reduce a complex and unsolvable puzzle of improvement into a rational and orderly set of proposed plans and activities.
- *Answering why*—The patience to develop the business case so that one can lead with facts and truth, and data to construct a solid story of change.
- *Answering what*—The ability to synthesize facts and decide on the correct strategic corrective actions.
- *Answering how*—The ability to understand and prioritize the true requirements of a challenge, and recognize internal shortfalls.
- *Answering where*—The ability to prioritize where the organization needs to focus improvement efforts.
- *Answering when*—The timing and sense of urgency required to move the business forward.
- *Know how*—Taking the time to build intelligence combined with objectivity, so that one avoids reactionary problem solving, underestimating efforts or hip-shooting leadership.
- *Needs-driven*—The ability to understand implementation requirements and admit to barriers to success and gaps in internal expertise.
- *Consequence enforcer*—The ability to take a tough stand on fact-based controversy or confrontation, or noncompliance to improvement goals and objectives.
- *Resource balancer*—The ability to help the organization balance priorities instead of the perceived piling of additional assignments on current workloads.
- *Skill builder*—The ability to recognize skill and experience gaps, and inject these competencies into the organization.

Passion

Passion is the compelling emotion that drives leaders to success. Passion is the fire in the belly that gets leaders and organizations through all obstacles to success. In all of our Lean Six Sigma benchmark deployments, these engagements were started with significant leadership mentoring until the failure-is-not-an-option momentum was established. These were not flowery words; executives and the organization deployed Lean Six Sigma in a manner where there were no individual failures, no leadership failures, and hence, success. Deployments were truly team-based where everyone helped each other through individual projects and other deployment issues. It is always amazing to watch particular individuals who some may have written off rise to the occasion and accomplish what others in the organization thought was nearly impossible. When leaders possess and transfer passion to the rest of the organization, it is powerful stuff. Organizations with the fire in the belly are more successful than *I-already-know-how-to* organizations because there is always an immense force to figure out the unknowns. In a previous book, we refer to these experiences as eureka moments or personal discovery moments. When organizations and individuals experience these victories, it builds commitment, confidence, and an even larger fire in the belly. After decades of business experience, an individual with deep passion will always outperform the passive individual with knowledge. A person with passion will learn, apply their education, and gain knowledge—and continue to repeat this cycle. Many people with knowledge are the I-already-know-how-to people who typically sit idle and tell others how much they know. Under the category of passion, the supporting best practice leadership behaviors include:

- *Motivating*—The ability to activate and energize goal-oriented behaviors in the organization.
- *Challenging*—The ability to positively call out individuals to explain, justify, or rationalize plans and activities.
- *People-oriented*—The ability to encourage employees to use all of their talents and skills and to be productive in an organization where learning is a priority.
- *Team builder*—The ability to mentor people to work in cohesive, cross-functional teams, regardless of their home organization.
- *Inclusive*—The ability to recognize and tap people's experiences and expertise from a variety of backgrounds.
- *Unmeddling*—Recognizing that leadership is not meddling in, or second-guessing other's roles and responsibilities. Leadership is developing others to conduct themselves with excellence in their roles and responsibilities so that meddling is not required.
- *Engaging*—Developing positive, enthusiastic, and affective connection with people regarding their work in a way that motivates an employee to invest in getting the job done—not just *well* but *with excellence*, because the work content energizes the individual.
- *Empowering*—The ability to give away power and authority to the organization because the organization has developed the sense of responsibility to accept power and authority and act in a correct manner.
- *Developmental*—The ability to encourage and mentor systematic growth in individual job content skills, broader business skills, communication skills, interpersonal skills, or supervisory and leadership skills.

Discipline

Discipline is the ability to follow rules of conduct and expectations for the organization in a manner that establishes logical business conduct and order. The other side of discipline is *walking the talk*. Discipline lays down the moral compass and serves to guide organizational behaviors to pursue the right decisions and achieve the right results. Discipline that encourages root-cause problem solving develops abilities in individuals to make choices that will help grow the business over the long term, rather than to take advantage of the short term. Discipline forces people to follow a proven path and not jeopardize the future for some short-term, knee-jerk actions. The new economy has introduced competitive forces that are reducing the ability of organizations to maintain discipline. In a world of *now, any color, any volume, any size and shape, and changes in demand* become normal customer expectations and discipline is being replaced with chaos. Leaders must realize that chaos is not necessarily bad because there is ultimately order in chaos. Chaos is just the hypersonic ride to the next level of order and the next level of discipline. Chaos brings out the best in people because they do not have time to think, pontificate, or consider reasons for not changing. Chaos is also an enlightening organizational state because it exposes an individual's true capacity and capability for change. The supporting best practice leadership behaviors of discipline include:

- *Commitment*—The ability to make a personal pledge or emotional contract to a particular course of action without being disrupted by other arising issues.
- *Objectivity*—The ability to express or deal with facts or conditions as perceived or measured, without any bias and distortion by personal feelings, prejudices, interpretations , political implications, or personal implications.
- *Patience*—The ability to endure and stay focused in the most difficult situations.
- *Communication*—The ability to foster interchange of the right thoughts and actions by translating information into understandable messages.
- *Competence*—The ability to engage and complete various actions, to demonstrate true commitment and demonstrate that one is not asking the organization to do something that they will not do themselves.
- *Common sense*—The ability to exhibit sound, logical, and practical judgment.
- *Consistent*—The ability to display cohesive, noncontradictory behaviors.
- *Constancy*—A behavior that relates to the quality of unwavering direction and steadiness or faithfulness in action, affections, and purpose.
- *Structured*—The ability to create, follow, and reinforce accepted standards of conduct such as DMAIC and root-cause problem solving.
- *Balanced*—The ability to strive for a fact-based state of equilibrium or parity characterized by understanding and stabilizing the organization's driving and restraining forces.
- *Realistic*—The ability to deal with people, objects, actions, or business conditions sensibly and levelheadedly as they reveal themselves in actuality.
- *Focused*—The ability to concentrate on a particular challenge and to create clarity that allows others to concentrate on a particular challenge.

- *Attentive*—The ability to listen to all sides of an issue with objectivity, and without interrupting and providing an answer. Also the ability to mentor and ask the right questions and develop subordinate decision making.

Conscience

Conscience is the leadership ability to distinguish whether the organization's actions, or an individual's actions, are right or wrong. Some refer to this as the inner voice of the subconscious mind. The subconscious mind is always acting as a secondary reflector of leadership thoughts and ideas. This inner voice is shaped by values or emotional rules established in one's personal, social, cultural, educational, and business life. Conscience is the inner voice that justifies and rationalizes what is right and what is wrong. When leaders go against what the inner voice is saying, the result is a guilty conscience, emotional anxiety, and a disengaged organization. The inner voice is right most of the time because it knows us better than others do and probably even more than we know ourselves. Conscience is the daredevil child of the intuitions we have held internally since childhood because it is always acting as a secondary reflector of one's thoughts and ideas. Intuitions about conscience are correct most of the time because it is the response of synchronism between our mental and physical being. Stated simply, most leaders know the difference between right and wrong, and there are many cloudy spaces in between. Intuition supplemented by data and facts reduces the risks of right or wrong. Eventually the inner voice, our best listener, picks us up and alerts us to learn from our experiences, get on with business, and leave the past behind. The supporting best practice leadership behaviors of conscience include:

- *Trust*—The reliance on another individual's integrity, abilities, commitment, enabling behaviors, performance, and mutual surety. Trust is the nucleus of leadership.
- *Authenticity*—The truthfulness of origins, attributions, commitments, sincerity, devotion, and intentions.
- *Candor*—The quality of being frank, open, and sincere in speech or expression.
- *Character*—The moral and ethical traits and qualities of a leader as observed by the organization.
- *Ethical*—A leader's observed moral principles and values.
- *Respectful*—The ability to exhibit positive esteem and in turn, receive the respect of others.
- *Transparency*—The ability to act in a what-you-see-is-what-you-get manner, and work *with* the organization.
- *Dignity*—The ability to grant the right of respect and ethical treatment to others.
- *Admissive*—The voluntary admission of truth, even if is a mistake. Also the acceptance of other's mistakes and the mentoring of corrective actions as part of the normal learning and development cycle.

- *Accessible*—The ability to be reachable and in the presence of the organization. Also the ability of others to work with leaders without fear.
- *Integrity*—The honesty and consistency of actions, values, methods, measures, principles, expectations and outcomes as demonstrated by both communications and actions.
- *Recognition and rewards*—The ability to celebrate and recognize organizational successes, reward high-performing individuals and teams, but follow the "Great job!" comments with: "How good do you think we can get? What are the team's next actions?"
- *Inspirational*—The divine influence, action, or power of leaders to motivate intellect or emotions, or to influence great behaviors followed by great actions and great satisfactions.

We have used the content of these best practice categories in various 360-degree participative exercises with the executive team or Lean Six Sigma steering team. Walking into a new organization and telling a CEO or their executive staff that they are the problem is a delicate, consulting-career-limiting decision. Leadership is the major influence on a successful Lean Six Sigma deployment. When these leadership and cultural behaviors are out of kilter, executives must pause, look in the mirror, and confront these success-limiting behaviors. It is often useful and informative to develop an attribute-based profile of an organization's readiness to tackle a large-scale strategic initiative such as Lean Six Sigma. The purpose of this exercise is not to point fingers but to promote awareness of these best practice leadership behaviors and understand the potential gaps that exist in their behaviors and cultural norms. It is often a humbling experience for organizations to review their radar chart profiles objectively and without displaying any defensive behaviors. Executives become executives not just by their successes, but because they have also learned from their mistakes. In every case where this exercise was conducted, the executive teams rose to the occasion, worked through the issues and have grown to become a better leadership team. There is a strong correlation between how executives lead their Lean Six Sigma initiatives and what their organizations achieve in terms of financial benefits and lasting cultural change.

Some organizations have skipped over the formal leadership strategy and vision infrastructure and have instead opted to jump into the training and improvement tools. For these organizations, this *leap of faith* has resulted in a huge *heap of waste*, lost momentum, and a culture that is not interested in another improvement program. Organizations beginning their Lean Six Sigma initiatives should heed the experiences of successful deployments because the annual improvements of 3 to 10 percent of revenues are both achievable and necessary in the new economy. Organizations with stalled Lean Six Sigma deployments need not be frustrated or give up because their deployments are salvageable with the 18 Accelerators of Lean Six Sigma results.

References

Babich, P. 2005. *Hoshin Handbook.* Total Quality Engineering, Inc., Poway, CA.

Burton, T. T., Moran, J. T. 1995. *The Future Focused Organization.* Prentice-Hall Publications, Upper Saddle River, New Jersey.

Jackson, T. L. 2006. *Hoshin Kanri for the Lean Enterprise.* Productivity Press, Boca Raton, FL.

Taylor, F. W. 1911. *The Principles of Scientific Management by Frederick Winslow Taylor.* A monograph. Harper & Brothers, New York, NY.

Chapter 4 Take Aways

- The objective of Accelerator #1: Strategic leadership and vision includes the following objectives:
  - Establish stakeholder engagement and commitment
  - Build a leadership deployment infrastructure
  - Assign a formal executive leadership team and a balanced deployment core team
  - Identify executive sponsors
  - Create a shared sense of executive knowledge via champion-level Lean Six Sigma education and executive coaching and mentoring
  - Establish high-level strategic improvement needs
  - Begin to build stakeholder commitment and engagement

- There is not much new in business improvement when you peel back the layers from the onion. We refer to this as the same-box-with-a-different-ribbon syndrome. The name of the box changes, but the contents of the box remain essentially the same. If you go back and read some of the early twentieth-century writings of Henry Ford, Frederick Taylor, or Frank and Lillian Gilbreth, they were right on the mark of what we are still trying to get right 100 years later. Regardless of the *ribbon du jour*, business improvement is more leadership and common sense than it is rocket science and tools.

- The DMAIC methodology within Lean Six Sigma provides an effective structure, discipline, and standard for business problem solving. The DMAIC methodology also provides a common, universal language of improvement throughout the organization.

- Lean Six Sigma is the most robust and all-encompassing improvement methodology in existence. Yet many elements of Lean Six Sigma are decades old and are derived from the discipline of industrial engineering. Reading the 1911 book *The Principles of Scientific Management* by Frederick Taylor makes one realize that much of Lean Six Sigma today is Taylorism improvement on steroids.

- An objective business diagnostic is the foundation of a successful Lean Six Sigma deployment or any other strategic improvement initiative. The diagnostic provides the compass and working roadmap for the deployment because it provides the up-front deep-core drilling to the organization's key strategic, business, and operations issues.

- Most organizations have a well-defined strategy that is intended to align the actions of all individuals, teams, and business units to achieve corporate goals. But when it comes to execution, the process breaks down—especially during times of significant business change. Policy deployment is a cascading step-down planning and execution process that helps in developing and organizing the strategic plan, midpoint plans, and the annual operating plan.

- The improvement vision communicates the compelling need to change and the consequences of doing nothing. The improvement vision communicates a strategy of improvement at a high level, telling the organization the *why, what, where, how,* and *when* of change. *Why* is the most important question. If people do not understand *why* there is a need to change, the vision will not accomplish the momentum of drawing together the organization around a common theme.

- Leadership implementation infrastructure involves defining the organization and reporting structure, feedback and review processes, corrective action processes, and critical metrics for the Lean Six Sigma deployment. This also includes the clarification of roles and responsibilities of the CEO and executive team, the executive deployment champion, the executive sponsors, leadership champions, process owners, team leaders, team participants, and on-demand project resources.

- Best practice leadership behaviors can be grouped into the following five major categories:

  1. Vision
  2. Knowledge
  3. Passion
  4. Discipline
  5. Conscience

5

Accelerator #2: Robust Deployment Planning

This accelerator identifies the major themes of improvement that are required to meet or exceed the business plan. It also involves a formal process for stepping down the major improvement themes into specific project and improvement opportunities. In our deployments, we have developed several templates to guide our clients through this process. Although these will be covered in greater detail, we will introduce you to them now:

- *Macro Charter*—A template used to collect and identify potential project information such as a description of a problem, probable root causes, cost of quality or waste, proposed project name, project objectives, improvement goals, benefits, and deliverables.
- *Project selection*—This template allows executives to evaluate projects against each other relative to business plan contribution. Projects are scored and ranked against attributes such as cost reduction, growth, level of resources, time, availability of data, capital investment, etc. The object is to remove subjectivity or executive preference, and instead, focus the organization's limited resources on critical projects that will take the least amount of effort and create the greatest impact.
- *Project or resource alignment*—This simple template evaluates potential participant resources against a variety of required skill sets and direct experiences, facilitates in the identification and selection of team leaders and team participants, and helps to objectively align people with projects.
- *Team assignment*—Another objective within deployment planning is to spread and develop critical mass as much as possible. We exercise the one-resource, one-team rule that forces a deeper development of bench strength. When everything needs the involvement of a handful of people in the organization, something is definitely wrong.

- *Project charters*—This is the team's reference document for their specific project. Project charters define a specific team leader and team, executive sponsor, and the project title. Project charters also include a crisp problem statement, probable root causes (clue data), project objectives, scope, boundaries, performance metrics, current baseline performance and cost of poor quality (COPQ) data, improvement goals, quantified benefits, expected deliverables, and a rough timetable for the project. Project charters are living documents that continue to evolve and target in on more specific opportunities as the team works its way through the DMAIC methodology.
- *Micro Charters*—A template used to facilitate a uniform process for identifying, assigning, completing, and summarizing Kaizen or Quick Strike improvements.

Figure 5.1 provides an overview of deployment planning relative to the other Lean Six Sigma accelerators. In Chapter 4 we discussed policy deployment—a formal practice used in strategic planning and in managing complex projects or initiatives with many components, each of which requires alignment, execution, measurement, and feedback for the plan. Policy deployment has been accomplished in two ways:

1. Policy deployment is a formal planning process that enables alignment between the strategic plan, the operating plan, and medium-term, short-term, and daily business activities. Policy deployment also incorporates execution plans, measurement, and feedback for all plans at all levels of planning. Policy deployment is effective in aligning key business process activities and other general business activities of the enterprise.
2. Policy deployment is a formal planning process that enables alignment between the strategic plan, the operating plan, strategic improvement initiatives, and daily improvement initiatives.

Although both can be handled via formal policy deployment practices, it is within the second that we have experienced a high level of administrative tinkering to keep everything aligned. The improvement activities under the umbrella of business excellence (e.g., Kaizen, Lean, Six Sigma, enabling InfoTech, etc.) are much more dynamic than the well-defined key business processes, operating plans, or strategic plans. Often, these improvement activities are launched or shifted around in response to critical customer needs or complaints and emerging global market opportunities. If an organization attempts to align every major Lean Six Sigma project and every localized Kaizen or Quick Strike activity, their improvement initiative will soon be replaced by the administrative requirements of policy deployment. Common sense tells us that all of these improvement methodologies require balance and mental awareness. Some 12 to 15 years ago, many organizations dabbled with a popular process for evaluating proposed new product features and functionality called *quality function deployment* (QFD). Followed blindly, the objective of improving product development was replaced with the tedious analysis and maintenance of QFD matrices, which actually

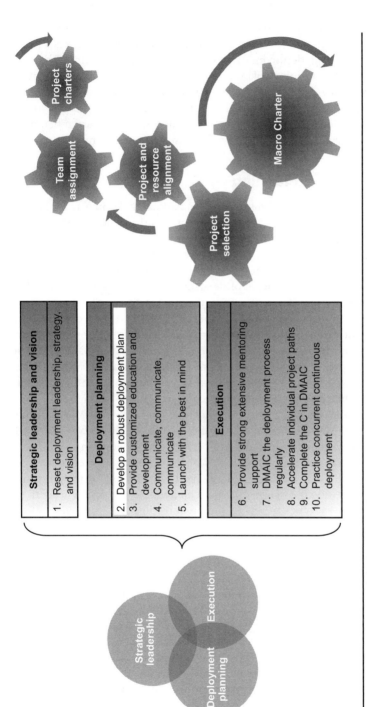

Figure 5.1 Elements of deployment planning.

made the product development cycle worse. If an organization spends more time on planning the improvement than they spend improving, there is a fundamental problem with their deployment process. When Lean Six Sigma becomes overshadowed by the training, planning, management, and measurement processes inherent within Lean Six Sigma, it is time to stop the process. For the specific improvement initiatives identified in a Lean Six Sigma deployment, there is a simplified version of policy deployment called Macro Charter planning, developed as an integral part of our Scalable Lean Six Sigma™ model.

Macro Charter Planning

One of the most frequent mistakes organizations make in a Lean Six Sigma deployment is the failure to define, scope out, and charter projects at a level of detail where they are legitimately *doable* for the organization and *assignable* to an improvement team. As organizations work through their business diagnostic and policy deployment efforts, they begin to develop improvement opportunities at a theme or boil-the-ocean level of detail. Some examples of this include improving the customer experience, improving new product development, reducing warranty and returns, or improving sourcing quality. When organizations assign improvement projects at this level of detail, teams flounder with an assignment that is too ambitious, too ambiguous, and effectively impossible. The result is an unsuccessful project and team experience. Taking this a step further, when teams and people experience these outcomes, the organization loses their commitment and interest because they tried Lean Six Sigma and it did not work. People not only internalize this bad experience, but they share it with others in the organization. In the examples cited above, there could be 20 to 50 separate targeted improvement projects to move these performance needles in the right direction. This is related to the core competency of Improvement Excellence™. The organization is anxious to achieve improvements as soon as possible, but they fail to take the time to define, scope out, and characterize projects with data and facts. In the process, they fail to set up the organization and improvement teams for success.

The Macro Charter

The Macro Charter (see Figures 5. 2, 5.3, and 5.4) are planning templates that logically break down the ambiguous inputs and improvement opportunities from the business diagnostic and higher-level policy deployment activities.

As we stated previously, the business diagnostic results in a significant amount of attribute data (e.g., perceptions, observations, intuitive inputs from structured interviews) and variables data (e.g., standard financial reports, daily and monthly performance reports, etc.). This is accomplished by preliminary analysis in each of the fuzzy areas to further refine more specific opportunities. The objective is to shake out the 80 percent of the problems and the corresponding 20 percent of

Business diagnostic summary

Business unit	Primary functional area	Problem discussion summary	Effect on business	Probable root causes	Key business processes affected
Consumer products	Sales & operations planning (focus PURELY on demand forecasting)	Low forecast accuracy leading to premium freight, inventory, OTD and customer service issues; Europe 70% of sales — can better manage variation than us with 30% of orders with wider variation); don't access sell-through info, access sell-to info to dealers; don't know sell-through to ultimate customers (Media Market in Europe, like xxxxx); not getting (any or reliable) sales forecasts from regions; not a priority for the sales group, not measured for performance; handle everything the same, proliferation of products and SKUs; sales does not recognize problems — top $ forecast is accurate; constant changes throughout month especially last week	More of a Pareto relationship in Europe than US with lower volumes; priority, lack of process (evolving); frequency of review; dropping in requirements without impact on whole; revenue-driven; way too much manual intervention	Forecast, master schedule, MRP but can't handle multi- whse; SAP process will be automated by April; currently analyzing product data to clarify root causes, where to focus to get largest, quickest, improvement, etc.	Same
Aerospace products	Quality	Warranty and nonwarranty returns are growing significantly; some returns have been in system for as long as 268 days; many "no problem found" returns — send back to customer and falls again; rev updates not getting done; customers are unhappy because we are not turning these around fast enough; customers applying their own billing adjustments causing waste in invoicing and collections; nonwarranty returns in queue represent $8.2m in incremental revenue	Lost revenue opportunities, customer complaints, potential catastrophe at customer, excessive costs of onsite repair, airline costs, expedited freight, disruptions, etc. when products fall and customer has no spares	Warranty and nonwarranty turnaround not a priority, sales talks customers into buying more new products, giving deep concessions when there is a warranty problem, probably giving away new products; product documentation weak on rev level change dates, difficult to tell what configuration customer purchased, may have sat in warehouse for 6 months before purchase	Sales, warehouse, quality, customer service, finance (returns and billing processes)
Consumer products	Operations	Poor on time delivery; sales sells and the organization falls down; customers angry, complaining about OTD and availability of stock, threatening to cancel orders; don't order enough inventory, vendor quality issues, designs failing in field; shipping department takes too long lunches and too many breaks	Losing market share, one of our largest retailers threatening to throw us out; lots of expediting, crisis meetings, running around, nobody really knows why, just fighting flames, dealing with same problems over and over	Consumer market moves fast, customers will buy competitor's product if ours not available; China manufacturers and suppliers need to be more flexible, not responding fast enough; wrong metrics — inventory, costs, efficiency and utilization can be OK but have terrible OTD	S&OP, order entry, supply chain

Figure 5.2 Macro Charter, Tab 1.

root causes. Figure 5.2 illustrates that improving sourcing quality can be broken down into six separate projects, segmented by specific vendors and groups of products with the highest defect or field reliability failures. At the risk of challenging conventional quality philosophies, organizations do not need to deal with every sourcing quality issue to make a big improvement hit. In effect, the Macro Charter promotes the notion of knocking down the tallest poles in the Pareto chart and then moving on to additional improvements. This scoping, breaking down, and characterization of obscure and fuzzy improvement activities is conducted from left to right across the template through a process called *funneling* or *chunking*. This scoping is also conducted from top to bottom as larger opportunities are broken down to multiple specific projects. Finally, scoping is conducted by the interpretation of preliminary clue data and facts, where multiple projects may either be consolidated or further segmented into more specific improvement projects. These projects may be further refined after they are assigned to improvement teams that throw the lower Pareto pole project segments back into the hopper for a future effort by the existing or new team. These initial Macro Charter activities usually result in more projects than an organization has the capacity to launch all at once. The executive core team regulates the level and scope of launched improvement initiatives based on organizational capacity and resource constraints. The Macro Charter rules prevent Lean Six Sigma from initiating activities for activities' sake and taking on an ineffective life of its own. Over time, the Macro Charter becomes the Lean Six Sigma project hopper of queued up, scoped, chartered, and assignable improvement projects. Maintenance of the Macro Charter is the responsibility of the core executive team. The Macro Charter template includes the following components:

Tab 1—Business Diagnostic and Policy Deployment Inputs

- Business unit
- Primary functional area
- Problem discussion summary
- Effect on business
- Probable root causes
- Key business processes affected

At this level of the Macro Charter (see Figure 5.2) there are many inputs, observations, and usually an abundance of conflicting data. Further fact-finding and analysis is required to separate the wheat from the chaff, and funnel or chunk out specific projects with specific objectives, improvement goals, and deliverables.

Tab 2—Definition and Scoping of Specific Projects

- Problem statement
- Project name
- Project objectives and scope

- Key performance metrics
- Baseline performance
- Improvement goal
- Benefits statement
- Quantified benefits
- Project deliverables
- Barriers to success

At this level of the Macro Charter (see Figure 5.3) there is much analysis and deep mining of data occurring in the background. The result of this deep-core drilling is the ability to translate world hunger projects into specific, well-defined *doable* projects. For example, a single problem discussion summary in Figure 5.2 (sales and operations planning) has been separated into four specific but inter-related improvement projects in Figure 5.3 (sales and operations planning improvement, customer rationalization, product rationalization, and premium freight reduction). In addition, there is substantial detail determined prior to handing these projects off to an improvement team. It is typical for the initial business diagnostic to result in 30 to 40 or more potential specific improvement project opportunities. If Quick Strike or containment opportunities are identified during the business diagnostic, they need not go through this funneling activity. These Quick Strike opportunities are reviewed with management as they are uncovered, and many short-term containment or improvement actions are made on the fly. The Macro Charter methodology allows executives to step back and objectively synthesize the results of the business diagnostic with the identification of specific improvement opportunities. This process also provides a rare opportunity for executives to step out of their daily routines and view their organization from a different perspective. Collaboration and constructive discussions on the identification and prioritization of improvement opportunities clarifies improvement and places it within believable reach. This process establishes continuity and consensus on strategic improvement needs.

Tab 3—Project Chartering

- Executive sponsor
- Process owner
- Team leader
- Team participants
- Extended team resources
- Standard team meeting schedule
- Next four- to six-week plan
- Initial mining data

At this level of the Macro Charter (see Figure 5.4), the actual chartering process takes place. This does not occur in a casual manner. The Lean Six Sigma executive core team has numerous discussions and debates about how to put the

Project definition and scoping

Problem statement	Project name	Project objectives and scope	Key performance metrics	Baseline performance	Improvement goal	Benefits statement	Quantified benefits	Savings category	Project deliverables	Barriers to success
Forecast accuracy is extremely low; not enough effort is put into S&OP process to tie sales, supply chain, and finance together. All products treated equally; measure and report out forecast error monthly, no corrective actions or accountability	S&OP Improvement	Improve forecast accuracy (the combo of forecast and MPS that drives MRP)	Forecast accuracy; forecast error, by product, category, region, sales associate, customer, distributor, etc.	Current US is 40–50%; EMEA is 60–70%	Shoot for 80–90%+	Forecast accuracy will improve OTD and F/G turnover	$784K	A, B, D	Accurate forecasting process with proven best practices and metrics	Sales not interested, wants to sell and hit $ goals; new forecasting process will expose waste and accountability
There is no distinction of customers; treat a $100 customer exactly as a $150M customer; often at expense of premier customers; invoicing costs more to apply individual discount agreements than the value of the order; obvious negative margins on too many orders. 14 customers represent over 90% of U.S. sales, sell to 3874 customers	Customer rationalization	Develop more targeted sales, customer service and fulfillment practices that recognize distinctions between customers; eliminate excess hidden costs to service low volume, unprofitable market segments; look for other options to smooth out selling cycle, might consider new policy for small customers to deal direct with dealers but determine based on data	$ revenue by market, region, distributor, customer; P&L $ by same	Billing employs 6 fte people ($238K) to deal with errors on orders under $250; sales spending too much time on same (COPQ being determined)	Work with product rationalization team; reduce low and negative margin orders, including cost of quality to sell and service smaller customers	Significant COPQ reductions and waste from handling low and negative margin customers; sales will have more time and resources to focus more on top 50 customers, tall pole	This project will reduce COPQ by $370K – $438K	A, B, C, D, E	Recommended actions to reduce, realign customers to appropriate channels	Sales does not want to lose the flexibility of selling to these customers
Too many products, many with low and negative margins, especially the disruption and expediting costs; sales meets $ goals but XYZ falls short on P&L, asset mgmt. goals	Product rationalization and pruning	Reduce the number of SKUs through data-driven logic and analytical science; also develop a formal ongoing process to evaluate and phase out old SKUs	Number of SKUs; profitability by category; product, SKU	Current 876 SKUs	Reduce the number of active SKUs by at least 25%	40% of order entry time is spent on orders under $250; estimate a P/N reduction of over 6000 R/M components; many products with negative margins	Eliminate negative margins on $170M revenues ($18M drain to profits); improve ave. profit margin by 6 points	A, B, C, D, E	Recommended SKU reductions with justification; ongoing SKU rationalization process with metrics	Sales will not give up SKUs will complain that they can not sell X without offering Y; some customers prefer older products
Spending $25M/year on premium freight from suppliers; 36% of F/G receipts to Denver warehouse are premium freight, then excess inventory next months; sales instructing warehouse to ship premium freight; premium freight is a free for all, everyone using as a security blanket, no process or controls	Premium freight reduction	Define best practice to control and reduce premium freight by 75%; to beat goal by year end	Premium freight $; look at premium freight by supplier, category, product, by time of month, etc	Current $25M	Reduce by 75%	Defining root causes of premium freight will identify future projects; these savings are hard $, bottom line savings	This project should reduce premium freight by $15M – $18M	A, D	Premium freight procedure, controls, and ongoing metrics; visibility to root causes (who, when, why, approved, etc.)	Will need to do a much better job in S&OP to enable this; engineering and supply chain groups will argue they need this to get products out on time

Figure 5.3   Macro Charter, Tab 2.

Project chartering

Project name	Project objectives and scope	Executive sponsor	Process owner	Team leader	Team participants	Extended team resources	Standard team meeting schedule	Next 4-6 week plan complete	Initial mining data
SOP improvement	Improve forecast accuracy (the combo of forecast and MPS that drives MRP)	Steve Boeder	Dave Johnson	Christine Williams	John McKrill, Scott Claywell, Larry Bonner, Amanda Griggs	Jeffrey Spands, William Heidke Lamborne, Randy Rodregas	Monday, 11AM–1PM, executive conference room	Y	Pareto analysis by revenue $, customer, dealer, distributor, region; prior Pareto forecast accuracy by product line
Customer rationalization	Develop more targeted sales, customer service and fulfillment practices that recognize distinctions between customers; eliminate excess hidden costs to service low volume, unprofitable market segments; look for other options to smooth out selling cycle. Might consider new policy for small customers to deal direct with dealers but determine based on data	Sandra Smith	William Trask	Steve Miller	Ben Burton, Sandra White, Tim Hardwig	Marc Flint	Tuesday, 1PM–3PM, conference room 1	Y	Pareto analysis of revenue $ by customer, gross margin by customer & by product
Product rationalization and pruning	Reduce the number of SKUs through data-driven logic and analytical science; also develop a formal ongoing process to evaluate and phase out old SKUs	Bradley Jones	Brenda Rooks	John Bender	John Lawson, Craig Allen, Roger Marconi, Richard Caldwell	Sales — TBD	Wednesday, 10AM–12PM, conference room A-2	Y	Analysis of products and revenues, volumes, gross margins
Premium freight reduction	Define best practice to control and reduce premium freight by 75%; to beat goal by year end	John Moore	Melanie Shafer	Richard Hertz	David Arthur, Robert Mondavi, Katherine Hall, Raymond Partridge	Kelly Quigley, Tammy Lamborne, Randy Rodregas	Thursday, 9AM–11AM	Y	Premium freight dollars by month

Figure 5.4 Macro Charter, Tab 3.

organization's best foot forward while balancing daily activities and deployment requirements, and optimizing the deployment as a great professional development opportunity. One of the goals in this activity is to select and assign resources from a particular project area who should already be concerned with improving the area defined in the problem statement and project objectives. Rather than viewing Lean Six Sigma projects as a responsibility *in addition to* normal workloads, it is an individual's normal duty, but one in which they are being equipped with new skills and improvement tools. It is impossible to achieve this alignment unless the executive core team follows the deliberate process of chartering.

In practice, jumping over Tab 3 and prioritizing projects (project prioritization matrix) saves a little time with chartering details. The Lean Six Sigma executive core team can return to Tab 3 after project prioritization and focus chartering efforts on the top-priority projects. Time is saved on chartering activities for projects that may fall down the priority list. However, Tab 3 is a must before improvement projects are actually assigned to a team. Projects that remain in the Macro Charter hopper in the first go-around will eventually float to the top of the priority list.

During Macro Charter development, the executive team may immediately assign Kaizen improvement (containment) activities to a particular manager or department supervisor as quick containment actions. These actions are common sense improvements and do not require deep knowledge of DMAIC or Lean Six Sigma. Every improvement opportunity does not require a formal Lean Six Sigma project or a complex statistical analysis. Another role of the executive core team may be to launch specific projects even if they did not score highest on the priority list because it may be a foundation or dependency project for other projects in the hopper. The Macro Charter methodology endorses the old Chinese proverb, "It is possible to move a mountain by carrying away small stones."

Project Prioritization Matrix

The project prioritization matrix (see Figure 5.5) is used by the executive core team to rank the relative importance of each project against the strategic plan and operating plan, and other critical factors or constraints unique to a specific client's Lean Six Sigma deployment. Other considerations might include personal and organizational development or career exposure opportunities for the organization's high-performing employees. Projects are scored and ranked against attributes such as cost reduction, growth, strategic positioning, or market availability. Other attributes may include the level of required effort, availability of the right resources, time, risks, availability of data, capital investment, etc. These attributes may also be assigned a rating for relative importance. Specific improvement projects are listed in rows, and the evaluation attributes are listed across the top of the template. Each attribute factor is assigned a weight from 1 (not important) to 10 (very important). Each project is evaluated in terms of how it contributes to the attribute criteria using the same 1 to 10 scoring procedure.

Project prioritization matrix

*=Reverse scoring, High score=low cost, low difficulty

Project name	Project objectives and scope	Growth impact	P&L impact	Cash flow impact	Strategic position	Resource availability	Availability of data	Level of difficulty*	Probability of success	Timeliness of completion	Ease of implementation	Cost of implementation	Weights	Total score
Weights		9	10	9	7	5	6	4	6	5	7	9		
SOP improvement	Improve forecast accuracy (the combo offorecast and MPS that drives MRP)	7	9	9	7	8	8	9	7	8	8	9		629
Customer rationalization	Develop more targeted sales, customer service and fulfillment practices that recognize distinctions between customers; eliminate excess hidden costs to service low volume, unprofitable market segments; look for other options	4	9	7	6	5	7	7	7	6	6	8		510
Product rationalization and pruning	Reduce the number of SKUs through data-driven logic and analytical science; also develop a formal ongoing process to evaluate and phase out old SKUs	6	9	9	6	7	7	8	7	6	6	8		569
Premium freight reduction	Define best practice to control and reduce premium freight by 75%; to be at goal by year end	5	10	8	8	9	9	9	9	9	9	9		651

Figure 5.5   Macro Charter, Tab 4.

The matrix multiplies the project rating by the criteria weight in each cell and accumulates the total score across the matrix. The object is to remove the subjectivity, business unit, or individual executive preferences, and focus on the organization's highest impact improvement opportunities with limited capacity and resources. The total scores for each project are meaningless; the relative ranking of projects against each other is what really matters. The executive core team is also responsible for rationalizing and scrubbing the project prioritization matrix. Rationalizing and scrubbing is not to be interpreted as arbitrarily changing ratings to make favorable projects float to the top of the list. Sometimes reviewing the attribute ratings of certain groups of projects results in a justifiable modification, and hence a revision in project scores and project priorities. One of the largest benefits of the project prioritization matrix is in building executive commitment that simplifies the executive sponsor and project chartering efforts.

Project or Resource Alignment

Another key requirement of deployment planning is making sure that the proposed improvement activities are spread across the organization and participants to create the initial momentum and critical mass. Project or resource alignment is the final check to validate that proposed improvement projects are staffed for success. One of the things to look for at this stage is the diversity, depth, and balance of mixed skill levels, and process knowledge of the proposed teams. For accounting and financial projects, having accounting resources who understand the financial accounting system, general ledger, and chart of accounts is a must. Otherwise, the team will exhaust time trying to understand accounting rather than completing their project. Another example is new product development where a proposed improvement team needs resources who are involved in product development on a daily basis. We want to avoid having five design engineers or five cost accountants on a team.

There are occasions where a team leader without expertise in a particular area may be used for total objectivity and possibly a career exposure opportunity. For example, a bright woman from human resources was assigned to lead a team on reducing tooling costs. Because she was not tainted by specific screw machine experience or other engineering factors, she had to follow the DMAIC methodology precisely, and subsequently made her team follow it as well. She was a great team leader and brought out the best in her team. Within four months they identified over $430K in tooling and downtime cost reductions. There are no set-in-stone rules for staffing teams, but it is a leadership responsibility to set up the projects and teams for success. During this stage, the executive core team is aligning projects to individual participant functional areas to minimize the in-addition-to-my-normal-work feelings of the team leader and the team.

At this stage it is necessary to look for individuals who may have been assigned to multiple teams. During the dialogue about how best to staff improvement projects, there is a natural tendency for executives and managers to select their go-to people—the people they trust the most at getting things done. Through discussion after discussion, project after project, there are always a few individuals assigned to multiple teams. We encourage organizations to follow a single-team position, single-individual rule so the deployment learning and execution activities are widened across as many people as possible for the proposed projects. The other factor to consider at this point is the realization of an individual's commitments as a team leader or member as well as their daily commitments. There are some occasions where a particular member is slated for an improvement team, but may be buried already with complaints from the largest customers. A word of caution here—it might be the old we-don't-have-the-time-to-do-things-right-but-we-always-find-the-time-to-do-things-over syndrome. Asking the question "Why?" five times about a major customer complaint may result in a good reason for this busy individual to participate on a team.

There are so many positive experiences in a consultant's career that come to mind while writing this book. We were going through the Macro Charter effort with one client and a restless executive said, "Is all of this necessary? Why don't we just form some teams and get them going on something?"

Before I could respond, the CEO said, "Yes it's necessary and revealing. We're going to get this right. You can't just throw a group of pathetic people together, give them a vague assignment, and call them a high-performance team. You build-in high performance up front."

That was much more compelling and gutsy than my response would have been. On a more serious note, a well-orchestrated Lean Six Sigma deployment is a tremendous learning and personal development experience for the organization. When executives stick it out for the long haul, root-cause problem solving and fact-based decision making become the new cultural norms. Executive debates and controversy are healthy emotions when reaching for success with Lean Six Sigma. When the broader components of Lean Six Sigma become an inherent behavior in enough people in the organization, fact-based decision making becomes a self-managing peer process.

Team Assignment

The final step of this segment is the official assignment of specific individuals as team leaders, team participants, and extended team members. This is a formal process where each team is stepped through their project by the executive core team, executive sponsor, and process owner(s). The group reviews the problem, project objectives, scope, improvement goals, preliminary clue data, expected deliverables, project timing, and a work plan for the next four to six weeks. These project parameters are negotiable as the team digs into more data, as they are actually in a better position to refine these project parameters. Although this seems like a lot of groundwork, the team leaves the starting gate with a solid understanding of their assignment. Team assignment is the official launching of improvement teams, and is followed by communicating these details to the organization. In Chapter 4, we discussed the improvement vision and executive commitment to provide more details in two to four weeks. Now is a good time for the CEO and executive core team to update the organization with summary-level details developed in the Macro Charter, and the official improvement teams. During this communication, one must not forget to explain that everyone cannot participate up front, but mention the rollout plans for Lean Six Sigma with the expectation of opportunities to participate in the near future.

Earlier in this chapter we discussed resource and project alignment to optimize the perception of improvement as a part of, instead of in addition to, one's normal work responsibilities. Having discussed this goal, there are always exceptions to the process. During the creation of teams and assignments, another motivation may be to designate participants for the purposes of career exposure or to evaluate how individuals perform outside their normal routines. It is typical for some resources to end up working in areas that are totally new to them, and it is difficult to view these assignments as anything but an addition to daily work (rather than part of the daily workload). Sometimes these assignments are given purposefully to evaluate how a particular individual performs in more of a leadership role across new and broader functional areas. Sometimes the same-people-same-thinking-same-process-same-results people are left out intentionally. In these examples, the team assignments often tend to be the most interesting projects. An individual working in an area with little to no experience is not tainted by the habits and thinking of the normal process or area experts. These individuals have no choice but to lead and follow their team through the DMAIC methodology, discovering root causes and opportunities that have been previously missed or discounted by the typical firefighting activities of resident employees. In the process, everyone benefits from more knowledge and empathy of other people's roles and responsibilities. As a reminder, this is not a bad reflection on the resident experts—it is the power of structured root-cause problem solving, looking at process through a different lens and with more robust improvement tools.

A few years back, we worked with a client to improve yields in a proprietary restricted area of their operation. This organization had their secret room—a clean room where a proprietary assembly process was located, and where access was limited to only a few key employees. This was a complex high-tech assembly area that had 60 percent yields on a good day. There was a belief that 60 percent was the best they could do because of the design—an assumption they made because they had been at that level for years.

We were looking at a perfect Lean Six Sigma pilot candidate. Why? Because this is the type of situation where everyone walks around back-patting and telling each other how technical and smart they are, and legends soon become facts. This process was supported by Tom Smart, an arrogant senior-level engineer who had designed and developed the assembly and test equipment since day one. This was a highly profitable product and Tom had the president's ear. He could out-talk, out-excuse, and out-blame anyone in the organization about the details of the clean-room processes. Unfortunately, it was all based on his perceptions, opinions, and experiences. Since access to the process was limited, it became impossible to do anything without overpowering Tom. Sadly, the organization felt stifled with Tom's close-mindedness, protective behaviors, and the potential threats of shutting down the process if changes other than his were made. Neither Tom nor anyone else in the organization understood the true root causes of process variation. One day in a meeting, Tom became so angry when questioned about key process variables and root-cause data that he refused to participate in a Lean Six Sigma project. It was a silly standoff based on this argument: "You people just don't understand the complexities and I can't show you or tell you because it's proprietary."

The vice president of operations sponsored a Lean Six Sigma yield improvement project with the condition that only two team (internal) members were allowed into Tom's clean room (and a silent condition that Tom would not be on the team). Tom did all he could to undermine the project. He told the team that they were wasting their time because he already knew (and was working on) the real problem of purchasing's low-cost suppliers who could not provide parts as good as the previous higher-priced suppliers. Tom never paid much attention to supplier quality data, which was analyzed by the team. The team validated that the same recurring yield problems was present with the previous suppliers. The initial analysis isolated most of the rolled throughput yield fallout to a tungsten inert gas (TIG) welding operation, a technology over fifty years old. Tom replied, "I'm the company's TIG expert, it's running fine, and you should be working on the real problems."

The team conducted Internet searches and learned a lot about TIG welding, key process input variables (KPIVs) and key process output variables (KPOVs) without even peeking through the drapes of the secret room. The team also found several completed TIG welding yield improvement references and articles on the Internet. We created a *design of experiments* (DOE) plan for the TIG welder on the white board of a remote conference room, and generated the Minitab data collection worksheets for the two authorized team members. The two authorized team members and the operator ran the trials and collected data. During the study, the operator was pleased that the team was looking at the right areas and shared ideas (ones Tom had previously shot down) with the two team members. Within three weeks, the team analyzed the DOE results and were able to develop, implement, and replicate process setting changes on the TIG weld operation that improved yield to 75 percent (about a $600K per year in savings). Tom Smart was furious with the study results and put up a last-ditch fight against implementing the recommendations. He went to the president and told him that the yield improvement team breached the company's security in the secret room and that the outside consultants were given confidential facts about their proprietary process. This rapidly escalated into an urgent meeting with the president and his staff. In the final showdown, the yield improvement team presented their project to the executive team and described how they acquired their knowledge about TIG welding on several public websites. They walked everyone through their fact-based and air-tight DMAIC phases of the project. They mentioned that the consultants helped them only with the DOE setup and running and interpreting the Minitab analysis, but never entered the clean room. We acknowledged our limited TIG yield experiences with previous automotive industry Lean Six Sigma projects and agreed that our primary purpose was leading the way for the team and helping them to analyze the process and draw the right data driven recommendations for improvement. The team shared the normal TIG yield results with key factors set on Tom's settings, and the higher TIG yield results on their proposed and replicated settings. The more Tom interrupted, the more the executive team shut him down. The team also shared over a dozen additional yield improvement ideas and expressed their interest in continuing with their efforts because they thought that they could eventually raise yields to 95 percent or higher. The team's well-executed and fact-based yield improvement project won out over the deep hole that Tom and his ego had dug for them. The secret room was now open for more improvement business. There is no secret to Lean Six Sigma's success, just common sense and persistence at chasing down root causes with a different set of eyes and improvement tools. The facts, empowerment, and results win out over politics and nonvalue-added games.

Using the Macro Charter for Planning and Project Management

The Macro Charter becomes a useful living template for a Lean Six Sigma deployment. Some of our clients have created a tab to post actual results and other project details to the Macro Charter. At the conclusion of every project is also a formal lessons-learned activity in which teams have the opportunity to comment on how their project or the deployment in general could be improved. This information is used by the executive core team and executive team to steer or reset the course of the deployment. Successful Lean Six Sigma deployments are not a steady-state cookbook of tasks. Active and creative leadership in the leadership strategy, deployment planning, and execution phases is what makes these deployments so successful. There is a constant stream of information and activity around how the deployment can get even better. Organizations that have used this methodology successfully have used the Macro Charter in several planning and analysis activities such as:

- Sorting and displaying launched and planned projects by business unit, key process, or functional area, and anticipated benefit timelines to determine how the organization's formal Lean Six Sigma initiative will contribute to the operating plan or financial plan. Some committed organizations are also aggressive and build the planned savings into their budgets.
- Analyzing projected and cumulative rates of improvement over a specified timeline and adjusting the deployment to maintain or improve the rate

of improvement. Typically, the rate of improvement becomes difficult to grow as the initial "sweet improvement fruit" is harvested during the first two years. Organizations maintain or increase the rate of improvement by new thinking, new innovation, new boundaries, new people, and improving the deployment process.

- Evaluating the relative value of launched and queued up projects by business unit, functional area, or as a baseline to measure actual project performance. This is another check to validate the load of projects across business units that may need to improve the most. This is also another check to make sure that Lean Six Sigma is positioned as an organizational improvement initiative, not a manufacturing or quality initiative. It is typical for many teams to actually exceed the anticipated benefits of their projects. Some of this happens by a natural lean toward fact-based conservatism on defining projected benefits, but most of this occurs because true root-cause problem solving reveals opportunities that were hidden and unknown to the organization.

- Evaluating current and planned professional development needs, developing backstop organizational skills and capabilities, or recognition and rewards.

- Providing a knowledge repository for completed, launched, and planned improvement projects. For completed improvement projects, the Macro Charter is usually supplemented with a searchable directory of detailed DMAIC information for each project. Future projects are able to leverage off the work of previous projects for needs such as process SIPOCs (supplier, inputs, process, outputs, customers) and value stream maps, root-cause considerations of previous projects, references for all Lean and Six Sigma tools and applications, or additional extended team members who might be useful on a current project.

The Macro Charter is a living template. It should be updated in real time as new information is discovered about queued up projects, or a totally new planned project is placed in the hopper. The Macro Charter provides all the current characterization information for all projects. After its initial creation, the Macro Charter is the active hopper of current and planned improvement projects. The hopper helps to keep the momentum high because there should always be more improvement opportunities than there is capacity to complete improvement opportunities. It is the responsibility of the executive core team to manage the hopper so that there is always a clean inventory of characterized, mission-critical improvement opportunities ready for assignment. The executive core team periodically needs to empty the trash and emotions out of the Macro Charter decision-making process. The hopper should not be the trash compactor of unqualified improvement ideas, and it should never be empty. When organizations let this happen, they are admitting that they no longer need to improve and, thus, are losing the *continuous* aspect of continuous improvement.

Individual Project Charters

The first assignment of a launched improvement team is to create their project charters (see Figure 5.6). This is the team's reference document for their specific project. Project charters define a specific team leader, team, executive sponsor, and project title. Project charters also include a crisp problem statement, probable root causes (clue data), project objectives, scope, boundaries, performance metrics, current baseline performance and COPQ data, improvement goals, quantified benefits, expected deliverables, and a rough timetable for the project. As the team progresses further into their project, the project charter may be refined or more targeted as the parameters of their project become more defined. Project charters are living documents that continue to evolve and target more specific opportunities as the team works its way through the DMAIC methodology.

The Micro Charter—Quick Strike Area Improvements

The Macro Charter incorporates an *above-the-line* and *below-the-line* process for identifying potential project opportunities. *Above-the-line* items are fully characterized and prioritized projects. These projects are either in an assigned or planned status. There are two different *below-the-line* categories:

1. *Below-the-line, Section I*—These are potential project ideas where there are questions about feasibility, benefits, or if it is even a real project or a symptom of another opportunity. Project ideas in this section need more fact-finding and data analysis to verify whether it is a real recurring problem or an emotionally stimulated problem. There are always situations where people will define problems with their emotions instead of with the facts. Project ideas in this category may make their way up the list, may fall off the list, or may become rolled into another defined opportunity.
2. *Below-the-line, Section II*—These opportunities may or may not be legitimate improvement opportunities, but it is certain that their resolution will not require a formal project with a formal team. Some of these are legitimate Quick Strike or Kaizen opportunities, and are assigned to the area manager or supervisor for further investigation and resolution.

Another element of Scalable Lean Six Sigma™ is called *basic improvement skills* (BIS). Prior to initiating Kaizen or Quick Strike activities in a particular department, the manager or first-line supervisors attend a one-day BIS education session. During this session, participants are exposed to the application of simple data analysis tools, Quick Strike templates, and the DMAIC methodology retrofitted for these types of improvement activities. At this level, DMAIC is a structured set of the right questions to ask when walking through a Quick Strike activity. Next, the managers and first-line supervisors are developed via a train-the-trainers effort. In turn, these individuals provide a short two- to four-hour education module to their people followed with a Quick Strike assignment

PROJECT CHARTER

Project name: Billing Errors	**Annual savings:** $ 6.7M cash flow, $70K avoidance
Green belt: Gretchen Hancock	**Champion:** Mike Hall
Team members: Robin Hood	**Business unit:** All
Sandy Ramsey	
Start date: 6/6/2009	**Target completion:** 12/10/2009

Problem statement:	* Billing errors are caused somewhere in the quote through invoice process (wrong price, incorrect quantity, RMAs, manual NRE billings, etc.). * Extend A/R, creates NVA in reconciling invoices and correcting errors before we can collect our money.

Project objectives:	What improvement is targeted and what will be the impact on critical business metrics?				
		Projects Y's	**Baseline**	**Goal**	**Units**
	Primary metric	Reduce billing	3	1.5	% qty
		errors	2.5	1.25	% $
	Secondary metric	Education	unknown	100%	
	Other metrics				
	Counterbalance				
	Financial impact				

Benefits and improvement goals:	* Reduction in payment delays * Reduce manual corrections/transactions * Accurate cash availability * Improves monthly revenue projections (accurate baseline) * Enhance business control processes

Baseline performance:	* Perception of high percentage of errors
	 * Actuals Mar–May 2009
	    - 3% credit transactions (non RMA)
	    - 2.5% of revenue
	 * Delays in payments

Current performance:		% credit transactions	% credit of dollars	Comments
	Mar–May	3.03%	2.50%	
	June	1.30%	0.41%	
	July	1.61%	1.40%	
	Aug	3.26%	1.21%	MPO contract closure
	Sept	1.21%	0.59%	
	Oct	1.58%	0.86%	
	Nov	1.88%	0.24%	

Support required	IT for SAP reporting only (minimal $)

Figure 5.6   Project charter.

The manager and area supervisors provide mentoring support to their people, or reach out to people outside of their immediate area for assistance. This element of Scalable Lean Six Sigma™ ensures a consistent improvement structure and language of improvement throughout the entire organization.

BIS demonstrates that improvement is not limited to a top down process. Employees throughout the organization and at all levels are encouraged to identify and participate in Quick Strike improvement opportunities. A Micro Charter is another template used in a Lean Six Sigma deployment to promote early involvement in department or area focused Kaizen or Quick Strike activities. The Micro Charter includes a consolidated tab of all open and completed Quick Strike activities, and a tab for each area that displays their particular open and completed Quick Strike activities. It provides a standard process and structure for identifying, prioritizing, assigning, tracking, completing, and summarizing Quick Strike activities. Since the Micro Charter is in spreadsheet format, it can be easily manipulated to view projects by area, projects completed by associate, savings by department, organization, or business unit, and many other options. We are advocates of integrating Micro Charter activities into individual performance reviews, reinforcing the notion that improvement is an expected part of everyone's job.

Keeping the Lean Six Sigma Lifecycle Alive

Organizations missing or underestimating the importance of deployment planning lose the sense of urgency over time. Weaknesses in the elements of deployment planning described in this chapter are the major causes of deployments running out of steam. For nearly four decades, organizations have allowed continuous improvement to follow a birth-death lifecycle. In the beginning, there is interest followed by some improvements. Then something changes (usually good news) that shifts the focus away from improvement, then something else changes that again shifts focus to the next improvement program. It is time to reverse this birth-death cycle of improvement, and this is so simple to achieve with the right leadership and infrastructure.

If an organization is really committed to continuous improvement, it is impossible to run out of things to improve. Over the next decade, the face of Lean Six Sigma and improvement in general will evolve, but the basics of success will remain pretty much the same. We are entering a new era of improvement that we call *Adaptive and Innovative Lean Six Sigma*. This is improving an organization's capability to sense, interpret, decide, act, and measure improvement activities with the integration of technology with an expanded, innovative application tool set, and in real time. These types of improvement are rapidly becoming a differentiator in this new economy. Whether it is developing software applications in India or designing new products in California, building products in China, synchronizing a global supply chain, or selling multiple versions of the same product in a dozen different countries and markets, improvement is necessary to survive. Organizations must improve for the long haul if they wish to be competitive in the next decade and beyond.

The Macro Charter and Micro Charter instruments, combined with the supporting infrastructure described in this chapter, keep improvement opportunities current, aligned to customer and business needs, and ready to go. These instruments also create a positive psychological effect because they visibly identify and queue up more opportunities, promote raising the bar, and provide the impetus for improving how an organization improves. Deployment planning is an important factor in enabling Improvement Excellence™—the mastery of developing and implementing successful strategic and continuous business improvement initiatives, transforming culture, and enabling organizations to improve how they improve.

References

Blanchard, K., Miller, M. 2009. *The Secret: What Great Leaders Know and Do.* Berrett-Koehler Publications, Thousand Oaks, CA.

Burton, T. T., Moran, J. T. 1995. *The Future Focused Organization.* Prentice-Hall Publications, Upper Saddle River, NJ.

Burton, T. T., Sams, J. 2005. *Six Sigma for Small and Mid-Sized Organizations: Success Through Scaleable Deployment.* J. Ross Publishing, Fort Lauderdale, FL.

Iacocca, L. 2008. *Where Have All the Leaders Gone.* Scribner Publications, New York, NY.

Chapter 5 Take Aways

- One of the most frequent mistakes organizations make in a Lean Six Sigma deployment is the failure to define, scope out, and charter projects at a level of detail where they are legitimately *doable* for the organization and *assignable* to an improvement team. As organizations work through their business diagnostic and policy deployment efforts, they begin to develop improvement opportunities at a theme or boil-the-ocean level of detail. Some examples of this might include improving the customer experience, improving new product development, reducing warranty and returns, or improving sourcing quality. When organizations assign improvement projects at this level of detail, teams flounder with an assignment that is too ambitious, too ambiguous, and effectively impossible.

- The Macro Charter is a deployment planning process used to collect and identify potential project information such as a description of a problem, probable root causes, cost of quality (or waste), proposed project name, project objectives, improvement goals, benefits, and deliverables.

- Project selection is a deployment planning process that allows executives to evaluate projects against each other relative to business plan contribution. Projects are scored and ranked against attributes such as cost reduction, growth, level of resources, time, availability of data, capital investment, etc. The object is to remove subjectivity or executive preference, and focus the organization's limited resources on critical projects that will take the least amount of effort and create the greatest impact.

- Project or resource alignment is a deployment planning process that evaluates potential participant resources against a variety of required skill sets and direct experiences, facilitates in the identification and selection of team leaders and team participants, and helps to align people with projects with a level of objectivity.
- Team assignment is a deployment planning process for resource improvement activities. One objective is to spread and develop critical mass as much as possible. In our deployments, we exercise the one-resource-one-team rule that forces a deeper development of bench strength. When everything needs the involvement of a handful of people in the organization, something is definitely wrong.
- The Macro Charter methodology allows executives to step back and objectively synthesize the results of the business diagnostic with the identification of specific improvement opportunities. This process also provides a rare opportunity for executives to step out of their daily routines and view their organization from a different perspective. Collaboration and constructive discussions on the identification and prioritization of improvement opportunities clarifies improvement and places it within believable reach. Finally, this process establishes continuity and consensus on strategic improvement needs.

Guest Article Contribution

Elpitha Votsis is vice president of finance at Harman Music Group (HMG), a business unit of Harman Professional (HPro) and part of Harman International Industries. Elpitha is the executive deployment champion for their Lean Six Sigma and continuous improvement initiatives, and is a passionate, disciplined, high-energy executive with outstanding interpersonal and project management skills. Elpitha earned her black belt and is also certified by PMI® as a Project Management Professional. Prior to joining HMG, Elpitha worked for 10 years as controller of EDO Corporation, a defense industry company and another 10 years as vice president of finance for a division of Baker Hughes, an oil industry company.

Continuous Improvement Initiative at Harman Music Group

Elpitha Votsis

VP of Finance

Harman Music Group

HMG embarked on its Lean Six Sigma journey four years ago. Senior management recognized the need for process improvement in a methodical formalized way that would change the culture of the organization, streamline processes, and eliminate waste. With increased competitive pressure, it was obvious that the company needed a lean and efficient infrastructure to give it a competitive advantage by eliminating waste to increase profitability. We were so fortunate to be well on our way to realizing savings when the economic crisis hit our business during the fall of 2008, and we were able to maintain our profitability as a percent of sales even when our revenue levels dropped 30 percent.

With the help of the Center for Excellence in Operations (CEO), we launched our Lean Six Sigma initiative in 2006. Initially, employees viewed this as the most recent fad—something temporary that would pass with time. CEO was able to get us started by helping us to plan and organize the deployment, provide customized Lean Six Sigma education, and mentor our initial 22 improvement projects to a successful conclusion. This initial experience with Lean Six Sigma demonstrated the power of improvement, and HMG recognized the importance of adopting and perfecting the process internally to keep it alive. HMG has succeeded in keeping Lean Six Sigma and continuous improvement alive, and well integrated into their culture. This has been accomplished through several practices:

- The number one secret is to have a senior executive champion the project. Someone who has a proven track record of accomplishments, has authority, and is well respected by the employees. Without senior management support and involvement, such initiatives will fail. Senior management needs to walk the talk.

- HMG formed a core team with our president, vice president of operations, vice president of engineering, and me—executive vice president and CFO—to review the macro project charter, rank projects in order of importance based on our business strategy, and decide on which projects the teams will work on during the fiscal year. This team also decides on who will lead each project as a green belt. These lead people are assigned to select their team members based on skill sets that they think are needed to complete the project.

- HMG holds the teams accountable for results. The team always takes the time to set clear expectations and hold regular meetings to check on the teams' progress. The teams are expected to hold weekly recurring meetings and to make assignments for each team member that would require one to two hours of effort during the week. The team members are expected to come to meetings with their assignments completed and ready to discuss with the other team members so that the project can move forward. Based on this concept, each project (depending on the number of members on the team; usually three or four) dedicated resources for six to eight hours per week working on their project. In addition, I meet with each team monthly to receive a status update on the project.

- The teams are expected to use the DMAIC process and are not allowed to move to the next phase until each step is completed (in order) and approved by me. This has become HMG's common language of continuous improvement. The teams are given a problem statement and high-level objectives and their first task is to complete their individual project charter, which includes defining the problem statement, defining project objectives and scope, identifying current baseline performance, identifying improvement goals, defining benefits to the company, and calculating potential savings.

- We provide training to employees so they develop the skills needed to be successful. We have engaged a local university to hold ongoing training and development for both green belts and yellow belts at our facility. Employees attend classes during regular business hours, which show the company's commitment to this initiative. The training is running parallel to the projects, and employees use their projects to apply skills they learn in the classroom and are encouraged to bring challenges to discuss with the teacher and their peers.

- HMG is committed to removing ambiguity from projects by breaking them down into chunks that the team can accomplish in the time allowed. Small wins give confidence to the teams; each success reinforces the fact that they can make a difference. Large projects are therefore broken down into several phases and the teams can close and implement each phase independent of the next. Be happy with small incremental improvements as over time they can add up to a lot of savings.

- All teams are required to produce the following prior to project completion
  - Process flow chart
  - Business process procedure released with an engineering change notice signed by all major stakeholders
  - Train all employees using the process (training sign-off sheet)
  - Develop an audit form that the auditors can use to verify compliance with the new process
  - Develop a formula to calculate on-going savings (after go-live) compared to the baseline
  - Submit a new project for FY11
  - Presentation slides with short description of project and major accomplishments to the core team

- We audit improvements and new processes for as long and as often as necessary to ingrain the importance of improvement in the organization and to ensure the improvement is sustained so employees do not return to comfort zones after the completion of the project. We have trained six improvement auditors, and at the end of each project, each green belt is required to submit an audit sheet that contains key tests that the auditor can use to verify and validate financial savings and compliance with the new process.

- Each process owner calculates and reports the monthly savings of the improvement compared to the baseline. I personally receive such calculations and prepare a schedule of consolidated savings for the month and cumulative year-to-date, and we use this as a KPI in measuring the company's continuing performance with improvement.

- We involve as many employees as possible to raise awareness and integrate the continuous improvement methodologies in the culture of the organization. At any given time, we have one-third of the employees working on Kaizen, Lean, Six Sigma, IT, or other improvement projects. These employees are from all functional areas—hourly, salaried, and production workers as well as management.

- Last but not least, we recognize the efforts of the teams in front of all employees during our monthly employee meeting and give them a small gift as a token of appreciation. Since Harman has a consumer products division, it is easy and cost effective to reward people with cool products (e.g., several varieties of iPod players, docking stations, and PC speakers) that have a perceived high value.

HMG's initial Lean Six Sigma deployment of 2006–2007 has evolved to an expected behavior and norm of our culture. We have progressed to the point where our people are regularly identifying new opportunities and volunteering to be part of an improvement team. Improvement is built into performance reviews, and improvement is an expected part of people's jobs. We are fortunate to have begun our improvement initiatives and to have continued these initiatives through the recent recession. Despite our progress and results to date, HMG is continuing to learn, and improve, how we can improve even further.

6

Accelerator #3: Provide Customized Education and Development

The objective of this accelerator (see Figure 6.1) is to shy away from the traditional boilerplate education structure and develop the custom-tailored curriculum and module content that delivers the specific skill-set needs of a client who has a particular set of challenges and projects. Scalable Lean Six Sigma™ has discouraged education on rarely used topics and theory and has focused instead on a more targeted, hands-on approach with the practical and most widely used improvement tools. In addition, this customized education includes skill-set development on the soft non-tools side of improvement such as project leadership and management, performance measurement and design, teaming and team dynamics, change management, and other improvement leadership topics.

Understanding Different Improvement Methodologies

In our Scalable Lean Six Sigma™ deployment model, we have always presented DMAIC (define-measure-analyze-improve-control) methodology as the standardized structure, discipline, and common universal language for all improvement methodologies. Kaizen, Lean, Six Sigma, and other previous improvement initiatives were all introduced as disconnected, stand-alone improvement approaches with their own unique vocabularies and tools, and their own approaches. In the beginning, they also had their own deployment organizations. This only caused confusion. Depending on the slickness of the consultant or trainer, organizations viewed these as independent, mutually exclusive improvement methodologies and selected their preferred approach. They internally debated these improvement methodologies, trying to decide which methodology

155

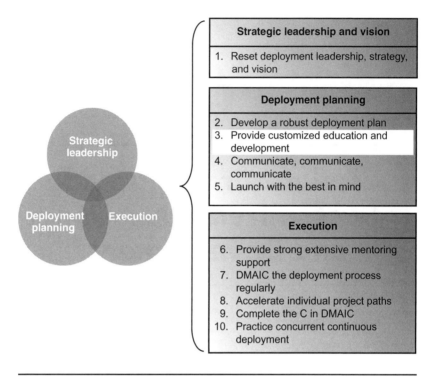

Figure 6.1   Elements of deployment planning.

was best, which was the fastest, which fit best in their business, and what was the most popular in other organizations. This was analogous to debating which tool in a toolbox is best before one defines the repair job: a screwdriver, a wrench or a drill? It depends—just as it depends with improvement in business. Organizations often deployed incorrect improvement methodologies to opportunities with sub-optimized results. People in organizations were confused and began asking questions such as, "What are we doing today? Kaizen? Lean? Six Sigma? What happened to value stream mapping?" The discussions about business improvement in many organizations often resemble the famous baseball comedy act of "Who's On First?" by Bud Abbot and Lou Costello.

Even today, there are experts peddling their stand-alone Kaizen, Lean, Six Sigma, 5S, Outside In, or other single-point acronym improvement program as the magic bullet and ends to success. Some trainers are knowledgeable of just Lean, others are knowledgeable of just Six Sigma, and both criticize the other's offering. Most do not understand the synergy of integrating both methodologies. Others have never been able to pick their heads up out of the Lean or Six Sigma tools themselves and recognize what really matters in a successful deployment. Some consultants remind us of French chefs, recommending their own version with a dash of 5S, a pinch of setup reduction, a smidgen of kanban, a cup of one-piece flow, and no need for IT. Blindly applying tools in the absence of improvement strategy creates what we call transparency improvements. Sure, there may be some initial small benefits—every organization has *no brainer* improvement opportunities. For the most part, these improvements (and associated efforts) are short-lived and totally transparent to the customer or the organization. By definition, these improvements are a nonvalue-added activity.

We spoke with an executive of a small company who has been working on and off with a local Manufacturing Extension Partnership (MEP) organization for the past three years. He commented, "I know Lean is the right thing to do and we have achieved some benefits, but it's hard to stay committed to it just because it's the right thing to do."

Sorry, but in this challenging economy it is not the right thing to do under those conditions. This comment is not directed at the MEP, but it is a good demonstration of how the tools by themselves limit sustainable improvement. Books and DVDs are being published that pitch how the tools should be implemented and in which order, but fail to address the most important factors of a successful or benchmark Lean Six Sigma deployment. Just about every reference is geared to improvements on the shop floor. The supposed experts claim the same approaches are applicable to the office, but they do not provide solid examples or case studies of improving areas such as new product development, invoicing, the supply chain, and many other ripe areas of improvement (be sure to read Chapter 14). The experienced practitioner understands and knows that the same approaches may be applicable in concept, but must be deployed with creative and innovative retrofits. Transactional and knowledge processes are technology-integrated and people-intensive processes where performance and behaviors are influenced by many factors beyond the direct process itself. Factors such as relationships, personalities, experience, maturity, political motives, egos, personal investment, security, insecurity, performance criteria, organizational balance of power, perceived priorities, and leadership expectations have significant impact on transactional processes. This is neither good nor bad—it is just a fact that influences how to improve transactional processes. There is not much human drama to deal with in a CNC machine, but there is a high level of human drama to deal with in many transactional processes. Back in the 1990s, we were working with an emerging high tech company on their Lean initiative. The printed wiring board work cell team was experiencing defects with a set of boards, and the operators documented the cause as violations in layout design guidelines and the insertion of components in the wrong sequence on work instructions. These are product development issues created by brilliant engineers, who never have the opportunity (challenge) to build the products that they design. I sat down and attempted to build a board and experienced their concerns firsthand. The president of this company walked over to see what I was doing and to find out why the PWB cell was shut down. I explained that the line was down because the boards were not manufacturable and required significant rework. I also explained (with the help of the operators) that the clown who designed the board layouts and created the work instructions did a horrible job and obviously did not make his living building PWBs. The president replied, "I designed these boards." He sat down and tried to build a board and within two minutes he said, "You're right. The board designer was me, I told engineering to design it this way, and—I'm the clown. Shut it down until we figure out how to fix the problems."

This is an example of human drama (luckily he was a good sport), but it easily could have gone down a different road with a different cast of characters. Hopefully, this book fills in most of the blanks and grey areas about deploying various improvement tools successfully toward a benchmark Lean Six Sigma deployment.

Customization Best Practices

A critical element of a successful Lean Six Sigma deployment is understanding the confusing puzzle of DMAIC, the wide spectrum of improvement tools, and how they all fit together to create success. The improvement methodologies and tools are important because they represent the *means* to achieve improvement. Although the improvement tools themselves represent about 10 to 20 percent of the success, they are collectively important but they are not the *ends*. People in organizations are comfortable applying a single improvement tool at a time. This results in creeping incremental improvements that often backslide to old norms without leadership and infrastructure. The real leverage is derived from understanding these improvement tools and how to apply them concurrently to a major improvement initiative. For example, if a team is improving global sales and operations planning (S&OP), that multimillion dollar project contains several Six Sigma, Lean, and Quick Strike opportunities, all of which are well orchestrated and executed to create a breakthrough improvement. This occurs because there are dependencies in projects such as this one, and concurrent improvements create incredible *interaction* improvements (e.g., when an improvement in one area creates residual improvements in other areas). When the right leadership and infrastructure is in place, continuous improvement on S&OP follows.

A note of caution is in order here. Experience in defining and structuring improvement projects is critical here. In the S&OP example, we want to avoid the boil-the-ocean syndrome, but we also do not want to granulate this opportunity so finely that we miss the dependencies, essentially slowing down improvement efforts.

Accelerator #3, customized education and development, is the enabler of understanding the various elements of Lean Six Sigma and how to deploy the right improvement opportunities for the highest impact opportunities to achieve breakthrough results. Customization best practices are shown in Figure 6.2. Customized education and development incorporates the following focus:

- *Cascading*—Education designed to deliver a uniform base of skills and knowledge to people at different levels in the organization, and to deliver

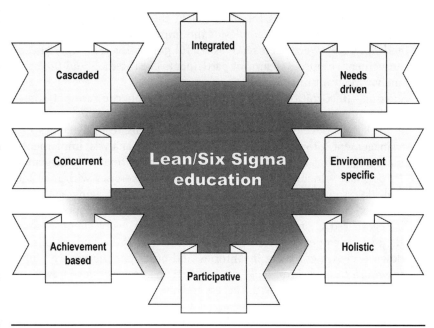

Figure 6.2 Customization best practices.

the non-tools skills for success in their specific organizational roles (e.g., executive leadership and behaviors, CEO and executive staff roles, executive sponsor expectations, project management, teaming, change management, performance management, recognition and rewards, supervisory mentoring skills, etc.). At the grass-roots level is basic improvement skills (BIS), which includes simple templates structured around the DMAIC methodology so that the DMAIC thoughtware is deployed uniformly across the organization. Cascading also promotes involvement of customers, suppliers, and other external stakeholders.

- *Integrated*—Replacement of boilerplate Lean and Six Sigma education with a more integrated approach to improvement. Success lies in understanding the vast array of elements and tools within Lean Six Sigma and in deploying them correctly to the right opportunities. Breakthrough improvements occur through cross-application of the right improvement tools.
- *Needs-driven*—Curriculum design based on the organization's history, specific needs, and planned improvement opportunities. The goal is to provide education that goes deep into the true needs of specific organizational areas, and avoids complicated statistical tools and theory that is unlikely to be used in a client's operating environment.
- *Environment-specific*—Integrate education with real-life examples and data from the client's environment. The business diagnostic provides the opportunity to learn about the nature of improvement needs and define

client-specific examples for inclusion in the education curriculum. The availability of real-life examples of the improvement tools and templates and how they were used serve as useful guides for less experienced improvement resources. Teams of participants use the tools and their data to analyze relevant improvement opportunities.

- *Holistic*—Recognition that all improvement properties are not addressed by the tools alone. Education includes soft skills development in areas such as leadership development, teaming fundamentals, team dynamics, change management, project management, cost/benefit analysis, implementation planning, selling, support-building skills, and performance management.

- *Participative*—Includes hands-on participatory exercises with relevance to real life issues. This may include waste walks, role playing, and custom-designed simulation exercises. For example, we have developed HalfFast™, a Lego-based Lean exercise that is designed for every client to simulate their specific operating environment. The names of their operations, scaled down cycle times, yields, inventories, and other parameters are built into the *Batch Push* vs. *Lean Pull* exercise. Participants experience how to apply the improvement tools with success and an immediate connection to their workplace.

- *Achievement-based*—Education followed by successful application to a real improvement opportunity, followed by teaching and mentoring others. All of us have experienced attendance at a workshop or seminar, placed the binder on the bookshelf, and then went back to business as usual. The best way to learn anything is to apply it to a real situation, repeatedly apply the new knowledge, then repeatedly teach and mentor others. Scalable Lean Six Sigma™ endorses certification of candidates achieving a black, green, or yellow belt status from a professional development perspective. However, creating belt factories for the sake of belts is wasteful. All other participants in BIS or other education are asked to complete a mandatory improvement project, Quick Strike, or some other documented improvement. Everyone must follow the standard and deliberate DMAIC methodology, and demonstrate their improvements with facts.

- *Concurrent*—Education where delivery is designed in parallel with application. Traditional education has individuals sit through days of training while they are worrying about everything else that is not getting done. Concurrent education is segmented into smaller incremental modules and delivered in parallel with DMAIC tasks of individuals' projects. Another example is BIS education followed by an area walkthrough, and identification of Quick Strike opportunities. The objective of concurrent education is to tighten up the learn and apply cycle.

Organizations have fumbled with respect to their Lean, Six Sigma, or Lean Six Sigma initiatives. First, there was this widespread *train-the-masses* approach in the absence of an improvement strategy, vision, deployment plan, and other infrastructure requirements. This approach to education is like a vector without direction. People return from these sessions and look for a situation in which they can apply the tools and do so with mixed successes and acceptance. A second problem occurred by using the boilerplate education curriculums of the successful pioneers.

A large amount of this education is generic and commoditized, focusing mostly on the mechanics of the improvement tools. People return from these sessions with great confusion about how to apply the tools to a specific improvement opportunity in their environment. In the majority of cases, education has missed the customization mark as outlined earlier. The benefits of incorporating these customization attributes into Lean Six Sigma are obvious, particularly after people leave the classroom. Their ability to apply, learn from the experiences, acquire new knowledge, and grow professionally is much greater than the slam-dunk, train-the-masses approach. Mentoring is an important part of individual development, as we will discuss in Chapter 9.

A positive step toward improving education is to better understand the internal workings, improvement methodologies and tools, and applications of Lean Six Sigma. The remainder of this chapter will describe the elements of Lean Six Sigma in more detail.

DMAIC—The Foundation of Lean Six Sigma

The DMAIC methodology is the standardized structure, discipline, and common universal language for all improvement methodologies. Lean Six Sigma as well as any other strategic improvement initiative requires a standardized problem-solving structure and a common language of improvement. In the TQM era of the 1980s, the PDCA (plan-do-check-act) cycle served as this common structure, and DMAIC is a more thoroughly updated version of PDCA. The largest benefit of DMAIC is to force people to ask the right questions as they proceed through a logical business problem-solving effort.

As our Scalable Lean Six Sigma™ deployment model has evolved, we have developed several helpful templates to reinforce the use of DMAIC as the foundation of Lean Six Sigma. Figure 6.3 provides the standard DMAIC template for a project requiring more of a Six Sigma approach. DMAIC templates exist for projects that require more of a Lean and Kaizen approach. These versions include similar deliverables but list the appropriate Lean or Kaizen tools for each phase. There is also a DMAIC template used for localized Quick Strike improvements as part of the BIS initiative mentioned earlier. When these DMAIC templates are placed side by side, the Six Sigma version appears to be the most complicated and populated, while the BIS template includes only the 20 questions in the DMAIC phases for a simple improvement activity. All versions promote following the common DMAIC methodology as the standard improvement approach and language. The DMAIC template is the visual gate-keeping form that is maintained by the project leader and reviewed regularly with the deployment sensei and executive core team. An underlying purpose of DMAIC is to define a practical

CEO The Center for Excellence in Operations, Inc.

6σ Project Status

PROJECT INFORMATION

Project:

Objective:

COPQ - Internal	$
COPQ - External	$
Annual cost savings	$

ATTACHMENTS

- Problem statement
- Baseline performance
- Project objective
- Project scope
- Deliverables
- Financial benefits

△ Deliverable   ☐ Tool   ▲ In process   ▲ ■ Complete

Define
- △ Problem definition
- △ Objectives
- △ Scope
- △ Boundaries
- △ Preliminary analysis
- △ Initial benefits
- ☐ ☐ Project charter
- SIPOC diagram

Measure
- ☐ ☐ CTQ's, FDM
- KPIV's, KPOV's
- △ Updated objectives
- △ Quantified problem
- △ Improvement goals
- △ Project team
- △ Project plan, Gantt
- △ Baseline performance
- △ A3 analysis template
- ☐ Value stream map
- ☐ ☐ Fishbone/CED diagram
- Cp & Cpk
- Gage R&R, MSA OK

Analyze
- ☐ △ DFMEA/PFMEA
- △ Sampling plan
- Initial data collection
- ☐ Basic stats
- ☐ Box, dot plots
- ☐ Causal
- ☐ Confidence intervals
- ☐ T–tests
- ☐ ANOVA
- △ Revised A3
- △ Update process map,
- PFMEA, & fishbone
- △ Revise project plan
- Containment actions

Improve
- △ Screen experiments
- ☐ Shainin, multi-vari
- ☐ Hypothesis tests
- ☐ Regression, correlation
- ☐ DOE design
- ☐ DOE experiments
- ☐ Mathematical models
- △ Recommendations
- △ Documentation
- △ Education
- Implementation plans

Control
- ☐ ☐ DOE
- △ EVOP, RSM
- △ Implement changes
- ☐ Replication experiments
- ☐ Handoff plan
- △ Lean, 5s, Poka–yokes
- △ Update ALL documentation
- △ Education
- △ Monitor improvement
- △ Document improvement
- △ Summarize benefits
- △ Define next project
- △ Management presentation
- △ Process owner handoff

Figure 6.3   Standard DMAIC template (Six Sigma)

problem (D), translate this problem in to a characterized analytical problem (M), analyze root causes of performance (A), develop data driven recommendations (I), and implement and monitor improvements (C). To accomplish this, several improvement tools and deliverables within each phase are listed, and a checklist format is used to verify the correct application of the tools and completion of the required deliverables. Not all improvement tools and deliverables are required for every improvement project. The objective is to use the template as a guide to select and deploy the right tools for a particular opportunity. DMAIC provides a repeatable, proven approach to solving business problems. On the surface, DMAIC seems quite logical, but in practice, most people are better at maintaining and working around problems than they are at solving problems with a solid root-cause approach. In practice, DMAIC is much more than a gate-keeping process or roadmap for projects. In effect, it serves as the GPS for the project by creating cohesion for project objectives, improvement goals, the solution approach, and application of the right improvement tools, teaming activities through root-cause analysis and bulletproof project results.

The purpose of multiple templates is to align the improvement approach with the improvement requirements of a project. In the enterprise or extended enterprise and in the realities of business improvement in general, there is a continuum of different types of business problems. If we blindfolded ourselves and randomly selected touch points in the total value stream (i.e., procurement, inventory management, customer service, sales, marketing, finance, quality management, engineering, new product development, IT, supplier management, logistics, third-party distributors, the production floor, etc.), this continuum of issues is a reality. No single improvement tool or fixed set of tools addresses all improvement requirements of all possible projects. The project objective and the complexity of the problem's root causes are the two major drivers that determine which tools to deploy to the improvement opportunity. Organizations that attempt to implement a single-point improvement initiative (e.g., just Lean or just Six Sigma) limit their effectiveness in conducting true root-cause problem solving. Executives who attempt to lead improvement by introducing their organizations to improvement tool after improvement tool often end up with a confused organization and an alphabet soup of short-lived improvements. Success requires a delicate balance defined by leadership and infrastructure. In the absence of implementation infrastructure, many organizations began with basic improvement activities in the Kaizen and Lean areas, and this approach is effective at getting at the organization's low-hanging fruit. When an organization limits itself to a single-point improvement initiative or does not fully understand the differentiators of various improvement tools and how to deploy them, they end up with the wrong results. With improvement, this is no different than trying to use a hammer for a painting task. We visited a company that had spent a year on Kaizen blitzes in its complex, multi-station welding line area and was disappointed with its scrap reduction progress. It selected Kaizen because its consultant led it to believe that Kaizen took less time and investment to implement than did Lean or Six Sigma. The wrong problem and the wrong improvement tools equal the wrong results.

Improvement Excellence™: Lean Six Sigma and Beyond

Figure 6.4 provides a framework for Improvement Excellence™. It is our version of Lean Six Sigma and incorporates the infrastructure elements and an enterprise-wide scope. As previously mentioned, the foundation of this framework is DMAIC, leadership, and infrastructure. This is the same leadership vision and strategy, deployment planning, and execution that was highlighted earlier in Figure 6.1. The scope of Improvement Excellence™ is enterprise-wide, particularly in the opportunity-rich knowledge and transactional processes. This is a huge shift from previous improvement initiatives that have primarily focused on manufacturing and the shop floor. This shift should have happened sooner, but many factors such as outsourcing and true root-cause problem solving redirected the course of improvement. A good question to ask is, "What are the root causes of the big problems in manufacturing?"

Previous improvement initiatives have focused on many symptomatic problems in manufacturing such as inefficiencies in flow, excess handling and rework, lower-order quality issues, or material out of specification. We cannot provide a valid generic answer to the root-cause question at this time, but if one work

Figure 6.4   Improvement Excellence™: integrating Kaizen, Lean, Six Sigma, and enabling IT.

through this question with a big-picture view, the root causes of the largest opportunities lie outside the manufacturing area (i.e., product line planning, sales and order fulfillment, forecasting, product proliferation, new product development, incapable suppliers, S&OP, distribution and logistics policies, warranty and return practices, global commercialization, pipeline inventory management, hardware and software integration, acquisition processes, packaging and shipping practices, etc.). The scope and focus of Lean Six Sigma has shifted from manufacturing to the knowledge or transactional processes. This shift continues as organizations are now interested in improving activities such as strategic planning, acquisitions, innovation and technology management, new product management and market research, point-of-sale analysis, benefits effectiveness, and global planning and logistics.

Confusion between Kaizen, Lean, Six Sigma, and other improvement initiatives exist because there is so much overlap in the improvement objectives and improvement tools. For example, value stream mapping is a useful tool for Kaizen, Lean, or Six Sigma projects. Kaizen, Lean, and Six Sigma use sidebars such as eliminating waste, reducing variation, reducing defects, eliminating nonvalue-added activity, reducing cycle time, or striving for perfection—this is just different jargon for improvement. Eliminating variation in a Six Sigma project reduces defects, eliminates waste, and reduces cycle time. Eliminating waste in a Lean project may or may not reduce defects or deep-rooted process variation. Six Sigma statistical tools and Minitab can be used for better understanding process capability and limitations of kanban and pull systems, balancing and synchronizing engineering workloads, analyzing root causes of billing errors, isolating S&OP variation, simulating design for manufacturability conditions, etc. Many other tools packaged solely as Lean or Six Sigma tools can be used across the board with improvement projects. The remainder of this chapter provides a new overview of the improvement tools and discusses the conditions and circumstances for deploying these tools correctly to the right improvement opportunities. At the conclusion of our discussion, it is our intent to convince the reader to never discuss Kaizen, Lean, or Six Sigma as stand-alone improvement programs or in isolation of each other. Integration of DMAIC and the improvement tools in Lean Six Sigma deployments—beyond the name itself—is a major enabler of benchmark results.

Kaizen

On the left side of the Improvement Excellence™ framework are the Kaizen improvement opportunities. The roots of Kaizen are derived from the Japanese word *kai* meaning *to take apart*, and *zen* meaning *to make good*. Kaizen is the gradual, incremental, and continual improvement of activities to create more value and less nonvalue-adding waste. Often, these are referred to as the *no-brainer* improvement situations that require little to no analysis to implement. Kaizen is about going after the obvious low-hanging fruit, or the fruit on the ground. Many of these improvement opportunities may not even require a team because they are *just-do-it* improvements. Some of these require just action because the conditions are apparent in terms of what needs to be done. It is a matter of locking something down for a few hours or a day and implementing the improvements. A simple example of Kaizen is housekeeping and the general physical organization and appearance of a work area. Kaizen-like events—and in particular, deployment of the 5S principles (sort, set in order, shine, systematize, standardize)—are simple and effective improvement tools to clean up, reorganize, and increase visibility of standard practices. These simple improvements provide a solid foundation for the more advanced improvements necessary in the area. Sometimes, the answer to a simple improvement opportunity is not so obvious and may require an additional but simple analysis. This is where the natural overlap occurs between Kaizen and Lean or Six Sigma. The most basic blocking and tackling tools of Lean and Six Sigma (e.g., Pareto analysis, check sheets, cause-and-effect diagrams, spreadsheet analysis, etc.) are also helpful for the low-dive root-cause situations. A solid Kaizen effort uses a simplified version of the structured DMAIC methodology and is always data- and fact-driven, whether it is data we can sense or data from simple analysis.

Kaizen is an improvement process that is applied to achieve event-specific continuous improvement. The distinguishing characteristic of a Kaizen improvement opportunity is that it is readily achievable with either little or no analysis. The improvement may not be the ultimate solution, but it is a noticeable and measurable incremental improvement. Kaizen events may focus on an activity within a single department, or focus on a more cross-functional improvement activity. Even in larger strategic improvement projects, there are several Kaizen opportunities that shake out during value stream mapping or root-cause problem solving activities. There could also be a simple improvement requiring further analysis with the Lean tools, a core improvement requiring the surgical Six Sigma tools, or another improvement project for the project hopper. This underscores the importance of understanding the various improvement opportunities and tools in Lean Six Sigma, their key differentiators, and how best to deploy specific improvement tools to specific improvement opportunities. There is no need to wait until the end of the larger project to make the improvements. However, there are typically formal rules of action that depend on how (or if) the improvement impacts others and on the expertise needed to implement the change (e.g., maintenance, purchasing, or finance). Kaizen is a low-cost, low-risk common sense approach to incremental improvement on the spot. In summary, the Kaizen philosophy is best suited to Quick Strike opportunities and quick containment measures in a process. Granted, it may not be the optimal solution, but it is incrementally better than the original process. It is not a matter of choosing between Kaizen or Lean; it is more about the characteristics and conditions of the improvement opportunity. The improvement opportunity is the driver of selecting the right improvement approach and tools.

Lean

The center of the Improvement Excellence™ framework includes the realm of Lean. James Womack and Daniel Jones identified five key principles of Lean in their landmark 1996 book *Lean Thinking—Banish Waste and Create Wealth in Your Corporation*. This book provided the initial vision for organizations to implement Lean thinking across the enterprise in both manufacturing and soft areas of an organization. An updated and expanded version of Womack and Jones' five principles of Lean includes the following:

- *Principle 1*—Accurately understand customer value propositions and specify value from the customer's perspective for products, services, and support.
- *Principle 2*—Identify the value stream for how products, services, and support are conceptualized, developed, designed, and delivered to customers, and remove both value-consuming and nonvalue-adding waste in the supply chain.
- *Principle 3*—Make the product and services flow with effectiveness and efficiency and without disruptions in core business processes.
- *Principle 4*—Achieve synchronous responsiveness, planning, and delivery of products, services, and support based on the pull by the customer.
- *Principle 5*—Strive for perfection by constantly analyzing and improving the value stream with the appropriate and applicable improvement methodologies and tools.

Lean typically includes improvement tools such as 5S, visual management, value stream mapping, work cell design, kanban and pull systems, quick changeover, total preventive maintenance, etc. Lean tools are best suited for projects seeking to simplify and standardize processes, reduce cycle times, eliminate unnecessary process steps or waste, or synchronize individual processes into a more continuous flow. Many Lean efforts are more like *compensating improvements* in practice because people often apply the Lean tools in a way that compensates for deep-rooted process variation. Techniques such as kanban, buffer inventories, work cells, and repetitive scheduling practices improve the flow, but they do not address the deep-root causes of process variation. At the risk of sounding like a broken record, it is improvement-limiting to separate Kaizen, Lean, and Six Sigma as stand-alone initiatives.

Originally, the foundation of Lean was based on the Japanese word *muda*, which defined seven categories of waste. These seven categories are easily remembered with the acronym TIM WOOD:

1. Transportation
2. Inventory
3. Motion
4. Waiting
5. Overproduction

6. Overprocessing
7. Defects

There have been several versions of the seven wastes (or the eight wastes) over the years, and people traditionally go through the mechanics of characterizing the obvious wastes into these categories. Two things are certain: these categories need a good update and redefinition to reflect the large transactional content of process improvement, and it is much more important to mine and identify visible and hidden waste in general than it is to categorize the obvious topsoil waste. This situation points out the need to integrate Kaizen, Lean, and Six Sigma to become successful fast enough in the new economy. In a more updated version, Lean by itself is usually focused on eliminating or reducing the simpler categories of the (now) nine enterprise wastes (see Figure 6.5). This is our updated version to reflect the improvement realities throughout the enterprise. The nine enterprise wastes include:

1. *Overconsumption*—Consuming more assets or resources than necessary in a finite process window. Includes building unnecessary inventory, consuming assets and resources inefficiently, ineffectively misusing or constantly shuffling engineering talent, having excess or mismatched finished goods, having planning and supply chain fluff due to unreliable forecasts, and having optimistic or unrealistic customer commitments.
2. *Wait time*—Waiting for anything that disrupts normal continuous and efficient process activities. This includes waiting for material, engineering prints, regional forecasts, executive approvals, suppliers, miscellaneous idle time, and delays that the customer will not be willing to pay for.
3. *Transportation*—Excess movement and handling. Includes moving and storing work in progress in a temporary location, premium freight, flying people overseas to fix problems, repackaging damaged products in a distribution center, ridiculous e-mails that disrupt normal work activities, expediting and firefighting, and changing the focus of people's responsibilities.

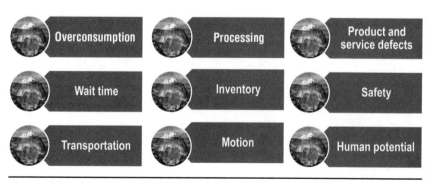

Figure 6.5   The nine enterprise wastes that inhibit Improvement Excellence™.

4. *Processing*—Scrap and rework from production operations, billing errors, incorrect purchase orders, repeat engineering after design verification reviews, journal entry adjustments during financial close, releasing non-configurable or nonmanufacturable orders, application of incorrect discounts, and over planning or under planning due to inventory accuracy.

5. *Inventory*—Excess and obsolete production inventory is the most familiar. Also includes excess or duplicate office supplies, low utilization of IT hardware and office equipment, low utilization of lab and test equipment, excess MRO supplies, excess and obsolete field service and repair inventory, excess furniture, and excess office space or other underutilized assets.

6. *Motion*—Workarounds for broken or incapable processes. This includes additional nonstandard assembly tasks, doing things over because they were not done right the first time, engineering changes after product release, correcting billing errors, engineering design modifications after constant functional specification changes, rescheduling suppliers due to late deliveries, meetings, forecast revisions, different versions of spreadsheet data, and board design spins due to moving specifications.

7. *Product and service defects*—Direct defects in products or services that reach the customer and are discovered after delivery. May include a dead-on-arrival television, a software update that does not work, missing owner's manual or operating instructions, faulty or unclear owner's manual or operating instructions, unfulfilled or late delivery commitments, incorrect transactions that cause trial balance adjustments, unexplainable budget overages, or less-than-desirable customer experience.

8. *Safety*—Conditions that represent potential harm or injury to process suppliers, owners, customers, or other stakeholders; an oily floor, unsafe office and environmental conditions, office and other work area ergonomics, storage, handling, and disposition of hazardous waste, and lack of preventive or other procedures.

9. *Human potential*—The waste of underutilizing and under-employing people, which is the largest waste in transactional processes. Includes institutionalization of bad practices, poor prioritization of goals or responsibilities or development projects, lack of formal and standardized processes, incorrect metrics, failure to communicate and listen, encouraging a functional versus cross-functional process focus, several versions of the supposed facts, lack of empowerment and involvement, organizational churn, reactionary problem solving, expediting, and emergency meetings.

The more complex forms of waste can be mined using the basic Six Sigma tools. Based on our latest experiences and organizational sources of root causes, Lean Six Sigma efforts should be focused about 75 to 80 percent on transactional process improvement and 20 to 25 percent on manufacturing improvement. In most organizations, it is exactly the opposite. There is one exception discussed in Chapter 14, outsourcing process improvement (a transactional process with a total supply chain embedded within it) requires a somewhat higher focus on offshore manufacturing operations than we stated previously. Many of the traditional Lean tools have more of a production floor orientation and should be applied with discretion to transactional processes. As we have mentioned repeatedly, the real improvement opportunities for organizations lie in their transactional and knowledge processes. It does not make sense in this economy to squeeze a few seconds out of production cycle time when organizations can knock down tens of millions of dollars from warranty and returns, obsolete inventory, or new product development. The five principles of Lean are fundamental to the elimination of waste and must be embraced across all functions within the organization as well as applied up and down the value chain by suppliers and customers. It is important to get the entire organization thinking in terms of process and focused on understanding value streams and the waste embedded in these processes. In transactional improvement projects, the most useful Lean tool is a more advanced and thorough form of value stream mapping. Adding information, cash, decision, resource, and deliverables flows to value stream mapping provides a clear picture of business processes. This is not to say that the other tools are not applicable. With creativity, tools such as cell design or 5S can be applied to co-locate key cross-functional people to a central operating location or clean up and reorganize a research and development laboratory or warehouse respectively. A few years ago, a team was assigned a project of improving the process of creating an expensive retail mail order catalog. Individuals from different areas of the organization were relocated to a war room environment where they were concurrently developing and improving the design and production of the next catalog. The team developed and detailed a more real-time value stream and timeline map, including all the event steps, disruptive decision points, rework efforts, and event and cumulative cost of catalog production. During the project, the wastes became evident as executives and managers strolled into the war room and left sticky notes saying, "See me, this needs to be changed."

They characterized the largest waste and cost drivers in the process. There were many unnecessary changes made too far downstream in the process, creating a significant amount of creative and administrative rework. A few could not see the waste and claimed that this was merely the creative process at work. The team demonstrated that it required about 1.8 catalog's amount of effort and cost to create a single catalog, and the more visible cost of quality was over $400K per catalog. At three catalog mailings per year, these costs added up. The team reengineered the process with defined gates and checkpoints, moved decisions and approvals up front, and eliminated the emotional involvement in the process. *Cha-ching*—the team identified over 700K per year in savings within four months. The team also recommended that various creative people and suppliers be co-located permanently to act as the design center and control tower for catalog production. The organization decided to generate four catalogs per year and has added over $40M in new revenue. This is what typically happens in transactional process improvement: the gold just keeps on coming when a team mines and uncovers the true root causes, and there are usually additional residual, interaction improvement effects on other key business processes. Another plus with transactional process improvement is that eliminating waste does not usually result in eliminating jobs, but in making people's roles more productive, effective, and rewarding.

The conditions for using Lean improvement tools exist when the objective is to eliminate velocity and utilization-based waste in processes, value-consuming swirls driven by modifications and doing things over, lost process time and disruptions, misuse of critical resources, or reengineering and standardization of process or practices. These are improvements that cannot be sensed yet, but the process is defined and the inputs and outputs are known. There are many clues suggesting what is wrong, but the true root causes and effects are not quite clear. Finally, the path to improvement is better known and straightforward. These improvements do not require significant data collection, process flexing and experimentation, or complex solutions.

Six Sigma

On the right side of the Improvement Excellence™ framework is Six Sigma. In this space, improvement opportunities and their specific root causes tend to be totally unexplainable because these are processes that contain complex variation. Many improvement opportunities are also redefined or refined after initial root-cause efforts. Why does the molding machine produce scrap? What are the factors that contribute to excess or obsolete inventory or warranty and returns? Why is there so much downtime due to unplanned maintenance? Why is there so much variation in forecast error across 400 SKUs in 50 different countries? Why does every new product get released late, over budget, and with manufacturability issues? Why is absenteeism higher than in other companies in the comparability survey? These questions may or may not have the real problem embedded in their statements. The answers to these questions are complex: everyone may have an opinion or perception of the root causes, but nobody knows for sure, nor do they have answers that are backed by facts. These projects require a deeper dive into clues, analytical data, and evidence much in the same manner that a detective solves a cold case. Six Sigma has the reputation of *perfection-driven improvement* because it is a focused effort in which analytics, data, and facts are used to understand and reduce or eliminate true root causes of complex process variation. Six Sigma drives processes to a new level of performance and capability. These are the complex problems that lend themselves to the Six Sigma methodology and tools. The specific tools of Six Sigma can be grouped into a few logical categories:

- *The basic blocking and tackling tools*—These include a SIPOC (suppliers, inputs, process, outputs, customers) diagram, fishbone diagram or CED, checklists, Pareto charts, histograms, scatter diagrams and other Minitab graphs, time series and control charts, value stream mapping, worth factor analysis, failure mode and effects analysis (FMEA), basic statistical analysis, affinity and relationship diagrams, box plots, confidence intervals, structured root cause templates, process capability, variable and attribute measurement system analysis, and other simple analytical tools. These tools are used for descriptive statistics and shallow root-cause problem solving.

- *The advanced Six Sigma tools*—These include Multi Vari Analysis, regression and correlation, hypothesis tests, analysis of variance, screening experiments, design of experiments (DOE), evolutionary operations, Monte Carlo and simulation modeling, decision and probability analysis, and other technically involved statistical engineering tools. These tools are used for inferential and predictive statistical applications where the input factors and output responses are extremely complicated and not well defined

It is important to point out that complicated improvement opportunities and complex improvement tools are mutually exclusive. The root causes of complicated improvement opportunities are not initially known with a high degree of confidence supported by facts. There may be speculation and opinions, but there are no facts to pin down root causes. However, this does not translate into the need to use advanced Six Sigma tools. This is where improvement experience cuts through the maze of an improvement project and prevents intellectual people from running around with a bag of tools looking for a problem. For example complex, automated multistation discrete manufacturing and process equipment includes a multitude of variation sources. In addition, many of the input factors and their effect on output responses are unknown, and various interactions of factors affect the process in different ways. These physical processes are not understood well by operators, engineers, maintenance, or even the equipment manufacturers. This situation is potentially a good candidate for the advanced Six Sigma tools; however, we should always start with the basic tools first and wring out any obvious opportunities as a first step. The conditions and characteristics of the particular improvement project determine which improvement tools to use. In the case of transactional and knowledge processes, the advanced Six Sigma tools are almost never needed. In addition, many of the Lean tools with more of a manufacturing spin (e.g., kanban, pull, TPM, one-piece flow, visual factory etc.) are irrelevant in direct application. However, these tools can be applied conceptually with creativity and innovation. Transactional process improvements are typically achieved through the most basic Lean and Six Sigma tools. Basic blocking and tackling tools such as the SIPOC, value stream mapping, CEDs, FMEAs and basic analytics (e.g., simple graphs, Pareto analysis, basic statistics, etc.) are the most widely deployed and widely successful improvement tools. A major reason for the success of basic tools on complicated improvement opportunities is that the root causes are not buried too deep. It is relatively easy to dissect transactional process and identify root causes using the basic improvement tools. In the majority of cases, transactional processes have evolved over time with different individuals and organizational regimes. A Lean Six Sigma improvement project is often the first time that transactional processes are analyzed across functional areas with objectivity and facts. The moral of this story is to deploy the simplest improvement tools first, and let the conditions of the specific improvement opportunity be the driver in selecting and deploying the appropriate high-complexity improvement tools later.

Enabling IT and InfoTech

Integrated enterprise IT applications are an important part of the infrastructure mentioned in Figure 6.4. Information technology such as enterprise requirements planning (ERP), supply chain management (SCM), customer relationship management (CRM), supplier relationship management (SRM), product lifecycle management (PLM), business warehouse, collaboration networks and portals, the Internet, and all other enabling InfoTech play a critical role in the success of Lean Six Sigma. The major features and functionality necessary to support a Lean Six Sigma deployment are embedded throughout the total information architecture. More importantly, the functionality to measure, monitor, and sustain improvement is also readily available. The importance of enabling IT is never mentioned by most Lean and Six Sigma experts because it is the most misunderstood element of success. Organizations spend billions on IT infrastructure and the Six Sigma consultant sends people off to collect data with manual check sheets. Some consultants even promote the notion of *unplugging* IT and running the business with a 1970s version of the Toyota Production System complete with manual kanban cards and manually maintained visual displays. These people just do not get it. In today's competitive and ever changing environment, it is impossible to keep supply and demand synchronized with manual cards or manually maintained storyboards. It is also impossible to sustain improvement with manual or mechanical controls. Organizations must leverage their IT infrastructure and improve how they improve to keep up with changing competitive pressures and global market demands.

Organizations must have a single source of accurate information to achieve and sustain business improvement. Information is the foundation of improvement because "without data, you're just another person with an opinion." Another related comment is, "You don't know what you don't know. If you don't know, you cannot act correctly. If you cannot act correctly, you cannot improve." Another critical development is the availability of enabling technology to acquire accurate real-time information from processes, and move more into the sense-interpret-decide-act-monitor improvement space. Technology is available to enable process improvement in real time (e.g., electronic kanbans, performance dashboards, real-time project management, electronic notifications of process conditions, etc.). This should not be confused with e-mail and Blackberry-driven multiprocessing, where the results are often based on opinions and are questionable. Much of this type of decision making is automated intuitive problem solving, not root-cause problem solving. People become fooled by these technologies that enable pure multitasking and improve productivity. Chapter 15 will discuss emerging trends and their effectiveness in more detail.

Education with Immediate Impact

The ultimate goal of Accelerator #3, customized education and development, is to create an immediate and positive impact. In this new economy, organizations and their workplaces are in a constant state of flux and flex. The all too familiar batch-generic, train-the-masses, Lean Six Sigma education model needs a serious update for this economy. The traditional black or master black belt certification is not only overwhelming to most people, but much of the content is never used beyond the classroom. Scalable Lean Six Sigma™ uses a more targeted, digestible, and applicable education model that is realistic and produces rapid and sustainable results. The model embraces a quick but continuous educate-apply-learn-increase knowledge-grow cycle of improvement. Customization of Lean Six Sigma education or any professional development educational platform is significantly more effective. The parameters described in this chapter (e.g. cascading, integrated, needs-driven, environment specific, holistic, participative, achievement-based, concurrent) provide a proven model to customize educational offerings that injects new skills, enables direct application, results in personal eureka moments, and places the notion of Improvement Excellence™ in clear sight.

References

Burton, T. T. and Boeder, S. M. 2003. *The Lean Extended Enterprise: Moving Beyond the Four Walls to Value Stream Excellence.* J. Ross Publishing, Fort Lauderdale, FL.

Liker, J. 2004. *The Toyota Way.* McGraw-Hill Publishing, New York, NY.

Womack, J. and Jones, D. 1996. *Lean Thinking: Banish Waste and Create Wealth.* Simon and Schuster, New York, NY.

Chapter 6 Take Aways

- A critical element of a successful Lean Six Sigma deployment is understanding the confusing puzzle of DMAIC, the wide spectrum of improvement tools, and how they all fit together to create success. Improvement methodologies and tools are important because they represent the *means* to achieve improvement. Although the improvement tools themselves represent about 10 to 20 percent of the success, they are collectively important but they are not the *ends*.
- Customized education best practices include cascaded, integrated, needs-driven, environment-specific, holistic, participative, achievement-based, and concurrent attributes. The benefits of incorporating these

customization attributes into Lean Six Sigma are obvious, particularly after people leave the classroom. Their ability to apply, learn from the experiences, acquire new knowledge, and grow professionally is much greater than the boilerplate *train-the-masses* approach.

- Kaizen is the gradual, incremental, and continual improvement of activities to create more value and less nonvalue-adding waste. Often these are referred to as the *no-brainer* improvement situations that require little to no analysis to implement. Kaizen is about going after the obvious low-hanging fruit, or the fruit on the ground. Many of these improvement opportunities may not even require a team because they are *just-do-it* improvements. Some of these just require action because the conditions are apparent in terms of what needs to be done. It is a matter of locking down for a few hours or a day and implementing the improvements.

- Originally, the foundation of Lean was based on the Japanese word *muda*, which defined seven categories of waste. The five principles of Lean are fundamental to the elimination of waste and must be embraced across all functions within the organization as well as applied up and down the value chain by suppliers and customers. It is important to get the entire organization thinking in terms of process, and focused on understanding value streams and the waste embedded in these processes.

- Six Sigma has the reputation of *perfection-driven improvement* because it is a focused effort in which analytics, data, and facts are used to understand and reduce or eliminate true root causes of complex process variation. Six Sigma drives processes to a new level of performance and capability. These are the complex problems that lend themselves to the Six Sigma methodology and tools.

- Integrated enterprise IT applications are an important part of a strategic improvement infrastructure. Information technology such as ERP, SCM, CRM, SRM, PLM, business warehouse, collaboration networks and portals, the Internet, and all other enabling InfoTech play a critical role in the success of Lean Six Sigma.

- Scalable Lean Six Sigma™ uses a more targeted, digestible, and applicable education model that is realistic and produces rapid and sustainable results. The model embraces a quick but continuous educate-apply-learn-increase, knowledge-grow cycle of improvement. Customization of Lean Six Sigma education or any professional development educational platform is significantly more effective.

Guest Author Contribution

Eric Lussier is currently the vice president of operational excellence for WHX Corporation. He is a master black belt and registered professional engineer in the State of Tennessee and is responsible for deploying the WHX business system at all of the companies within WHX. His career has focused on applying industrial engineering and Lean Six Sigma methodologies to all processes in manufacturing companies over the past 17 years. As a lifelong learner, Eric is currently completing his doctorate degree through the University of Alabama, Huntsville, in Industrial and Systems Engineering with a concentration in Engineering Management.

Tailored Education and Development at WHX

Eric Lussier

VP of Operational Excellence

WHX Corporation

As vice president of operational excellence for WHX Corporation, the concept of customized education and development certainly rings true. WHX Corporation is a diversified global industrial company focused on delivering value to our customers through innovation, operational excellence, and superior customer service. As such, WHX has nine different operating units focused heavily in manufacturing various types of products. The primary commonality among these companies is the WHX business system, which effectively describes the customized education and employee development program that is available. This business system is at the heart of the improvement methodology for all companies and employees in the WHX family. This business system brings commonality in approach and focus for customer satisfaction and profitable growth to the diverse group of companies within the WHX family.

Strategy deployment forms the roof of the business system and serves to convert strategic plans into tangible actions ensuring alignment of goals throughout each company. The pillars of the business system are the key performance indicators used to monitor and drive improvement. The steps of the business system are the specific tool areas that drive the key metrics and overall performance. The WHX business system is a proven, holistic approach to increasing shareholder value and achieving long-term, sustainable, and profitable growth.

Similar to the Improvement Excellence™ concepts described earlier, this business system provides a myriad of tools to help drive improvements (see Figure 6.6). The focus is not on training everyone, rather it is about raising the overall level of education and skills of the organization to become more effective problem-solvers. The old adage of "if the only tool in your toolbox is a hammer then everything looks a lot like a nail" certainly fits here as tools have specific uses and address specific needs. WHX has assembled a holistic series of training focus areas to address not only operations and manufacturing but also the transactional processes including sales, marketing, human resources, accounting, product development, and information technology.

Within the WHX companies, the initial focus started with the Lean manufacturing tools. WHX took the approach of placing a seasoned and experienced lean champion at each facility in order to start looking at customer value, waste

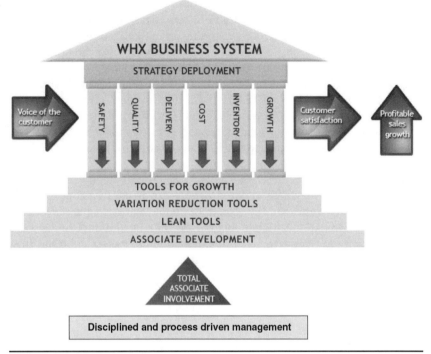

Figure 6.6 WHX business system.

reduction, and flow. This early emphasis on Lean allows for quick-hit improvements so that success can be built upon. Moreover, the Lean tools and Kaizen approach of improvement lay an effective foundation to address problems and opportunities as they are uncovered. All employees are trained in Lean 101 tools, which include the 5S+S (+S being *safety*) methodology, waste identification, and the Kaizen problem solving approach. All salaried employees are trained in a week-long Lean leadership curriculum, which exposes attendees to the standard Lean tools like value stream mapping, standard work cell design, setup time reduction, kanban, and flow. This week-long training follows a hear-see-do approach where the concepts are first explained in the classroom followed by real world application within an operation.

Besides Lean tools, employees have the opportunity to learn other tools focused on variation reduction (Six Sigma tools). Other training is available under *tools for growth*, which focuses on a process-driven methodology for sales and marketing. Finally, the strategic planning process for each company follows the *strategy deployment* process, which is also known as Hoshin planning. This process driven methodology ties everything else together and allows each organization to focus on achieving truly breakthrough results over and above budget.

To compete globally, companies must continue to challenge the status quo, improve processes, and deliver profitable business results. The path to achieve successful growth may be different depending on markets, competition, capabilities, and business conditions, but organizations must tap into the human potential and capabilities to drive innovation and improvements. As such, investing in the growth and development of employees is essential and should be part of any long-term business plan. Tailoring this development effort and providing effective tools to help employees analyze data and make better decisions based on data can become a strategic advantage to any organization. Within WHX, the business system is designed to provide an overview of what is available and considered world-class tools and training in order to leverage the human talent within our organizations. The challenge is to equip people and then develop a conducive environment where talented people can make decisions and drive a company forward. Investing in the growth of people and raising the level of education in any organization through customized training and development is one of the most important endeavors any organization undertakes, and it has the potential to deliver a return on that investment multiple times.

7

Accelerator #4: Communicate, Communicate, Communicate

This accelerator will address the fine art of communicating change, backed by a well-designed strategy to achieve specific organizational and behavioral responses. Accelerator #4: communicate, communicate, communicate (see Figure 7.1) is an important part of deployment planning. There is a strong linkage between communication and improvement: communication opens the organizational door to improvement and change. There is no such thing as too much communication, as long as the message is consistent and value adding to the recipients. Obviously, the best communication is value adding to both the recipient and the sender. The most important part of communication is to establish the recognition of the need to change, and why the organization must embrace change. The *why* of change is often explained inadequately or with emotional reasoning. Well-executed and frequent communication builds commitment and trust, reduces confusion, sets expectations, builds continuity and interest, removes the fear of change, provides a medium for publicizing success and recognizing people, and builds momentum for larger successes. Effective, continuous communication creates the needed momentum for improvement. When the communication message is off the mark or loses steam, a Lean Six Sigma deployment begins to slow down or stall out.

Similar to many other improvement tasks, communicating change is pursued with great intentions and the high-anxiety hormones of making something happen quickly. Communication to support a Lean Six Sigma initiative includes much more than calling a town meeting or casually mentioning the organization's intentions in a quarterly videoconference. Much of the communication behind Lean Six Sigma and other previous improvement initiatives has not been well thought out. Communication is a lot like the topic of leadership—everyone knows *how* to lead and communicate, but actions are often out of synch with intentions. Effectively communicating change requires design time and

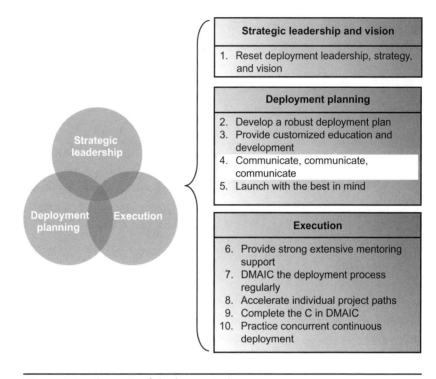

Figure 7.1   Elements of deployment planning.

concentration—two factors in limited supply with most executives. In the final analysis, many communication efforts end up being more symbolic than genuine, and definitely lacking in constancy of purpose (Deming's first point). During the past three decades, executives have communicated the strategic importance of initiatives such as TQM, Reengineering, Lean, Six Sigma, or Lean Six Sigma only to disband and dismantle these efforts by their actions. People have little love for symbolic communication and become either disillusioned or unplugged from improvement—the appetite for being involved in another improvement program can be standoffish. Symbolic communication weakens relationships and therefore reduces the objectives that organizations are trying to establish, embracing and transplanting best practices leadership behaviors (see Chapter 4) in other members of the organization. These include vision, knowledge, passion, discipline, and conscience.

One thing that is certain in this new economy is change. Improvement is evolving quickly from discrete programs of the past to the need for continuous real-time improvement. The bottom line is that organizations are faced with change that is real in terms of competitive survival, and real in terms of the effect on their people. Technology and the global economy will continue to push the required rate of improvement upward. Even today, change is occurring faster than many organizations can respond to it. Change is not only a core capability, but it is also a differentiator of competitive advantage.

Constant communication and reinforcement of reality is desperately needed in organizations—not communication for communication's sake, but communication with honesty, candor, facts, and consequences. People are human and need constant reinforcement of directions and expectations, especially in this new economy. They need to be informed and reminded of the emerging competitive forces that are impacting the organization and its people, and how the organization as a cohesive team will respond to these challenges. People also need an open conduit for communication and feedback. Unfortunately, there is no way to slow these trends. The only constant going forward is change, and the choice is simple. Organizations must step up and lead improvement and change, or sit around passively and become victims of another competitor's improvements and changes.

The Purpose of Communication

Many organizations have made hasty attempts to communicate change within their organizations. These efforts are pursued with the best intentions, but fail to address the root causes of current culture and behaviors. The purpose of communication is to create awareness, commitment, trust, inspiration, engagement, and other positive behavioral attributes of change. Communication efforts often downplay the need to understand the current drivers of people and behaviors, the potential root causes of resistance, or how people may react to the messaging. Further, the message itself has little to do with establishing the positive behavioral attributes of change. The purpose of communication is to build the human and emotional foundation for improvement and change. There are four key segments of communication:

1. Present state
2. Intermediate state
3. Future state
4. Activities of the change process

Why is the most important question to answer for individuals in the organization. People need to be informed of the reasons why the organization has to move away from their current as-is state, and of the consequences and risks of staying the same. They need to better understand the external market and competitive pressures that are driving the organization to change. They also need to understand the magnitude of these external market pressures and the sense of urgency for change. Communication is the medium that explains why the current state is no longer adequate, how the business environment is changing, why the organization must change to meet these new challenges, and what to expect if the organization does not change—particularly at the individual level.

Communication becomes challenging in organizations with a track record of failed improvement programs. The mention of the next improvement program leaves people with the feeling of, "Here we go again, it won't last long."

Another hasty communication effort is not what is needed in these situations. Executives must come clean with their people, whether it was their previous improvement program or not. People generally embrace an honest explanation. No excuses, no blame—just an honest explanation of the facts followed by an apology for bad performance and how it may have negatively impacted the organization. This is now a perfect position to begin communicating about the future and in particular, why the organization must get improvement right this time, and what will be done differently to get it right. History is a huge contributor to culture and the status of an organization's behavioral attributes of change. History may have created a negative grapevine and invisible resistance to change. Simply ignoring previous experience with improvement initiatives is a sure way to keep these undercurrents of resistance alive.

Communication is also challenging in organizations that are new to Lean Six Sigma and other improvement initiatives. For the most part, the communications model is straightforward for these organizations. However, the culture and behavioral attributes and readiness for change factors must not be overlooked. For these organizations, it is imperative to recognize past contributions and discuss the reality of external factors driving the need for change. This will associate change with changing external circumstances, rather than leaving the organization thinking that they have done something wrong. Ineffective communication in these organizations gets the rumor mill pumped up, and people begin to speculate on the underlying, and often imaginary reasons for change. There is nothing new here. In fact, it all comes back to recognizing Maslow's Hierarchy of needs. When a Lean Six Sigma initiative is introduced, it is natural in this economy for people to feel threatened by something that they know nothing about, how it will affect them, or how much additional work it may represent. When this occurs, people check in on their lower-level needs:

- *Safety*—Will I lose my job? How does it affect my pension?
- *Belonging*—Will I need to move? How will my organization and team change?
- *Esteem*—Will my social status be reduced? Will I have less influence?
- *Identity*—How will this change who I really am?
- *Prediction*—What will happen now? Is there a new future?

The purpose of any communication generally falls into one of two categories: to inform the organization or individuals; or to call the organization or people to action. Communication is not a perfect science, and people continually seek the intent and expectations of the message. Communication about Lean Six Sigma is an evolving process—it may answer a few questions or concerns, but it may also raise new questions and concerns.

The Most Important Message

The most important message about Lean Six Sigma or change in general is that change at an increasing rate is inevitable in the new economy. There is no such thing as staying the same in this economy. Either an organization is improving, or they are falling behind due to another competitor's improvements. The only status quo these days is rapid deployment, rapid response improvement. The risk of failure or disappointing performance can be reduced significantly by judiciously applying the 10 Accelerators of Lean Six Sigma results.

What Organizations and Deployment Leaders Can Expect

Initiating or restarting a Lean Six Sigma initiative follows a common generic path as shown in Figure 7.2. Organizations begin in their current or as-is state. The organization chugs along, following its accepted practices and operating norms. This is the comfortable status-quo stage of improvement. Change is driven by external forces, and there is a widespread recognition of the need to change. After due diligence and analysis of available options, the organization identifies its key improvement needs and decides to deploy Lean Six Sigma as an enabler of success. This is the rumblings-of-change stage of improvement. Prior to a vision, improvement strategy, or more detailed deployment planning, there is either a

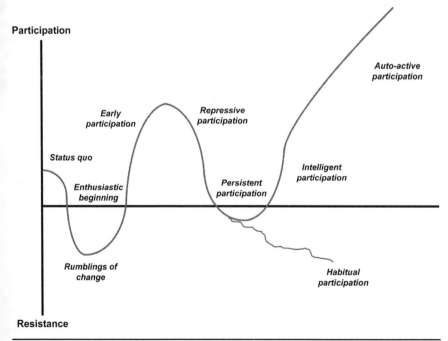

Figure 7.2   Desired improvement lifecycle.

formal business diagnostic or some informal bush-shaking and tire-kicking exercises to identify more specific improvement opportunities and how best to proceed with change. In the absence of information, people extrapolate what is about to happen or what might happen and internalize the perceived emotions of change, and resistance to change is a by-product.

Once the vision is communicated and more detailed deployment plans are developed, the initiative is launched. This stage includes formation of teams, assignment of improvement activities, education, and communication about the initial projects and participants. This is the enthusiastic beginning stage where people view Lean Six Sigma as a magic recipe for instant success. The early participation stage may include early successes, but more information and knowledge are known about the true magnitude and challenge of Lean Six Sigma. In the repressive participation phase, teams may experience failures and discover the difficulty and commitment to true root-cause problem solving. People learn that improvement requires effort and is much more difficult to achieve than the traditional practices of hip-shooting and winging it. In the absence of leadership and commitment, organizations may quietly retreat to old habits in the habitual participation stage. The persistent participation stage is when the team knows what they need to do to succeed, and they have too much invested to turn back. They see the light at the end of the tunnel. The intelligent participation stage is reached by application of the right methodologies and tools, and a visible improvement. Auto-active participation is the stage when teams and people subconsciously deploy the right methodologies to the right improvement opportunities without even thinking about Kaizen, Lean, or Six Sigma. The entire Lean Six Sigma deployment follows this same cycle. Leadership and improvement infrastructure determine the displacement, time, and flux of the cycle.

Concerns and Reactions to Change

An effective communications strategy around Lean Six Sigma or any other strategic improvement initiative recognizes the common thought processes that surface in people and organizations facing major change. It is a natural phenomenon for people to have initial questions and concerns about change, or initial reactions to change. A positive and effective cycle of communication breaks down these barriers and builds the emotional and behavioral foundation for change. Left unchecked, these factors can become serious detractors to a Lean Six Sigma initiative. Some of these factors result from an ineffective communications effort, and some of these factors are deeply embedded in personalities or cultural corners. Nevertheless, these factors must be dealt with in a communications strategy.

Initial Concerns About Change

Esteem needs drive people to rationalize change by seeking explanations from those executives and individuals leading and implementing change. These esteem needs include the requirement for information and knowledge that creates a better understanding of the need, process, and implications of change. In short, it is the filling in of their initial blanks of change. The first response of people is to question the need based on their own personal concerns and perceived concessions. This is an informative, listen-to-the-voice-of-the-customer moment for executives. The organization is also the customer of improvement and change. When people perceive or are affected by change, they will be evaluative and critical of leadership's values and behavioral standards of conduct. People may not fully agree with change, but it is important that they view change as an overall fair process. Lean Six Sigma has an overall positive reputation with people and organizations, and in fact, it is frequently accepted with a "Great, it's about time," and "I want to be involved" attitude. Lean Six Sigma suffers from the reputation of being a complicated massive training commitment that is expensive to implement; this is not true. A few years back, the initial introductions of reengineering and Lean coincided with massive layoffs and so much negative publicity that people wanted nothing to do with either initiative. One organization referred to their Lean initiative as *less-employees-are-needed* (LEAN). The recent meltdown has taken organizations on another ride through this repeating Omni pattern, where executives downsized their organizations while sending negative messages about their improvement initiatives. When one has a hard look at improvement, the opportunities are related to process, not people. Organizations are paying a heavy price for downsizing and failing to address their deeper process issues and reasons why people were employed in the first place. If executives are serious about regaining the commitment for Lean Six Sigma with their organizations, they need to make an investment in time and patience to rebuild a more positive perception and acceptance of the broader change management process.

Initial Responses to Change

People and organizations respond in several different ways to the initial introduction of change. Some of the common responses include:

- *Joining*—This is the best condition. People have listened to the message and wish to get on board early. They want to be part of the solution, not part of the problem. These people are generally open to change and thrive on challenges. They see the benefits of change, and view their participation as a career-expanding opportunity. Many of these people are also the field soldiers who can potentially convince others to step up and commit to change. Occasionally, an individual may join in instead of hedging to appear that they are on board. Joiners and hedgers are easily spotted by their behaviors and performance.
- *Hedging*—This is a condition where people are not for or against change. They are merely holding out, with the thoughts of change on their minds. These people become preoccupied with the perceptions of change, just

when they are needed to focus and commit to change. They are indecisive and waffle around commitment. Some of these people will join in after additional education and demonstrations of initial successes. Others will hedge until the risk of hedging is higher than the risk of boarding the improvement train.

- *Kibitzing*—This is the process of reaching out to others in the organization and sharing opinions and perceptions (with an underlying attempt to find all the answers). When Lean Six Sigma is introduced, there are many unanswered questions about the details because the initiative involves Greenfield improvements to key business processes. Socialization via opinions, perceptions, and fears can stir up the organization's emotional pot with imaginary concerns. These people need continuous communication, clarity, and examples to win them over.
- *Holding out*—These are people who are not committed but wish to hide their true feelings for political reasons. Their reasons are influenced by personal beliefs, values, career goals, or previous experiences. They continue to stay busy, keep a low profile, and convince others why the time is not right for their participation. They stay quiet, under the radar, and do not make waves. They have not decided to be part of the solution, so they are the silent part of the problem. It is not always their fault—the right communication can push their buttons and win them over. Some of these people will remain uncommitted and potentially a deterrent to those who are committed.

Most executives recognize that they cannot mandate the "joining" response to change. Managing the concerns and responses to change is necessary throughout a Lean Six Sigma deployment. Communication is mission-critical in the launch of a Lean Six Sigma initiative. Typically, there is an announcement at the start of the deployment (leadership, vision, and strategy) followed by a more detailed communication at the beginning of deployment planning. The remainder of the deployment is a continuous process requiring continuous communication to reinforce the process. In several deployments, we have tapped the expertise of our client's internal marketing and creative services organization to help design a communications strategy, including the messaging and media options, which we will discuss later in this chapter.

Overcoming Resistance to Change

Resistance to change occurs when there is a perceived threat to an individual. Figure 7.3 provides an overview of the natural resistance to organizational change. The two key words here are *perceived* and *threat*. In most cases, the basis for resistance is imaginary and self-perpetuated, and the risk of change is much lower than is the risk of staying the same. Some resistors are individuals who proclaim that they do not have time to improve while doing their regular jobs. They are

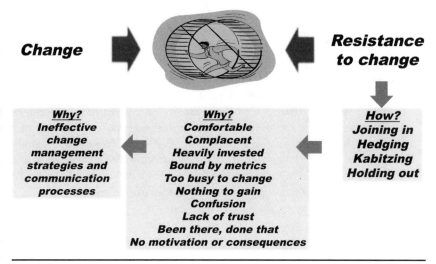

Figure 7.3   Natural resistance to organizational change.

too busy doing all the wrong things and cannot see that a little investment in improvement might result in less firefighting and more value-added time. Yet, they can always find the time to do things over. Many people are stuck in this emotional treadmill of behavior. Worse yet, many leadership behaviors help to build and promote this behavior. Perception is reality to these people and their managers, and it must be addressed by communication and other critical success elements of a deployment. Sometimes, stopping the insanity and sending these people off for an uninterrupted team improvement exercise is the best way to begin breaking down this vicious cycle of incoherent thinking.

Understanding Resistance to Change

Recognizing the root causes of resisting change is important in developing a communications strategy. These resistors are, for the most part, perceptions and opinions—a no-no in Lean Six Sigma. However, this is the human drama side of Lean Six Sigma where people's perceptions become reality in their own minds. Dealing with these resistors head on with an effective communications strategy will establish strong underpinnings for Lean Six Sigma success.

I Don't Want to Change Because . . .

There may be hundreds of reasons why people initially refuse to accept change. Typically, these reasons fall into the following categories:

- *People are happy with their current situation*—These are people who have served in the same steady-state position for a long time and find comfort in familiarity and routine. Change will upset the apple cart, and the destination of change does not look any better than the current position. These people need more awareness of reality, a new carrot for change, or a larger stick for their current position.

- *People are heavily invested*—Some people have spent time building their career in a social and organizational dimension. The social investment has created a sense of identity, and the organizational investment has created a sense of power and influence. Change represents a perceived sense of loss for individuals in this category. The combination of cross-process analysis, empowerment, and teaming is at cross-purposes with these individuals. They need to be shown the compelling reasons for change, a larger identity and the organizational opportunities available from change.

- *People are bound by metrics*—Some people are committed to achieving a specific objective, and involvement in change will disrupt or jeopardize success and individual performance. Individual metrics play a crucial role in a Lean Six Sigma deployment, and many of these metrics are localized, creating conflicts with the broader vision of improvement. The conflicts abound as performance metrics are directly tied to compensation.

- *People view improvement as additional work*—The first reaction of change with many people in organizations is incremental work—with no additional compensation and efforts that far exceed the perceived benefits. The journey of change is perceived to be uncomfortable, disruptive, and painful. These people require additional awareness and education. They must be moved by the opportunities presented by change, or experience higher pain and consequences in their current situation.

- *People see change as hollow*—People do not see the connection between all the commitment and effort that is being asked of them and how they will benefit from those actions. The *what's in it for me* and the attraction of change is missing, and change is perceived as an initiative to benefit a few individuals at the expense of others. People also do not see the connection between change and how they might step up and benefit without being recruited. Expanding the *why* of change is needed for these situations Lean Six Sigma is not a departmental goal; it requires focused efforts of the entire organization.

- *People are confused by the journey*—The idea of Lean Six Sigma sounds great, and people understand the *why* of change. However, they are missing the conceptual roadmap of *what, how, where,* and *when* change will occur. People have a lot of questions and are seeking more details to fill in the grey areas. This is usually attributable to ineffective communication with a vague vision and objectives, and a fuzzy deployment plans. People may converse with each other and speculate about the vision and deployment plans, and this is a bad thing. Unknowns create fear and resistance to change. People are unwilling to commit until they have a better understanding of how Lean Six Sigma will be rolled out to the organization, and they are comfortable with the plans.

- *People do not trust leadership*—This topic may be helped by revisiting the best practices leadership behaviors in Chapter 4. This is also a good topic to which you should apply the five *whys*. Whether imaginary or real, executives need to rely on their people to achieve Lean Six Sigma success. These issues may be imaginary or due to someone's perception, but they are at least temporarily real in the heads of the people that will be relied upon in a deployment. It is certainly worth taking the time to better understand the root causes of these issues and build the right countermeasures into the communication strategy. On the other hand, organizations should not spend the next year conducting touchy-feely exercises, delaying improvement. Balance and common sense is also necessary in all aspects of the deployment.

- *People have been there, done that, and got the tee shirt*—This was discussed earlier in this chapter. Before a Lean Six Sigma effort is launched or kick-started, some serious fence mending is warranted here. People in these organizations are just waiting for a deployment to stumble so they can pull out their *see-I-told-you-so* script. Skipping this fence mending and deployment renewal effort leaves the organization full of skeptics who will not step up and be committed, and who will help fulfill their *see-I-told-you-so* prophesy through their negative actions. Whatever happened in the past is yesterday's rain. Today is a new day. Build their concerns into the communication strategy. Sometimes these people need to be told to just get over it!

- *People are allowed to reject or obstruct change*—Some people have developed their knowledge and social and organizational power to such a level that they can get away with rejecting or not participating in change. Additionally, there are no consequences for refusing to participate in change. This barrier is prevalent, but not limited to privately owned organizations. These people fall into two categories: *passive* and *obstructive*. Passive people go about their business and pay little attention to change. Obstructive people reject change and involvement, and then attempt to use their power to reject or undermine improvement efforts. If an organization is serious about change, there are no exemptions from improvement. You are either on the train or lying on the tracks.

Understanding resistance to change involves more awareness and common sense than science does. One of the most positive aspects of management consulting is the constant communication and dialog with people in organizations. This communication involves understanding current business conditions, analyzing and reviewing current performance, working through strengths, weaknesses, and gaps in performance, and working with many people who are extremely helpful at expediting this foundation for improvement. Working with people, and listening to their issues and concerns, quickly builds trust. Sometimes it seems as if this is the first time an executive has sat down with these people and asked them about their challenges. People do not often share their knowledge and concerns with their own management groups, but they literally open their minds when someone makes the effort to listen, show interest, and empathize. These people have filled in so many organizational improvement puzzles than we could have ever understood by limiting our contact to the executive team and our own experiences. This has been an outstanding two-way learning process, and the importance of listening to the internal voice of the customer in Lean Six Sigma deployments is well recognized.

The Signals of Resistance

Resistance to change is usually obvious when an experienced executive is aware of the signals and looking for the signs of resistance. Most people will not approach the executive team and openly admit to resisting change, but some of these defectors will get away with as much as leadership allows them to get away with behind the scene. These signs are appropriately nicknamed *resistance flags* and include the following resistance activities:

- *Open resistance tests*—Some individuals will openly challenge the need, objectives, and approach of change to test the waters of commitment and knowledge. Their object is also to drive a wedge into the improvement initiative and test the explanation and response from leadership. The manner in which leadership responds to the challenge might influence the next resistance events. The best response is active listening followed by an unemotional, fact-based response. These resistance tests may be useful for inclusion in future communications.
- *Individual rejections*—Individuals may have a beef about change, and the manner in which this is handled depends on their level, influence, and power in the organization. This is not to discount any particular individuals, but to focus communications efforts on the areas with the highest influence for resistance. Again, the best approach is active listening followed by an unemotional, fact-based response.
- *Grapevine gossip*—Announcing Lean Six Sigma or any other major improvement initiative will not answer every question of the collective organization. There will be voids in information and there will be speculation to fill in these voids. The best way to handle the rumor mill is to keep an ear to the ground, listen to questions and concerns, openly discuss questions and concerns, and fill in the voids with additional useful information. Letting the rumor mill fester is a sure way to fill in the voids with fantasy negatively impacting commitment and trust.
- *Organized rejections*—This sign is obvious. A union, department, or group of engineers who are stressed out by their present overwhelming work loads join together to share their issues and concerns with the proposed changes. This is a sign of a deep divide and miscommunication, especially in the case of Lean Six Sigma. Resolution requires active listening followed

by convincing negotiations about workloads and priorities. It comes down to an honest negotiation of facts versus perceptions.

- *Passive resistance*—These people go through the motions of change. They may sit quietly in team meetings and agree with everything, but then do nothing to contribute to change. For these people, their heads and hearts need to be turned on to change. Much of this behavior is due to not knowing what to do to support change, and doing nothing is more comfortable than doing something and making a mistake. These people are best handled by a broader public assignment of activities, proactive mentoring, and accountability for results.

- *Active resistance*—This is where people take deliberate actions to reject participation in and acceptance of change. Many of these people may be turned around with additional useful information and demonstrated results from successful pilot improvement activities. This is a positive aspect of Lean Six Sigma. It is difficult to argue facts with fiction and opinions. Occasionally, there are active resistors who are blatant saboteurs of change. One of these characters can offset the good intentions of dozens of committed people if they are allowed to operate and sabotage improvement initiatives.

The last point reminds me of an experience we had while helping one of our previous clients implement Lean, and, in particular, a team implementing a pull system in a particular clean room area. The team designed and implemented a pull system in a unique process with outstanding results. WIP was reduced by 90 percent and defects were reduced by over 38 percent. This represented a projected $168K of annual savings. Suddenly, the pull system began causing several problems in the line with identifiable root causes. When the team babysat the process, it worked great. When they walked away, it would suddenly fall apart within the hour. The team discovered that their first line supervisor, who we later nicknamed Kanban Dan, was nervous about losing his power and authority and began sabotaging the pull system. The team felt deep ownership of their pull system and was on to Dan's tricks. When nobody was looking, he would destroy kanban cards, which is the equivalent of making the replenishment requirements disappear. He would shuffle the kanban cards, which is the equivalent of screwing up the FIFO priorities designed into the team's pull system. He would remove kanban cards and then replace them a few days later to create past due replenishments. This was only one of many games Kanban Dan played on his various people involved in improvement teams. When I learned of the sabotage from the team, I went straight to the CEO's office and shared the story with him. The CEO called an emergency meeting with the team and a representative from human resources. In the meeting, he acknowledged their issues and said, "I have empowered you to make improvements to our business. I am committed and serious about empowering you and supporting your success. I am also empowering you to decide what to do about Dan. Let me know what you decide to do and I will support your decision 100 percent."

The team decided to terminate Kanban Dan on the spot, and the human resources representative walked him out the door. This event turned out to be the strongest message about empowerment that I have ever witnessed. It also sent a clear message to the rest of the organization that you are either part of the solution or part of the problem. Executives need to take swift actions to shut down sabotage of improvement initiatives.

Developing an Effective Communications Strategy

The new economy is one where executives must point the organizational compass in every direction except where they have been in the past. Great executives and communicators recognize how confusing the business strategy may appear to the organization, and they carefully craft their communications *before* delivering any messages. For some executives, this comes naturally; for others, it is a struggle. Communication—whether positive or negative—must be deliberately crafted, candid, and positively framed to be well received. Several preliminary questions must be considered when creating any effective communication about strategic change:

- *Who are the stakeholders?*—Anyone impacted by change needs to hear the message. This includes internal and external audiences who may be directly or indirectly impacted by the change.
- *What is the communication objective?*—The message of change will differ depending on whether an executive is informing, educating, persuading, seeking support, or building awareness and clarity in direction. Communication of change must be focused on the particular objective of the message.
- *What is the general attitude?*—This relates to executive credibility. Like it or not, executives must think about how audiences perceive their personal credibility and trust, and how to build it if it is not there. The level of hostility, ambivalence, or full support will influence how the message of change will be received by the organization.
- *How do we communicate to different audiences?*—The message of strategic change must be identical and consistent between organizational constituencies. However, different audience groups may need a different version of the puzzle, different levels of detail, more specifics on the impact, and information about what to expect. Message of change is highly dependent upon a particular audience's connection to the change.
- *What is the method of communication?*—This relates to how the message of change will be communicated. It may include a shareholder's meeting, a quarterly review, a monthly newsletter, e-mail, webcasts, conference calls, payroll mailers, signage, and other media. The point here is that different methods of communication (media and hits) are necessary to reach and connect with different organizational constituencies.

- *What is the proper timing?*—There is no right time to change except now. The timing of communication should be considered when delivering the message of strategic change. The visible actions after the message are also important.
- *How will stakeholders participate?*—Communication must become an ongoing process where stakeholders and audiences feel free to participate and provide vital feedback about change. This builds buy-in and ownership for change. Communication of change should never be a one-way dialogue.

Communication is a process where stakeholders may reserve judgment when it is effective, but make their feelings well known when it is bad. When the CEO and executive team develop an effective communications strategy, the result is shared commitment, a uniform message, and constancy of purpose. When communications is short-circuited and informal, the results are usually disastrous.

Communication of Lean Six Sigma and Other Strategic Initiatives

Change must begin and be crystal clear in the heads of executives and managers. The purpose of communication is to create awareness, commitment, trust, inspiration, engagement, and other positive behavioral attributes of change. Communication is the sanity check for Accelerator #1—leadership vision and strategy. When developing a communications strategy, the Lean Six Sigma vision, deployment plan, and initial content of the Macro Charter will help to answer the *what, how, who,* and *when* questions of change. Figure 7.4 provides an overview of an effective Lean Six Sigma communications strategy.

An effective communications strategy requires several steps, which are outlined in the following paragraphs:

- *Educate executives on the subject matter content of Lean Six Sigma and related topics*—This is an absolute must because executives need to know what they are talking about when they communicate to their organizations. Executives need not become statisticians or technical experts, but they need to understand the fundamentals such as DMAIC, the basic improvement tools, leadership roles and responsibilities, teaming, and change management. Several years ago we were contracted to help an organization implement Lean. A few weeks into the deployment the CEO skipped the Lean executive overview education but continued to communicate the importance and need to implement Lean within his organization. During the internal practitioner workshop, he visited the HalFast™ Lego simulation exercise and observed the improvements between a batch-push system and a demand-pull system. Everyone in class understood why and how the improvements were achieved. However, the CEO accused us of playing a magic trick on the class and insisted that we reveal the magic. His own people were trying to explain that it was not magic. He could not

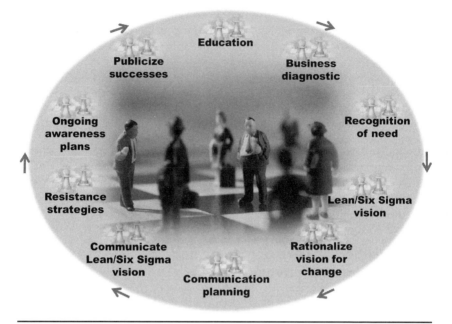

Figure 7.4 Effective communications strategy.

understand their explanations because he skipped the executive education and was clueless about the basics of Lean. Yet he was asking his organization to embrace Lean even though it was perceived that he had not embraced Lean himself.

- *Share and discuss the results of the business diagnostic*—A useful exercise is to review the business diagnostic with key managers and direct participants, and achieve consensus or shared awareness of the mission-critical improvement challenges. These individuals will provide excellent input to implementation planning and the communications strategy. This step builds commitment with key individuals in the organization prior to an official launch of a Lean Six Sigma deployment. This also supplements the informal rumor mill with a consistent set of facts about the need to change and the organization's key challenges.

- *Document the burning platforms and recognition of the need to change*—This includes a crisp and clear picture of business reality and the new challenges facing the organization. This is an opportunity to back up these challenges with data and facts from the business diagnostic. Recognition of the need must be perceived as being fact-based and data-driven instead of emotionally or personal-gains driven. The organization also needs to understand the consequences and risks of staying on the same course, the anticipated benefits of improvement, and the expected value proposition for individuals. Recognition of the need places all members of the organization in the same boat.

- *Develop the Lean Six Sigma vision*—The vision includes a bold and compelling image of the future in a presentation format. The Lean Six Sigma vision should be no longer than a few slides, and should be structured to answer the essential *what, how, who, when,* and *why* questions of the planned deployment. Additional information about the vision and its contents can be found in Chapter 4.

- *Dry run the vision*—The CEO and the executive deployment team should review the vision with a broad cross-section of selected executives and other key individuals, and solicit their initial reactions and suggestions. Several valuable discussions occur during the dry run, including how other influential people in the organization might react, or what anticipated questions the team should be prepared to answer. This step also builds commitment with key individuals in the organization prior to an official launch of a Lean Six Sigma deployment.

- *Decide how to communicate and launch the Lean Six Sigma deployment*—This involves thinking through the most effective means of communicating the vision and other messages to various employee segments in the organization. A well-designed communications strategy uses multiple media resources to reach certain individuals and achieve specific communication objectives. A single all-hands meeting or monthly videoconference is simply not enough. A combination of well-orchestrated organization-wide meetings, staff and step meetings, visuals, signage, videos, and other creative formats and ideas is the best approach to achieve a variety of positive Lean Six Sigma impressions and communications objectives.

- *Communicate the vision*—It is time to get the word out. No change is possible unless people understand and embrace the contents of the vision and are willing to step up and participate. The vision document itself helps in communicating the message, but the most powerful medium is executive behavior. Executives must demonstrate behavior that is consistent with the vision, and communicate the vision consistently as well. Another suggestion when communicating the vision is to personalize the message with specific examples and situations.

- *Plan for resistance*—Anyone who has lived through a successful Lean Six Sigma deployment understands that change introduces uncertainty and disruptions to the status quo. It initiates doubt about new requirements and excessive concerns about the future. This translates into personal anxiety, stress, conflict, and resistance. Resistance is a normal human trait that varies by personality, perceived effects, or how change is being introduced. It is much easier to deal with resistance head on through communication and awareness than it is to fight or deny it. People come around when their grey area is colored in with information.

- *Design an ongoing awareness plan*—This includes reinforcement with a continuous and consistent unified message, and decisions about how to trickle down a consistent message from executives to operators. Other things to consider include recognition of key individuals and teams, or communicating continuous reminders and hits via methods such as visuals, newsletters, mailing laminated pocket cards, workplace posters, digital storyboards, monitor messaging in cafeterias and other high traffic areas, and the like. The ongoing awareness plan is carefully constructed by defining objectives, then asking what to communicate, how to communicate, and when and where to communicate. This is much different from the coffee mug and tee shirt approaches of previous improvement programs. The difference is that it is well-planned to achieve a specific communication objective and is backed by substance and results.
- *Publicize successes*—This is an opportunity to accomplish several effective communications objectives. First, it is an opportunity to share improvement plans, internal and external customer updates and feedback, and showcase internal successes. Only a fool hedges or holds off from involvement when a dozen successes and the associated peer pressure is staring them in the face.

Accelerator #4, communicate, communicate, communicate is an important accelerator in a Lean Six Sigma deployment. Communication is the food that nourishes the ongoing process of deployment and execution. Communication is important at the beginning of a Lean Six Sigma deployment because it provides information about direction, initial fears and concerns, and expectations. Many organizations have not recognized the need to communicate throughout the deployment. It is just as important to communicate throughout a Lean Six Sigma deployment as it is in the beginning. As deployments evolve, there are several things to consider:

- The organization will have new questions, experiences, and valuable inputs about the deployment that may fine-tune the course of the deployment.
- People need to internalize the consistency in the vision and personally experience the progress and recognition from their efforts.
- People and priorities change, which may give off false messages about the importance of and commitment to Lean Six Sigma.
- People require constant reminder images and reinforcement of improvement for it to become continuous improvement.
- A deployment's progress is not linear; the rate of improvement oscillates over time, and communication helps to avoid falling into the negative slumps.

Effective communication keeps the attention and focus on a Lean Six Sigma deployment.

Change Management Essentials

Change is a process that almost every human balks at, even though the most positive career and life experiences have come about by change. When change is introduced, people internalize the perceived and often imaginary outcomes of change. No matter how much change is planned, the response is the same. The more unknowns affiliated with change, the higher the anxiety and the more negative perceptions there are about the change. Deep diving into people's thoughts usually reveals that they are not afraid of the change itself, they are afraid of the *perceived* loss, effort, commitment, discipline, sacrifice, the risk of failure, and disruption to their established norms. Leadership gets the organization through this very real dilemma.

One fact of improvement that has been repeatedly mentioned is a long pattern of pressure to change followed by reaching out and grasping the *fad du jour* improvement program. This was all done with the greatest of intentions, but it has confused organizations with inconsistent behaviors, inconsistent improvement direction, and inconsistent results. This is the cycle executives must break going forward with Lean Six Sigma and other improvement initiatives. Change management is about understanding how and why people feel the way they do about change, and building the right leadership responses into a communications strategy. The economy is demanding that organizations put the *continuous* back in continuous improvement.

The Power Hits

Effective change management efforts reach out and listen to the organization's questions and concerns, and clarify the confusion about change. Communications strategy is the media to accomplish this continuous process of managing change. One of the most powerful practices of executives is the use of continuous *power hits* within their organizations. Power hits are short, 15-second conscious messages that demonstrate commitment, interest, and expectations such as:

- How's your project going?
- Are you beyond D&M and into A&I yet (DMAIC status)?
- Looking forward to the team's improvements.
- Has the team identified root causes?
- This project is important.
- When do you expect to identify improvements?
- I'm happy that you are involved.
- I support you.
- Let me know what you need.

This becomes a challenge of asking the right questions, and proactively discovering and recognizing the contributions of people. Making the effort to stop by an education session or occasional team meeting also sends a strong message of commitment, interest, and expectations. Power hits are effective when structured and communicated effectively, and it requires a conscious effort.

During one multisite Lean Six Sigma education session, the CEO happened to be at the facility one day working on a monster opportunity with a huge potential customer. The participants in the class asked why he was not interested because he did not stop by and say a few words to the class. After all, he was in a nearby conference room. This executive was legitimately busy all day with a room full of potential customer executives trying to do great things for his organization. Dropping in for 30 seconds during one of his walk-bys would have made a big difference.

Executives are naturally busy people who are involved in a multitude of issues and stressful situations. They may disappear from the improvement scene with the best of intentions of the organization. However, when they disappear, people kibitz and have their own interpretations about what is going on, or exchange gibberish about the perceived changing level of interest. This is not right or wrong—just a fact of dealing with the human element of change. The good thing and bad thing about people and organizations is that they are always amazing. Many organizations are still experiencing shellshock from the latest economic changes. People are insecure about their futures and tend to extrapolate on the scenarios and situations that surround them. Executive behavior is a powerful metric—people observe and interpret the visual behaviors and signals around them to determine and respond to their own interpretations of the expectations. Consistent, unwavering, and clarifying behaviors drive the right actions and the right results.

Let's now revisit Lean Six Sigma and strategic improvement. These are proven approaches to achieve breakthroughs in business improvement. If we remove the hype and buzzwords, what is the underlying objective? Wearing the change management hat, Lean Six Sigma is about connecting reality and vision to improve fundamental properties of the organization such as leadership, direction, thinking, actions, behaviors, culture, and total stakeholder success. Embedded within our Scalable Lean Six Sigma™ model are several components that are consistent with change management. Years ago, we used a term associated with this objective called *organizational robustness*, which we described as an organization's capability to sense, interpret, adapt or respond, validate, and maintain competitiveness. At the end of the day, this is what organizations should be accomplishing. Organizations that develop these traits can usually implement any improvement initiative with nothing short of greatness.

How to Manage Change

There are several proven leadership approaches to handhold the organization through a major improvement initiative such as Lean Six Sigma. These approaches require patience, time, logic, and facts—and are much more difficult in practice to get right. All executives are under tremendous pressures in this economy, and the quickest leadership approach is issuing directives. Directives are great for unemotional tasks where the root causes are visible. Overuse of directives motivates people to look at the wrong issues, create band-aid improvements, or create more inefficiency. Some organizations become stuck in this silly *whack-a-mole* approach to improvement. Executives cannot expect to be successful in commanding their organizations to innovate, transform culture, or reduce new product time-to-market by 70 percent. Unfortunately, there are no shortcuts to reinvent organizations and transform culture. Lean Six Sigma addresses the more complex improvement issues that require a different, more holistic improvement approach and changes in thinking and behaviors. After years of involvement with Lean Six Sigma and many other strategic improvement initiatives, nothing in organizations will change much until people embrace and are ready and willing to change. Executives and managers need to deploy several familiar approaches to lead their organizations through change, namely:

- *Facilitation*—This includes openly collaborating with people to help their people to digest and embrace the vision, mentoring people and teams to a successful conclusion on improvement initiatives, and helping people find their personal discovery moments with change.
- *Education*—This includes increasing awareness and knowledge about the need to change, helping people to understand the organization's burning platforms and priorities for improvement, explaining the expectations and requirements for success, and making clear the consequences of failure.
- *Engagement*—This entails getting people involved up front in the business diagnostic, creating the vision, participating in the Macro Charter, and participating in other deployment planning activities.
- *Discussion forums*—These are smaller focus group meetings that facilitate listening and openly discussing questions and concerns, expectations, project ideas, and other potential detractors on people's minds.
- *Good teaming practices*—This includes pausing, active listening, acknowledging the other person's point of view, thinking before speaking, offering clear and consistent unwavering responses, and continually using data and facts.
- *Cross-learning*—These are regularly scheduled peer reviews where executive sponsors and team leaders can collaborate on the progress of their improvement activities and any other dynamics of change that they are experiencing within their teams and the project.
- *Best practice leadership behaviors*—These are the vision, knowledge, passion, discipline, and conscience behaviors discussed in Chapter 4.

Executives should do their best to follow these proven approaches. In some instances, there will be the naysayers who will not step up no matter what the organization does or accomplishes. Some of these people will resign because of the emotions of peer pressure, or because they are not interested in a future that includes Lean Six Sigma, improvement, or collaborating in teams. Following these approaches and other advice in the leadership vision, strategy, and deployment planning phases will initially win over a critical mass. These factors combined with execution will eventually engage the entire organization (with a few irrelevant exceptions) in the pursuit of Improvement Excellence™.

References

Scoble, R., Israel, S., Barbosa, D., and Merkle, G. 2009. *The Conversational Corporation: How Social Media is Changing the Enterprise*. Dow Jones and Company, New York, NY.

Senge, P. 2006. *The Fifth Discipline: The Art and Practice of the Learning Organization, 2nd edition*. Doubleday Publishing, New York, NY.

Chapter 7 Take Aways

- The purpose of communications is to create awareness, commitment, trust, inspiration, engagement, and other positive behavioral attributes of change. The most important part of communication is to establish recognition of the need to change, and why the organization must embrace change. The *why* of change is often explained inadequately or with emotional reasons. Well-executed and frequent communication builds commitment and trust, reduces confusion, sets expectations, builds continuity and interest, removes the fear of change, provides a medium for publicizing success and recognizing people, and builds momentum for larger successes. Effective, continuous communication creates the needed momentum for improvement.

- The most important message about Lean Six Sigma or change in general is that change at an increasing rate is inevitable in the new economy. The only certainty going forward is change and more change. Stakeholders need, expect, and want more from their other stakeholder partners. The risk of the status quo (or even mediocre improvement) is much higher than the risk is from solid improvement in this economy. Organizations must either step up and control their destinies or watch competitors control their destinies at their expense. There is no such thing as staying the same in this economy. Either an organization is improving, or they are falling behind due to another competitor's improvements. The only status quo these days is rapid deployment, rapid response improvement.

- Managing the concerns and responses to change is necessary throughout a Lean Six Sigma deployment. Communication is mission-critical in the launch of a Lean Six Sigma initiative. Typically, there is an announcement at the start of the deployment (leadership, vision, and strategy) followed by a more detailed communication at the beginning of deployment planning. The remainder of the deployment is a continuous process requiring continuous communication to reinforce the process.

- In most cases, the basis for resistance is imaginary and self-perpetuated, and the risk of change is much lower than the risk is for staying the same. Some resistors are individuals who proclaim that they do not have time to improve while doing their regular jobs. They are too busy doing all the wrong things and cannot see that a little investment in improvement could result in less firefighting and more value-added time. Yet they can always find the time to do things over. This may sound ridiculous, but many people are stuck in this emotional treadmill of behavior in organizations.
- One of the most powerful practices of executives is the use of continuous *power hits* within their organizations. Power hits are short, 15-second conscious messages that demonstrate commitment, interest, and expectations. Questions and statements like—How's your project going? Are you beyond D&M and into A&I yet (DMAIC status)? Looking forward to the team's improvements. Has the team identified root causes? This project is important. When do you expect to identify improvements? I'm happy that you are involved. I support you. Let me know what you need.—are extremely effective. Making an effort to stop by an education session or occasional team meeting also sends a strong message of commitment, interest, and expectations. Power hits are effective when structured and communicated effectively, and they require a conscious effort.

8

Accelerator #5: Launching with the Best in Mind

This accelerator means simply putting the best of everything into the deployment: best projects, leadership, overall resources, team leader, team members, innovative approach, implementation plans, use of limited resources, time and capacity, implementation path, and results. Figure 8.1 displays Accelerator #5, launching with the best in mind, and its relationship to the other accelerators. Although some organizations have attempted it, improvement is not something to be assigned to less-desirable people with time on their hands. We want to pull these people in and develop their expertise at some point, but not at the front end of the deployment. Sports teams do not start with their third string—they go with their best players. The same holds true with Lean Six Sigma and improvement in general.

During a dinner meeting with the CEO of one of our clients, he was sharing his perspectives about being customer driven. He discussed how he always embraced the notion of listening to the voice of the customer and focusing on the customer, up until his initial experiences leading the Lean Six Sigma deployment. He mentioned, "For as long as I have been an executive, everyone has promoted the customer-driven philosophy. I believe that there's something fundamentally wrong with this thinking."

We both talked and agreed that being customer driven is an empty wish unless it is backed up by the right actions. He added, "I'm on a new mission, although I probably can't state it publicly without being crucified. The customer is not number one to me anymore. My people and my organization are number one. If we don't have great, loyal people with talent and motivation, working together to do the right things, with shared success, we can't be successful with customers or anything else we try to do." This CEO's perspective is insightful in understanding Accelerator #5, launching with the best in mind.

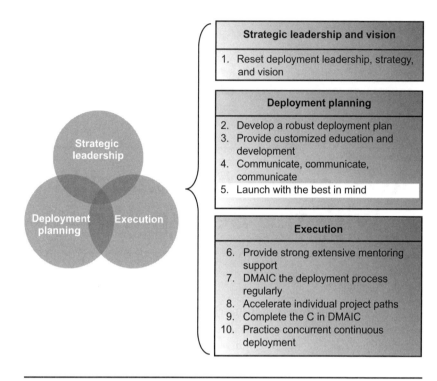

Figure 8.1   Elements of deployment planning.

The Underpinnings of Best

Best assumes that an organization has the best of everything to put into a Lean Six Sigma deployment because they have been investing in developing the best leadership, the best people, and the best culture. *Best* insinuates both developing the best and putting up the best—they go hand in hand, and it is difficult to have the latter conditions without the prior conditions.

During the economic meltdown, education and professional development spending funds are the first to be frozen. This has repeatedly been the case when organizations face negative dips in the economy. It is a familiar age-old pattern of freezes and layoffs. Executives view people not as an asset but as an expense and they cut the expense as much as possible in a recession. On the other hand, the best time to develop the organization's capabilities and skill sets tends to be when things are slow and people have more time to focus on development. In a down economy, organizations tend to be more selective about development budgets. Only short-sighted leadership pulls the purse strings fully closed in a down economy. For publicly traded organizations, these decisions are adversely influenced by Wall Street perceptions and the potential risk of a massacre on stock prices.

During the recent meltdown, most organizations did not invest in improvement, but instead chose to hunker down, cut costs and discretionary spending, make the books look good, and allow their business problems to grow. Many of these executives openly committed to a Lean, Six Sigma, or Lean Six Sigma initiative prior to the 2008–2009 period of the changing economy. Their decisions and responses to the economic meltdown melted down their improvement initiatives and employee loyalty. The leadership responses to the recent meltdown were negative for the most part, and the effort required to resuscitate improvement in these organizations is a significant leadership dilemma.

On the other hand, the leadership response to the meltdown in champion organizations was all positive. Champion organizations recognize that they need to inject new skills into their organizations to deal more effectively with the emerging challenges of this economy, and the best time to change is always *now*. For these forward-thinking organizations, the underpinnings of *best* is organizational and talent development. They recognize organizational development as a continuous living process of developing their most valuable asset—their people. They invest in this asset because the investment earns a lot more than the cost of capital.

This human capital philosophy does not waver in a recession. These organizations invested in improvement while they had the time to become better prepared for the upswing in the economy. It is a totally different perspective, and a better, healthier, and more responsible perspective. These organizations have been the exception throughout this recent meltdown.

In reality, most organizations have not only frozen professional development budgets, but they have frozen time, resources, and funding for improvement. What a concept! A well-executed Lean Six Sigma deployment can pay off at 20 to 50 times the investment annually, and organizations instead chose to tolerate a much higher level of inefficiency and mediocrity. They were convinced that saving their pennies while the hundred dollar bills continued to get away was the right thing to do. Worse yet, these short-sighted decisions permanently affect the professional and personal lives of thousands of employees. This is the repeating death cycle of improvement. This pattern has existed for three decades with different executives and different improvement programs in different organizations. Executives fail to recognize that their short-sighted actions actually create larger problems for the organization. Most across-the-board directives are inherently incorrect and cause organizations to focus on the wrong things. Blanket actions send horrible messages to the organization regarding commitment, wavering in or lack of direction, or uncertain and insecure futures. These recurring observations, trends, and cycles regarding improvement initiatives are not intended to discredit or degrade leadership. Executives must recognize the negative impact of these cycles on continuous strategic improvement, and they have to understand that these cycles must be broken if organizations hope to be competitive in the future. One thing for sure is that the need for improvement will always exist as competitive lever.

When executives are committed to improvement, strategically and for real, their decisions and behaviors are much different from their *frozen* counterparts. Organizations that continued with an aggressive Lean Six Sigma initiative through the meltdown have emerged from this economy thankful for their decisions. Many rode through the meltdown with millions more in newly executed improvements than they would have had if they had chosen to do nothing. In addition, these organizations have invested in more nimble processes and infrastructure to better deal with their emerging challenges. They have emerged from the economic meltdown much more agile and responsive than when they went in, and they have a stronger foundation to continue with improvement.

The Meltdown Is Over . . . What Next?

Whether an organization chose to aggressively pursue or freeze improvement during the meltdown is irrelevant in today's economy. The need for improvement is facing both types of organizations, especially those that are cautiously thawing out after the freeze. When organizations think about *best*, the first thing that they must focus on is creating a best company or best organization. When organizations strive for this status, they end up having the best of everything else needed for a successful Lean Six Sigma deployment. In fact, they have the best of everything needed for any successful initiative or venture. When striving for a best company or best organization, there are several things that executives must do better in the new economy:

- *Listen more effectively to the market and key customers*—There are so many emerging business requirements driving the need for organizations to improve. The sheer velocity of an emerging market and its customers is growing exponentially, faster than the ability of many organizations to keep up. Some executives say, "Boy, I'm glad I'm not starting my career now." This is unfortunate because the new economy has provided organizations with the most challenging and opportunistic time for improvement and competitiveness in history.
- *Tell the organization the whole truth*—People in organizations are much smarter and perceptive about the new economy and change. Future leadership needs to do a better job of communicating their intentions to the people in their organizations. People need to know what their leadership is planning to do, even if the message is negative.
- *Engage and empower people*—Empowerment is a misused word that has been casually thrown around in association with fad improvement programs. Most organizations are so far away from empowerment and engaging the full potential of their people. It is amazing to see how much knowledge people have about their roles and the organization in general. Yet they sit on this information because there is a feeling that nobody is interested and nobody cares. Engagement and empowerment are critical organizational goals in the new economy.

- *Learn how to deal with ambiguity quickly*—The future for executives and their organizations is the ability to sense, interpret, decide, act, and monitor progress in dealing with ambiguity. Organizations need to accept this fact and learn how to manage and deal with ambiguity effectively. As we learn from fractal physics, even in the most chaotic situations, there is a sense of order to all of it. Change, ambiguity, and discovering and improving the unknown are normal expectations in the new economy.

- *Build the formal foundation for organizational learning and development*— The future will be a difficult place for organizations who fail to embrace a more enlightened and long-term human capital philosophy. The real objective is to build organizational models where people continually expand their capacity to create the results they truly desire, where new and expansive patterns of thinking are nurtured, where collective aspiration is set free, and where people are continually learning to see the whole together as a winning team.

- *Lead with creativity and innovation*—This is an economy where the best organizations will reinvent business models and set radically different courses for their business. Leaders must check in on their behaviors and how they lead their organizations. This includes encouraging other executives and managers to engage in a dialogue with employees throughout the organization to make sure that change is well-communicated, planned, and executed. This is the time to think about possibilities beyond the box, lead and benefit from change, and transform and transcend culture.

- *Walk your talk, and keep talking and walking the line*—Executives are on center stage more than ever. People today are observing and reading their behaviors and actions as their prescription for survival. If changes to plans must be made, executives need to communicate these changes as soon as possible. The old adage "Tell them, show them what you told them, tell them what you showed them again" will close the loop and reinforce the message.

- *Praise, then raise the bar*—The new economy is an environment of either improving or falling behind. Leadership in the new economy must set high expectations for themselves and others in the organization. The world has evolved to a gigantic change machine, where the rate of change demanded by markets and customers is exceeding the bandwidth to change for many organizations. Striving for Improvement Excellence™ is becoming more of a competitive differentiator, because it is just too easy for everyone to knock-off or make a few small incremental improvements here and there in the organization. Nevertheless, there is always room for praise for previous successes, and this is the best time to elevate the sense of urgency and expectations. Raising the bar effectively energizes the organization because it keeps expectations high but within reach. It also sends a clear message that the organization is not finished with improvement, and that improvement really is a continuous process.

The remainder of this chapter will expand on how to create a best organization in this new economy, and how to put that best organization forward for a successful Lean Six Sigma deployment. Many of the necessary concepts have been placed in the hands of executives and organizations for years. The big difference in this new economy is execution.

Eight Factors that Influence Organizational Greatness

Rapid changes in the world are impacting how organizations conduct business. As a result, the old rules of how organizations develop and improve have been turned upside down. The new economy is demanding different types of leaders with a broader perspective and range of qualities. For organizations to succeed, they will need to understand what key leadership behaviors and practices are paramount in driving their organization toward mass-collaboration, business improvement, and growth.

This is much more than just getting people to make the right decisions and produce the right outcomes. It is about getting people to show commitment to the organization, passion toward their work, and a personal desire to grow and handle the challenges ahead. The best organizations have already figured this out and are busy implementing and executing positive change.

There are many possible attributes of best organizations ranging from growth opportunities to allowing pets at work. *Fortune Magazine* and numerous regional and local business periodicals frequently publish articles such as "The Best Companies To Work For," "The Most Innovative Organizations," "The Most Successful Companies," "The Best Health Care Providers," "The Best Restaurants," and "The Best Executives." Figure 8.2 includes the major common factors that influence greatness in organizations. These include but are not limited to:

- Innovation
- Global market position
- Leadership
- Financial performance and stability
- Product and service quality
- People and talent management
- Long-range investment plans
- Social responsibility

The remainder of this section describes these greatness factors in more detail.

Innovation

In the current economy, companies face not only more competitors but also new kinds of competitors who may play by different rules and come from different business, geographic, and social backgrounds. Without any market share to defend, new competitors have little to lose and much to gain—at the expense

Figure 8.2 Factors that influence organizational greatness.

of current industry leaders and other participants. Great organizations earn and keep their positions by innovation—sensing and translating customer and market opportunities, creating new and flexible business models, and building fast and fluid execution processes. Innovation includes the ability to:

- Understand business opportunities, recognize competitive forces, and embrace markets and customers
- Define clear strategies to operate beyond the normal industry rules and create superior, robust, user-delighting products and services
- Deploy technology to drive business goals and build new business models, organizational infrastructure, and discipline to execute quickly and decisively
- Leverage the full potential and talent pools of the entire enterprise and extended enterprise

The new economy is driving leaders and organizations to take more of an 80/20 view of the world, and halting the all-things-to-all-people business strategies of the past. Great organizations embrace product and service rationalization, focusing on the more successful segments of their business. They also seek key customer input and collaboration in every stage of the lifecycle—from conception to design and development, from marketing and product launch to distribution and logistics, from collaborative point-of-sales analysis and promotional design to ongoing sales and operations planning and after-sales service and support.

The world has moved from discrete snapshots to a continuous movie of evolving change. Great organizations take advantage of emerging technologies, which enable a new level of customer intimacy by changing the way enterprises connect, communicate, and build solid customer relationships. These organizations are moving from merely knowing the customer to truly embracing the customer through more predictive and preventive sense-interpret-decide-act-monitor business models. This connection, collaboration, and information exchange is carried over in the design of their products and services.

An organization that comes to mind here is Apple, with its portfolio of Mac, iPod, iPhone, iPad, iTunes, and customer support literally oozing with innovation. These products have not only reinvented Apple, but they have also revolutionized how people listen and communicate. The entirety of Apple and its brand oozes with innovation from marketing to point of sale, customer ease of use, and an emotionally pleasing customer experience. Even the retail packaging of their products communicates the message of a superior innovative organization.

Innovation in this area involves the creation of new adaptive business models and processes, products, and services that are faster and more delighting than the competition's product. Traditional business models, processes, and information systems have been built to be as efficient and effective as possible, but the ability to quickly adapt to changing scenarios has not traditionally been a top requirement. New business models and processes must be fluid yet formal, which sounds like an oxymoron. Fluid and formal means adaptive to emerging situations with a standardized response, and maybe a short lifecycle as the bar of market demands rises with new emerging situations. "That's not the way we do things around here" is an obsolete statement for innovative organizations. Adaptive business models and processes are developed via numerous combinations of evolving and innovative practices that increase an organization's capability to remain flexible and responsive to customers and markets.

Velocity and an 80/20 focus in the sense-interpret-decide-act-monitor cycle is across-the-board more important than perfection is when it comes to business process innovation. However, innovation is not the same thing as an organization running around with Blackberries and its hair on fire. Innovation is a deliberate reach for a breakthrough for an anticipated need that targets the few vital customers and markets. Innovation is a planned win-win for the organization and its customers and markets. Innovation is improved significantly with the presence of baseline information and facts and shared objectives and assumptions.

Best organizations are innovative by design. They focus on developing people and building the spirit and culture to continuously reinvent themselves and overcome any challenge or obstacle. As a result, they have their critical mass of innovative, continuously developing people who are encouraged by culture and metrics to grow and nurture an innovative organization. Innovation also requires that many organizations reconsider their more restrictive metrics and controls around idea generation and incubation. Best organizations recognize that restrictive metrics and a command-and-control environment restrain the innovative business models and processes needed in the new economy.

Global Market Position

Global competitiveness requires the ability to quickly and continually bring superior value to diverse marketplaces in the face of rapidly changing needs, technologies, and environments. These competitive forces and increased complexity are prompting major strategic and structural changes in organizations. Global markets represent growth opportunities and increased competitive pressures. Global market position is a function of several factors:

- Magnitude of new market potential versus the number and relative strength of new competitors
- Velocity, or identifying and understanding market opportunities and being the first to deliver to market
- Reactive measures, or how much incentive the competition has to challenge or counter the organization's global decisions. Reactive measures are usually based on total market share, profitability, or emotional factors such as national image or corporate pride. How large is the market? How much market share is at stake? How profitable is it? How emotionally attached is the competition to it?
- Attractive measures are the mirror image of reactive measures. This measures the relative importance of the organization's global decisions based on the same total market share, profitability, or other emotional factors. How large is the market? How much market share is at stake? How profitable is it? How emotionally attached is the organization to it?
- Relative clout measures the organization's and competitors' relative strength and position to launch or defend against a strategic move in a global market. Clout is determined by relative sales, distribution dominance, technology advantages, or sheer economies of size, scale, and capital strength. Relative clout measures the ability to retaliate, while reactive measures represent the propensity to retaliate.

An organization's current and planned global business strategy is a good indicator of their culture. Global competitiveness is not achieved through adhoc measures. Aggressive global business strategies require innovation and all of the other attributes of best organizations discussed in this section. Best organizations increase global competitiveness by recognizing the importance of organizational development. From Boston to Bangalore to Beijing, education and professional development is the engine of economic growth. Opportunities for continuous professional development have emerged as a key driver of competitiveness, ensuring that people have access to new knowledge, skills, and the latest technologies. Best organizations enable their aggressive global market strategies by leveraging the full potential of their intelligent, creative, adaptive, and courageous organizations.

Leadership

Best practices leadership behaviors were discussed in Chapter 4. To refresh your memory, best practices leadership includes:

- *Vision*—The ability to see beyond current challenges and define a new direction for improvement. Vision is the conceptual road map to a future state of prosperity and success.
- *Knowledge*—The ability to act based on facts and data. Knowledge is self-education and self-awareness that enables one to understand how the vision may be possible. This includes taking the time and having the patience to understand what really matters in a successful Lean Six Sigma deployment and any other strategic endeavor.
- *Passion*—The compelling emotion that drives leaders to success. Passion is the fire in the belly that gets leaders and organizations past all obstacles to success.
- *Discipline*—The ability to follow the rules of conduct and expectations for the organization in a manner that establishes logical business conduct and order. The other side of discipline is walking the talk. Discipline establishes the moral compass and serves to guide organizational behaviors to pursue the right decisions and achieve the right results.
- *Conscience*—The leadership's ability to distinguish whether the organization's or individual's actions are right or wrong. Some refer to this as the inner voice of the subconscious mind. The subconscious mind is always acting as a secondary reflector of leadership thoughts and ideas in the body. This inner voice is shaped by values or emotional rules established in one's personal, social, cultural, educational, and business life.

Best organizations have great executive talent who live the best practice leadership behaviors, and who mentor and develop the same behaviors from others. There is a strong relationship between how executives lead their organizations, the resulting organizational behaviors and culture, and the resulting performance in the marketplace. Best organizations encourage the development and attraction of great leaders and people, with a strong sense of team spirit and winning.

Financial Performance and Stability

The description of financial performance is straightforward. This includes the traditional P&L, balance sheet, cash flow, and other financial performance ratios. Stability is more complicated. True stability goes beyond the obvious financial statements. First, stability is not achieved by accounting games that smooth out the perceived variation in the business. Second, stability recognizes the presence of hidden costs followed by aggressive actions to eliminate hidden costs. Organizations cannot be best and broke at the same time. Best organizations recognize and are able to invest in their most important asset—people. In the new economy, financial performance and stability is becoming more dependent on people skills, behaviors, and shared commitment.

Product and Service Quality

The description of product and service quality is also obvious. Best organizations are known for products and services that delight customers. Products and services that exceed customer expectations and value propositions, create long-term brand loyalty. Best organizations strive to deliver quality beyond the initial products and services in areas such as sales administration, customer service and support, and supply chain management. These organizations are tuned into maximizing the total customer experience. Best organizations also have internalized product and service quality. People in these organizations treat each other as customers and suppliers while striving for perfection in everything from releasing a sales order to developing new products in half the time. External product and service quality cannot be achieved without internal product and service quality.

People and Talent Management

Talent management (see Figure 8.3) is a process of aligning resources and skill sets to business needs. Best organizations recognize the importance of talent management in the new economy because the need for change is challenging the capabilities of many organizations to respond successfully.

The process occurs by managing six clusters of talent management:

1. *Talent planning*—Defining and planning an optimal strategy for acquiring, developing, and retaining people with the types of skills required to support future needs. Talent planning also includes the identification of internal individuals with the potential for development, learning, and growth. Many organizations tend to limit their focus more on direct external replacements than they do on longer-range talent needs, sources, and strategies.

2. *Talent acquisition*—Attracting, recruiting, and acquiring new talent. This is a well-planned, proactive activity that targets specific talent sources. A critical element of talent acquisition is to provide information beyond the current open positions such as culture and values, professional development opportunities, flexibility, and work-at-home potential career development road maps.

3. *Talent deployment*—Verify that people's capabilities are understood and deployed to match present and evolving business requirements, and that they meet an individual's need for orientation, assimilation, performance and expectations, motivation, recognition, and career satisfaction.

Figure 8.3   Talent management process.

4. *Talent development*—Leveraging existing talent through targeted education, professional development, and an introduction to several career exposure opportunities and highly visible special assignments. This includes the identification and delivery of talent-development initiatives that expand current capabilities to support evolving business needs. Every organization should make their best effort to develop their existing talent pool, because replacement costs are high.

5. *Talent retention*—Hold on to the existing talent pool and in particular, the most valued resources and future leaders—the risk of departure to the competition is high, and the cost of replacement is high. The total cost of replacing these individuals usually falls between 30 and 80 percent of their salary.

6. *Talent rationalization*—Identification of employees who clearly do not have a future with the organization due to changes in circumstances or performance issues, and assisting these people through outplacement

and transition. This is the right decision for the organization and for the individual.

Talent management is a critical requirement in best organizations. Many organizations such as GE, Microsoft, Starbucks, Baptist Health Care, and Google have an active, formal talent management process. Another example, Colgate Palmolive, the $15 billion, 204-year-old giant, has tens of thousands of employees in 80 countries. It is undoubtedly the leading global consumer products giant on the planet. Its culture starts with over 3000 employees—almost 10 percent of its population—who work solely on talent management, training, and development. Raises are tied to three values: caring, teamwork, and continuous improvement.

Many are predicting that the most important corporate resource over the next 20 years will be talent—smart, sophisticated business people who are technologically literate, globally astute, operationally agile, and willing to grow through exposure to a variety of career assignments. There are many predictions out there that as the demand for talent escalates the supply will spiral downward, culminating in a corporate war for talent. To win the war, organizations will need to be skilled at hiring and promoting people and even more importantly, be able to keep others from stealing their talent.

In today's economy, baby boomers with significant business experience are beginning to retire at a rapid rate. This is creating a major imbalance between talent leaving and entering organizations. The emerging workforce is much different demographically from that of the past, and organizations are faced with enormous challenges in back-filling positions and succession planning. The success of organizations rests on the speed at which they can transform their people into intelligent, flexible, multi-skilled resources.

For best organizations, their future is all about creating a learning organization that can withstand constant change and can truly focus on continuous improvement and continuous success—collectively for the enterprise, and individually to the people who actively and openly contribute to the success.

Long-Range Investment Plans

Best organizations are not reactive and all over the map. They have well thought out long-range investment plans to develop new products, purchase new equipment, expand global markets, acquire other organizations, or invest in improvements to their business. Best organizations also have the financial strength and stability to invest in their futures. Long-range investment plans communicate strong messages about the future of organizations. At any given time, they may be missing the organizational skill sets to execute on their plans. Best organizations achieve their long-range investment plans by recognizing the importance of organizational development. During the past decade, organizations have morphed into transformational companies where there is a higher dependence on people, information, and decision making for success.

Social Responsibility

Social responsibility is commonly described by its promoters as aligning a company's activities with the social, economic, and environmental expectations of stakeholders. Social responsibility is a corporate commitment to improve community well-being through discretionary business practices and contributions of corporate resources. In several instances, social responsibility has become a multibillion-dollar public relations career specialty in the business world as public relations work diligently to cover the tails of fast food chains, the tobacco and alcoholic beverage industries, and most recently, Toyota's damage control commercials.

For the most part, social responsibility is a well-intended best practice in many best organizations. The Timberland Company is an extraordinary example of an organization walking the talk of social responsibility. Timberland implements this commitment through a series of community service activities in local government, day care centers, food banks, local ASPCAs, etc. At national sales meetings, participants leave their golf clubs at home to spend time on selected local community service activities. Timberland is one of the greatest social responsibility organizations and a great employer.

The attributes of best organizations provide the foundation for the title of this chapter—*launch with the best in mind*. The purpose of the previous information was to increase awareness about the link between *developing the best* and *having the best* to deliver in organizations. Many executives are still living with the repercussions of the economic meltdown and are reacting to many short-term issues with a multitude of directions. These executives have their organizations running around with their hair on fire, and the effect is demoralization and moving their organizations backward.

The largest investment in building a best organization is the emotional commitment of leadership. In the new economy, the cost of this decision is significantly less than the growing hidden inefficiencies and costs, and lost opportunities of failing to make this emotional commitment. Like any other investment, building a best organization requires time, patience, the right people, the right processes, the right actions, and the right measurement systems.

Empowerment and Engagement

As mentioned earlier, empowerment is a misused word that has been casually thrown around in association with fad improvement programs. Organizations wish to empower their people, but they do not have the proper structure and disciplines in place to make empowerment a normal behavior. Figure 8.4 provides a simplified diagram of empowerment.

From an executive and leadership perspective, empowerment is giving away power, authority, and accountability because:

- A sense of trust and mutual respect exists in the relationship

Empowerment

What is the true meaning?

Giving away power	Accepting power
• Trust	• Trust
• Mutual respect	• Mutual respect
• Faith that the recipient will act correctly and responsibly in an empowered state	• Skill and teaming competencies
• Power is "imaginary" for a single individual in an organization	• Responsible in actions and getting results
	• Willingness to share power, collaborate to achieve synergy and breakthrough results

Figure 8.4   Engagement and empowerment.

* There is complete faith that the recipient can and will act responsibly in an empowered state.

From the empowered perspective, empowerment is receiving power, authority, and accountability because:

* A sense of trust and mutual respect exists for the leader
* There exists both a desire and a capability to use skill sets and act responsibly to achieve objectives
* There is a willingness to share power, collaborate, and deliver results

What is the purpose of this empowerment discussion? Organizations have talked a good game concerning empowerment for the last thirty years, and they are still trying to get it right.

In the new economy, high-performance teams require on-the-spot high-performance people and rapid, high-performance results. In today's global arena, the lifecycle of teams is short and targeted. Empowerment is a necessity for best organizations that leverage the full strength of their people. Empowerment is also a necessity for organizations striving for best, or even for survival. Yet empowerment is impossible without the unwavering long-term commitment of human capital competency development.

The future belongs to executives and their people interested in learning, developing, and deploying new skills to challenging scenarios, and process innovation in general. For those who are through with learning and wish for things to stay the same, it is the end of the line. Organizations have run out of time to focus on small evolutionary improvement. These improvements are gradual, linear, sequential, and predictable within an existing business model of paradigm. The problem with evolutionary improvement today is that it is often slow, transparent to customers, and easily duplicated by competitors.

The new economy demands revolutionary improvement, which is geared toward breakthroughs and cultural transformation. Revolutionary improvement can be made predictable to people inside the organization through proper planning, deployment, and execution. Revolutionary improvement is no longer disruptive, and it can be achieved with the simplicity of evolutionary improvement with the right implementation architecture and best organization attributes in place.

Crafting a Learning Culture

The Fifth Discipline was written by Peter Senge in 1990. This book explored the need for organizations to become learning organizations to remain competitive.

> *Learning Organizations are organizations where people continually expand their capacity to create the results they truly desire, where new and expansive patterns of thinking are nurtured, where collective aspiration is set free, and where people are continually learning to see the whole together. The basic rationale for such organizations is that in situations of rapid change only those that are flexible, adaptive and productive will excel. For this to happen, it is argued, organizations need to discover how to tap people's commitment and capacity to learn at all levels. While all people have the capacity to learn, the structures in which they have to function are often not conducive to reflection and engagement. Furthermore, people may lack the tools and guiding ideas to make sense of the situations they face. Organizations that are continually expanding their capacity to create their future require a fundamental shift of mind among their members.*

> (Peter Senge, 1990)

Peter Senge was only 20 years before his time. At that time, a number of criticisms about the practicality of learning organizations surfaced. Some argued that within a capitalist system, Senge's vision of companies and organizations turning wholehearted to the cultivation of the learning of their members could evolve in only a few special instances. Others argued that learning organizations run counter to most companies where the bottom line is profit and time horizons are quarterly performance. In this environment the learning and development of employees and associates is simply too idealistic. On the other hand, many organizations took Peter Senge's advice and have gained significantly from becoming a learning organization. Organizations such as GE, UPS, Amazon, IBM, Disney, Microsoft, Shell Oil, Harley Davidson, and many others have institutionalized organizational learning as part of their culture.

Learning organizations are a necessity in the new economy. It is time to go back and dust off *The Fifth Discipline* because the contents are (for the most part) relevant to the challenges of today. Collaborative knowledge and development is necessary for visible challenges and for the challenges that are yet to be seen in this new economy.

Talent Management Matters

The greatest product line or financial strength is not always sufficient to sustain an organization's success over decades. In the new economy, talented employees and innovation are the differentiating factors. Technology and knowledge continues to replace physical human work, and this trend will only accelerate in the future. Organizations need the right organizational and talent-development policies and the best people to deliver on their strategic goals and objectives. Organizations that have invested in strategic improvement and talent development through this recent economic trauma are emerging much stronger than their *penny wise, pound foolish* counterparts (that chose to put a *freeze* on improvement and development). Intelligent organizations have the developed talent pool to control their business destiny, rather than hang around floundering or waiting for other competitors to control it for them.

Now that the critical foundations of organizational development and talent management have been mentioned, it is time to become more tactical about the Lean Six Sigma deployment. When we talk about launching with the best in mind, we are referring to the combination of best strategy (leadership, strategy, and vision), best structure (deployment planning), best processes and practices (execution), best people, best technology, and best metrics. Best actions create best practices and best results. Launching with the best in mind is covered throughout this book. Best strategy is covered in Chapter 4, and best structure is covered in Chapters 5 through 8. The conclusion of this chapter sheds more light on the resourcing and initial deployment details.

Best People

The Macro Charter referred to in Chapter 5 has a *resource selection* tab. Within this tab are the skills assessment matrix (see Figure 8.5) that evaluates the relative strengths and potential of proposed participants in a Lean Six Sigma deployment. This matrix evaluates individuals against nine project skills factors and one growth-potential factor. The golden rule of Lean Six Sigma and strategic improvement in general is to staff the initiative with the best people, but also recognize that *best* is attribute data. This increases the odds for success, and provides

Lean Six Sigma Skills Assessment Tool

Candidate Names	Skills Score	1 Team Facilitating	2 Analytical Problem-Solving	3 Objectivity & Process Orientation	4 Change Facilitation	5 Interpersonal Communication Skills	6 IT, Excel, Knowledge	7 Program & Project Mngmt	8 Analyze Costs & ROI	9 Business Process Knowledge	10 Talent Potential
Selection Criteria → WEIGHT >		10	10	10	10	10	10	10	10	10	10
MINIMUM >		7	8	7	6	7	6	6	5	5	5
Bob Lehman	510	5	6	5	6	5	7	5	8	4	6
John Smith	560	5	6	4	7	3	6	5	5	7	8
Christine Williams	880	8	9	8	9	8	9	9	9	9	10
John Bender	830	9	7	9	8	6	8	9	9	8	10
Richard Hertz	710	7	7	6	7	8	6	8	6	7	9
Sally LaPalme	800	8	8	8	8	9	8	7	8	7	9
John McKrill	590	6	6	6	6	6	7	6	7	5	4
Mike Jones	400	4	4	4	3	4	4	3	3	4	7
Scott Claywell	710	6	7	6	7	6	7	8	7	8	9
Larry Bonner	720	6	7	6	7	6	7	8	7	9	9
Amanda Griggs	640	5	5	5	6	7	6	7	8	7	8
Ben Burton	640	6	6	6	7	6	5	7	8	6	7
Sandra White	780	6	7	7	8	7	8	9	9	8	9
Tim Hardwig	620	6	6	6	6	6	6	6	6	6	8
John Lawson	750	7	7	7	8	7	8	7	7	8	9
Craig Allen	700	9	9	9	9	9	4	4	4	4	9
Roger Marconi	700	6	7	6	6	6	8	7	7	8	9
Richard Caldwell	610	7	6	7	7	7	6	4	4	4	9

RATE 1-10 According to Skills Proficiency Level Definitions

Figure 8.5 Skills assessment matrix.

growth opportunities for these future leaders. This practice also sends a clear message that the organization is committed to, and serious about, this initiative.

There is a risk that in the event that commitment wavers or drops off, the organization's best people will feel the disappointment of leadership's decision not to stick with improvement long-term. Some organizations have staffed their deployments with a combination of good people and underperforming people in hopes of pulling up the low performers. Their rationale has been that their best people are too busy with more important things.

Occasionally, one of these underperforming people rises to the occasion and surprises everyone with their efforts. Some people with potential have been left in one place in the organization for too long because they are the resident tribal knowledge expert. There is another risk here of allowing the underperformers who really are low performers to drag down the good performers. The main point here is that staffing a Lean Six Sigma deployment with inexperienced, mediocre, or disloyal resources just because they have time will put an organization on the road to failure.

Organizations must make the effort to staff their deployments consistent with organizational learning and development and talent management goals. Staffing a deployment is not an exact science or a binary choice effort. A good practitioner's rule of thumb here is to seek out the people with great attitudes, and then develop their talents via the deployment. Successful Lean Six Sigma deployments are resourced with the best leaders, best team participants, and best executive sponsors. Beyond improvement, a successful Lean Six Sigma deployment is a great talent-development opportunity. People with a strong internalized mindset for improvement are usually successful in every situation or role in the organization.

Best Approach

Best approach is arrived at through the activities in the Macro Charter and in particular, the project definition and project chartering activity. Best approach includes best-defined objectives and scope, best work plan, best thinking, best use of limited resources (team members), best use of limited time, and best use of limited capacity. Best approach requires time and effort up front, but saves 10 times the effort during the project.

There is no question that projects can and should be better scoped prior to assigning them to teams. The absence of strategy and structure not only places the deployment at risk, but also generates negative forces with people. This is a good time during the reading of this book for organizations to rethink the details of their Lean Six Sigma deployments. For some, the reluctance of people to engage in another improvement initiative should become clear. Great deployments can get additional and expedited results, and stalled deployments have the opportunity to become great deployments.

Where Is My Executive Sponsor?

A major enabler that accelerates a new team to a high-performance team is an engaged executive sponsor. Specific roles of the executive sponsor were discussed in Chapter 5. The best executive sponsors are those individuals who have actually led a project, used the DMAIC methodology, and successfully deployed the right improvement tools. These individuals lead from a superior position of strength because they are leading from direct experience and knowledge. There is a big difference between experiential leadership and intellectual leadership with respect to the executive sponsor role. Executive sponsors guide and mentor the team leader and the team to strive for best practices. In deployments this is a weekly activity. The executive sponsor asks the right questions, reviews progress and factual data, and makes sure that the team is following the proven DMAIC methodology. *Best* includes launching with the best, and delivering the best breakthrough process and best financial results.

Effective executive sponsors bring out the best in team leaders and teams when they encourage them to think outwardly and are outcome focused. This may include asking questions such as:

- How can we sense and prevent problems before they occur?
- What would zero changeover time look like and what would it enable us to achieve?
- How do we achieve instantaneous feedback and corrective action?
- What would it take to close the books in one day each month?
- How would we achieve a real-time quotation process?
- What are the conditions and indicators of process excellence?

In short, executive sponsors are the organization's frontline leaders in a successful Lean Six Sigma deployment.

Best includes both developing the best and putting up the best. These conditions are inseparable, and it is difficult to have the latter conditions without the prior conditions. The notion of best is similar to improvement—no matter what level an organization reaches, they can always do better. Improvement organizations must continue to strive for best, because the lifecycle of best is much shorter in this economy, and the definition of best continues to evolve.

Best today is probably equal to average or needs improvement two years from now. Best will continue to be a scenario that more organizations strive for, and as they are successful, the notion of *best* as we know it today will no longer be a competitive differentiator. Hopefully, the advice of this chapter will help your organization move toward the front of the best-in-class curve.

References

Boone, L. E., and Kurtz, D. L. 2011. *Contemporary Business 13th Edition 201 Update*. John Wiley and Sons, Hoboken, NJ.

Flood, R. L. 1999. *Rethinking the Fifth Discipline: Learning within the Unknowable.* Routledge Publishing, London.

Porta, M., House, B., Buckley, L., and Blitz, A. 2009. *Value 2.0: Eight New Rules for Creating and Capturing Value from Innovative Technologies.* The IBM Institute for Business Value.

Ringo, T., Schweyer, A., DeMarco, M., Jones, R., and Lesser, E. 2009. *Integrated Talent Management: Turning Talent Management into a Competitive Advantage.* The IBM Institute for Business Value.

SAP. 2009. *Time to Change: New Thoughts on Supporting Business Change Fast and Flexibly.* White paper. SAP AG.

Senge, P. M. 1990. *The Fifth Discipline: The Art & Practice of the Learning Organization.* Doubleday, NY.

Sullivan, J. 2005. *The Top 25 Benchmark Firms in Recruiting and Talent Management.* www.ere.net (accessed June 26, 2010).

Chapter 8 Take Aways

- When we talk about launching with the best in mind, we are referring to the combination of best strategy (leadership, strategy, and vision), best structure (deployment planning), best processes (execution), best people, best technology, and best metrics. Best actions create best practices and best results.

- *Best* assumes that an organization has the best of everything to put into a Lean Six Sigma deployment because they have been investing in developing the best leadership, people, and culture.

- *Best* includes both developing the best and putting up the best. These conditions are inseparable, and it is difficult to have the latter conditions without the prior conditions. The notion of best is similar to improvement: no matter what level an organization reaches, they can always do better. The golden rule of Lean Six Sigma and strategic improvement in general is to staff the initiative with the best people. This increases the odds for success, and provides growth opportunities for these future leaders. This practice also sends a clear message that the organization is committed and serious about this initiative. Innovation is necessary in the creation of new adaptive business models and processes, products, and services that are faster and more pleasing than the competition's. Traditional business models, processes, and information systems have been built to be as efficient and effective as possible, but the ability to quickly adapt to changing scenarios has not traditionally been a top requirement. New business models and processes must be fluid yet formal.

- Great organizations take advantage of emerging technologies, which enable a new level of customer intimacy by changing the way enterprises connect, communicate, and build solid customer relationships. These organizations are moving from merely knowing the customer to truly embracing the customer through more predictive and preventive sense-interpret-decide-act-monitor business models.

- Talent management is a process of aligning resources and skill sets to business needs. *Best* organizations recognize the importance of talent management in the new economy because the need for change is challenging the capabilities of many organizations to respond successfully to change. The success of organizations rests on the speed at which they can transform their people into flexible, multiskilled people.

- The new economy is demanding different types of leaders with a broader perspective and range of qualities. For organizations to succeed, they will need to understand what key leadership behaviors and practices are paramount in driving their organization toward mass-collaboration, business improvement, and growth. This is much more than just getting people to make the right decisions and produce the right outcomes. It is about getting people to be committed to the organization and passionate about their work, and to foster a personal desire to grow and handle the challenges ahead. The best organizations have already figured this out and are busy implementing and executing positive change.

- The future belongs to organizations that develop their competencies in attracting, acquiring, developing, and retaining talent. Collaborative knowledge and development is necessary for visible challenges, and for the challenges that are yet to be seen in this new economy.

Guest Article Contribution

Susan S. Underhill serves as vice president of Hewlett-Packard's Certification and Partner Learning Organization with global responsibility for development operations and worldwide marketing of certification and learning solutions across the breadth of HP's product, services, and solutions portfolio. Her organization provides valuable training and accreditation to both HP's partners and customers helping to ensure greater return on their IT investments. In addition, Susan leads the HP Learning Channel, an efficient global network of authorized training centers that provide local accessibility to high-quality partner training. Susan's team manages a growing, global community of 325,000 certified professionals and over 250,000 channel partners, keeping them current on the latest HP technologies and solutions.

Prior to her current role, Susan led the Americas Systems Integrator & Alliances team for HP Software. Before joining HP in 2000, Susan held several executive channel sales and marketing positions with leading technology companies including Bluestone Software, RSA Security, Skytel, and Lotus Development. She began her high-tech career opening and running ComputerLand centers.

A Recent Interview with Susan S. Underhill,

VP of Certification and Partner Learning,

Hewlett-Packard Company

Tell Me About Your Role at HP

As vice president of Hewlett-Packard's Certification and Partner Learning Organization, I have the global responsibility for strategy, development, operations and worldwide marketing of certification and learning solutions across the breadth of HP's product, services, and enterprise solutions portfolio. My organization provides valuable training and accreditation to both HP's partners and customers, helping to ensure a greater return on their IT investments. In addition, I lead the HP Learning Channel—an efficient global network of authorized training centers that provides local accessibility to high-quality partner training. My team manages a growing, global community of 325,000 certified professionals employed by our customers and channel partners, keeping them current on the latest HP technologies and solutions.

Why Is Global Certification and Partner Learning Important to HP?

Global certification and partner learning is a term that we use internally to refer to the team of people who develop and manage a broad range of programs and initiatives that touch, literally, hundreds of thousands of HP partners, customers, and employees around the world. Rather than talk about this team, I am going to describe how certification and partner learning contribute to not only HP's success, but the success of our channel partners and customers as well.

Let's start with certification. At its most basic level, certification is about competency—the combination of knowledge and skills to be able to perform a job well. In any profession, the more competent a person is at his or her job, the more likely that his or her projects will be successful and will provide a meaningful contribution to the greater good of the organization. Hiring managers for companies use certifications as a benchmark to understand what knowledge and skills a person brings to a position, and to put together teams of people that complement each other.

HP certification ensures that a person is competent to lead or participate in a successful IT-oriented project; for example, to virtualize the IT infrastructure that allows a company to be much more flexible with its business applications.

But HP doesn't stop at the single individual; we offer families of credentials built around a specific topic that help to foster and empower entire teams. I will give you an example. HP has a wide range of solutions that are sold through our channel partners, who in effect represent HP. We require our channel partners to prove their competency by having a certain number of HP certified professionals on staff in different roles. For instance, an HP accredited sales consultant would have the knowledge and skills to gather a customer's business requirements and recommend an appropriate HP solution that will meet those needs. He is assisted by an HP accredited presales consultant who can design a solution with the proper hardware and software configuration. Then, an HP accredited integration specialist would install the solution and ensure that it is working as the customer needs it to work. An accredited systems engineer has the expertise to integrate this solution with others that the customer may already have in place. Using four different credentials, HP has helped our channel partner to build a highly competent team that takes the sale from start to finish, and takes the customer from problem to opportunity.

This is clearly a win-win-win situation for customers, partners, and HP. The customer gets a solution that addresses his business needs, and he gets it faster and with fewer problems. The channel partner is able to sell more sophisticated solutions at a better profit. HP knows that we have a satisfied customer, and of course, we benefit from the sale that was transacted by professionals who are not directly on our payroll.

Partner learning can be, but is not necessarily, tied to certification. We often want to educate our channel partners without putting them through the process of passing an exam, or a set of exams, to prove their competency. For example, when we introduce new products and solutions to market, we provide training to our partners so they can learn how these new solutions can address customers' needs. This type of training might include *how* to sell in addition to *what* to sell. Partner learning is important to HP in that we want our partners to lead with the best possible solutions for our mutual customers. And it is important to partners so they can stay ahead of their competition and be true consultants to their customers.

Was HP Doing This Before the Economic Meltdown, or Is This a New Initiative?

Partner learning and certification have a deep history at HP, dating back at least two decades. We have always felt that it is important to provide and validate the skills and knowledge of our employees, customers, and partners. The state of the economy does not change the fact that we need well-trained people with proven expertise in IT.

What Are the Risks If HP Chooses To Do Everything on Their Own?

In the past few years, HP has built a worldwide network of training centers that we call *authorized training centers* (ATCs). These training partners are independent companies that meet a high threshold of requirements to be able to deliver HP-developed training. These ATCs are critically important to HP in that they allow us to meet the global demand for training, delivered in a local fashion.

It would be far too costly for HP to attempt to deliver all of our training without these partners. Many ATCs also provide training in complementary technologies, such as Microsoft operating systems or VMWare virtual technologies. HP leverages the ATCs' facilities and expertise at a significantly lower cost than if we had to do it on our own. This increases HP's reach and lowers our costs.

We also use third-party leverage in our certification program. Some of our advanced certifications require our candidates to have in-depth knowledge that can be developed outside of the HP certification program. For example, we leverage certifications from Microsoft, Novell, VMWare, CompTIA, and other vendors so that we do not have to develop non-HP content within our own courses. Again, it comes back to increasing our reach while keeping down our costs. Our certification candidates like leveraging the other certifications they have already earned, too.

What Is HP's Specific Talent Management and Talent Development Strategies?

I will tell you about our external talent management and talent development strategies. The development of internal personnel is not within the scope of my job. But when you think about it, every time my team trains or certifies a channel partner or a customer, it is like we are developing an off-payroll advocate for HP. In that sense, we *are* developing talent for HP, even though these people do not wear an HP badge. In fact, most of the training and all of the certifications for partners and customers are the same as what is available for HP employees.

In terms of talent development, we offer several paths that correspond to job roles that people have; specifically, sales, presales, technical integration, systems administration, and hardware support. Within each of those job roles, we offer several levels of certification, so someone can start at an entry-level position and work up to becoming more of an expert. We outline the path to get from Point A to Point B, provide the training, and then provide a wide range of tools and resources for that certified professional to use in his job.

HP is doing something that I think is totally unique in the IT industry today. Most IT vendors, including HP, offer certifications focused on a single technology or product—for example, storage solutions. That is fine, but we have observed that people who only hold single-focus certifications tend to work in a silo. So, someone who holds a storage certification is, by default, the storage person. Likewise, you have the server person, and the networking person, and so on.

But silos are inhibitors to business. An enterprise that wants to do amazing things needs workers that go far beyond their silos. Through HP's new converged infrastructure certifications, we are broadening a person's knowledge and expertise to span all of the major technologies of the enterprise datacenter—storage, servers, networking—everything that is needed to build a flexible IT infrastructure. Now, the storage person also has a good understanding of the other components of the data center and can help to reconfigure the infrastructure to respond to immediate business needs. No other IT vendor is putting all the knowledge and skills together in one training and certification development path to create the talent that is needed for tomorrow.

How Do You See Global Certification and Partner Learning Evolving at HP?

We are, in fact, evolving our program to make it much more responsive to customers' needs. We are building more training courses and more certifications that help develop the broadened skills I mentioned earlier. We will still have our product-focused certifications, but every person taking our foundational courses will learn how everything fits together in the converged infrastructure. We will help develop workers who are much more valuable because they will understand the larger IT picture and not just a niche product or technology.

What Advice Would You Offer to Other Organizations Relative to Strategic Partnering?

Partnering with other companies is absolutely the way to go. By leveraging their assets and resources, you can focus on the pieces that you do best and spend less money to get to where you want to be.

9

Accelerator #6: Provide Strong, Extensive Mentoring Support

Accelerator #6, strong mentoring support (see Figure 9.1), is the most important activity in a Lean Six Sigma deployment. Not surprisingly, it is also the most time and resource consuming activity. This is the *rubber on the road* accelerator, where opportunities and plans are transformed into real change (improvement) and tangible results. Unfortunately, mentoring is often viewed as a simple short-term activity that every black belt inherently knows how to do and should do, and improvement initiatives suffer from the lack of strong mentoring support. When a black belt mentors an improvement team, there is no guarantee that he has solid mentoring skills. For the most part, mentoring skills have been limited only to mentoring on the use of the tools—the insignificant part of Lean Six Sigma and improvement in general. Going through black belt certification prepares an individual for the most entry-level aspects of strategic improvement.

Mentoring Expertise Does Not Come with a Belt

Let us return to a discussion of Lean Six Sigma mentioned previously. During the last decade, organizations have spent billions of dollars on Lean and Six Sigma training. The large training firms all marketed their *train-the-masses* black belt programs as the methodology for achieving success with Lean, Six Sigma, and Lean Six Sigma. Those that did not understand Lean peddled stand-alone Six Sigma certification. Those who did not understand Six Sigma peddled Lean certification. Those that recognized that both Lean and Six Sigma were compatible and necessary promoted Lean Six Sigma certification. In all situations, the training firms placed all the emphasis on mastering the tools and

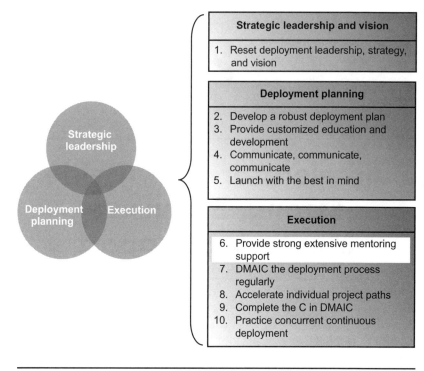

Figure 9.1   Elements of execution.

certification. Organizations were sold this promise of success through training the masses and belts.

Education and organizational development are a critical part of Lean Six Sigma success, but it is not the ultimate objective. A few years back, it was mind-blowing to observe how much organizations relied on individuals with belts as the answer to business improvement. A belt became the *punched ticket* to entry for most organizations that were hiring improvement resources. Demand and compensation for master black and black belts went through the roof as people jumped ship after their certification to take a higher paying position in another company. Many of these inexperienced belts joined the large training and consulting organizations. It was a false expectation to believe that an individual with a belt could be lowered into the organization and make a dramatic difference. Lean or Six Sigma certification focused on training individuals on a narrow set of improvement tools. Some of these individuals had strong prior background and experiences, and they were able to make a big difference with the addition of Lean Six Sigma certification. But the majority of belts are missing the most important leadership, experience, and knowledge skill sets of strategic improvement. Furthermore, their organizations are missing the enabling leadership and infrastructure core competencies for Lean Six Sigma success. This has become a repeating pattern of massive education followed by hopes and wishes for instant gratification improvement. Today, the majority of people with belts are not actively engaged in strategic improvement and root cause problem solving.

Organizations have been trying to get teaming and empowerment right for the past thirty years. A deep dive into this situation reveals that organizations have endorsed the mechanics of teaming but, for one reason or another, have not nurtured the human drama, knowledge gaps, and relational aspects of teams. The mechanics of working in a team are simple, but emotional intelligence along with the leadership, behavioral, developmental, and knowledge factors determine team performance. Effective mentoring expertise does not come wrapped in a black belt. Going through the mechanics of define-measure-analyze-improve-control (DMAIC), the Lean and Six Sigma tools, and teaming are not enough for rapid deployment and rapid results. The leadership and behavioral issues come in when the need arises for executive coaching and adjustment, technical team help and development, performance and feedback, barrier and conflict resolution, process owner and organizational consensus, and dealing with other team dynamics or political situations. The knowledge issues come in when executives and teams do not fully understand business processes, the interrelationships of key business processes, how to adapt Lean Six Sigma to nonstandard problem situations, or how to remain on the critical path to success.

Effective and well-executed mentoring has been missing in many Lean Six Sigma deployments. Many of the leadership, behavioral, and knowledge issues have been allowed to remain open with indecision. The consequence is that team performance is diminished as they struggle with these issues on their own, and improvement is usually short lived. Emotional intelligence helps organizations learn, recognize, adapt, and manage the relational situations with Lean Six Sigma. Leveraged mentoring—helping and nurturing teams to grow beyond knowledge of the tools and take responsibility for working through all aspects of their projects to a successful conclusion—is what creates the personal discovery moments, develops real talent, changes culture, and accelerates the pace and sustainability of improvement.

In the new economy, organizations that are interested in rapid deployment, rapid results, and sustainable continuous improvement can no longer afford the osmosis-based, on-the-job training of their belts. Success with strategic improvement initiatives requires a grasp of the voluminous and continuously evolving skills, knowledge, and experiences gained through leadership vision and strategy, deployment planning, and execution in a variety of organizations. Successful strategic improvement and the notion of Improvement Excellence™ is a core competency. The world is changing rapidly and much of the improvement progress made in organizations during the past five years are now obsolete or insufficient for the future. Global competitiveness combined with the recent meltdown has become a significant subtractive force against improvement, which makes the need for continuous improvement that much greater. At the same time, organizations must now focus on improving how they improve. We have built a compelling case that a different Lean Six Sigma deployment model is needed in this economy to achieve rapid deployment, rapid results, and sustainable continuous improvement. A different mentoring model is also needed to achieve different results. We refer to this mentoring model as leveraged mentoring.

Leveraged Mentoring

Deployments of the past have seriously underestimated the importance of mentoring. In the majority of situations, mentoring has been an afterthought or symbolic activity that the organization knows how to do on their own. Based on the recent 80 percent failure rates of Lean, Six Sigma, and Lean Six Sigma deployments, this is an area of the deployment process that needs improvement. Mentoring is the most important factor in the execution phase of Lean Six Sigma infrastructure, and many organizations have underestimated that importance. The resources and time consumed for mentoring represent more than 75 percent of successful Lean Six Sigma deployments, in contrast to less than 10 percent for training. Beyond the initial serious attention to mentoring is the approach to mentoring for longer-term success.

In the short term, there is a significant opportunity to reduce project completion cycle times and results, and develop people in the improvement methodologies and tools. This requires project leadership and mentoring by experienced professionals who have a thorough understanding of key business processes, a deep knowledge in leading and implementing large-scale business improvement, and several previous experiences with the same or similar projects. Leveraged mentoring is exactly what it says: leveraging the combined skills, knowledge, and experiences in a manner where improvement teams are allowed to develop and grow, while trying not to reinvent the wheel. Leveraged mentoring proactively manages the activities of integrated improvement teams while balancing the day-to-day concerns of the business with its broader strategic improvement needs. Figure 9.2 displays the elements of leveraged mentoring.

For the longer term, the objectives of leveraged mentoring reach far beyond mentoring a team and an improvement project. Leveraged mentoring involves teaching, coaching, mentoring, and developing people to teach, coach, mentor, and develop others in the organization. The larger objectives of leveraged mentoring are to act as the flywheel in building and developing a learning organization that is capable of achieving its strategic goals and Improvement Excellence™. Leveraged mentoring in a Lean Six Sigma deployment should not only achieve improvement project objectives, but begin to develop the next generation of leaders, managers, and employees. Leveraged mentoring is one of the *how* of talent management discussed in Chapter 8. Over time, leveraged mentoring grows into a much larger power of organizational trust, multidimensional learning and development, and collaborative teaching, coaching, and mentoring across the organization. Just as DMAIC becomes the accepted language and structure of improvement, the resultant behaviors from larger scale and repetitive leveraged

Figure 9.2 Leveraged mentoring.

mentoring become positive contributions to the organization's code of conduct. The following paragraphs describe the major elements of leveraged mentoring in greater detail.

Executive Industry Experience

The most important element of leveraged mentoring is executive industry experience. The reality here is that organizations, admittedly or not, are missing the core competency of Improvement Excellence™. When an organization embarks on a major strategic opportunity such as Lean Six Sigma, there is always the false sense of executive confidence in deciding how best to proceed with the deployment. Credit is due to executives for these decisions because the deployment must begin somewhere. However, a scant deployment launch can result in organizational confusion and a lot of lost time and opportunity. Before an organization thinks about specific project mentoring, the delicate process of executive mentoring and the development and infrastructure building must take place. This is the process of putting the first two major accelerator categories in place: strategic leadership and vision; and deployment planning. Three important attributes of the executive industry experience element of mentoring include:

1. *On demand*—The seasoned mentoring professional has established the right deployment measurement and feedback processes, and understands where and what type of mentoring is necessary at all times. They provide mentoring support as quickly as possible to resolve any issues, conflicts, or bottlenecks with the executive leadership team, executive sponsors, the deployment process, process owners, or teams and their individual projects.
2. *Leveraged*—The broader aspects of the deployment and individual projects benefit from the skills, knowledge, and implementation experiences of dozens of previous deployments and thousands of successfully completed projects.
3. *Targeted*—Mentoring is proactively provided based on continuously reaching out and identifying critical leadership, deployment, or project needs.

This element of leveraged mentoring also includes ongoing mentoring on broader executive and leadership issues related to the deployment such as ongoing commitment, communication, organizational development, conflict resolution, and performance management. Finally, this element of leveraged mentoring allows for the integration of improvement and culture change throughout the organization. Executive industry experience enables mentoring at all organizational levels on all of the *make-or-break* organizational and people issues of a deployment.

Lean Six Sigma Experience

This element of leveraged mentoring is straightforward. This includes mentoring on the DMAIC methodology and specific improvement tools of Lean Six Sigma and broader knowledge and experiences with other strategic improvement methodologies and approaches. An important factor in this area is the ability to help improvement teams understand opportunities well enough to select and deploy the correct improvement tools. Too often, this process tends to be a misguided teaming effort where improvement tools are either restricted or naively applied in hopes of finding a solution. Improvement teams waste valuable time and resources in their inexperienced journey through DMAIC, and a trainer limited to the mechanics of Minitab or the tools themselves is not of much help. Narrow experience increases the risk of the *right-data, wrong-tool, wrong-answer* problem. Knowledge and proven expertise of the methodology and tools are essential, but the more important ability is in mentoring on the deployment of the right improvement tools to the right opportunities in a project. Another critical factor here is creativity and innovation in applying the philosophy and intent of Lean

Six Sigma to the high-impact, enterprise-wide transactional processes. In retrospect, there has been too much tunnel-vision mentoring by improvement consultants focused on the mechanics of the process and the tools themselves. The new economy is a new world, and Lean Six Sigma, or improvement in general, requires new thinking and new deployment best practices.

Business Process Improvement Experience

This element of mentoring is often overlooked. In many deployments, the same individuals teaching the mechanics of Minitab and the improvement tools end up mentoring improvement teams. Most of these individuals are less experienced on information technology and business process knowledge than the team they are mentoring. Add ego into the equation and the mentoring may well end up directing the team down the wrong road. Business process improvement experience includes deep expertise and knowledge of business processes, and experience in analyzing and improving these complicated and multistaged transactional processes. This experience is invaluable in mentoring and managing conflicting objectives to improving particular business processes. Areas such as new product development or sales and operations planning must balance the needs of sales, marketing, finance, engineering, manufacturing, and the supply chain while meeting or exceeding ultimate customer requirements. This element of leveraged mentoring also recognizes the integration and interaction of business processes so that improvement teams can avoid suboptimized improvement—improvements in one localized area that may negatively affect the end-to-end business process. For example, some Lean zealots promote the notion of unplugging IT and managing the business visually with manual kanban cards. This system worked well for Toyota fifty years ago, but it is impossible to manage a system like this in real time, synchronized across the total supply chain. Another example is many of the mundane tasks such as BOM, packaging and document specifications, CAD changes, or design reviews in new product development that often get postponed only to create serious customer and supplier issues down the road. Business process improvement knowledge and expertise is a major factor in accelerating projects and the overall deployment.

External Best Practices Experience

This is another overlooked element of mentoring. Organizations have plowed full speed ahead with their Lean Six Sigma deployments with little input on best practices, and on how to discover and architect their own best practices for their own environments. Rather, the common practice has been to quickly copy and emulate the surface-level practices of other well-publicized Lean Six Sigma deployments, but many of these approaches are short lived and ineffective.

In a single organization, it takes years of continued involvement, dozens of projects, and a broad array of interpersonal experiences before a black belt is prepared to serve as a serious improvement leader. This experience is not best practices experience, but merely internal improvement experience. During even the most aggressive process of *nose-to-the-ground* improvement, it is possible to miss out on how other organizations are dealing with the competitive pressures—especially in this economy. The seasoned external mentoring professional not only obtains the voluminous and continuously evolving skills, knowledge, and experiences gained through a variety of organizations, but they are also often the Lean Six Sigma best practices architects in these organizations. They collaborate with many other external organizations and have a more complete data set of best and emerging business improvement opportunities and practices. They also gain valuable experiences through porting and adapting of best practices across various industries and cultures. In short, they are actively engaged in improvement 100 percent of the time. This element of leveraged mentoring helps improvement teams strive for the best, with some inclination of how to achieve best.

We wish to clarify a potential misunderstanding about leveraged mentoring. This mentoring approach leverages the combined skills, knowledge, and experiences in a manner where improvement teams are allowed to develop and grow without reinventing the wheel. In practice, there is a delicate balance between coaching and mentoring, and giving a team their orders. Directing a team's every move undermines the development and success of the team, where leveraged mentoring strengthens the knowledge, experiences, and capabilities of the team. Leveraged mentoring lets the team know that they are fully empowered, fully supported, and bound for a successful outcome. It is a different and much more professional approach than dictating directions and instructions to teams.

The following story is an example of ineffective leveraged mentoring: prior to a recent deployment, an organization hired a deployment leader solely for their black belt status. The leadership of this organization was sold on the need for their own resident black belt before the deployment began. They had no knowledge of a black belt's roles, responsibilities, or interpersonal skill set requirements in their unionized environment, but they knew for sure that they needed one. The vice president who they were in the process of terminating played a major role in the hiring process, and was attracted to someone with his own qualities. They hired a deployment leader who came from a *kick-butt-take-names* command and control culture. As it turned out, this individual earned their black belt certification of from one of those accelerated *fly-by-night* Six Sigma training courses, had questionable experience and knowledge with the basics of Lean and Six Sigma, never heard of Minitab, and became severely combative when challenged about their supposed background and expertise. Great . . . the organization has an arrogant know-it-all deployment leader with limited business experience and little interest in listening to others or facilitating a team spirit (but has the belt). The new deployment leader rejected any deployment approach that differed from the well-publicized big-bang, top-down, train-the-masses approach, and constantly meddled in team meetings, talked down to team members, mandated the use of templates from a previous employer, steered their progress in circles and then fixed the blame on the team for nonperformance. However, this individual was much more polished in executive reviews and had a reason, corrective action, and schedule laid out for everything. This deployment leader was blindly following a *mechanical* course of action while concealing the facts behind fancy PowerPoint presentations. The deployment was significantly reengineered, and the deployment leader was replaced with a more competent individual.

The organizational acceptance, enthusiasm, progress, and results began pouring in after a few weeks as if Dorothy threw a bucket of water on the wicked witch of the North. A big negative with Lean Six Sigma is that ineffective mentoring is more widespread in organizations than most are willing to admit. In fact, it is more the norm than the exception. There are many people with belts going through the motions, but they are not mentoring and growing people to be capable of mentoring others, and they certainly are not building this core competency of Improvement Excellence™ in their organizations. In all fairness to these individuals, they are working in the absence of leadership and infrastructure, and have not received the development opportunities to grow into great mentors.

There are three take aways from this short example: first, leveraged mentoring is a core competency based on skills, knowledge, and experiences developed over time and in a variety of mentoring situations. Second, the objectives of leveraged mentoring reach far beyond the improvement projects at hand and include any and all implementation issues across the enterprise. Third, beware—there are many black belts out there with their tickets punched, but who have questionable credentials, experience, and an unproven track record of improvement success.

DMAIC—The Mentoring Road Map

DMAIC is the accepted structured approach and universal language of improvement. DMAIC has a strong analogy to a roadmap or atlas, because in practice it becomes evident that the true benefit of DMAIC comes from the universal ability of people to follow a repeatable, proven approach to solving business problems. Over time, DMAIC becomes the standard communication protocol for improvement. On the surface, this seems quite logical, and this is the most powerful development within Lean Six Sigma. For the past three decades, the world of improvement has chosen to take a more nonstandard structure and branded approach to problem solving resulting in cycles of programs, confusion by the buzzwords, and disappointment with results.

The DMAIC methodology is not just a problem-solving process. DMAIC is the universal improvement language of the seasoned mentor, who is trying to install DMAIC as the common cultural standard and protocol for improvement in the organization. Following this structure, and coaching others about how to use this structure to their advantage, is a major enabler of Lean Six Sigma success. Like leveraged mentoring, DMAIC grows into something much larger and more powerful—it becomes the new way that people think, act, and work and breeds the expectation of the same in others in their organizations. The underlying philosophy of DMAIC and the power of fact-based, data-driven, root-cause problem solving is a tremendous competitive advantage in the new economy.

Successful mentoring is dependent on closely following the DMAIC methodology. DMAIC is not a simple recipe and it should not be limited to a linear problem solving framework. It is a conceptual structure that can be adapted to a wide array of problem-solving issues. The DMAIC methodology (see Figure 9.3) provides an effective structure and gate-keeping process of improvement with formal and deliberate checkpoints. The specific elements of each phase are not all used all of the time, but exist for practical application when their use is warranted. In the case of an atlas, not every page of the atlas is used for every trip. The pages used depend on the objectives and destination in mind. Likewise, in DMAIC, the specific steps and tools applied depend upon the specifics of the particular problem.

Additionally, similar to taking a trip, the secret to successfully completing the journey is to first understand where it is you want to go (define). Once the starting point is established, it becomes critical to characterize the problem and the process (measure). At this point, improvement teams define potential root-cause diagrams, value stream mapping, and other analyses that quantifies the current process and its associated baseline performance. Moving further into the DMAIC process, teams perform root-cause analysis and other analytics to diagnose and analyze the current process (analyze). At this point, the problem is more defined and better understood than it ever was before. The onion layers have been peeled back, and the true root causes are known and calibrated. Next is the point where improvement alternatives and options are evaluated (improve), and the best improvement course of action is decided on by the team. Last is the implementation of recommendations (control) and the handoff to process owners.

The DMAIC process is logical, and it is the lifeline of strategic improvement. Unfortunately, DMAIC and structured root-cause problem solving is the first casualty in times of crisis. Recently, one executive who experienced the power of DMAIC through a successful project commented, "This is definitely a better way to solve problems. We just don't have the time to follow DMAIC all of the time." As we have mentioned previously, this is symptomatic of a leadership problem and falls outside of the domain of Lean Six Sigma. It takes strong and seasoned mentoring to take DMAIC from a novel concept for a few teams to an accepted standard of behavior and logical thinking in organizations.

In practice, DMAIC is not a true linear process. Black and green belt candidates go through an official review and signoff for each phase. However, individuals often find themselves looping back to a previous phase to clarify forward direction or to conduct an additional analysis based on new information. The journey to Lean Six Sigma is more important than the destination itself. The reason for this is the fact that this journey, when planned and executed correctly, redefines and reinvents culture and organizational capabilities. DMAIC fundamentally changes the way people think, work, communicate, and interact with each other internally as well as externally with customers and suppliers. Later in

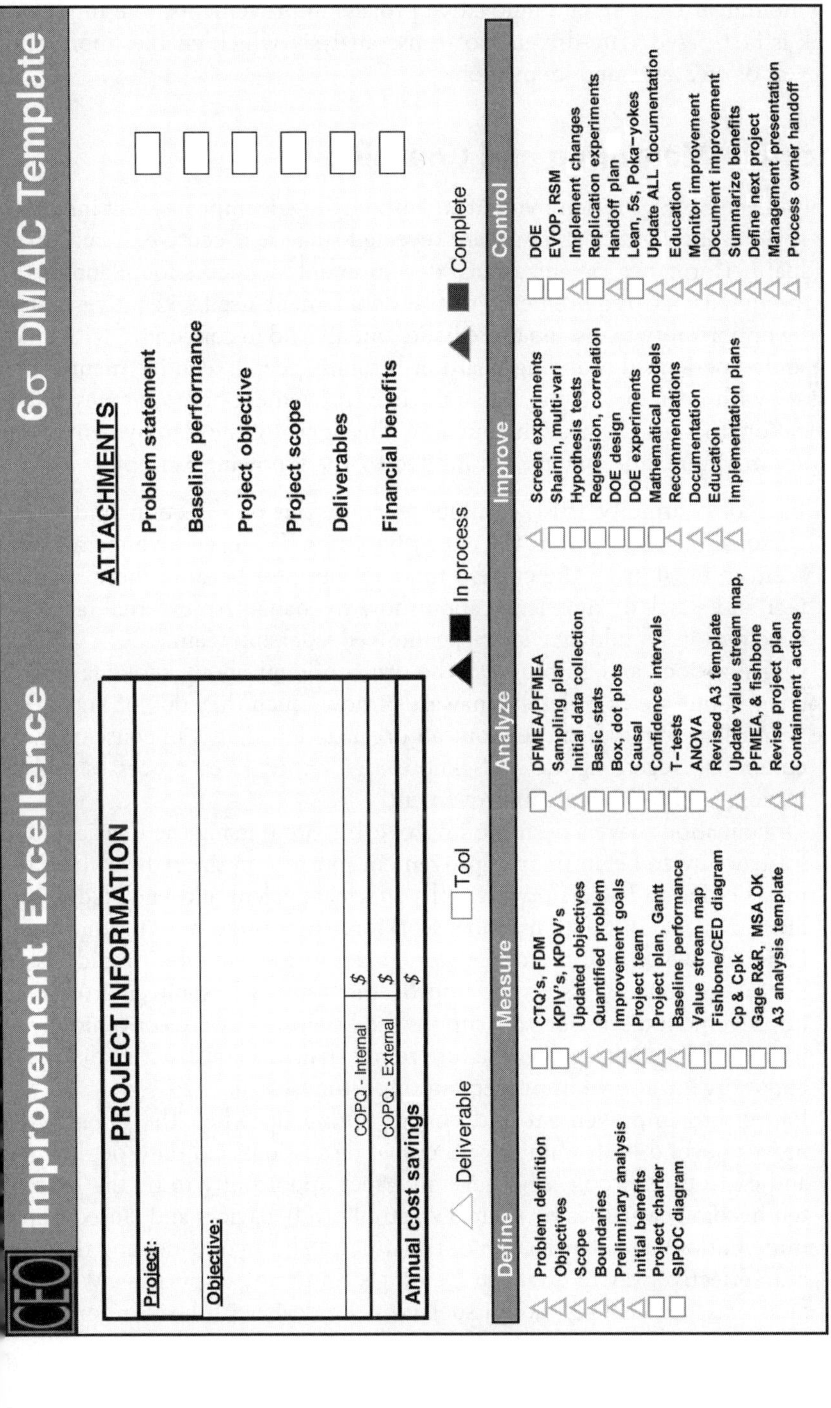

CEO Improvement Excellence — 6σ DMAIC Template

PROJECT INFORMATION

Project:

Objective:

COPQ - Internal	$
COPQ - External	$
Annual cost savings	$

△ Deliverable   □ Tool   ▲ In process   ■ Complete

ATTACHMENTS

- Problem statement
- Baseline performance
- Project objective
- Project scope
- Deliverables
- Financial benefits

Define
- Problem definition
- Objectives
- Scope
- Boundaries
- Preliminary analysis
- Initial benefits
- Project charter
- SIPOC diagram

Measure
- CTQ's, FDM
- KPIV's, KPOV's
- Updated objectives
- Quantified problem
- Improvement goals
- Project team
- Project plan, Gantt
- Baseline performance
- Value stream map
- Fishbone/CED diagram
- Cp & Cpk
- Gage R&R, MSA OK
- A3 analysis template

Analyze
- DFMEA/PFMEA
- Sampling plan
- Initial data collection
- Basic stats
- Box, dot plots
- Causal
- Confidence intervals
- T–tests
- ANOVA
- Revised A3 template
- Update value stream map,
  PFMEA, & fishbone
- Revise project plan
- Containment actions

Improve
- Screen experiments
- Shainin, multi-vari
- Hypothesis tests
- Regression, correlation
- DOE design
- DOE experiments
- Mathematical models
- Recommendations
- Documentation
- Education
- Implementation plans

Control
- DOE
- EVOP, RSM
- Implement changes
- Replication experiments
- Handoff plan
- Lean, 5s, Poka–yokes
- Update ALL documentation
- Education
- Monitor improvement
- Document improvement
- Summarize benefits
- Define next project
- Management presentation
- Process owner handoff

Figure 9.3 DMAIC methodology.

this chapter, we will provide information about how DMAIC can be applied to totally nonlinear creative and innovative process improvements. The fundamental link is fact-based, data-driven root-cause analysis, which enables more effective levels of creativity and innovation.

Executive Mentoring and Coaching

During a Lean Six Sigma deployment and other strategic improvement initiatives many related organizational issues are revealed such as executive commitment, individual performance, organizational development, or succession planning. Beyond the details and requirements of the deployment itself, executives benefit from the opportunity to discuss these issues openly and in confidence with an external and experienced sounding board or business peer. Executive mentoring is necessary with Lean Six Sigma and strategic improvement because many related organizational issues are brought out into the open by the deployment. Some examples might include, but are not limited to, the following examples:

- Lack of continuity, trust, confidence, consensus on direction, and serious personal conflicts within the executive team. The executive team cannot seem to break from the current mode of business because there is both a fear and a lack of knowledge about how to change. An external facilitator is helpful in rebuilding a strong, cohesive leadership team.
- Organizations and employees who are confident about knowing how to change, but are completely unaware of how much they do not know. This permeates activities throughout an organization that is unconsciously incompetent regarding the skills, knowledge, experiences, processes, and behaviors vital to strategic improvement.
- Organizations have a desire to improve, but are missing the inertia and infrastructure to begin their improvement journey on the right course. This may be due to leadership strengths and fears, talent and knowledge gaps, organizational distractions, and a workforce that is too busy to improve.
- Political, ownership, and other barriers get in the way of a candid discussion about strategic issues and improvement needs. In some environments improvement discussions are suppressed because they are conveniently interpreted as an admission of failure rather than as a constructive discussion about organizational improvement opportunities.
- Barriers to improvement and change spring up when the organization moves beyond both training and casual discussions and onto deployment and execution. People who have a perfect opportunity to be the hero often become casualties by their own stubborn behaviors and closed minds. Interventions and clarification of the situation by an outsider and the team is an effective way to establish Deming's continuity of purpose. When the facts exist for change, these issues must be dealt with head-on or an improvement initiative will derail quickly.

- CEO, executive sponsor, or other executive behaviors are well meant, but are taken out of context by the recipients of their message. Mentoring and coaching on individual behaviors is received positively by most executives who recognize their limitations and are willing to learn and grow from their deployment experiences.
- News delivered by an objective external resource is sometimes received with a higher degree of urgency and with seriousness, rather than passively analyzed for political motives and other hidden agendas.
- CEOs and executives receive value from candid discussions and objective feedback about their people, growth potential and options, organizational dynamics, or performance related issues.

The CEO and executive staff appreciate the opportunity for an objective sounding board on these and other strategic issues that arise during a deployment such as customer retention, organizational realignment, input on organizational changes, and fast-track career planning of superstar resources. Executives in benchmark Lean Six Sigma deployments recognized their organization's and their own personal limitations. They reached outside of their organization and found a proven Lean Six Sigma implementation firm and their seasoned *sensei* to help their organization to benchmark performance. It is no surprise that the executives of these organizations have grown to become the sensei to the people who helped launch their initial Lean Six Sigma journey. This is the essence of Lean Six Sigma success, arrived at through effective leadership mentoring and coaching.

Mentoring Wicked Problems

There are numerous situations where the traditional sequential *waterfall* application of DMAIC must be creatively modified to fit unique improvement situations—areas such as software development, research and development, technology development, and some aspects of advertising and new product development. Many projects in organizations, particularly the technology-related projects, are about dealing with *wicked problems*. These challenges are typically characterized by significant ambiguity and uncertainty, no single correct and fixed definition of the problem, multiple views about the problem with conflicting solutions, lack of information, different participants with different motivations, and multiple connections to other problems.

Indeed, it is the *social complexity* of these problems, not their technical complexity, that overwhelms most current problem solving and project management approaches. In wicked problem terminology, these initiatives begin as a *mess*—the correct technical term for a complicated issue that is not clearly defined or formulated. Recognize that all messes are not automatically wicked problems; some are tamed easily with direction, definition, and focus via the traditional DMAIC approach. However, many of the legitimate messes deal with dynamic and extremely complex problems that are difficult to define and solve via the traditional DMAIC approach. The more people with different views and objectives collaborating on a particular initiative, the more socially complex the initiative becomes. This is referred to as *fragmentation*. The only response to fragmentation is to create a shared understanding and commitment, and team cohesion. The nature of these challenges is about first moving from chaos to some level of order, and then maximizing the probability of customer and market success, while closely managing and minimizing time, economic uncertainties, and risks.

About 35 years ago, scientists began writing articles and describing these situations as wicked problems. A wicked problem is one for which each attempt to create a solution changes the understanding of the problem. Wicked problems cannot be solved in a traditional linear fashion, because the problem definition evolves as new possible solutions are considered or implemented. Furthermore, proponents claim that wicked problems can rarely be solved completely.

The term was originally coined by Horst Rittel at the University of California. Wicked problems always occur in a social context—the wickedness of the problem reflects the diversity among the stakeholders in the problem. Some specific aspects of wicked problems include the following characteristics:

- *You do not understand the problem until you have developed a solution*—Indeed, there is no definitive statement of *the problem*. The problem is ill-structured and an evolving set of interlocking issues and constraints.
- *Wicked problems have no stopping rule*—Since there is no definitive *problem*, there is also no definitive *solution*. The problem-solving process ends when you run out of resources.
- *Solutions to wicked problems are not right or wrong* –They are simply better, worse, good enough, or not good enough. Solutions, like beauty, are in the eyes of the beholder.
- *Every wicked problem is essentially unique and novel*—There are so many factors and conditions, all embedded in a dynamic social context, that no two wicked problems are alike, and the solutions to them will always be custom-designed.
- *Every solution to a wicked problem is a one-shot operation*—Every attempt has consequences. As Rittel says, "One cannot build a freeway to see how it works." This is the catch 22 with wicked problems: you cannot learn about the problem without trying solutions, but every solution you try is expensive and has lasting unintended consequences, which are likely to spawn new wicked problems.
- *Wicked problems have no given alternative solutions*—There may be no solutions or there may be a host of potential solutions that are devised, along with another host of solutions that are never even thought of.

Individuals involved in complex technology roles tend to view DMAIC as a traditional waterfall approach to problem solving that is irrelevant to their particular needs. This occurs with good reason because DMAIC is primarily a methodology that uses linear thinking for the most part. Many business improvement opportunities might be complex, but the big difference is that they are *tamed* by the ability to define objectives, scope, goals, benefits, and next steps. Involvement in a global software development initiative (e.g., operating systems, software languages, web-supported applications, utilities and libraries, interfaces, remote team development, and dozens of other complex combinations of choices) quickly convinces a seasoned mentor that DMAIC as a concept of fact-based improvement is still applicable, but not as a linear tame problem-solving methodology. One quickly realizes the limitations of plain vanilla DMAIC in dealing with these most complex situations.

Mentoring and Taming Wicked Problems

The DMAIC methodology is cleverly modified to accommodate creativity and innovation (see Figure 9.4). There is no doubt that innovation benefits from information and a mentoring methodology that tames wicked problems. Unlike the traditional sequential methodology, wicked problems can use what we refer to as a randomized DMAIC methodology, moving around to each phase and identifying both known and desired situations. The purpose of this approach is to lead a team through the typical stages of a wicked problem (e.g., a mess, a complex problem, a puzzle, and a solution). This type of mentoring facilitates and manages a team through the centrifugal fragmenting forces that delay or compromise a valid project solution. Some of the effective mentoring strategies for taming wicked problems include the following techniques:

- Collaborate with others in open brainstorming sessions, and map the various interpretations and positions of the participants to create a higher degree of shared understanding
- Try to identify the wicked problem in smaller, manageable dependent and independent chunks and separate cause-and-effect elements of the problem
- Lock down the definition of the problem by taming the forces that drive complexity and variation (e.g., controlling the functional specification in development projects)
- Assert that the problem or parts of the problem are solved because dealing with the downstream consequences might be easier than attempting to solve an unsolvable problem
- Specify objective parameters for success, including how the team will determine success and what they will measure to validate success
- Cast the problem like a previous problem, temporarily filtering out the elements that complicate the problem
- Down-select a broad complicated set of problem characteristics into simpler characteristics or options for defining and moving forward on the problem

Taming wicked problems

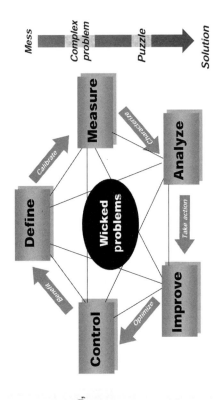

Mess
Complex problem
Puzzle
Solution

Define — Calibrate — Measure — Characterize — Analyze — Take action — Improve — Optimize — Control — Benefit

Wicked problems

Randomized DMAIC followed by sequential DMAIC

Collaborate with others in brainstorming sessions
Define problem in manageable chunks
Lock down the problem definition
Assert that the problem is solved
Specify objective parameters to measure success
Cast the problem like a previous problem
Stop inventing solutions and stick to one option

Wicked problems

1. You don't understand the problem until you have the solution.

2. The end of the project is unclear . . . it stops when you are sufficiently satisfied and/or run out of time and resources.

3. Solutions to wicked problems are not optimum, not right or wrong — and are often determined by creative consensus.

4. Every wicked problem is essentially unique and novel. Experience develops over time.

5. Every solution to a wicked problem is a one-shot deal. Every attempt has consequences and irreversible costs.

6. Wicked problems have no given alternative solutions. It's a matter of creative judgment to determine what should be implemented.

Examples
Software development
Rapid product or technology development
Global supply chain strategy
Advertising strategy
Poverty, hunger, terrorism

Figure 9.4 DMAIC and wicked problems

Much of the underlying philosophy and intent of DMAIC is useful in this process. There are a number of effective improvement tools for defragmenting and taming wicked problems. The general category of these tools is called *morphological analysis*, which is the study of the shape and arrangement of parts of an object, and how these parts *conform* to create a whole or gestalt. Some of the more useful morphological improvement tools include dialogue mapping, relationship mapping, affinity mapping, decision analysis, utility mapping, and simulation modeling techniques. These are all spatial mapping tools designed to help teams find the order in chaos, and to visualize the relationships between ideas and how they might tame their wicked problems. The randomized DMAIC methodology helps the team through the mess and complex problem stages.

Once the team reduces a wicked problem to a manageable and more defined solvable problem, the traditional sequential DMAIC methodology helps teams to knock the ball out of the park. The lesson from this section is that DMAIC and Lean Six Sigma can actually improve the creativity and innovation process in organizations. However, the methodology must be creatively modified to enable and multiply innovation.

Mentoring Larger Strategic Issues

Given the complex nature of organizations, improvement needs to look far beyond the success of a few improvement teams or even multiple teams to achieve success. When one thinks about it, transforming culture in organizations, global business strategy, reengineering the global supply chain, building customer intimacy, or designing products in half the time all begin as wicked problems with varying complexity. These issues remain in a wicked state when organizations allow themselves to remain focused on improvement at these levels. Leadership is the mentoring force that strives for the taming of wicked problems via dissection into manageable opportunities for improvement. If leadership is incapable or lacks the time and resources to get an aggressive start on taming the wicked elements of their organization, they will fall behind quickly.

Part of this mentoring is achieved through the business diagnostic described back in Chapter 4. However, there is an ongoing need in organizations to scan the marketplace for new requirements, synthesize these broad complex issues into manageable and scopeable improvement initiatives, and fill in the strategic gaps to success. Mentoring on these larger strategic issues is not a skill to be turned on by the flick of a switch. Seasoned mentoring professionals become seasoned because their mentoring is a full-time career, dealing with these similar challenges in a variety of other organizations and cultural settings.

The future of strategic improvement is becoming more complex and more necessary for success. Organizations need to become much more serious about improvement, collaborate with a proven and trusted improvement partner, and develop this core competency internally. As we stated in a previous chapter, organizations as a whole need to become knowledge organizations and gain a kind of literacy or fluency in the competencies of Improvement Excellence™. Beyond DMAIC and the Lean Six Sigma methodologies and tools, this includes crafting coherence and shared commitment, formal infrastructure and protocols, best practices leadership behaviors, and seasoned mentoring practices that enable the creation of the organization's future.

References

Conklin, J. 2005. *Dialogue Mapping: Building Shared Understanding of Wicked Problems*. John Wiley & Sons, Hoboken, NJ.

Rittell, H., and Webber, M. 1973. *Dilemmas in a General Theory of Planning*. An introduction to wicked problems from working papers in Urban and Regional Development, University of California at Berkeley.

Chapter 9 Take Aways

- Leveraged mentoring is exactly what it says: leveraging the combined skills, knowledge, and experiences in a manner where improvement teams are allowed to develop and grow without reinventing the wheel. Leveraged mentoring proactively manages the activities of integrated improvement teams while balancing the day-to-day concerns of the business with its broader strategic improvement needs. Leveraged mentoring is a different and much more professional approach than dictating directions and instructions to teams.

- DMAIC is the universal improvement language of the seasoned mentor who is trying to install DMAIC as the common cultural standard and protocol for improvement in the organization. Following this structure and coaching others about how to use this structure to their advantage is a major enabler of Lean Six Sigma success. Like leveraged mentoring, DMAIC grows into something much larger and more powerful: it becomes the new way that people think, act, and work. The power of fact-based, data-driven root-cause problem solving is a tremendous competitive advantage in the new economy.

- Leadership mentoring is always required in strategic improvement initiatives. Executives in benchmark Lean Six Sigma deployments recognized their organizations and their own personal limitations. They reached outside of their organizations, found a proven Lean Six Sigma implementation firm, and found their seasoned sensei to help their organization to benchmark performance. It is no surprise that the executives of these organizations have grown to become the sensei to the people who helped launch their initial Lean Six Sigma journey. This is the essence of Lean Six Sigma success, arrived at through effective leadership mentoring and coaching.

- Many projects in organizations, particularly the technology-related projects, are about dealing with *wicked* problems. These challenges are typically characterized by significant ambiguity and uncertainty, a lack of one correct and fixed definition of the problem, multiple views about the problem with conflicting solutions, a lack of information, different participants with different motivations, and multiple connections to other problems. Indeed, it is the *social complexity* of these problems, not their technical complexity, that overwhelms most current problem solving and project management approaches. In wicked problem terminology, these initiatives begin as a *mess*—a complicated issue that is not clearly defined or formulated.

- Unlike the traditional sequential methodology, wicked problems can use what we refer to as a randomized DMAIC methodology, moving around to each phase and identifying both known and desired situations. The purpose of this approach is to lead a team through the typical stages of a wicked problem (e.g., a mess, a complex problem, a puzzle, and a solution). This type of mentoring facilitates and manages a team through the centrifugal fragmenting forces that delay or compromise a valid project solution.

- There are a number of effective improvement tools for defragmenting and taming wicked problems. The general category of these tools is called *morphological analysis*, which is the study of the shape and arrangement of parts of an object, and how these parts *conform* to create a whole or gestalt. Some of the more useful morphological improvement tools include dialogue mapping, relationship mapping, affinity mapping, decision analysis, utility mapping, and simulation modeling techniques. These are all spatial mapping tools designed to help teams find the order in chaos and visualize the relationships between ideas and how they might tame their wicked problems.

- Organizations need to become much more serious about improvement, collaborate with a proven and trusted improvement partner, and develop this core competency internally. Organizations as a whole need to become knowledge organizations, and gain a kind of literacy or fluency in the competencies of Improvement Excellence™. Beyond DMAIC and the Lean Six Sigma methodologies and tools, this includes crafting coherence and shared commitment, formal infrastructure and protocols, best practices leadership behaviors, and seasoned mentoring practices that enable the creation of the organization's future.

Guest Article Contribution

Sherry Gordon is the president of Value Chain Group, a supply management and performance excellence consultancy. She was previously vice president of supplier performance at Emptoris, president and founder of Valuedge (acquired by Emptoris), and a consultant with Arthur D. Little. Sherry is a pioneer in enterprise measurement and process improvement techniques and is considered a thought leader in supplier performance management. Her most recent book is Supplier Evaluation and Performance Excellence: A Guide to Meaningful Metrics and Successful Results.

Understanding and Improving Supplier Performance
Sherry R. Gordon, President
Value Chain Group

Often when firms adopt Lean and Six Sigma methodologies, they focus on fixing internal operational problems. Assuming that they prioritize and choose improvement areas based on strategic imperatives and customer impact, firms often address the most controllable issues that lie within their four walls. The approach of *Doctor, heal thyself* before trying to heal others makes sense, as poor and broken internal processes need to be addressed first. It does not take long, however, before companies discover that they cannot achieve better enterprise performance without first-rate, high-performing suppliers.

Increasingly, the performance of firms depends on the performance of the extended enterprise. The ability not only to manage but also to improve the performance of an extended enterprise with its external network of suppliers has become critical. A number of factors have converged to create this situation:

- Increased outsourcing and reliance on suppliers for both goods and services
- Globalization of business and supply chains
- Increasing complexity in managing a diverse and global supply chain
- Improvements in enabling purchasing and supply chain technology
- Increasing levels and frequency of supply risks

Firms are often depending on suppliers as if they were a cookie jar, as they have realized that suppliers are not just a cost, but a potential revenue source that corporations can tap to make bottom-line numbers. That is, improvements in materials costs reduce the cost of goods sold (COGS) and go straight to the bottom line. Therefore, companies have pursued low-cost country outsourcing to reduce COGS. They have also pressured suppliers to continually lower prices in order to meet their own profitability targets. But these tactics do not come without inherent risks. Doing business with offshore suppliers requires additional skills, both to choose and work with good suppliers and to ensure that the many hidden costs do not outweigh the savings. The risk and incidence of supplier bankruptcies has increased during the global recession, exacerbated by additional price pressures from customers.

With the growth of outsourcing, suppliers have become increasingly critical to the success of the enterprise. Firms are realizing that they need to pay more attention to selecting and working with the right suppliers and to managing and improving their performance. But why is good supplier performance so important? The supply base of most firms is full of hidden cost drivers such as quality rejects, quality escapes to customers, shipping errors, customer complaints, excess inventory, excess freight, call center expenses, warranty costs, performance failures—all of which can be the result of supplier performance problems.

For every dollar spent on critical suppliers, what percentage is lost to poor performance factors, such as poor delivery or quality performance? For every percent of improvement in supplier quality or delivery performance, how many more dollars would be saved? Or, how many fewer sales dollars would you need to make up for poor supplier performance? Lean and Six Sigma tools can help firms identify the supplier contribution to these issues. The following challenges exist in identifying these issues:

- How can firms select the right suppliers?
- How can firms improve the performance of their key and critical suppliers?
- How can firms prevent supplier problems from occurring?

Good supplier performance is a key ingredient in enabling firms to achieve business and extended enterprise performance excellence. But how can firms manage or even influence the performance of outside suppliers? Supplier performance management (SPM) is being widely adopted as a method to understand and improve the performance of the extended enterprise. SPM can be defined as "the process of evaluating, measuring, and monitoring supplier performance and suppliers' business process and practices for the purposes of reducing costs, mitigating risk, and driving continuous improvement."[1] The SPM process in the context of the Six Sigma DMAIC process is illustrated in Figure 9.5.

1. *Understand, define, and align supplier performance management strategy*—The strategy to manage and improve supplier performance cannot be developed in a vacuum. It should be derived from and aligned with the company's overall goals and strategies. Alignment with an organization's corporate strategy helps to ensure that appropriate suppliers are selected, adequate resources are applied, and senior management support is maintained.

2. *Develop the SPM plan*—In this step, a multifunction team is selected, usually led by procurement, and it develops a plan for performance management. The planning phase includes making decisions and creating implementation timetables about areas such as supply base segmentation, a process for choosing which suppliers to measure; a supplier evaluation strategy; performance expectations; KPIs and scorecards; data collection approaches, sources, and techniques; use of technology; internal and external stakeholder communications before, after, and during the process; action planning around supplier performance results; and supplier development and continuous improvement.

3. *Develop performance expectations and measurement criteria*—In this phase, the team explicitly states and documents supplier performance expectations. A supplier performance expectation can be defined as "a specific statement of a business practice, process, policy, or the results anticipated or required from a supplier's performance or behavior in relation to the customer."[2] Supplier performance expectations, aligned with purchasing

---

Gordon, Sherry R. 2008. *Supplier Evaluation and Performance Excellence*. J. Ross Publishing, p. 4.
Ibid. p. 83.

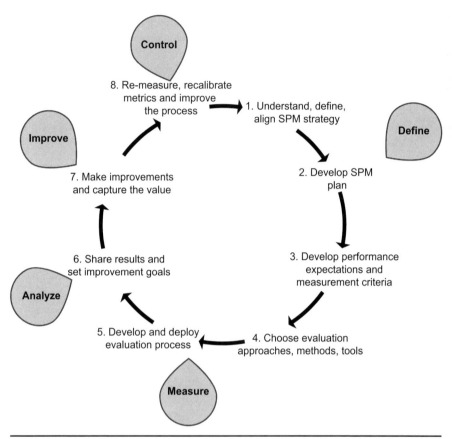

Figure 9.5   Supplier performance management in the context of the Six Sigma DMAIC process.

and overall corporate strategy, should be communicated to suppliers and be used as the basis for developing performance metrics.

4. *Choose evaluation approaches, methods, and tools*—Often the desired metrics exceed a company's ability to collect and respond to them. Supplier evaluation is about choosing the few vital metrics rather than a large quantity of metrics. Also, it is important to choose metrics aligned with strategy, rather than using metrics that are readily available, to avoid the danger of measuring what is easily measured instead of what should be measured. Other decisions in this step include deciding which tool or tools to use, such as scorecards, site visits, and questionnaires to gather performance information. Ongoing supplier performance measurements should feed into the initial supplier qualification process, which should also reflect the impact and importance of certain performance criteria on the smooth functioning of the business.

5. *Develop and deploy the supplier evaluation process*—Many companies find that implementation of an evaluation process is less risky and more successful when done as a phased rollout with a subset of suppliers rather than as a big-bang, full implementation. Phased rollout gives both customer and supplier staff time to learn the process, test, recover from mistakes, and improve the process.

6. *Share results and set improvement goals*—Communications cannot be over-emphasized. Scorecards should be made readily available to suppliers as soon as they are created. Customers should regularly communicate with suppliers regarding performance, corrective actions, continuous improvement, and issues internal to the customer that may be adversely impacting the supplier. Just launching scorecards to suppliers without communication before, during, and after about the intent, meaning, and consequences of the scorecards defeats the purpose of having them. Another often-neglected piece of communications is internally to stakeholders and senior management. If people outside of the purchasing or quality function are unaware of the successes, support will fade and the budget will disappear.

7. *Make improvements and capture the value*—A key reason for measuring supplier performance is to improve it. Without action, SPM is ineffective and will quickly degrade and lose support. Performance management is logical, but is often neglected. Firms get so caught up in what metrics to put on scorecards that they often lose sight of why they are doing SPM—to uncover risks, hidden cost drivers, and opportunities for improvement. It cannot be overemphasized that the value must be captured, documented, and regularly presented to senior management. For example, a large global information services company regularly tracks the savings it gets from its SPM process. Savings have come from many areas such as supplier ideas, quality improvements, and financial penalties levied against suppliers that do not meet their contractual service level agreements.

8. *Re-measure, recalibrate metrics, and improve the SPM process*—As in all good continuous improvement, processes should be revisited regularly for improvement opportunities. Also, companies find that some metrics are more useful than others and that suppliers and stakeholders will have suggestions for improving the process.

Improvement is a two-way street. Leading companies use not only supplier scorecards, but also reverse scorecards to give suppliers the opportunity to measure and improve their performance as a customer. Often, customer companies have poor or broken processes that adversely impact their suppliers' performance. Reverse scorecards help to uncover these problems. Customers need to view performance improvement as a mutual goal and be willing to improve themselves. SPM provides a path for building mutually beneficial relationships with key and critical suppliers.

SPM can help firms better understand their suppliers' capabilities and gain better insights into their performance. It also helps firms set criteria for new supplier on-boarding and an approved supplier list; rationalize the supply source based upon performance information; disengage with low performers and high-risk suppliers and give more business to high performers; work jointly on product or service development projects with suppliers; and help identify, prevent, and mitigate supply risk.

All firms try to pursue competitive advantage. Competitive advantage, by definition, is fleeting. A better goal is to pursue sustainable competitive advantage.[3] This has been defined as "an advantage that enables your business to survive against its competition over a long period of time."[4] Selecting the right suppliers, understanding supplier performance, and improving supplier relationships will help firms in their journeys toward improved extended enterprise performance and the goal of sustainable competitive advantage.

---

[3]Rogers, Stephen C. 2009. *The Supply-Based Advantage*. AMACOM, pp. 1–2.
[4]Vadim Kotelnikov. 2007. "Sustainable Competitive Advantage," www.1000advices.com/guru/strategy (10/31/2007).

10

Accelerator #7:
DMAIC the Deployment
Process Regularly

Variation exists in all processes, including the Lean Six Sigma deployment process. There is no magic mantra for success; the series of events that happen during a deployment are unpredictable and therefore subject to course corrections. Things such as delays in projects, a team pulled from another project and assigned to an important customer issue, the departure of an executive or team member from the organization, misunderstandings in project objectives, shifting in priorities, problems with acquiring data and information, workload conflicts, absenteeism, dysfunctional behaviors, poor team performance, a trip to a supplier, unexpected quality or engineering development problems, and thousands of other events introduce variation and disruptions to the implementation process. Successful Lean Six Sigma deployments require the leadership, DMAIC (define measure analyze improve control) thinking, and know-how to recognize these detractors and take the right swift actions to reset the course. This is the essence of Accelerator #7: DMAIC the deployment process (see Figure 10.1).

The objective of Accelerator #7 is twofold:

1. First, the deployment must remain in focus with customer and market needs because these requirements are evolving and changing rapidly. Coupled with this, keeping improvement initiatives aligned and directly linked to customer and market needs. Executives need to recognize that this is a commitment and a deliberate targeting effort, not another informal token agreement.

2. Second, the prioritized, queued, and in-process improvement initiatives must be completed efficiently and effectively and produce tangible mutual benefits for customers and the organization. This involves dealing

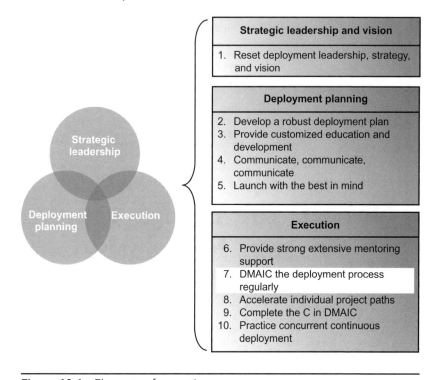

Figure 10.1 Elements of execution.

with the normal issues of change and the specific events of improvement initiatives mentioned previously.

This accelerator is more of a *micro-control* on the deployment, focusing on the technical and human dynamics of individual projects and teams. In the next chapter, we will discuss Accelerator #8: accelerate individual project paths, which is more of a *macro control* and integration of all accelerators. Together, these accelerators keep a Lean Six Sigma deployment synchronized to customer and market needs. When these accelerators are practiced successfully, a deployment eventually transforms itself into a normal everyday way of working and thinking.

For decades, organizations have been throwing around words such as *customer focused*, *customer-driven*, and *customer intimacy* as hollow slogans to guide their business affairs. Many have stressed the importance of creating a seamless customer chain, striving to meet or exceed ultimate customer demands on a macro level, and striving for improvement by recognizing and satisfying internal customer and supplier requirements. In the real world, every individual is a supplier, enabling process owner, and customer to someone else within and outside of the enterprise. As organizations embarked on various improvement initiatives, the acknowledgement of these customer and supplier relationships began on a good note. The ugly fact is that most improvement initiatives of the past three decades have talked about being customer focused in theory, but certainly were not customer focused in continuous execution. Many improvement initiatives have been too inwardly focused, where the customer was a few improvement czars trying to demonstrate their own success by implementing the tools everywhere. The term *customer-driven* means exactly what it says: improvement initiatives must be designed around customer and market needs and produce tangible, measurable, and mutually beneficial results. To be successful with Lean Six Sigma, organizations must make the effort to understand, align, and directly link customers and strategic improvement initiatives. The marketplace is the *Hemi* that drives strategic improvement across the enterprise. This is a mandatory Step 1, outlined in Accelerator #1: strategic leadership and vision. They must acknowledge any change and evolution in customer and stakeholder requirements, then respond and keep their daily Lean Six Sigma deployment activities synchronized to the marketplace. This is the purpose of DMAICing the deployment process.

Customer Centricity—From Idea to Pleasurable Customer Experience

In the post-meltdown, it is both surprising and alarming that the leadership practices in organizations actually result in contempt, whether implicit or overt, for their customers. Many organizations are responding to change with too much of an inward survival focus, and they are losing touch with rapidly evolving customer and market needs. This inward focus is also the root cause of fad improvement programs having come and gone, and along with it the permanence of customer satisfaction. The parade of improvement programs have resulted in many hollow slogans—lots of temporary sizzle but little lasting substance. Much of this has been due to the lack of intimately focused and pointed strategic leadership and vision, deployment planning, and execution infrastructure that is portrayed throughout this book.

The latest directive in the new economy is customer centricity. This is a journey, not a destination, albeit a rapid journey, in the new economy. Customer centricity involves placing the emotional connection and the wow factor into the customer experience. Individual products and services continue to converge into a commodity hell where there is less of a distinction from competitor to competitor. Becoming customer-centric means looking at an enterprise from the *outside-in* rather than the *inside-out*—through the lens of the customer and market, rather than through marketing or engineering perceptions of product requirements. Customer centricity goes well beyond providing the product or service itself. It is the value stream that begins with a product or service idea and ends at the pleasurable customer experience (e.g., from idea to pleasure). Customer-centric organizations truly understand the problems that customers face, and try to provide mutually advantageous bundled solutions.

Organizations such as Best Buy, Lowes, Staples, and many others are aggressively pursuing customer centricity as a strategic edge. Best Buy has taken the time to understand their customers and their specific needs, and has started selling customer-bundled solutions instead of standalone products.

As part of its research, for example, Best Buy discovered that 55 percent of its customers were women, and that for the most part, they loathed their shopping experience at the retailer. Men look for a specific product, at a discount price. Women want not just a digital camera or high-end receiver, but audio and printer cables and other home theater or imaging accessories. Women also care far more about these things than price. Equally important, they want help with installation, while most men prefer to try to put things together themselves. Children now have special play areas while their moms browse the store. To help with installation, the company acquired a Geek Squad. Mom can buy a flat screen TV and have it running before the family's favorite show airs.

Lowes has followed a similar customer-centric strategy where moms can actually touch, see, and feel how products will work at home, whereas Home Depot has remained more of a lumberyard atmosphere for the guys. Staples has also done a great job of providing a one stop solution center for the office.

A favorite admired and customer-centric organization of all times is Harley Davidson. Harley provides customers with the "ultimate freedom lifestyle" experience from their daily routines. First, it begins with innovative products that cater to a diverse array of Harley enthusiasts. Whether you are male or female, tall or short, new or experienced, functional or image conscious, a chrome or performance fanatic, prefer standard or custom options, or ride to the local store or across the country—the local Harley dealer will match your needs to their best motorcycle model. They provide a unique product solution based on specific customer needs, where superior product quality and reliability is assumed as a given.

fact. Then, they recommend that you complete the motorcycle safety course to build rider awareness, 360-degree defensive driving, and confidence. The purchase of this American-made art form is then an emotional experience, and this is a small ($25K) component of the total experience.

Of course, most people never leave the store without purchasing the latest $500 Harley branded leather jackets (two—one for you and one for the significant other) and other motorclothes. Add to that $1000 in chrome accessories; $1500 for louder, high-performance exhausts; $200 in Harley-branded riding goggles, gloves and tees; and maybe a Harley collar for the dog or Harley bib for the new grandson. The purchase comes with a one-year membership to the Harley Owner's Group (HOG), where customers discover many new friends and connections from diverse backgrounds—doctors, attorneys, electrical contractors, school teachers, postal workers, nurses, CEOs, social workers, realtors, software engineers, supply chain directors, chefs, sheriffs, and many others. HOG sponsors weekly rides, professional development courses, social meetings, regional meets, and other charitable events for its members. Their infamous *Fly and Ride* program provides members a means to fly just about anywhere in the world and rent a Harley from the resident dealer. HOG also promotes teamwork, fun, friendships, dealer loyalty, and safe riding skills development.

Most riders check out, *ooh* and *ahh*, and appreciate the bikes of their counterparts. Most seek to create their own personally customized touches on their bikes, be it with custom paint, more chrome or bling, or an aftermarket alligator seat. The service department provides all maintenance, repair, and custom add-on services via experienced technicians who treat your bike as if it were china dinnerware, and it is always delivered sparkling clean. Every trip back to the dealership is the HD revenue-generating experience (HD stands for "at least a hundred dollars") for the dealer and an emotional experience for the customer. The rides are pleasurable adventures that might include anything from a trip to the summit of Pike's Peak to a friendly chat with a group of 80-year-old tourists in Bar Harbor, Maine. It is nearly impossible to visit the local dealership without running into other friends. When it is time to purchase a new bike, customers do not have to think about where to go, and the products hold their value. The emotional experience of buying a Harley can be summarized thusly: buying a Harley includes consulting and product selection, safe driving skills development, the motorcycle purchase, the image created by the motorclothes, the pride of customization and accessorizing, fun and reciprocal friendships, technical collaboration, adventure, and freedom of expression.

Experiences such as these create customer centricity and unwavering brand loyalty. Many enthusiasts assemble their personal collections of Harley dealer tee shirts from all over the world. Harley Davidson customers go as far as to display the brand proudly on jewelry, rear windshields of automobiles, or on their person as a tattoo. Watch out, World—we might be seeing more people with logos for Apple, Google, Amazon, Wal-Mart, or your organization as a tattoo in the future.

Executives have learned that achieving customer centricity is a long-term journey that includes making a formal effort to define known and unknown customer and market needs while improving the internal planning and execution processes. Lean Six Sigma is a powerful enabler of improving both sides of this challenge. Improvement Excellence™ and the notion of improving how organizations improve require a continuous critique and enhancement of the overall deployment processes, which are:

- Strategic leadership and vision processes
- Deployment planning processes
- Execution processes

This constant DMAICing of the Lean Six Sigma deployment process generates ideas for improvement in customer and stakeholder focus, velocity, magnitude, and rate of improvement. Improvement initiatives have their ebbs and flows, peaks, and backslides. Like any other process, the deployment process can and needs to be improved continuously. Eventually, the effects of improving the deployment process are visible beyond the improvement initiatives themselves. Leadership vision and strategy, deployment planning, and execution infrastructure elements align customer and market needs with improvement initiatives so that the results are visible to customers and the marketplace in general. Lasting customer centricity and loyalty is achieved through Improvement Excellence™.

Avoid the Clone, Create Your Own

Organizations deploying Lean Six Sigma travel through distinct stages on this journey to customer centricity. This is not an easy journey to nirvana; it is a tough journey of persistent and continuous improvement. Figure 10.2 highlights the five stages of customer connectivity in Lean Six Sigma deployments. Some organizations are successful for years within certain stages of the journey. The good times do not last forever in any organization. In times of change, many organizations fall short of reaching the higher stages of customer connectivity because they lose sight of, and do not understand, new customer and market needs. To complicate matters, many are missing the core competency of Improvement Excellence™, or they have ineffective planning and execution processes to deliver unmatched value propositions. The result is simply a customer disconnect, which is a sure way to blow strategic business improvement initiatives. This customer disconnect also creates a massive Doppler effect from the customer to all other upstream supply chain processes. It is the *tail of the dog* syndrome where the further upstream that an individual resides, the more disconnected they become from external and internal customer reality. This is true with Lean Six Sigma and with the total business in general. These typical stages include:

1. *Customer awareness*—Organizations find it difficult to acknowledge that its customers are even out there. Such organizations tend to be product-centric and are challenged with identifying their customer base. Companies at Level 1 are product focused and have an *if-I-build-it-they*

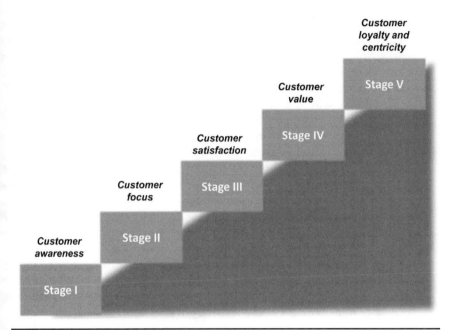

Figure 10.2   Stages of customer connectivity.

will-buy-it mindset. The focus is on technological excellence with some diffuse understanding of customers who may buy the product.

2. *Customer focus*—Companies here have begun acknowledging customers and seeking ways to determine which are most profitable. Companies at Level 2 have a basic understanding of their customers, typically coming from some market research and segmentation studies. They start talking about customers and distinct segments and believe that this alone is an indicator that they have now made the shift toward an outside-in perspective. Frequently, such firms still remain fundamentally oriented toward pushing products, albeit in a more refined and targeted way. Their market research starts to permeate their sales efforts, but does not have much of an impact on their product development and other upstream activities.

3. *Customer satisfaction*—These organizations are attempting to define and measure customer satisfaction and attempt to meet or beat competitors. To their credit, these organizations are actively talking to customers through limited survey methods and are seeking actions to improve customer satisfaction. Frequently, companies at this stage report customer satisfaction data regularly and tie satisfaction levels to internal compensation models.

4. *Customer value*—These organizations have begun looking at how they deliver value to particular customers. This is the early state of customer

centricity. The focus here migrates from selling products toward solving customer problems. In so doing, firms become adept at comprehending what their customers' deep-rooted issues are and look for ways to position themselves to address those issues. They ask, "What benefits are we really providing, and can we extract a price or a margin for that value?" They know why their customers buy, and they differentiate how they treat targeted customers and markets based on specific needs that drive satisfaction and competitive advantage for each segment. In trying to go from insight to action, these firms seek to make their internal silos more permeable, while also building bridges across them wherever necessary. They shift their culture so that some of these ideas begin to permeate and shape the behaviors and actions of their employees.

5. *Customer loyalty and centricity*—Organizations are more attached to the process of solving customers' problems than it is to the actual products and services it offers. This intellectual, structural, and emotional transition means that the company is no longer concerned whether the inputs it uses to solve customers' problems are its own or is assembled through a network of partners. Success is achieved through constant and effective collaboration. These companies enjoy repeat business, heightened customer demand, and improvements pertaining to margin. They can reduce costs for things deemed unimportant by customers and can demand premium prices for products and services perceived as vital. Organizations that fall into this category deploy a variety of robust improvement methodologies and a variety of tools. These organizations just do not assemble information—they actually synthesize information into actions and have a strong understanding of where they should invest to see the most return.

Now we will take a critical look at how the majority of Lean Six Sigma initiatives are designed and launched. During the past few years, Lean Six Sigma has basically followed a *herd* strategy in most organizations. As we have mentioned extensively, the primary focus has been on education and belts, blindly following and cloning the recipes of the early Lean Six Sigma successes. It is typical for organizations to have dabbled in improvement for years while being totally out of touch with the deliberate evolution to customer connectivity. For the past three decades, organizations have been cloning the improvement programs of other organizations and then wondering why their efforts are transparent to customers and other key stakeholders. For too many of these fad improvement programs, the customer has been limited to the circle of internal people trying to keep these initiatives alive while falling on the organization's deaf ears.

In spite of all this improvement activity, it seems like there is more low hanging fruit (improvement opportunities) than ever before in most organizations. Today is a great time to renew this lasting sense of urgency and commitment due to customer disconnects or confusion about how improvement can enable custome connectivity. The dynamics of the global economy wipe away improvement progress faster than organizations are capable of implementing improvements.

There should be no surprises today. A Lean Six Sigma deployment should not be a clone of someone else's program focused on the tools themselves. Rather, Lean Six Sigma should be postured within the organization to recognize current customer service capabilities and limitations. The improvement strategy and deployment initiatives should be moving the organization toward a more favorable customer-centric stage. In real life, this is a difficult process to keep aligned because the targets are moving, and customer expectations continue to rise.

Aligning Strategic Leadership and Vision

In the initiation of Lean Six Sigma and other strategic initiatives, the business diagnostic serves as the primary driver to align business strategy and improvement strategy. When this methodology is followed, the vision of improvement is based on widely recognized facts, and becomes crystal clear to the organization. The business diagnostic begins this improvement alignment process, but a more institutionalized ongoing process is necessary to identify new opportunities and keep the organization's improvement priorities aligned with customer requirements and business strategy. There are essentially two ways to make improvement alignment a living process:

1. Build improvement goals into the annual operating plan. In other words, budget a level of improvement and its associated financial impact on strategic performance. The budgeting process should demand periodic reviews of activities planned, in process, and completed by the financial responsibility area. The budgeting process should also require cumulative progress toward the budgeted improvement goal. When goals are built into the operating plan, it motivates leaders and managers to strive for favorable budget positions via targeted improvement initiatives. Rather than wait for a black-belt project, these leaders and managers step up and take ownership because they are accountable for performance. The universal DMAIC methodology will help to promote true root-cause problem solving. These improvements might be within or external to the formal Lean Six Sigma initiatives.

2. Institutionalize a planning process that continuously identifies customer and market opportunities, gaps in organizational performance, and other strategic improvement opportunities for the Macro Charter hopper. The inputs to this process are outside-in, inside-out, top-down, bottom-up, middle-out, or cross-functional (i.e., some organizations have formal processes to collect knowledge and facts from anyone in the organization who interacts or "touches" the customer). The results of this process will confirm or reprioritize needs currently identified in the Macro Charter, and some of this process will uncover new strategic improvement needs. This

planning process occurs quarterly in conjunction with the current deployment review and impact on strategic metrics. The result is a living process where improvement activities are aligned to dynamic strategic needs. The effectiveness of execution is also reviewed with the executive team, and the deployment is tweaked accordingly with leadership consensus.

How does an organization know if it is achieving success? Like all other processes, they need to define the critical metrics, and then close the performance loop with periodic measurement. The Scalable Lean Six Sigma™ model encourages the agreement on five or six key business metrics to gauge the effectiveness of Lean Six Sigma and other strategic initiatives. Per the business plan and the improvement strategy, these metrics follow the balanced scorecard rules and have a baseline level and a goal by which success is achieved. Although the specific calculations may differ from organization to organization, these metrics usually include:

- Customer satisfaction
- Market and revenue growth
- Profitability
- Balance sheet and cash flow
- Economic value added
- Human capital improvement

A successful strategic improvement initiative must achieve results that are pegged to the categories above. The Scalable Lean Six Sigma™ model recommends major reviews of these metrics on a quarterly basis. To the extent possible, organizations should be measuring the influence of their specific improvement initiatives on the continued well-being of these metrics.

There will be other normal business activities besides Lean Six Sigma that may be contributing to achievement such as successful promotion programs, new product launches, or supplier development efforts. Of course, there may be activities that also detract from success such as losing a major customer, premature commercialization of new products, surprise quality and reliability issues, or sales and operations planning in this new economy. However, during a finite window such as a quarter, it is straightforward to link recent improvement project performance to these metrics.

Keep in mind that major targeted improvement projects should have significant financial involvement in scoping, baseline process metrics, and financial validation of improvement claims, as we outlined in earlier chapters. When the financial strategy, deployment, and execution practices are working well, it becomes easier to identify and fold in the influence of specific projects on these higher level strategic metrics. The bottom line here is that leadership vision and strategy is measurable, and organizations must demonstrate that their improvement initiatives are directly impacting their strategic metrics. If organizations are not seeing a positive impact on their strategic metrics, they are throwing good money after bad money. It is time to conduct some quick root-cause problem solving and modify the improvement strategy, deployment, or execution processes.

Deployment Planning Metrics

Lean Six Sigma and other strategic initiatives look so easy and logical on the surface, but the fact is that it is a complex process to achieve the right results and sustain continuous improvement. The problem is in the details of strategy, planning, and execution—particularly in the new economy. Most executives have approached various improvement initiatives with the best of intentions. However, the high failure rates with improvement are due in part (and in good faith) to executives' own anxiety levels, but much of it is due to a lack of candor on the part of their guiding experts. Executives have been misinformed and uninformed when it comes to strategic improvement. This is no surprise because many executives and consultants have had the book knowledge, but were light on deep change leadership and implementation experience and demonstrated successes.

History demonstrates that Improvement Excellence™ is a core competency missing in many organizations. There has always existed this lack of, or reluctance to understand what it really takes to be successful with strategic improvement. Coincidently, there has always existed the impatience to understand the *whys* and *hows* of the current situation. Whether we are talking about Lean Six Sigma or any other previous, current, future improvement initiatives, organizations will continue to overpromise and under-deliver until they acknowledge and deal effectively with this common dilemma. Lean Six Sigma and other strategic improvement initiatives are extremely difficult to implement successfully, and even more difficult to sustain as a cultural norm.

Like any other process, deployment planning requires metrics and performance measurement. To gauge the effectiveness of the deployment, several formal metrics are used:

- Planned improvement activities (improvement projects, Quick Strikes) by organizational area with anticipated time-phased benefits
- Improvement activities (improvement projects, Quick Strikes) by organizational area with planned time-phased benefits
- Current individual project and cumulative benefits and rate of improvement based on completed and planned improvement activities
- Showcasing of best projects and sharing attributes of success with others in the organization
- Depth and breadth of improvement by organizational area, and confirmation of activity levels to the right strategic areas
- Inventory of assigned and available talented improvement resources, and plans for developing improvement talent across the organization
- Ongoing dialog with deployment participants about what is working well, where people need additional help, and what aspects of the deployment can be improved (this is literally a continuous improvement initiative on

the deployment and execution process by the direct participants with speedy corrective actions)

One challenging bullet point is in measuring the rate of improvement. Idealistically, executives would like to see their organizations increase their rate of improvement. The reality is that the rate of improvement goes through lifecycles, even in benchmark Lean Six Sigma deployments. In the beginning, there are usually so many opportunities identified from the business diagnostic that the rate of improvement can be increased for one or two years. Once the initial improvement opportunities are implemented, it becomes increasingly difficult to mine new opportunities, and implement new improvements that are of the same magnitude of savings as the initial stream of projects. The rate of improvement may crest or begin to descend, but this is initially not an indication of a bad thing. Every organization has their own maturity rate of improvement. The only way to increase the rate of improvement at this stage is by a paradigm shift such as:

- Expanding improvement initiatives throughout the enterprise on new areas such as the premium freight, invoicing and collections, acquisition process, new product development, finished goods stocking policies, customer service, engineering changes after new product release, obsolete inventory, warranty and returns, etc.
- Expanding improvement initiatives externally in the extended enterprise such as outsourcing process improvement, supplier development, customer collaborative design, supply chain synchronization, special customer and distributor processes, collaborative sales and operations planning, etc.
- Shifting focus from manufacturing to the transactional processes in both areas above
- Innovating a different deployment model (e.g., Scalable Lean Six Sigma™) for strategic improvement
- Innovative thinking about improvement applied to areas such as research and development, new product planning and brand management, technology development, advertising and promotions, competitive analysis, etc.

The rate of improvement is an excellent metric for sustainability and continuous improvement. The key to a successful deployment planning is not in waiting for something to fail. It is the proactive shaking of the bushes to anticipate and prevent deployment planning activities from failing, and simply to continuously improve the deployment planning process. Foresight and corrective actions are critical elements of Improvement Excellence™ or improving how an organization improves.

Execution Metrics

Execution is a more focused process with the intent being success—one project at a time. If this is done effectively, the whole is also successful. The execution process includes two types of metrics:

1. *Informal action-oriented metrics*—These may be informal but they include the sense-interpret-decide-act-monitor behaviors of a seasoned mentor. Some of the common informal action-oriented metrics in Scalable Lean Six Sigma™ deployments include:
   o Daily check-ins with the executive deployment leader
   o Frequent dialogue and feedback with team leaders and executive sponsors
   o Sharing of events of the day and heads-up topics
   o Daily interactive and interference mentoring on topics such as team and team member performance, lack of executive mentoring and commitment, coaching on executive behaviors, functional or political conflicts, clarification of expectations, etc.

2. *Formal measurement practices*—These are deliberate metrics describing the effectiveness of individual projects and deployment progress to plan. These metrics lead to more formalized actions to a particular team or to the deployment in general. Some of the common formal measurement practices in Scalable Lean Six Sigma™ deployments include:
   o Green-yellow-red (GYR) deployment management, where projects and teams are slotted into their appropriate color based on progress. Green is good, yellow is okay but potential danger, red needs improvement immediately. These charts are generated every one to two weeks then shared with the CEO and their staff, the executive deployment team, executive sponsors, process owners, and the team.
   o Weekly formal executive deployment team reviews. Ideally, these meetings are limited to one hour—thirty minutes for reviewing GYR project status and team performance issues and thirty minutes for discussing how to improve the deployment process and integrate improvement throughout the organization.
   o Weekly 15-minute update to CEO and executives in their staff meeting. Improvement progress is a formal agenda item on the CEO's staff meeting. This update is provided by the executive deployment leader and is a short version of the executive deployment team review above. Members of the executive deployment team are also on the CEO's staff.
   o Financial validation of results for each improvement project, and a structured project close process (control, in Chapter 12).
   o Cumulative benefits mapping, or mapping the cumulative verified results by project and by improvement category.

Figure 10.3 provides an overview of these planning, deployment, and execution metrics. The key to success lies in proactively managing these metrics to successful conclusions. Organizations have focused more on the projects themselves while allowing their deployment processes to take on a life of their own. Success with Lean Six Sigma cannot be allowed to happen based on chance or

Balanced scorecard approach

Improvement strategy
Customer satisfaction
Market and revenue growth
Profitability
Balance sheet and cash flow
Economic value added (EVA)
Human capital improvement

Deployment planning
Planned improvement activities
Current improvement activities
Completed improvement activities
Cumulative improvement
Rate of improvement
Depth and breadth of improvement
Talent bench inventory
Talent bench plan

Execution
Sense-Interpret-Decide-Act-Monitor
Daily executive leader reviews
Interactive/interference mentoring
Real time dialogue/feedback
GREEN-YELLOW-RED management
Weekly deployment review
Weekly CEO and staff review
Individual project success
Financial validation
Structured closure

Aligned and linked metrics

Figure 10.3   Critical Lean Six Sigma metrics strategy, deployment, and execution processes.

perception. Success is a choice that is achieved by deliberate management of the critical deployment success factors.

Success by Avoiding Metric-mania

One of the familiar scenes in organizations is this tendency to measure and post everything in the organization. Many organizations have their familiar war room or performance binders full of charts on just about everything imaginable. We refer to this as *metric-mania*—the need to cover one's backside by measuring everything. This practice demonstrates that there is an understanding of what is going on because it is quantified and tracked. It must be a balanced scorecard because it includes metrics for everything. People justify their actions with the statement, "What gets measured gets attention," which is true only to a certain extent. The corollary "Be careful what you measure because you might just get it" is also true. There are several problems associated with practicing metric-mania:

- It is unactionable because there is no distinction between outcomes, root causes, and dependencies. Further, it most likely does not measure true root causes or include the right metrics.
- These war room metrics are usually updated well after the path of the problem has turned cold.
- It confuses the organization because they cannot decide what to do or where to begin to improve performance, so the metrics practice becomes an information sharing process with no conclusions, action items, or improvement plans.
- It encourages opinionated and perception-based conclusions by attempting to explain relationships between metrics. Charts may go up or down but the explanation of *why* is subjective. Therefore, the corrective actions are usually subjective (firefighting).
- It encourages finger-pointing, justification of poor performance, lack of ownership, and lack of accountability.
- It is a monumental task to update and take the right corrective actions with a repeatable and reliable process.
- It clearly demonstrates that the wrong metrics drive the wrong behaviors and achieve the wrong results.

The last point is a strong conviction. Two things that become clear after significant experience with improvement: all organizations measure many of the wrong things and fail at measuring the true root causes of process performance. Several improvement projects with our clients have focused on identifying the factors that are most influential in achieving growth and profitability, and a residual finding is always a mismatch in performance metrics. In other projects, it becomes clear that existing metrics are measures of symptomatic issues rather than of root causes. In our Scalable Lean Six Sigma™ model, one of the most interesting factors has been this identification and ongoing measurement of root-cause metrics.

This represents a major enhancement to the balanced scorecard approach because it makes a formal distinction between root-cause metrics (factors or inputs) and effect metrics (responses or outcomes).

The evolution of new metrics that measure and monitor root causes of performance is the missing strategic lever to continuous improvement. In most organizations, there are no distinctions made between the two different types of metrics, so the measurement system increases the complexities of tracking down root causes of various performance issues. Prior to Lean Six Sigma, organizations did not have the structure and surgical improvement tools to peel back the veneer layers of their organization and conduct true root-cause problem solving.

Get It Right Upfront

A major improvement opportunity for organizations lies in investing in the methodologies and capabilities to continually listen to customers, gather meaningful data and insight from and about customer hits and misses, and ultimately integrate that data and insight into the business. When companies uncover the truth about why customers are dissatisfied or leave, the reaction tends to be emotional, muddled, and wrought with politics such as who is to blame, who owns the problem and who will make the right corrective actions. The problem with achieving alignment and customer concentricity is that organizations are not equipped with internal processes to leverage all areas of customer information across the business, such as what happens when customers defect or are at risk of defecting, who owns the analysis of customer retention and where happy and unhappy customers go to tell their stories.

The 10 Accelerators of Lean Six Sigma results are proven best practices in many benchmark deployments. Granted these are intensive processes, but they are effective given the limitations of listening to the customer in real time. Many organizations think that they have already incorporated these factors into their deployments but their performance and financial results demonstrate something different. Some executives view the accelerators as a waste of time because their organizations already know how to do all of these things. Organizations need to have patience and take the time up front to get these accelerators right, because it is a complicated and unfamiliar process. It should be obvious by now that strategic leadership and vision and deployment planning lays the groundwork for a grand slam Lean Six Sigma deployment because it is targeted at customer and market requirements, has well-prioritized and defined improvement activities, is implemented by the best people and teams, is implemented by teams that have received the best customized education, and is implemented with great commitment, communication, precision, constant attention, and solid mentoring support. The proven best practices of strategic leadership and vision, deployment planning, and execution produce benefit equivalent to 3 to 10 percent of revenues.

Chapter 10 Take Aways

- Successful Lean Six Sigma deployments require the leadership, DMAIC thinking, and know-how to recognize these detractors and take the right swift actions to reset the course. This is the essence of Accelerator #7: DMAIC the deployment process.
- The latest directive in the new economy is customer centricity. This is a journey, not a destination (albeit a rapid journey) in the new economy. Executives have learned that achieving customer centricity is a journey that includes making a formal effort to define known and unknown customer and market needs while improving internal planning and execution processes. Lean Six Sigma is a powerful enabler of improving both sides of this challenge.
- Improvement Excellence™ and the notion of improving how organizations improve requires a continuous critique and improvement of the overall deployment processes that includes:
  - Strategic leadership and vision processes
  - Deployment planning processes
  - Execution processes
- This constant DMAICing of the Lean Six Sigma deployment process generates ideas for improvement in customer and stakeholder focus, velocity, magnitude, and rate of improvement.
- The rate of improvement goes through lifecycles, even in benchmark Lean Six Sigma deployments. In the beginning, there are usually so many opportunities identified from the business diagnostic that the rate of improvement can be increased for one or two years. Once the initial improvement opportunities are implemented, it becomes increasingly difficult to mine new opportunities and implement new improvements that are of the same magnitude of savings as the initial stream of projects.
- The rate of improvement may crest or begin to descend, but this is initially not an indication of a bad thing. Every organization has their own maturity rate of improvement. The only way to increase the rate of improvement at this stage is by a paradigm shift.
- The key to success lies in proactively managing deployment metrics to successful conclusions. Deployment is a series of processes that can be measured, managed, and controlled. Success with Lean Six Sigma cannot be allowed to happen based on chance or perception. Success is a choice that is achieved by deliberate management of the critical deployment success factors.

Guest Article Contribution

Robert Q. Watson is a senior Lean Six Sigma consultant at INOVA Hospital. Previously, Bob held several senior management positions with The Juran Institute, The Center for Excellence in Operations (CEO), and

General Electric. Bob is a master black belt and has worked with dozens of clients in North America, Europe, and Asia.

Reducing Emergency Department Length of Stay by Two Hours
Robert Q. Watson, Senior Lean Six Sigma Consultant
INOVA Hospital

The INOVA Mount Vernon Emergency Department in Virginia had struggled for months with excessive length of stays (LOS) for its patients. Length of stay is the amount of time a patient is in the emergency department, beginning when a patient registers in the emergency department (ED) and ending when the patient is discharged from the ED. In 2008, the average LOS for *discharge home* patients (those patients who are not admitted and have dispositions to leave the ED) was approximately four-and-one-half hours, creating patient and community dissatisfaction with the emergency department service.

Benchmarking data from Premier (2007) showed that emergency departments in the top 25 percent (overall) had length of stays of roughly two-and-one-half hours. Clearly, the hospital had to review its current process and look for ways to improve performance while maintaining the same high standards for patient care.

Overview

Mount Vernon is a 237-bed hospital with floors for rehabilitation, joint replacement, psychology, medical and surgical procedures, and critical care. It also has a small ED that is split between a two-bed fast track area (includes a waiting room with chairs and wheel chairs) and an 18-bed unit for more acute patients. A simple example of how patients would flow through the emergency department is shown in Figure 10.4.

The ED treats an average of 80 new patients per day. Between 18 and 20 percent of those patients are admitted to the hospital for additional treatment. As the number of inpatients increases, the impact on the ED is negative, leaving few beds available. The result is that emergency patients who require admission may have to wait in the ED until inpatient beds become available. This effectively reduces the number of available beds for incoming patients and can increase the length of stay as patients wait for an emergency bed.

Quality Tool—Abbreviated Kaizen with Value Stream Mapping

A kaizen is a concentrated short-term effort made by work area staff to improve a work area process. At Mount Vernon, the focus was on short time and quick implementation. Each event lasted three days with the outcome being the implementation of a process change. This rapid-fire approach works well in the hospital setting because securing staff members for one or two weeks can be difficult (what most companies commit for a kaizen).

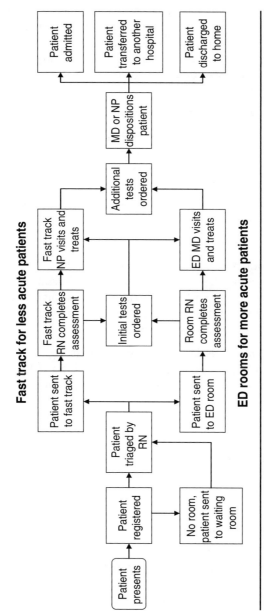

Figure 10.4 Fast track and more acute flow through emergency department.

Each kaizen began with a short overview on key techniques that the team would utilize: value stream maps, data analysis, problem and goal statements, work standardization, and throughput concepts. The balance of the first two days was spent completing a current state value stream map that would revise the current work practices to develop a future state map and implement a quick trial. The final day was spent understanding new process data collection and finalizing work standards for the process to immediately go live. These abbreviated events allowed us to quickly change processes and work standards over the course of several months.

Recognize the Need for Improvement

The first step to improvement is to recognize that you have a problem and develop a vision that can guide the organization through the cultural and process changes that will be necessary to raise performance levels. The community's dissatisfaction with the ED service was highlighted and acknowledged, and became the basis for authoring a vision of excellence. The next step was to communicate this vision throughout the organization, since the ED interfaces with all other departments in the hospital.

A process needs to be measurable before it can be improved. Therefore, data gathering was conducted, which established a baseline of 300 minutes for patients who were being discharged to go home. Benchmarking research from Premier was conducted to understand what other hospitals were doing, and the Mount Vernon ED established goals for the key tasks of LOS for discharge home patients. The following is the list of established goals:

1. Time patient arrives in room (best was 9 minutes)
2. Time medical provider arrives in room (best was 14 minutes)
3. Time it takes medical provider to make disposition (top 25 percent took 82 minutes)
4. Time from disposition to patient discharge (top 25 percent took 20 minutes)

The research formed the basis of the methodology that was utilized. Establishing the LOS goal and the goals for each task was a key step. It gave the organization a common performance target to shoot for.

Establish a Foundation for Success
Document and measure the process

An ED tracking system was implemented in November 2008 to track key information about patients: chief complaints, acuity level, diagnosis, and patient disposition. Key steps were time-stamped to understand how long each step took. The key process steps that could now be timed were:

a) Registration time
b) Triage time

c) Time patient arrives in ED room
d) Time medical provider first visits room
e) Time medical provider takes to disposition patient
f) Time from disposition to patient leaving ED (to go home, to an admitted room, or transferred to another hospital)

The timing could also be segregated by doctor, RN, shift, etc., to better understand where the delays were happening and why. It was reinforced from the beginning that the tracking was not in place to take punitive steps toward any individual, but rather to understand the process and what areas needed help. Graphical displays of the key metrics were distributed daily and displayed monthly (see Figure 10.5). Since we measured performance, we could begin to understand what parts of the process needed to be fixed and begin root-cause analysis to define corrective actions.

ED floor leadership has to be strong

Strong ED frontline leadership proved to be as critical as the establishment of the vision, metrics, and goals. The shift management coordinators and charge nurses are the frontline support who carry out the vision and mission. They need to be involved in the establishment of goals and development of any new processes. They need to measure and hold the staff accountable for their performance and take appropriate action when processes or procedures are not being followed.

Methodology for Improvement
Determine what is important

Once baseline metrics were obtained and the vision and mission were communicated, the task Mount Vernon faced was where to apply focus. Metrics obtained along with cross-functional meetings with the ED, floor units, and ancillary operations (radiology, laboratory, housekeeping, etc.) were conducted to identify the critical needs in the ED. Whenever agreement was difficult to obtain, the group would always ask, "What is in the best interest of the ED patient," or "If the ED patient was your loved one, what would you desire to be done?"

The group eventually rallied around a single patient-based principle: "The patient comes to the ED to see the doctor." Based on that notion, it was decided that getting the patient to the doctor as soon as possible was the ultimate goal. As the project progressed, additional principles were added to the primary goal. The result was the final list of guiding principles as highlighted below:

1. Get the patient to the care provider (doctor) as soon as possible
2. Order what you need as soon as possible
3. Execute the order as soon as possible
4. Review order results as quickly as possible following completion

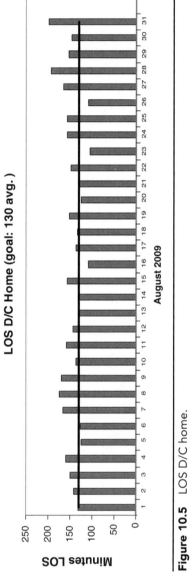

Figure 10.5   LOS D/C home.

The next steps involved working through each of the guiding principles.

Streamline the triage or bedding process

The first change activities focused on the front-end processes of getting a patient triaged and into a bed (see highlighted boxes in the ED process flow in Figure 10.6). Spaghetti diagrams were utilized in this step to better understand patient registration and ED staff movement. Since the ED nurses and technicians were involved in creating the new process, buy-in was readily obtained.

The team decided to modify the triage process and have only a quick triage prior to moving a patient to a room (after patient was registered and a wristband was applied). This quick triage involved obtaining patient vitals, the chief complaint, and the initial acuity level. The initial acuity level is the Emergency Severity Index that stratifies patients into five groups from one (most urgent) to five (least urgent) on the basis of acuity and on clinical staff resource needs.

After the triage changes were made, we discovered that the ED doctors were seeing the patient multiple times prior to the nurse completing the triage. This was a cultural change for some nurses, but ultimately they came to appreciate some of the benefits. An obvious benefit was that it enabled the nurse to obtain the MD orders more quickly. The bedside nurse could combine the nurse assessment or triage (see shaded boxes in flow below) with execution of the orders (i.e., blood draws) and further accelerate the care of the patient.

The new process facilitated the first two guiding principles: get the patient to the care provider as soon as possible and order what you need as soon as possible (see Figure 10.7). The overall performance gain was over 20 minutes.

Streamline the discharge to home process

The portion of the ED process from doctor disposition (to home) to patient discharge was also addressed early in the improvement endeavor. All nurses and charge nurses were trained to review the ED status board regularly. The ED doctors were also charged with verbally calling out whenever they discharge a patient to go home. Individual nurse performance times on the disposition to discharge were tracked regularly and the comparative times were posted openly for review. Coaching was instituted where necessary. The goal was to complete the patient discharge instructions and get them on their way within 20 minutes of disposition. Total time savings from this change has been approximately 10 minutes.

Measuring length of stay performance for MDs

How you are measured is how you perform. This is true in any situation and in any industry. The ED doctors are no different. They are a competitive group and are always striving to be the best. The doctor disposition time was monitored and separated by doctor and graphed on a monthly basis. After dissecting the data, the key element discovered was the different charting methods employed by the doctors. It was found that newer doctors had a tendency to over document. These

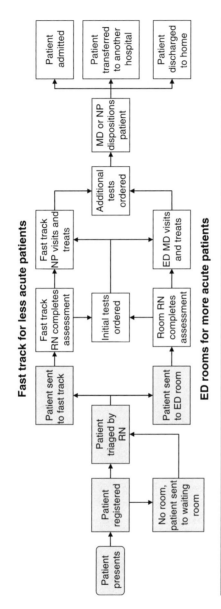

Spaghetti Diagram – Movements by process operators (RNs, technicians, and registration) were drawn on a floor layout. Patient movements were also drawn. This helps visualize the excess movement between areas and facilitates moving of some process steps closer to each other to remove wasted operator and patient movement.

Figure 10.6   ED process flow.

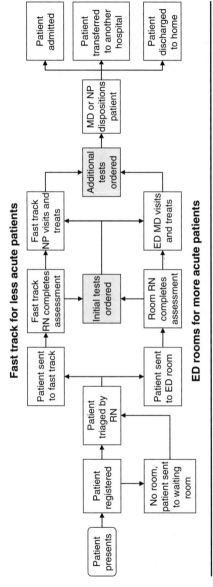

Figure 10.7 Combining nurse assessment/triage with execution of the orders.

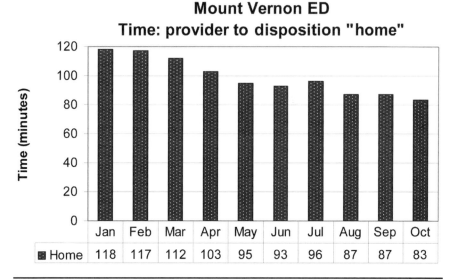

Figure 10.8   Mount Vernon ED.

doctors were then counseled by the ED medical director. Overall, the length of stay (LOS) decreases in this area were approximately 35 minutes, as shown in Figure 10.8.

Implementation of an ED fast track for less acute patients

The ED leadership recognized early in the improvement process that lower acuity or less complex patients were spending more time in the ED than their condition warranted. It was felt that if a fast track process was established for these types of patients (manned by a nurse practitioner), they could be more quickly treated in the ED while allowing the ED to focus more resources on the more severely ill patients.

Principles 1, 2, and 3—get the patient to the care provider as soon as possible, order what you need as soon as possible, and execute the order as soon as possible—were addressed with the fast track approach and it achieved its goals of enabling less acute patients to be seen and dispositioned more quickly. Use of the patient waiting area dropped significantly and LOS times for the fast track patients stabilized at around 90 minutes. Another advantage was the reduction (75 percent) in the number of patients who were leaving without being seen (LWBS), which actually added to the total revenue gathered by the ED (see Figure 10.9). The impact to overall LOS was a reduction of more than 15 minutes.

The overall LOS metric is shown in Figure 10.10 and plotted on a daily basis to keep focus and understand when to take actions.

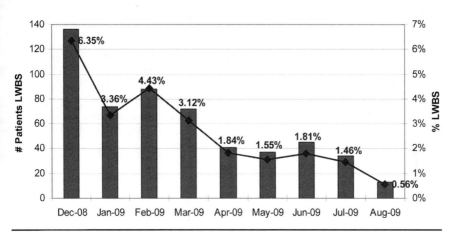

Figure 10.9   2009 LWBS.

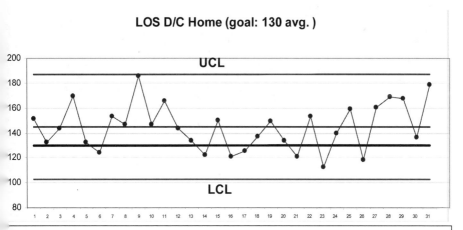

Control charting—Charts showing average patient length of stay for each day. The variation from day to day was used to calculate the control limits (moving range or the absolute value difference in average times from one day to the next was used). The monthly average per day along with process goal line was also shown on this graph.

Figure 10.10   LOS D/C home control chart.

What's Next?

Huge improvements have been made in reducing ED patient length of stay from 270 minutes to less than 150 minutes (see Figure 10.11). Patient satisfaction has risen dramatically because of this, although it is still not where it needs to be. The ED is the main gatekeeper for hospital admissions, and a good, safe, and fast experience is a great start to establishing a satisfied patient.

Another side benefit that we have also noticed is a big reduction in ED patients who leave without being seen. This is a community satisfier since patients are being treated more quickly, instead of deciding to leave out of frustration because of not being allowed to see a doctor in a timely manner. It also adds to the hospital's bottom line because more patients are being seen—a true win-win.

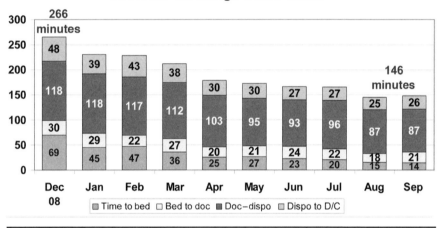

Figure 10.11   IMVH ED discharge home times.

11

Accelerator #8: Accelerate Individual Project Paths

This accelerator deals with improving the effectiveness of all the other accelerators. A Lean Six Sigma deployment (or any other strategic improvement initiative) cannot be successful with a launch and hope strategy. Executives and in particular, the executive deployment team, must proactively manage the infrastructure factors that most influence a successful outcome. Otherwise, the strategic leadership and vision, deployment planning, and execution processes run out of control. In essence, the executive deployment team is placing specifications and best practices standards around the various elements of strategic leadership and vision, deployment planning, and execution (see Figure 11.1). The largest challenge is in knowing and understanding these factors and how they interact with each other. The objective is to grow the positive interactions of these factors, or recognize and implement swift corrective actions when the interactions of these factors are producing negative effects on the deployment.

A successful Lean Six Sigma deployment is highly dependent upon how well these infrastructure factors are managed. Picture this management process as making the right decisions and taking all of the right actions to keep all the relevant factors within the bandwidth of superior performance. This includes everything from selecting and scoping the right projects to building high-performance teaming relationships to recognize drifts in performance and developing extremely talented root-cause problem solvers throughout the organization. Executives must look beyond the Lean Six Sigma deployment because the real benefits are derived from the *spillover effect* on daily business practices. This spillover effect is the evolution of DMAIC and improvement tools deployed to a project, to the way individuals think, work, and improve in day-to-day work. This occurs when, and only when, people view improvement intuitively and spontaneously as *part of*, rather than *in addition to* their normal roles and responsibilities. As we have

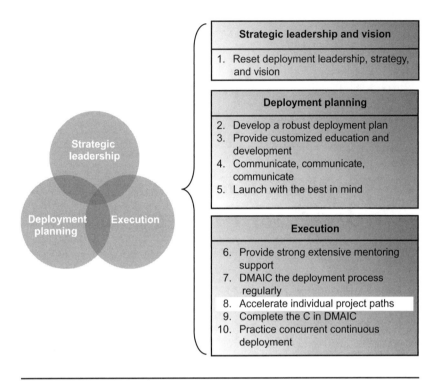

Figure 11.1   Elements of execution.

previously mentioned, deep implementation know-how and experiences count a lot more than self-proclaimed knowledge of individual improvement tools.

Viewing Accelerators Systematically

As a refresher, Accelerator #8: accelerate individual project paths, is the *macro control* of the deployment and integration of all accelerators. Accelerator #7: DMAIC the deployment process regularly (Chapter 10), is more of a *micro control* on the deployment, focusing on the technical and human dynamics of individual projects and teams.

This accelerator was initially viewed as a proactive process to implement improvement initiatives quicker, with the goal of realizing the benefits quicker. In the earlier years of the Scalable Lean Six Sigma™ deployment model, the primary focus was on Accelerator #2 (develop a robust deployment plan, detailed project definition, and scoping via the Macro Charter) and Accelerator #6 (provide strong extensive mentoring support, particularly leveraged mentoring).

Initially, constant attention to these two accelerators produced the rapid deployment, rapid results characteristics of our model because individual improvement projects were accelerated to completion. With more deployments and experiences, the importance and leverage derived from other accelerators became obvious, but it was this positive interaction of everything working in harmony that produced the real breakthroughs in improvement and benchmark deployment successes.

The positive interaction of all accelerators produced the same effects on the overall deployment as the initial two accelerators produced on individual projects. The attributes of rapid deployment, rapid results, breakthroughs in performance, internalizing and institutionalizing Improvement Excellence™, and benchmark deployments are all derived from achieving excellence in implementation infrastructure and in the details of the accelerators. Hence, the accelerators should be managed as a network of enabling processes (see Figure 11.2). Accelerators can be deployed to any strategic improvement initiative to drive up the levels of high performance and success.

The purpose of Accelerator #8 is to proactively manage the interaction of all accelerators to positive levels of performance. It is deliberately positioned in the middle of the other accelerators because it is not intended to be a post-mortem effort. Rather it is a *living* post mortem and serves as a real-time integration function. To accomplish this effectively, executives must first view implementation infrastructure and the accelerators as a systematic network of connected subprocesses. In addition, executives must understand how the inner workings of one accelerator influences the performance of one or more of the other accelerators, and take the appropriate continuous improvement actions. A few obvious examples of these interactions are:

- *Glossing over of strategic leadership and vision*—This has been a familiar practice in most Lean Six Sigma deployments. Without a solid improvement strategy and vision, everything else has the potential to miss the mark (because there is no defined mark). Lean Six Sigma is difficult to discuss, difficult to communicate, difficult to deploy, and difficult to execute. When strategic leadership and vision and deployment planning is done effectively, execution is simpler and quicker. People become believers quicker, and improvement is assimilated into the organizational fabric quicker.

- *Selection of projects that are not strategically important*—This is exactly what most deployments have done. The traditional deployment focused on training with a message of, "You're scheduled for black belt training, bring a project to the first class." This produces a lot of work on the remaining accelerators with questionable benefits, particularly for the customer. Worse yet, it does not allow team participants to realize success or a eureka moment, and they may become nonbelievers instead of supporters of Lean Six Sigma.

- *Poorly defined and scoped projects*—This is also a familiar practice in traditional deployments. Executive sponsors and teams waste time and hidden costs trying to figure out their mission. Strategic leadership and vision and deployment planning are both complex and time consuming. However,

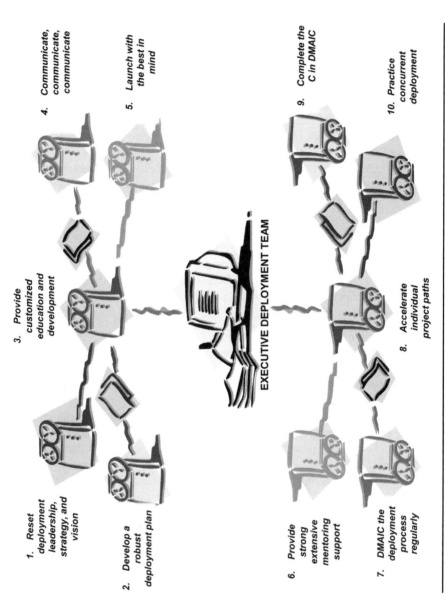

4. Communicate, communicate, communicate

5. Launch with the best in mind

9. Complete the C in DMAIC

10. Practice concurrent deployment

3. Provide customized education and development

EXECUTIVE DEPLOYMENT TEAM

8. Accelerate individual project paths

1. Reset deployment leadership, strategy, and vision

2. Develop a robust deployment plan

6. Provide strong extensive mentoring support

7. DMAIC the deployment process regularly

Figure 11.2 The connected accelerator network.

every hour spent on these tasks saves 10 to 50 times that amount through-out the course·of a deployment. This single factor negatively impacts all other accelerators to follow, resulting in lost time and other hidden costs of the deployment.

- *Boilerplate Lean Six Sigma education*—This has also been a familiar prac-tice and a personal peeve. How does one know what education and skill injections are necessary, or how many black belts or green belts are nec-essary without first spending time understanding the organization's cur-rent strategic challenges, improvement needs, or organizational readiness? People become frustrated when they cannot see the connection between education and improvement assignments and how to best deploy the right improvement tools to their situation. This is a guaranteed road to failure, especially without seasoned mentoring support.

- *Disengaged and disconnected leadership*—This is a situation that typically has its peaks and valleys during a deployment. This shift in focus and at-tention may occur for good reason, but it quickly communicates the wrong messages and begins to unravel improvement progress. Employees are watching executive behaviors and interpreting the expected response. A real or perceived message that Lean Six Sigma is less important than daily firefighting is a sure way to stall improvement progress.

- *Failure to communicate*—This has negative consequences on those putting forth the effort to improve. Improvement is an uphill battle that requires significant nonvalue-added interventions on accelerators because people do not understand the *what, why, where, when,* and *how* of Lean Six Sigma or other improvement initiatives.

- *Staff improvement with the undesirables*—It is a copout to make the argu-ment that the best people in all organizations are always too busy. Many organizations have attempted to implement improvement by drawing on the most available resources. They are available for a reason, and that is a different talent management problem. Visible commitment and success means playing hard with the first string—the best resources. Without the best people committed and engaged, the deployment will become bogged down with the need for nonvalue-added support.

Executives and their organizations must view the larger picture of Lean Six Sigma and strategic improvement. Success does not come about by fixed mind-sets on the improvement tools themselves. Strategic and sustainable improve-ment is about people and culture change, and accordingly, a complex challenge that does not yield to quick fixes or conventional wisdom. Executives must lead and develop growth mindsets in their organizations where people believe that they have reservoirs of untapped potential to improve. An organization's limit to improvement is its own self-imposed limit. Success requires proactive and systematic leadership of the accelerators. Improvement Excellence™ is the true core competency, and glaring gaps exist between current leadership skills and leadership skills needed for sustainable improvement and change. The most important future leadership skills are the competencies incorporated into strategic leadership and vision, deployment planning, and execution—and in the individual components of the accelerators.

Managing and Accelerating Performance

Managing the accelerators is a deliberate and systematic process. Why? The accelerators create strong interactions with each other in practice—positive, neutral, and negative interactions of change. An organization cannot be great at one or two accelerators and expect to achieve deployment success. Allowing the dynamics of a deployment to evolve without recognizing the power and influence of these accelerators is a sure way to railroad success. The successful executive deployment leaders and their teams understand the dynamics of these accelerators and how to manage the details to multiple successful conclusions. They also have the benchmark Lean Six Sigma deployments to demonstrate the impact of the accelerators.

One of the practices encouraged by the executive deployment team is to continuously seek out actual known or potential deployment detractors, whether it be a particular strategic issue or the performance of an individual on a team. Next, it is useful to associate these detractors with the most related accelerator. Finally, the executive deployment team further probes into the current situation and discusses corrective actions around the best practices guidelines of each accelerator. Frequent open discussions with the executive deployment team about accelerator performance is a healthy process. In the beginning, it may seem like an intimidating process. Within a short time, it promotes interest and attention to the human dynamics and key factors that really matter in a successful change initiative. This process builds the internal core competency of Improvement Excellence™ through the continuous analysis and improvement of the overall deployment and its ultimate success. In many deployments, best practices are discovered through this proactive accelerator management process.

The specific objectives, details, and best practices of each accelerator are provided in their respective chapters. When working with executive deployment teams, a formal accelerator gate-keeping checklist is used until executives have internalized the processes of the accelerators. Changing culture in organizations requires complex change simultaneously at many levels. Organizations tend to build a kind of immune system to fend off disruptive influences—at least for those that are disruptive to the task at hand. Early awareness and consequent action helps to address the natural response of an organization to resist change. The lasting goal of improvement is to positively change individual behaviors, which in turn changes culture and institutionalizes continuous improvement. The improvement tools are the easy part, but managing the human drama of the overall deployment with formal infrastructure and processes has the most influence over Lean Six Sigma success. The accelerators are also the factors that most influence individual behavior and culture change.

Easy as A, B, C, D, E, and F

Let's take a layman's look at the accelerators and their purpose in a Lean Six Sigma deployment. Figure 11.3 provides the A, B, C, D, E, and F of deployment success.

The purpose of the 10 Accelerators can be simplified to five letters—A, B, C, D, E, and F.

A for Alignment. This is a key objective across all accelerators, and especially in initializing the deployment with Accelerator #1. Alignment is the process of linking customer and market needs with strategic improvement initiatives and includes three dimensions:

1. *Vertical alignment*—This is the linking of strategic leadership and vision and deployment planning to specific improvement projects and daily improvement activities. This is accomplished through the Macro Charter and policy deployment best practices discussed in Chapters 4 and 5.
2. *Horizontal alignment*—This is the linking of strategic leadership and vision, and deployment planning across organizational functions. Horizontal improvement is necessary to work in teams and tackle complex, cross-functional process improvement opportunities.
3. *Lateral alignment*—This is the free integration of strategic improvement across organizational silos and organizational hierarchies, recognizing that everyone is an improvement associate in key business processes and has the responsibility, capacity, and capability to improve.

B for Boundaries. Collectively, the accelerators aim to recognize and knock down the barriers to success. This includes the elimination of organizational structures, processes, procedures, and practices that were once effective, but are

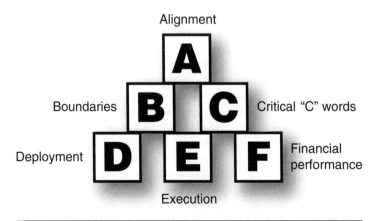

Figure 11.3 The ABCDEF's of deployment success.

now barriers to improvement and Lean Six Sigma success. The accelerators are taking out the things that block progress, and replacing them with things that build and enable progress. The other relevant element here is that there are no organizational boundaries, and no upside boundaries to improvement. In other words, *B* really stands for no boundaries—no limit to success.

C for the Critical C-Words. Think about the accelerators as a systematic set of processes to plan, deploy, and execute on improvement initiatives. The following list includes a baker's dozen of critical C-words that influence these processes and the deployment as a whole:

- Character
- Commitment
- Courage
- Candor
- Communication
- Consistency
- Charisma
- Creativity
- Competence
- Compassion
- Common sense
- Controversy
- Confrontation

When the positive side of these attributes is missing or weak, the success of a Lean Six Sigma deployment is eventually at serious risk. The accelerators are promoting the positive practice of these words by the CEO and the executive team, senior and middle management, executive sponsors, process owners, and every other associate involved with improvement.

D for Deployment. This pertains specifically to the accelerators that comprise deployment planning. Deployment translates strategy into the right aligned improvement actions via detailed project scoping, education and skills development, resourcing, communicating, and launching for success. Too many deployments include either the wrong improvement actions or a disconnected series of improvement-for-improvement's-sake activities. In many organizations, Lean Six Sigma and other prior improvement programs have become more of the process for dealing with problems, rather than the enabler of strategic and continuous improvement.

E for Execution. This pertains to the accelerators that comprise the *execution* part of infrastructure. Execution refers to the efficient implementation and follow-through of improvement, including control (The C in DMAIC) and sustainability. Many deployments begin with high expectations, but tend to fall down in the execution phase. Conversational improvement is easy; rubber-on-the-road improvement and continuous improvement are much more challenging.

F for Financial Performance. The golden rule of successful Lean Six Sigma deployments is that everything begins and ends with financial performance—one project at a time. Deployments should strive to achieve this objective but also recognize strategic opportunities that may be difficult to quantify along traditional lines yet open the door to many new improvement opportunities.

Lean Six Sigma Assessment Process™

The ultimate measure of Lean Six Sigma or any other improvement initiative's success is financial performance. If there is not a measurable improvement in both strategic and operational financial performance, it is time to return to the drawing board and figure out how to improve the deployment.

Financial performance is an outcome. Executives cannot dictate improvements in financial performance with Lean Six Sigma. However, organizations have the ability to dive deep into the potential root causes of our current performance and (hopefully) point our Lean Six Sigma deployment in a more positive direction. Another formal practice used in measuring Lean Six Sigma success is our Lean Six Sigma Assessment Process™ based on our strategic leadership and vision, deployment planning, and execution infrastructure, which is closely aligned with the 10 Accelerators. This assessment process is not an ongoing process. Rather, it is useful when assessed at the beginning, every few months, the end of the first year, and occasional subsequent milestone points. The Lean Six Sigma Assessment Process™ has been used effectively when there is a need to discuss the deployment from a wide variety of executive perspectives. This process builds unity and constancy of purpose: Deming's first point, which is still important today.

Chapter 11 Take Aways

- A successful Lean Six Sigma deployment is dependent on how well the accelerators are managed. The largest challenge is in knowing and understanding these factors and how they interact with each other. The objective is to grow the positive interactions of these factors, or recognize and implement swift corrective actions when the interactions of these factors are producing negative effects on the deployment.
- The attributes of rapid deployment, rapid results, breakthroughs in performance, internalizing and institutionalizing Improvement Excellence™, and benchmark deployments are all derived from achieving excellence in implementation infrastructure and in the details of the accelerators. Hence, the accelerators should be managed as a network of enabling processes.
- Improvement Excellence™ is the true core competency, and glaring gaps exist between current leadership skills and the leadership skills needed for

sustainable improvement and change. The most important future leadership skills are the competencies incorporated into strategic leadership and vision, deployment planning, and execution—and in the individual components of the accelerators.

- Another formal practice used in measuring Lean Six Sigma success is our Lean Six Sigma Assessment Process™. The process is based on our strategic leadership and vision, deployment planning, and execution infrastructure. It is not an ongoing process. Rather, it is useful when looking at the beginning, middle, and end of the first year, and occasional subsequent milestone points. The Lean Six Sigma Assessment Process™ has been used effectively when there is a need to discuss the deployment from a wide variety of executive perspectives.

12

Accelerator #9: Complete the C in DMAIC

C, or *control*, is the most important phase of the define-measure-analyze-improve-control (DMAIC) cycle. This is the actual point of implementation, the realization of improvement, and process owner hand-off for sustainability. Over the past several years, we have observed some organizations that make their way through the DMAI phases of Lean Six Sigma and then fall down on C. It almost appears as if their continuous improvement efforts end with the PowerPoint presentation of what they are going to do.

It turns out that C is also the most difficult phase in DMAIC and implementation in general. There are several important activities that must take place to ensure a smooth transition from a team project to the improved and sustainable process norm, and these will be pointed out in detail in this chapter. After involvement in thousands of improvement projects, the real pushback comes when it is time to actually change. People intellectually accept or tolerate improvement as long as everyone is limited to talking about it. Even the best projects are subject to comments such as, "I'm not sure I agree with your recommendations" or "I didn't think the project would take us in this direction." Or, better yet, "I did not expect this project would result in my needing to change."

Improvement will never last unless the executive deployment leadership, executive sponsors, improvement teams, and process owners work judiciously through these issues. With improvement, perceptions of change are reality. This requires more effort, education, or dealing with controversy, but the improvements are far more lasting that the over-the-wall or unconditionally imposed improvements. A reality in business and in life is that nothing changes until people are ready and willing to change.

The Scalable Lean Six Sigma™ deployment model incorporates an accelerator dedicated to the smooth ending and transition of improvement initiatives to ensure sustainability and true continuous improvement. This final phase in DMAIC (see Figure 12.1) is the one that keeps removing the *continuous* from continuous improvement.

Control Plan

The control plan is used in Lean Six Sigma and in particular, in the control phase of DMAIC. In this context, the control plan is a detailed guide for identifying and monitoring all activities required to transfer improvement ownership from the team to the process owner. In the Scalable Lean Six Sigma™ model, the control plan has two control mechanisms:

1. The improvement team control plan
2. The process owner control plan

Improvement Team Control Plan

This side of the control plan provides the specifics required by the team to wrap up their project. The most important task is in the hard and soft validation of

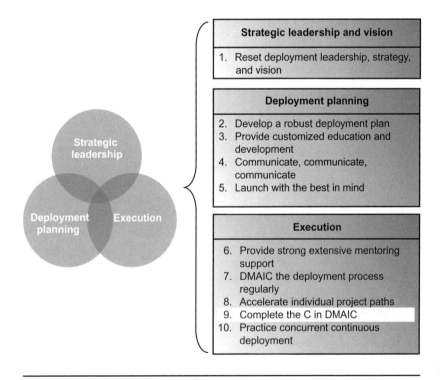

Figure 12.1 Elements of execution.

their project. First of all, did the project achieve the original objectives and goals? Second, did the project achieve the anticipated benefits, and how do we know for sure? This side of the control plan outlines the specific tasks that the team must complete in Gantt fashion, prior to process owner transition. Verifying the improvement, designing the ongoing performance measurement system, documenting new procedures and policies, and education planning are a few examples of what may be found in the improvement team control plan.

Process Owner Control Plan

This side of the control plan provides the specifics required by the process owner and organization regarding the new process, how to operate and manage the new process, how to measure and monitor its performance, and how to further improve it. The process owner control plan is also designed as a checklist in a Gantt format, with the full identification of handoff tasks, responsibilities, timetables, and deliverables. Rather than leave transfer of ownership up to happenstance, the control plan provides a structured and formal process for the handoff. This formal process forces people to ask the right questions and deal effectively with the transition. Using the Deming Plan-Do-Check-Act (PDCA) analogy, the improvement team control plan is the *P* component, and the process owner control plan is the *DCA* component. The specific details of the control plan will be covered in the remaining sections of this chapter.

Six Elements of Control

Control includes six major elements:

1. *Validation of improvement*—This element verifies that the recommended actions have actually improved the process. For some organizations, their approach is sufficient if someone says, "Oh yea, things are much better now." That is not good enough for a benchmark Lean Six Sigma deployment. Validation occurs through measurement of the key process metrics before and after the changes. Sometimes validation is achieved by positive and negative replication of results (shifts back and forth from old to new processes, demonstrating the respective negative and positive oscillations in performance). Improvement should demonstrated by a positive movement in the metrics. The benefits derived by improvement must be validated by the financial organization.

2. *Sustaining measurement systems*—This element defines performance ownership, what metrics will be monitored by the process owner, corrective action guidelines for slippage in improvement, periodic audit and validation plans, and integration into the overall performance measurement process. This includes tracking of both primary metrics and critical root-cause metrics, and practices to expose and prioritize ongoing root causes.

3. *Process owner transition*—This element includes all activities that must take place (e.g., new procedures, templates, visuals, education, IT modifications, knowledge transfer, etc.) to transfer ownership of the improvement initiative to the process owner. This element addresses all questions related to transfer and continuation of improvement, dismantling of the improvement project team, and freeing up resources for new improvement initiatives. Process owner transition included both the hard process improvement details and the emotional, interpersonal, or human drama issues of improvement and change.

4. *New improvement opportunities*—This element has to do with defining additional improvement opportunities that are either directly or indirectly related to the current improvement project. The team is in a great position to comment on further improvements to the existing project, or other unrelated project opportunities that may inhibit further improvements. These ideas go into the Macro Charter hopper for further investigation and prioritization against the existing content of planned improvement projects. Some of these may also go directly to a functional manager or supervisor for Quick Strike improvement. The other piece of this element is asking each team member to identify and commit to an improvement activity in their immediate areas, using the methodology and knowledge gained in their project.

5. *Knowledge repository*—This element is twofold. First, the executive deployment team officially closes out an improvement project in a formal team meeting. The purpose of this meeting is to capture any additional lessons learned firsthand, and integrate them into the overall deployment. Second, the executive deployment team must build a formal process to archive the knowledge, experiences, analysis, and other relevant information for future teams. This repository of knowledge is available and accessible for future improvement initiatives as both living and learning examples, and to reduce redundancy in improvements (e.g., using value stream maps or FMEAs from previous improvements).

6. *Celebration*—The final element of control is celebration, which incorporates much more than a few token pats on the team's back. One important aspect of celebration is organizational reinforcement through the showcasing of success. The other aspect is recognition and reward for the team and extended participants. Celebration must also become a deliberate formal process because this is an opportunity to leverage Lean Six Sigma and strategic improvement.

Figure 12.2 provides an overview of these key control elements. As simple, logical, and straightforward as these elements may sound, they are often the casualties of a deployment. Many of these casualties are unintentional because there is a failure to recognize the human dynamics of control. Some of this is attributable to time constraints and superficial commitments, which are not valid excuses. Most of it is driven by a lack of understanding about what it takes to verify

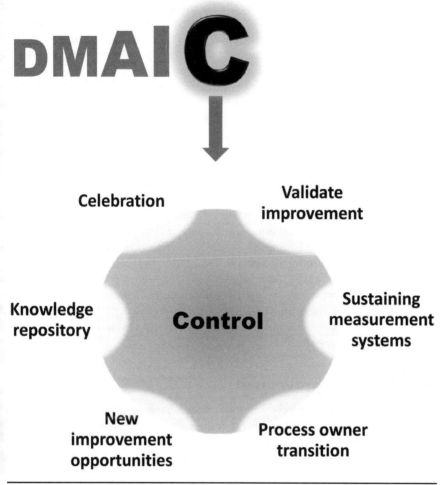

DMAIC

Celebration

Validate improvement

Knowledge repository

Control

Sustaining measurement systems

New improvement opportunities

Process owner transition

Figure 12.2 The key elements of control in DMAIC.

mprovement, and then successfully transfer the knowledge of the team to the process owner and his or her direct people and organizational interfaces.

Think about the typical context of improvement for a minute. A team may spend months working through the DMAIC methodology and verifying improvement, then they might spend an hour or so instructing everyone who was not involved in the project how to sustain improvement—with a much more limited background, education, analysis, and problem familiarity than the team has. Since day one with Lean, Six Sigma, or Lean Six Sigma, it has never made sense to pull people out of their organizations, make them full-time black belt improvement gurus, and ask them to implement improvement as a perceived outsider. This is not a black belt or Lean Six Sigma problem, this is a leadership problem, and a misunderstanding of strategic and sustainable improvement problems.

Some executives might react with the thought, "It's easy to point the finger at leadership." In all fairness, this was the boilerplate guidance provided by the gurus from other large organizations and training firms. The Scalable Lean Six Sigma™ model has always rejected this stringent requirement of a separate centralized department of full-time black belts. A better practice is to carefully select projects and teams where improvement is directly related to their daily work, then provide them with the infrastructure, a new methodology and new tools, and leveraged mentoring to ensure their success. It becomes much easier to integrate and sustain improvement with this "daily work integration" approach, and the knowledge resides with the organization. Organizations need to take a step back and get beyond this blame game.

An underlying theme throughout this book is root cause problem solving. The Scalable Lean Six Sigma™ model has evolved by a fanatical focus on the root causes and detractors from successful deployments. We are blessed by a long list of clients who were also willing to innovate and improve how they improve with us. The bottom line is simple: if Lean Six Sigma is not working to expectations, the only way to improve is by dealing with the root causes, be it leadership or a specific technical team issue. One of the objectives throughout this book has been to provide benchmark infrastructure examples, develop a better understanding of these non-tools infrastructure requirements of success, and discourage organizations from oversimplifying the realities and requirements for continuous improvement.

Validation of Improvement

Validation verifies that the recommended actions have actually improved the process. By the time a team reaches control in their improvement projects, they have a good understanding about why the details of D, M, A, and I exist as a formal methodology. In the *measure* section, teams are required to complete two deliverables baseline performance metrics and validation of the measurement system itself.

Teams verify that the variation or perceived waste is not derived from a measurement problem in the process. Examples might include the variability of gauges and measurement equipment in operations, or treatment of charges and categorical transactional groupings through the quality system, the chart of accounts, the month end close, returns and allowances, or time and materials charges in the engineering development system.

Measurement error is much more obvious in physical processes than it is in transactional processes. For example, if an organization has 25 customer service people tracking customer complaints using 50 different categories of complaints there is probably significant inconsistency and therefore a measurement problem. Teams must isolate variation and waste derived from the measurement system from the process itself. They must fix the measurement system before proceeding further with their projects. If this is not fixed up front, the data will lead teams down the wrong path of improvement and achieve the wrong results. Validation of improvement assumes that an effective measurement system analysis was completed up front, and that variation or waste has not been produced by inconsistencies in reporting or measurement.

Validation of improvement can be completed in a number of ways. Essentially, teams measure the process before and after improvements and demonstrate the positive effects of their improvements. They must also demonstrate that their improvements are not luck, based on other factors such as changes in revenues, timing changes, or modifications to the accounting and reporting processes.

The financial organization plays a key role in validation. The financial organization assists individual teams with improvement and savings assumptions, classification of savings, providing standard rates for savings calculations, prevention of double counting savings, and validation of claimed savings achievements. A financial representative should be a member or extended resource for every improvement project.

Validation needs to occur until there is enough factual evidence and data to be statistically convincing. Replication experiments and other simulation techniques are often useful because they demonstrate *what-if* conditions in validation. The objective here is to demonstrate that what-ifs from the new process are superior to the what-ifs of the old process. Another objective is to predict tolerations and bandwidths of process capability as the key input factors shift around. This is the most effective verification technique for winning over the nonbelievers. The final task of validation is to place the new process in an in-control (predictable) state.

Sustaining Measurement Systems

Sustaining measurement systems is the first step in the transfer of operational financial ownership, and accountability of sustaining improvement. There are several details to this control element:

- Define the control plan. How will the new process be managed, monitored, and sustained? The control plan is a detailed what-needs-to-happen plan to successfully transfer ownership.
- Define the key process inputs and outputs, and determine how to calculate, display performance, and manage the new process. This includes recommended performance dashboards and other visual displays and how to maintain them.
- Define how the process owner and the organization will hold and improve the gains of the team, including how to detect slipping performance, substandard conditions, root causes, and other detractors from sustaining performance.
- Provide education and hands-on application support regarding the data acquisition, calculation, and interpretation of performance metrics or corrective actions.
- Develop a response plan to help manage when inputs, process elements, or outputs indicate a potential performance shift or when out-of-control

situations arise. This might include advice on what parameters to watch, corrective actions for known situations, or a simple troubleshooting guide.

Sustaining measurement system tasks are an important part of the control phase. It all comes back to the basics of measurement. What gets measured gets attention. Furthermore, if people cannot measure their process they cannot improve it, because *they don't know what they don't know,* and therefore cannot take the right corrective actions. Performance measurement and metrics should always follow a balanced scorecard approach.

Process Owner Transition

Process owner transition includes all activities related to transferring ownership from an improvement team to the process owner and the organization. Specific details of this transfer should be identified in the control plan mentioned previously. There are several issues that must be addressed during this formal handoff:

- *Documentation and standardization*—It is often necessary to document new procedures and templates, revise work instructions, and provide additional tools or guides for the new process. Part of this task might also include guides for mistake-proofing the new process, or measures for sensing and preventing process detractors. Lack of standardization around best processes and practices introduces variation and allows waste to creep back into the process.
- *Education and training*—To supplement documentation and standardization, people often need education, training, or instructional guidance on how to function within the new process on a daily basis, and clarification of new roles and expectations. It may be necessary to monitor learning of the new process until it is mastered by the responsible individuals.
- *Ownership responsibilities*—This is a clear description of the process owner's role in the daily management, performance monitoring, and improvement of the new process. Part of this task should include a formal provision for periodic review and audit of process owner progress. The objective is to transfer knowledge and project learning from the team to the process owner. Designated team members should be on call during the handoff to ensure a smooth transition.

It becomes easier to visualize how the elements of control are simplified and streamlined when the improvement team and process owners are one and the same. Improvement teams should always include a balanced and diverse group but process owner and participant members help to expedite and raise the effectiveness of the control phase.

New Improvement Opportunities

It is astonishing how much some people know about improvement but will never speak of it. Some of this is attributable to culture, and some is attributable to lack of communication and interest. It is equally astonishing how much the improvement teams learn about the business and additional improvement needs. These improvement needs take the form of direct follow-on activities to existing improvement initiatives, or indirect variation and waste in other key business processes that influence the performance of existing improvement initiatives.

A good example of this is new product development. Part of the influence resides within this key process and how engineering and technical resources work their way through the major phases of development. Situations such as poor market knowledge, optimistic sales projections, changes in priorities, specification creep, pressures to select the lowest cost offshore suppliers, and pressures to meet unit price targets often have a much larger impact on performance than the process itself.

During their projects, teams have learned so much about their process and about the interactions and influences of other unrelated processes. Formal dialogue during and at the conclusion of improvement projects is an effective way of mining and identifying additional opportunities, or in learning what worked well and not so well in the deployment (although this is an open and more real-time dialogue and corrective action process during their individual projects). Organizations interested in a benchmark Lean Six Sigma deployment need to aggressively seek out these *do-differentlys* and trust the judgment of their skilled improvement resources. The best time to capture these opportunities is when the knowledge and experiences are fresh in the minds of the executive deployment team, executive sponsors, improvement teams, and process owners.

Within the control phase, the Scalable Lean Six Sigma™ model requires improvement teams to identify an additional improvement project, and individual members to identify an additional improvement initiative in their daily roles. These practices keep the momentum for improvement alive. One caveat here: this idea generation should be placed in the Macro Charter hopper where the potential opportunity can be verified and scoped in more detail with data and facts, and prioritized against other proposed projects in the hopper.

Knowledge Repository

This is a leverageable area of improvement, and an area where many organizations fall down. There have been several projects where a team came up with recommendations only to have someone say, "Oh, that's the way we used to do it." Some have even admitted things such as, "It worked better than what we are doing now. We just changed it, but I don't remember why."

In other situations, teams may drive blindly down their own road of improvement and be unaware of value stream maps, FMEAs, analytical studies, maintenance projects, or other activities where some of the knowledge required already exists from previous improvement initiatives. Granted, the business may have changed significantly since these efforts were completed. However, a value stream map or defects Pareto chart developed by a team six months ago probably has a lot of relevance to current conditions. Some of these documents and analyses are also useful in replacing fiction with facts in the normal daily meeting routines.

Beyond an improvement project, Lean Six Sigma provides an advanced opportunity for many to contribute, learn, and understand the details of the business. The intranet and knowledge management software has made this process easy to maintain. Typically, organizations establish a Lean Six Sigma directory that includes folders for the deployment planning (e.g., Macro Charter and project prioritization, resource availability and development, executive deployment team leadership activities, education, and improvement activities).

Improvement activities can be organized further by specific projects, participants, DMAIC templates and analysis, and the like. Several organizations have developed the capability to access their improvement activities through such things as function, improvement topics, and keyword searches. New teams are encouraged to use this repository for related information, template and analytical examples, or technical or subject matter guidance from others in the organization. This provides a unique opportunity to tap the knowledge of others directly or digitally, and improve the efficiency of improvement.

Celebration

A major aspect of celebration lies in demonstrating success to the organization. This is best accomplished through awareness and communication, showcasing team success and project accomplishments, allowing teams to become lead spokespeople for change, and reinforcing strategic improvement as a competitive weapon.

The other aspect of celebration is the genuine recognition and reward process for team performance and accomplishments. The reward needs to be genuine, setting performers visibly above nonperformers and making their accomplishments a big deal to the organization. Why? Because the successful completion of an improvement project that saves a few million dollars *is* a big deal. Recognition is the public acknowledgement and gratitude for the team and individual efforts.

Recognition might include a spot in the organization's newsletter or intranet site, a recognition dinner event (including spouses or significant others), or special status on an employee ID badge. Reward is usually more tangible and might include anything from stock options to a nice embroidered laptop bag or golf shirt, or a gift certificate for the company store. The big difference here is the word *genuine*, which is significantly different from the empty slogans, banners, tee shirts, and coffee mug collections with past fad improvement programs. Figure 12.3 provides an example of a simple DMAIC control checklist for the six key elements of control.

When Is a Project Complete?

In Lean Six Sigma and other strategic initiatives, the answer to this question can be quite confusing. There is no single global answer to cover every improvement initiative. Some might argue that a project is complete when the objectives are met. Others might argue that a project is complete when the improvement is less than the effort to improve. Still others might argue that a project is complete when enough improvement is achieved and resources can be put to better use on other initiatives.

On a case-by-case basis, these answers are all correct. However, there is a real danger in blindly completing projects based on an across-the-board version of one of these statements. Strategic improvement in a holistic sense is a *wicked problem* of sorts. No matter how much effort is consumed on front end planning and project scoping, the actual improvement potential is not known until the latter phases of DMAIC. This effort is well worth the time in terms of efficiencies and risks downstream in the DMAIC process.

Using the Macro Charter methodology, improvement projects are identified, planned, and scoped serially although they are prioritized in relation to each other. Sometimes the potential benefits are significantly understated because the mining found larger opportunities or residual effects were not predictable. The issue here is breaking these opportunities into more manageable chunks, and possibly keeping the team together for subsequent phases. Sometimes potential benefits are overstated because the problem is smaller based on facts than it was based on perceptions and opinions, or just because it turned out that way. The following practice guidelines shed light on this complex question:

- When a project has met all of its initial objectives, and the team's analysis demonstrates that the initial project sizing and scope were correct, the project should go through the structured closeout process.
- When a project has achieved benefits, but not to the extent of the original sizing and scoping, the executive deployment team needs to take some lessons-learned time to improve the Macro Charter process. If the team has reached diminishing returns, the project should go through the structured closeout process.
- When a project is scoped and the team finds that the initial project is really several projects, the executive deployment team and the project team should revise objectives and scope, and place the newly defined projects in the hopper for further analysis. Teams should never flounder with *boil the ocean* assignments, but sometimes this happens unintentionally.
- When a team finds more opportunities than originally anticipated, there are two options: (1) Keep the team intact and go for the additional opportunities beyond the original project objectives and scope, or (2) Break the opportunities into smaller modular chunks and keep the team together for an extended period of time and on multiple assignments.
- Initially, multiple teams are required to provide enough focus and manpower on process improvement. In some improvement situations with overlapping and residual impact, it makes sense at some reduced urgency point to consolidate into a single, more focused team. An example might be the

	Responsibility	Status	Complete?
1. Validation of Benefits			
Develop team segment of control plan			
Post-improvement sample			
Comparison of pre- and post-improvement conditions			
Quantification of hidden costs and benefits			
Expected benefits by time horizon documented			
Replication and what-if verification			
Validation by financial organization			
2. Sustaining measurement system			
Develop process owner transition segment of control plan			
Define KPIVs, KPOVs, performance calculation procedures			
Define how process owner will sustain improvement, detect out-of-norm conditions			
Mistake-proofing practices			
Document a simple troubleshooting guide – how to detect slipping performance and initiate the right corrective actions			
3. Process owner transition			
Documentation and standardization of new process			
New templates, checklists, work instructions, etc.			
Education and training – process operations			
Education and training – I/O participant expectations			
Ownership roles and responsibilities			
Corrective action and response plans			
Co-monitoring, team and process owner			
Decide on official cut-over situation by situation			

	Responsibility	Status	Complete?
4. New project opportunities			
Additional directly related improvements			
New potential projects (direct, internal to process)			
New potential projects (indirect, external to process but influences performance of process)			
Define and commit to functional area improvement activities and time (spillover effect)			
Lessons learned, do differently			
5. Knowledge repository			
Complete documentation and organization of project into DMAIC phases (all evidence, etc.)			
Archive project in master Lean/Six Sigma directory			
Work with IT to create keyword accessibility			
Official executive deployment team sign-off			
6. Celebration			
Organizational improvement exhibition			
Reward and recognition process			
Official reward and recognition ceremony			

Figure 12.3   DMAIC control checklist.

consolidation of an order management and invoicing team at some point, because the single team can now prevent both order entry and billing issues.

The fact remains that organizations cannot predict the interaction effects of many concurrent improvements. This is not a bad thing, just a fact of strategic improvement. Recognize that there are risks and diminishing returns for allowing projects to complete prematurely or too late. The executive deployment team, executive sponsors, and process owners are the best judges of these particular situations. The control phase and the control plan will provide a solid guide for making these decisions. A disciplined and structured closeout process will also enable pulling the trigger at the right time.

The answer to the question, "When is a Project Complete?" is multidimensional and can only be answered by observing the dynamics of the live project pool, and then proactively squeezing as much improvement out of the combined portfolio as possible.

Control the Journey and Control Success

The new economy is a watershed moment for Lean Six Sigma and strategic improvement in general. There is an abundance of improvement methodologies and tools, but the missing link has been the deliberate implementation architecture of strategic leadership and vision, deployment planning, and execution. The ugly fact is that success with strategic improvement is a matter of commitment and choice.

There are so many critical activities that can take a deployment off the tracks. A great improvement strategy and vision without the right actions is nothing more than hopes, dreams, and wishful thinking. Improvement activities focused on tools but in the absence of strategy and vision is nothing more than consumption of time and resources. A great strategy and vision, followed by great effort and an unsuccessful implementation is a short lived, nonvalue-added improvement.

Control is the most critical part of DMAIC. Treating the tasks of control casually and haphazardly is a sure way to fail at improvement. In the short term, process owners and their people will have difficulty repeating and sustaining the results of the team, and they will slide back into business as usual when leadership becomes focused on another issue. In the long term, the infrastructure and skills are not in place to sustain gains and improve the process further. The same gradual performance backsliding will take place. The journey of improvement is difficult because people are human and are susceptible to human error and variations in consistency, perceived expectations, and performance.

On the other hand, the successful journey of improvement is controllable by commitment and choice. Behavioral alignment is the correcting force to sustain continuous improvement. Many forms of behavioral alignment techniques such as leadership, communication, measurement, mentoring, proactive deployment management, reinforcement, recognition and rewards, and periodic audits are the most prevalent in benchmark Lean Six Sigma deployments. Organizations may not want to commit to this tough work of a successful improvement journey, but they cannot take away the proven successes of the accelerators of Lean Six Sigma results.

Chapter 12 Take Aways

- C, or control, is the most important phase of the define-measure-analyze-improve-control (DMAIC) cycle. This is the actual point of implementation, the realization of improvement, and process owner hand-off for sustainability.
- The control plan is used in Lean Six Sigma and in particular, in the control phase of DMAIC. In this context, the control plan is a detailed guide to identify and monitor all activities required to transfer improvement ownership from the team to the process owner. In the Scalable Lean Six Sigma™ model, the control plan has two control mechanisms:
  1. The improvement team control plan
  2. The process owner control plan

- The six elements of control include validation of improvement, sustaining measurement systems, process owner transition, new improvement opportunities, knowledge repository, and celebration. Each of these elements includes specific tasks to smooth the transition of improvement from teams to process owners.
- The new economy is a watershed moment for Lean Six Sigma and strategic improvement in general. There is an abundance of improvement methodologies and tools, but the missing link has been the deliberate implementation architecture of strategic leadership and vision, deployment planning, and execution. The ugly fact is that success with strategic improvement is a matter of commitment and choice.

13

Accelerator #10:
Practice Concurrent
Continuous Deployment

The traditional roll out of a Lean Six Sigma deployment occurs in waves, similar to groups of soldiers completing basic training and military boot camp. The term *wave* refers to a sequential process for developing people and completing projects. There is a defined start and end time to a wave, as well as a deadline for certification. The implication of waves is that all projects are equal and begin and end at the same time. Waves tend to stretch out the smaller content projects and compromise the larger content projects in the interest of everyone marching to the same certification deadline and scheduled graduation day. In reality, each improvement project has different objectives and scope, different resource requirements, different skill sets, and certainly different timetables for completion. Yet the traditional train-the-masses wave approach treats all projects identical in terms of these properties. Between the so-called waves, a lot of progress and momentum can be lost waiting for the last projects to reach completion or the next batch of projects to start.

In contrast, concurrent continuous deployment (see Figure 13.1) is the continuous development of people and completion of improvement projects, and is based on current critical needs. Although a deployment may begin with teams and projects leaving the same starting gate, improvement activities do not need to begin and end at the same time. Concurrent continuous deployment embraces proactive management of projects, priorities, and resources that are always ready to go. Individual project launches are staggered based on resource availability and improvement capacity is managed. Concurrent continuous deployment optimizes the opportunities for improvement by *overlapping* wave activities and reducing aggregate cycle time for the overall deployment progress. This significantly

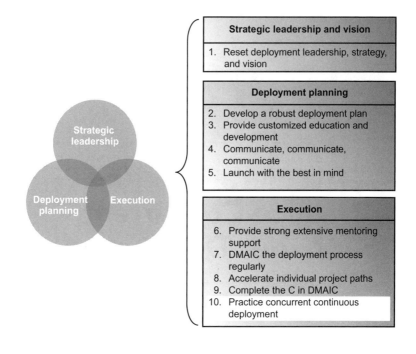

Figure 13.1   Elements of execution.

reduces the traditional wave wait time and resource conflicts of a *batch* deployment, and increases the capacity of improvement by as much as 30 percent in the same window of opportunity. Simply stated, concurrent continuous deployment enables organizations to achieve more with less.

Rather than wait for completion of waves, organizations achieve flexibility in the better matching of opportunities to improvement efforts. Concurrent continuous deployment is an acceleration process that has evolved out of the Scalable Lean Six Sigma™ model, and has enabled organization after organization to rack up their magnitude of realized improvement in record speed. This velocity attribute of concurrent continuous deployment is what keeps the attention and momentum for improvement high and continuous. The Lean Six Sigma deployment takes on the characteristics of a freight train and becomes difficult to slow down or derail.

The Logic of Concurrent Continuous Deployment

Concurrent continuous deployment has evolved by borrowing a few Lean improvement methods from the past such as continuous flow, bottleneck and throughput management, quick changeover, dynamic finite scheduling, and standardized work. These methods are integrated with best project management and concurrent engineering practices in an attempt to optimize resources and results. The following section provides a brief review of these concepts.

Continuous Flow

The notion of continuous flow production applied to concurrent continuous deployment eliminates many wasteful activities in the Lean Six Sigma deployment. Continuous flow production promotes the practices of small lot sizes (e.g., scoping improvement projects into many smaller manageable chunks), and continuous progressive activity (e.g., by eliminating wait time, overloading and wasted resources, and other inefficiencies). In a continuous flow production environment, production is regulated where each part is pulled through at an ideal rate of one piece at a time, and this greatly reduces the manufacturing lead time. In a project environment, continuous flow promotes the overlapping of projects based on improvement pull and availability of the right resources. This improvement pull is the voice of the executive deployment team, and is based on their identification and prioritization of strategic improvement needs via the Macro Charter process. This practice also reduces cycle times over the traditional batch sequential wave approach, and enables organizations to better match the timing and execution of improvement needs and improvement projects.

Throughput Management

This concept strives for getting the most throughput and results in the shortest amount of time. Leveraged mentoring plays the most critical role in this process by giving the appropriate attention to projects where it is needed the most. The objective here is to help teams eliminate or reduce the bottlenecks and dependencies in their improvement projects. Recall that leveraged mentoring includes Lean Six Sigma knowledge, business process improvement experience, industry best practices experience, and executive industry experience. The objective of throughput management is also to search out and eliminate the broader deployment barriers and bottlenecks, and recognize the leverage points to achieve a desired rate of improvement in the deployment. This is just like production throughput where revenue and delivery performance are heavily influenced by throughput. To achieve a rate of savings by a given time, organizations must synchronize the correct type and level of improvement activity.

Quick Changeover

In a production environment, quick changeover enables increased flexibility to changes in demand and the ability to build in smaller lot sizes, which better matches customer demand patterns. Two accelerators play a vital role here:

1. Accelerator #2: robust deployment planning, where scoped and prioritized improvement activities are ready to be assigned

    2. Accelerator #9: complete the C in DMAIC, where there is a formal and structured closure process to improvement activities

In a project environment, the critical resource is the right people with the right skill sets at the right availability. Quick changeover promotes the elimination of any wastes between ending one improvement project and launching another. In a production environment, we strive to keep the bottleneck operation available. In strategic improvement, the bottleneck is leadership and people related. Improvement is analogous to production flow, and availability of the right people with the right skill sets is analogous to the throughput, capability, and capacity of individual production operations. Quick changeover promotes the constant redeployment of improvement resources to additional improvement activities so the larger dynamic of continuous improvement becomes internalized without thinking about Lean Six Sigma. Quick changeover facilitates the spillover of improvement knowledge gained from specific structured projects into daily work.

Dynamic Forward Scheduling

This is a practice that requires constant attention by the executive deployment team. The objective here is to look ahead and anticipate completion of improvement projects. The official launch date for new projects is a formal process, similar to scheduling production based on need dates and equipment availability. The other side of this is taking the projects that are ready to go in the Macro Charter and resourcing them based on the availability of the right people and other talent development goals. One mistake to avoid here is always calling upon the same go-to people. They are great and know how to get things done, but severe overloading the best people often places them in positions where they become frustrated and ineffective at any single assignment. Part of the objective here is to build deeper bench strength by developing more go-to people. There are many dormant people in every organization with the potential to grow into additional go-to people and sometimes the best improvement resources. Organizations can never hope for continuous improvement unless they develop a deep bench of improvement-enabling people.

Standardized Work

This is accomplished through the religious practice of the 10 Accelerators. The architecture of strategic leadership and vision, deployment planning, and execution provide the standardized process of successfully deploying Lean Six Sigma or any other strategic improvement initiative. The DMAIC methodology is the common language of improvement throughout the organization. The infrastructure provides a disciplined and structured process that the organization eventually understands and marches to. However, this infrastructure is not so rigid that it kills the opportunity to be innovative. In the next chapter, the topic of transactional process improvement will be covered, and the reader will learn that success requires dealing with broader and more complex systems issues, innovation, imagination, and discretion to harvest these opportunities.

Best Practices Project Management

There are many books available on this topic alone. Another great resource is the Project Management Institute that offers certification courses on this topic. At the risk of oversimplifying, the objective here is to make sure that all deployment activities (from executive deployment team activities to individual improvement project tasks) are broken down and managed in a Gantt format. At any moment, it should be easy to review the status of projects or other deployment activities in terms of current position, detailed definition of next steps, timing of next steps, responsibilities and assignments, and specific deliverables. The last point is important. Having a project with a lot of steps marked complete, complete, complete and nothing to show for it is a doomed project.

Another key enabler of project management is to gauge the impact on resource loading if certain changes are made to the improvement schedule. Improvement must not allow itself to become *accelerator entrapped* as we discussed in Chapter 2. Project management is not loading up the improvement pipeline and then moving on to something else. Project management provides the opportunity to realistically develop, load, and manage critical resources while getting everything done that needs to be done. Projects are much more nebulous than a production line is. It is much easier to walk out to a production line and estimate status than it is to walk into an engineering organization and put one's hands around the portfolio status of new development projects. The only hope of managing a Lean Six Sigma deployment or any other strategic initiative is by incorporating best project management practices into the equation.

Concurrent Engineering

In a Lean Six Sigma deployment, concurrent engineering promotes the idea of moving away from improvement projects scheduled as independent waves toward improvement projects scheduled based on need and resources. In effect, it is the overlapping and parallel processing of waves of improvement projects. To do this well, the executive deployment team needs to know the status of all in-process and planned activities in the deployment. This is a deliberate and proactive leadership process where executives manage the deployment to optimize results, resources, and learning. Applying concurrent engineering to the deployment establishes a formal sustaining process of improvement by setting the expectation verbally and visually that improvement is a continuous process. Improvement is a condition of successful employment and everyone is expected to develop their own expertise with improvement.

Figure 13.2 displays the real benefits of combining these forces. The diagram demonstrates the additional resources and capacity that can be gained through

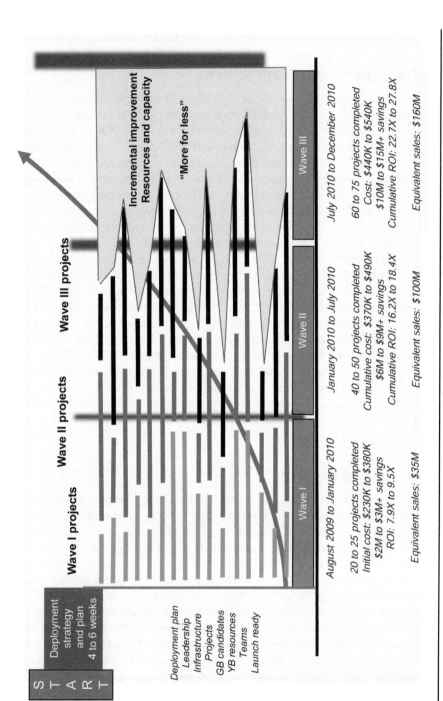

Figure 13.2 Concurrent continuous deployment (model reflects a $500M business unit).

better definition and scoping, deliberate scheduling around resources and constraints, concurrency and parallel deployment, and meticulous project management. Concurrent continuous deployment is the accelerator that enables organizations to get *more for less*, which is a great bargain in this economy. This is the application of the right methodologies and tools to maximize resources (utilization and development) and output (improvement results).

The diagram reveals an interesting story about the Scalable Lean Six Sigma™ deployment model. Concurrent continuous deployment is highly dependent on infrastructure (the first nine accelerators). This effective use of limited improvement resources and flawless execution enables organizations to lift their cumulative rate of improvement—in effect, generating more benefits in less time. Another way to view the diagram is to observe the capacity for additional improvement initiatives that is freed up over time. Again, this translates into more for less.

Let's discuss this specific benefit for a moment. *More for less* might be translated by some as *equal for less effort*. This is so far away from what concurrent continuous deployment is all about. Organizations can never become complacent or satisfied with their improvement initiatives just because they are achieving more for less, or more than the organization next door. In the new economy there are global forces threatening to equalize improvement gains as quickly as they are generated. Things such as raw material price increases, additional premium freight, or market-driven price concessions can rapidly wash away the progress from improvement. The only way to stay ahead of the power curve is with a fanatical focus on improving the rate of improvement.

We all live in a new economy characterized by *either get better* or *fall behind*. There is no such thing as staying the same anymore. As soon as organizations take their eye off the improvement ball, their improvement initiatives decline quickly and the results quickly follow. This is particularly true for organizations crawling out of the meltdown, where their people are constantly reading and interpreting leadership directions, and falling in step with what they perceive to be the priorities. To be quite candid, daily business and improvement have again been separated by many organizations during the meltdown, even though they are one and the same. It is no wonder that we now sit with yet another 80 percent Lean Six Sigma failure rate and organizations patiently waiting for the next *improvement du jour* to come along.

No matter how executives slice it, improvement is always mandatory for continued business success including before, during, and after an economic disaster. Maybe it was necessary to separate improvement from the immediate survival responses to the recent meltdown. However, remaining in this hip-shooting survival mode, or being fooled into believing that chaos is "very fast" improvement is not a long-term success strategy. No matter what lingo or label we choose for improvement, it is ludicrous to postpone or freeze improvement initiatives because:

- Improvement has a much higher ROI than the reactionary tactics used by organizations to make their financials appear to look better during this recession and recovery

- Improvement is the process of getting people to think and act differently, ask the right questions, and transform current conditions to more desirable future performance levels
- Improvement in the right mission-critical areas builds significant competitive advantage
- Improvement is always possible and necessary, especially now

The problem with improvement initiatives is that over time, it is extremely difficult to either maintain or increase the rate of improvement unless there is a lasting executive commitment, a formal monitoring infrastructure, and serious positive interventions. The 10 Accelerators and the overall infrastructure helps the executive deployment team identify these positive interventions so the improvement curve can remain on a positive slope. Strategic leadership and vision, deployment planning, and execution provide the formal processes to *improve how we improve*. Without these proactive and positive interventions, improvement initiatives go through a normal lifecycle and eventually decline into the sunset. Lack of implementation infrastructure allows improvement initiatives to lose momentum and eventually die out.

The Business Mastery Model of Improvement

Organizations have been inundated with improvement tools, and they certainly do not need another set of buzzwords to emerge successfully in this new economy. There is still too much attention on the *fluff stuff* (education on the tools) and not enough attention on the *right stuff* (leadership and infrastructure, deployment, execution processes). This continued fascination and focus on the tools themselves is a sure way to create confusion and eventually stall out an improvement initiative.

One of the secrets of improvement success is to break the pattern of the last three decades. Like hungry trout at the first hatch, executives looking for the quick fix have seemingly snapped at whatever improvement spectacle is dangled in front of them. This has been a constriction in leadership and imagination to think that strategic and continuous improvement is this easy. Too many organizations have blindly jumped into their improvement initiatives without first thinking about the specific objectives and purpose of improvement, or how to organize for a successful journey. Eventually, improvement becomes a buzzword mania of tools and techniques, the showboating of fabricated benefits, and illusive financial results. This is exactly why we have observed poor-performing companies receive Best Plants and Shingo awards, or Baldrige Award recipients filing bankruptcy.

How could this have happened? The biggest reason is that the examiners take the word of these organizations and do not take them deep enough into the details and facts. The Gemba boards, charts, and banners, the color-coding of everything from raw material totes to work instructions and employee uniforms and the other visible application of the tools looks impressive on the surface. Recently I visited another organization just beginning Lean, and toured their manufacturing area with the VP of Operations. During the tour I noticed that not a single employee talked or acknowledged our presence, so I asked an operator his thoughts about Lean. As he shrugged his shoulders and gave a blank stare at his VP as if looking for clues about what to say, the VP of Operations interrupted and said to the operator, "Never mind, I'll answer his questions." As we walked away he commented to me, "These people don't understand Lean. I'm the only one in the company with Lean experience. I redesigned their work areas into cells for them. You saw the kanbans and floor stock. Each area has its performance boards, and we review these every week and they still are not doing what they were told to do. I've had to write up a few of them." His clarification showed why you could cut the "us" and "them" characteristics of their culture with a knife! Many organizations like this one begin with the best of intentions, but end up being symbolic tool exhibitors—the substance and cultural fabric is missing and their improvement initiatives fizzle out. What is needed is the leadership committed to building the proven success infrastructure of strategic leadership and vision, deployment planning, and execution. These competitive weapons do not come to organizations by osmosis.

Let's return to the basics. Mastery is the internalized desire to become better at a particular talent. Think about what people do during their discretionary time. Why do people choose to play a musical instrument, fly fish and tie their own lures, ride mountain bikes on dangerous terrain, play in an adult hockey league, research and collect wine, and thousands of other activities? Because it is outside of the routine, autonomous, challenging, fun, developmental, results in a sense of accomplishment and satisfaction, and the experience adds to the desire to improve their particular talent. This is what mastery is all about: creating the environment of purpose. Business mastery is about creating an environment of *purpose plus profit* (versus just profit). When purpose and profit motives become unhitched in organizations, the risks (and often the outcomes) are poor performance. These outcomes show up in the form of reactionary leadership, short-sighted decision making and firefighting, poor customer service, poor quality and reliability of new products, inefficient global supply chains, customer returns and allowances, hidden and tolerable visible wastes, lack of teamwork, and an uninspiring work environment. People work long hours, follow directives, stay out of trouble, and collect a check—but the genuine commitment is not there, and they can't wait to return to their purpose-driven discretionary time. Like it or not, the recent meltdown has been the root cause of this organizational damage. It's like a spin on the famous saying from the Forrest Gump movie, "mastery is as mastery does." Executives must step up and trade in this negative effect for a more desirable organizational effect. Leadership in the new economy needs to build more capable and transcendent purpose-driven organizations characterized by innovative thinking, mastery, challenge, contribution, accomplishment, and talent development. The business mastery model builds the executive vision and roadmap for this operational and cultural transition.

A few years ago, we developed the business mastery model (see Figure 13.3) to help executives and organizations step back and realize the larger objectives of Lean Six Sigma and strategic improvement in general. One of the best practices of improvement is to revisit the objectives, purpose, and other basics of what organizations must improve within the business, independent of the improvement jargon. This leads organizations down a preferred improvement path where the business objectives define specific improvement initiatives, and drive the deployment of the right improvement methodologies and tools to the highest impact opportunities. Organizing and setting up a strategic improvement for a successful journey takes leadership commitment, time, effort, and patience—and unfortunately, more than too many overanxious organizations are willing to invest.

The idea behind the business mastery model was to step back and detach organizations from the buzzword mania and fascination with the improvement tools, or hang-ups about being different. Too often, organizations have begun

Figure 13.3   Business mastery model.

their improvement journeys with massive training on improvement jargon and tools followed by forced application of the tools to a particular situation or issue. In retrospect, the historical and current approaches to improvement are often analogous to walking into Grand Central Station and hopping on any train, before knowing the purpose, destination, and objectives of the trip. Rather than focusing on applying improvement tools, the model provides the opportunity for organizations to view the facts and strategic purpose of improvement in more practical and realistic business terms.

The business mastery model is combined with the business diagnostic process described in Chapter 4, and the objective is to help build a strategic operating model, and identify competitive strengths, weaknesses, and gaps in performance by each of the mastery components. The process works well because it leads executives in a direction of developing the improvement strategy and deployment plan, rather than jumping at immediate solutions. Originally, the business mastery model incorporated benchmarking data to help gauge progress and gaps. Over time and especially in this new economy, benchmarking data is helpful but becoming less relevant because the many best practices are now being created faster than our ability to collect and analyze meaningful benchmarking data.

This is a radical departure from the 1990s where some organizations spent more time collecting, analyzing, and presenting benchmarking data than they did in actually improving their business. We are living in a world where new leadership and improvement paths are being taken by those organizations that are clever enough to innovate and discover them. Strategic improvement is becoming a more complex and complicated core competency—one where the sprinkling of cookie-cutter Lean and Six Sigma concepts and going through the motions of developing belts is not going to cut it. To succeed in the new economy, organizations must evolve and deploy improvement deeper into the interdependent transactional processes of the enterprise and extended enterprise. The business mastery model helps to build the holistic vision of strategic improvement in the following areas:

- *Industry model mastery*—All industries have their accepted business norms and practices. These industry models are sometimes used to justify how the entire industry handles certain business issues such as returns policies, dealer and distributor practices, lead-time expectations, warranty and customer service policies, and many other factors. Global competitiveness is forcing organizations to question aspects of their industry models and reinvent new value propositions for customer and market needs. The objective of industry model mastery is to uncover the unspoken and unknown market needs and differentiate performance and capabilities from what the rest of the industry is doing. Examples of this include the availability of Apple iPhone software applications, healthcare institutions shifting focus to prevention and wellness, additional services provided by upscale automobile dealers such as breakfast, a wash, a free rental, pizza, and a play area for children, and the Harley Davidson ultimate freedom lifestyle experience described in Chapter 10.

- *Innovation mastery*—This is the combining of *innovation* and *process*, which sounds like an oxymoronic endeavor. Process conjures boundaries, structure, and controls, while innovation is best fostered in unfettered surroundings. The objective of this mastery component is to identify innovative, best practices improvement opportunities that wow the marketplace and provide a competitive advantage. Today, organizations are managing inputs on a global scale across every boundary one can imagine—across engineering disciplines and in concert with all the other business disciplines in multiple countries. Innovation mastery is setting the bar and building best practices that are unique and extremely difficult to replicate over time. Innovation mastery is a team sport that is dependent on a culture of information exchange, knowledge sharing, and openness. It takes people working together across different groups, disciplines, and organizational lines to make it happen. It also takes real leadership in charting the course and inspiring people to reach for the highest level of performance, supported by a never-ending focus on integrity.

- *Customer mastery*—This business component relates to the organization's ability to identify known and unknown marked needs, and then translate those needs into innovative product and service offerings. In effect, it is the creation of new value propositions that exceed the offerings and value of competitors. The other side of innovation mastery is product lifecycle management and product rationalization. Apple is one of the most popular examples with its iPod, iPhone, and iPad technology and its new line of user-friendly Mac personal computers. Most organizations have a significant opportunity to improve their business by focusing on new product identification and introduction, new product development, and customer or product rationalization. The key to success lies in unlocking innovation and thinking beyond the box. Organizations also recognize that they are not in a one-size-fits-all business, and they manage different customer and product segments in different ways to optimize growth and profitability.

- *Value chain mastery*—This mastery component deals with achieving flexibility, responsiveness, synchronization, and instantaneous response and adjustment across the total supply chain. Globalization and outsourcing has achieved incremental revenue and cost reduction benefits for organizations, but at the same time, it has removed flexibility and responsiveness. Value chain mastery is about creating supply chain superiority from forecasting and supply-demand management to continuous pipeline flow and rapid-reflex execution. A valuable reference for value chain mastery is the supply chain operations reference (SCOR) model, which provides a familiar plan-source-make-deliver-return framework of supply chain excellence. Value chain mastery incorporates the enabling strategy, planning and execution processes, information, technology, inventory management and logistics, capital assets, transportation, and other management best practices, and the right event-driven metrics. The supply chain provides extensive opportunities for revenue growth, improved profitability, and superior competitiveness. Organizations such as Dell, Nokia, Proctor and Gamble, IBM, Walmart, Anheuser-Busch, Coca-Cola, Best Buy, and many others are the poster children of value chain mastery.

• *Integration and data mastery*—Executives are making critical business decisions every day based on the information available to them. This information can come from a variety of sources including data from the formal business architecture, kluge Excel spreadsheets and Access data bases, opinions from peers and colleagues, unsubstantiated e-mail, voice mails and telephone calls from around the world, a personal sense of intuition or business judgment, or other internal or external data sources. The problem in most organizations is that despite the millions in IT investment, there are still too many versions of the facts, a lack of the facts, or too much manual effort to search for the facts. Off the record, most executives will admit to making important decisions on the basis of inadequate information. This suggests that problems in decision-making are arising in the quality, volume, consistency, and timeliness of information. What is needed is a believable 360-degree view of their enterprise from an integrated enterprise architecture. This includes the right event driven metrics that enable people in organizations to sense-interpret-decide-act-monitor (SIDAM) their end-to-end business processes in real time. Real-time visibility provides not only a means to verify and justify results, but also full confidence that small and midsize companies are leveraging consistency, accuracy, and timeliness via a single data source to make better, faster decisions.

• *Human resource and talent mastery*—Prior to the meltdown, improvement and people development initiatives were rolled out through more of a batch train-the-masses approach. These hit or miss, throw-it-up-on-the-ceiling-and-see-if-it-sticks approaches require too much effort, overhead, and time—in fact, more than the new economy is willing to permit if organizations wish to reclaim their competitive momentum. Now, human resource and talent mastery has become a global challenge with global implications. A more continuous and targeted talent development and talent management process is needed in the new economy. Best organizations believe in the importance of human capital and acquire, develop, and grow their organizational talent continuously through good and bad times. These organizations build a strong culture that embraces improvement and change and allows for issues and challenges to be accepted as thinkable and doable challenges, not as insurmountable disasters. This is the exception to how most organizations have reacted to the recent meltdown. This mastery component deals with developing a best-in-class workforce made up of the most loyal and talented people. Predictions about the workforce in this new economy estimate that as the demand for talent escalates, the supply will spiral downward, culminating in a corporate war for talent. To win the war, organizations will need to be skilled at hiring and promoting people, and even more importantly, able to keep others from stealing away their talent. In today's economy, baby boomers with significant business experience are beginning to retire quickly. The emerging workforce is much different demographically from the past, and organizations are faced with enormous challenges in backfilling positions and succession planning. The success of organizations rests on the speed at which they can transform their people into flexible, multiskilled and multidisciplined people.

The business mastery model provides a practical roadmap for relevant discussions about improving business performance and competitiveness, while discouraging the temptation to think about how quickly organizations can implement and finish their continuous improvement activities. Lean Six Sigma and other strategic improvement directives are complicated initiatives to implement correctly, reap the results, and stay the course.

The recent meltdown certainly has neutralized many of the positive business improvements that organizations have implemented during the past few years. It is an unrealistic expectation that these inefficiencies can be fixed in a few weeks or a few months. If it were that easy, we would not be looking at the parade of failed improvement programs over the past three decades and organizations would have figured out how to resolve all of their critical strategic issues. Improvement Excellence™ is a legitimate core competency that will raise organizations out of the ashes to new levels of competitiveness and superior performance. Strategic improvement is an executive commitment to a new organizational lifestyle and culture, and the business mastery model is a rock-solid first step in this process.

The business mastery model has proven to be an effective means of avoiding the distraction of the tools themselves and focusing on the real things that matter in an organization's deployment. When improvement initiatives such as Lean Six Sigma do not go as planned, it is usually because the implementation infrastructure and processes were not defined. A well-structured strategic leadership and vision, deployment planning, and execution infrastructure is the largest enabler of concurrent continuous improvement.

Improvement Excellence™—The Foundation of Business Mastery

At the heart of the business mastery model is Improvement Excellence™, the foundation mastery. The only way to transcend the present state into a more desirable and profitable one is through well-designed, planned, and executed improvement. The heart is a deliberate analogy because like the human body we cannot function physically, emotionally, or passionately without a heart. Improvement Excellence™ is the *Hemi* engine that drives superior performance across all components of the model. However, it is the outer ring of components in the model that shape and determine the strategic leadership and vision, deployment planning, and execution infrastructure.

There is a critical law about strategic improvement that is experienced by only the most committed professionals. The things that matter most about strategic improvement are the things one learns after they think they know it all. Organizations that underestimate or oversimplify the mission, choose focus on generic education and the tools, or go through the motions are stuck in their own Achilles' heel of improvement. People in these organizations who think they know how to improve and then hang around pontificating to each other are often the largest obstacles to improvement. Many of these organizations have little to show for their illusive expertise in knowing how to improve. One executive recently commented, *"We know how to do everything that your firm does but can you email me your methodology and implementation plans from a few recent projects? I know we can do this on our own."* Over the years, I have lost count of how many of these individuals called months later, looking for new employment!

There is a very simple test to determine if you know how to improve: *demonstrated results* from a proven track record of planning, deploying, implementing, and sustaining improvement successfully. Organizations that truly know how to improve, are doing so with a formal improvement initiative and achieving breakthrough and sustainable results. Additionally, their demonstrated results are proportional to how much they truly know about how to improve. The remainder of these organizations just continue talking about how to improve. This is not a criticism, just another fact and a huge barrier to success. Improvement Excellence™ and *improving how we improve* is an evolving core competency that produces strategic value. Those who acquire it correctly and continuously develop this core competency will achieve unlimited strategic value in their business, particularly in this challenging economy. Those who treat it with the simplicity and trivia of more boilerplate training and filling in the forms will join the 80% failure side of improvement. The only thing that is simple and trivial to Improvement Excellence™ is the familiar moral to its story: do all of the right things right the first time, or avoid the trouble, time, resources, costs, and cultural risk of another failed fad improvement program (and accept the consequences of inferior industry performance). Improvement Excellence™ is not optional in the new economy.

No matter how much an organization improves, the limits of improvement are their own self-imposed limits on the organization. These limits can only be heightened through the creative evolution and deployment of improvement to new strategic opportunities. This represents the challenge and upside power of improvement because the largest opportunities for improvement are those that we do not know about yet. It is time to face the competitive music, blow off the improvement dust, address new improvement opportunities, and achieve new levels of improvement and performance.

Despite the recent meltdown and slow recovery, there are more opportunities for improvement than ever before, although this might be hard to believe for organizations involved in various improvement initiatives for the past three decades. At the same time, there is a strong reluctance to invest in improvement and go for the real opportunities to improve global competitiveness. Improvement programs have had several rides up and down these lifecycles for the past three decades, and the leadership behaviors through this recent meltdown are causing Lean Six Sigma and other improvement initiatives to follow suit.

Leadership will make the difference between new successes or another failed improvement program. Organizations are now at a critical juncture where they will lose big time if they allow Lean Six Sigma and other recent strategic improvement initiatives to fizzle. The choice is simple: organizations can choose to either step up and improve how they improve, reaping the benefits of their successes (Improvement Excellence™), or stand passively on the sidelines and watch their latest Lean Six Sigma initiatives melt away (self-fulfilling and self-destructive improvement).

The Black Hole of Improvement

In astronomy, *black holes* are the evolutionary endpoints of stars at least 10 to 15 times as massive as the earth's sun. If a star that massive (or larger) undergoes a supernova explosion, it may leave behind an enormous, burned out stellar remnant. With no outward forces to oppose gravity, the remnant will collapse inward on itself. The star eventually collapses to the point of zero volume and infinite density, creating what is known as a *singularity*. Singularity is a term often used to refer to the center of a black hole, where the curvature of space-time is maximal. At the singularity, the gravitational tides diverge and no solid object can even theoretically survive hitting the singularity.

Mathematically, a singularity is a condition when equations do not give a valid value that can sometimes be avoided by using a different coordinate system. Around the singularity is a region where the force of gravity is so strong, that not even light can escape. Thus, no information can reach us from this region. It is therefore called a black hole, and its surface is called the *event horizon*. The event horizon is the distance from a black hole within which nothing can escape. In addition, nothing can prevent a particle from hitting the singularity in a short amount of proper time once it has entered the horizon. In this sense, the event horizon is the point of no return.

So what does all of this have to do with Lean Six Sigma, strategic improvement, accelerating results, and Improvement Excellence™? The black hole analogy is relevant to the course of improvement initiatives during the past three decades, and mimics what will happen to Lean Six Sigma if organizations do not shift from survival mode to success mode soon. In all honesty, Lean Six Sigma and other strategic initiatives *are* extremely difficult to sustain, particularly with all the other new requirements that the new economy has placed on organizations

The initiatives have a familiar pattern of lasting and producing benefits for a while, but then they reach the singularity and event horizon zones and eventually disappear down the black hole.

A simplified example of the black hole analogy is a person with a kayak. If the person is kayaking in the summer on Lake Erie near the Cleveland shores, everything is great. This is the same as an improvement initiative that is working well and producing results and culture change. If this person is kayaking on Lake Erie the following spring near Buffalo and enters the mouth of the Niagara River, he or she may experience strong currents and frequent chaotic swirls, but still be able to paddle and avoid danger. This is the same as an improvement initiative hitting a few bumps but getting back on course with a few corrective actions. But, if the person does not pay attention and drifts nonchalantly down the Niagara River, he or she will soon reach singularity where the current is noticeable and begins to significantly impair his course. This is the same as an improvement initiative that begins to fall apart due to lack of commitment, leadership, priorities, or other factors. The only thing that saves the kayaker and the improvement initiative at this point is serious leadership, external intervention, and corrective action. If the kayaker does not pay attention and goes beyond Navy Island, he is in the *event horizon* where the current is too strong—the point of no return. Finally, the kayaker is doomed and travels over the falls—the black hole—and disappears from sight.

Executives have lived through this cycle with previous improvement initiatives for the past three decades. One moment, the improvement initiatives are in the forefront, supported, and producing great results for the organization. Then, they lose importance and finally fade into the sunset. If you ask the people in these organizations what happened, everyone has a different opinion, but, nobody seems to know for sure. Organizations may pass the buck with their discussions, but the buck stops with executive leadership.

The most disturbing reason cited for failure is a change in executive leadership where improvement is not on the new person's agenda. This is as foolish as removing growth, market share, and profitability from the executive agenda. This is a cultural blow to organizations that experience good things coming out of their Lean and Six Sigma initiatives and suddenly receive the edicts from above to cut back on improvement. The more improvement lifecycles that an organization experiences, the less likely it is to step up and actively participate in another one.

Avoiding the Black Hole of Improvement

The answer to this issue is in the infrastructure stressed throughout the book: strategic leadership and vision, deployment planning, and execution. This includes leadership and business issues, organizational challenges, culture and cultural drivers, attitudes and management styles, code of conduct, beliefs, values, historical experiences with improvement, and readiness for improvement—all of which are attainable via the business diagnostic.

Organizations avoid the black hole of improvement by one of two means: (1) executives must lead upstream and not allow forces to jeopardize improvement progress, or (2) executives must intervene soon enough and make the right corrective course actions. Both of these require formal processes (i.e., the 10 Accelerators) for prevention.

The process that breaks down the barriers and detractors of strategic improvement the most is direct executive engagement and architecting of the strategic leadership and vision, and deployment planning infrastructure elements. These processes create a clear and concise view of what is working well, what is broken, a vision of what is possible and achievable, a validated analysis of potential benefits, a realistic plan and direction for moving forward, and the true barriers to success. What makes this story so compelling is the objectivity, independence, and undisputable data and facts that comprise the improvement vision and deployment plan. As has been stressed many times throughout this book, this infrastructure is what gets organizations off the dime and energizes their strategic improvement initiatives and sustains long-term success.

Integrating the 10 Accelerators

The rewards of actively pursuing an integrated business improvement strategy can be significant, and failing to do so can be somewhere between unsuccessful and catastrophic. The largest shift that organizations must make in the new economy is to integrate the philosophy of improvement into the total business—for the long haul and for real. Success with improvement is no different from success with an acquisition, success from a new product, success by penetrating new market opportunities, and other business initiatives. The best strategy in the world will fail without a solid implementation process and clear measurable results.

A large amount of symptomatic improvement effort in the absence of strategy alignment, and direct linkage to business objectives may produce some short-term results. A focus on the tools of improvement instead of the cultural process of improvement will be short lived. Failure to conduct due diligence about what needs to be done to create strategic success will result in wasted efforts toward improvement. The 10 Accelerators of Lean Six Sigma are the basic building blocks found within the strategic leadership and vision, deployment planning and execution phases of a deployment. They provide the proven roadmap, structure, process, performance measurement, and human systems for a successful Lean Six Sigma and other strategic initiatives. Collectively and at a minimum, the 10 Accelerators are a guaranteed insurance policy against failure with Lean Six Sigma. But for the most part, the 10 Accelerators are the practical secret of rapid deployment and rapid results, and sustainable strategic improvement.

There is a world of difference in results when organizations commit to the patience, time, resources, and processes to get it right the first time. Organizations are bound to make mistakes with Lean Six Sigma and other large-scale improvement initiatives. However, the biggest mistake organizations can make is to conveniently rationalize away the facts, problems, and root causes of their deployment—or any other business endeavor for that matter. These accelerators repeatedly have created the rapid deployment, rapid enduring results characteristics of our Scalable Lean Six Sigma™ model.

In the new economy, organizations must create the strategic leadership and vision, deployment planning, and execution infrastructure. Then, they must build the benchmark implementation process that leads to breakthrough results and cultural transformation. Organizations that continue with postponing, shortcutting, or flippantly dabbling with strategic improvement will pay the consequences of lost market presence and decreasing financial performance. A well-structured and well-executed strategic improvement initiative carries over into every other organizational activity and changes the way that people think and work. Remember, it is always more costly and time consuming to do things wrong and do them over again than it does to do them right the first time.

References

Anderson, D. M. 2004. *Design for Manufacturability & Concurrent Engineering: How to Design for Low Cost, Design in High Quality, Design for Lean Manufacturing, and Design Quickly for Fast Production.* CIM Press, Cambria, CA.

Bolstorff, P., and Rosenbaum, R. 2003. *Supply Chain Excellence: A Handbook for Dramatic Improvement using the SCOR Model.* AMACOM, New York, NY.

Goldsby, T., and Martichinko, R. 2005. *Lean Six Sigma Logistics: Strategic Development to Operational Success.* J. Ross Publishing, Ft. Lauderdale, FL.

Skarzynski, P., and Gibson, R. 2008. *Innovation to the Core: A Blueprint for Transforming the Way Your Company Innovates.* Boston: Harvard Business School Publications, Cambridge, MA.

Chapter 13 Take Aways

- Concurrent continuous deployment is the continuous development of people and completion of improvement projects based on current critical needs. Although a deployment may begin with teams and projects leaving the same starting gate, improvement activities do not need to begin and end at the same time. Concurrent continuous deployment optimizes the opportunities for improvement by overlapping wave activities, and reducing aggregate cycle time for the overall deployment progress.

- There is a critical law about strategic improvement that is experienced only by the most committed professionals. The things that matter most about strategic improvement are the things one learns after they think they know it all. No matter how much an organization improves, the limits of improvement are their own self-imposed limits on the organization.

- The business mastery model enables organizations to revisit the objectives, purpose, and other basics of what must improve within the business, independent of the improvement jargon. This leads organizations down a preferred improvement path where the business objectives define specific improvement initiatives, and drive the deployment of the right improvement methodologies and tools to the highest impact opportunities. As the model points out, strategic improvement is about evolving key business components that are universal in most organizations to breakthrough levels of superior performance.

- Organizations avoid the black hole of improvement by one of two means: (1) executives must lead upstream and not allow forces to jeopardize improvement progress, or (2) executives must intervene soon enough and make the right corrective course actions. Both of these require formal processes (i.e., the 10 Accelerators) for prevention.

- The largest shift that organizations must make in the new economy is to integrate the philosophy of improvement into the total business—for the long haul and for real. In the new economy, organizations must create the strategic leadership and vision, deployment planning, and execution infrastructure. Then they must build the benchmark implementation process that leads to breakthrough results and cultural transformation.

- The 10 Accelerators of Lean Six Sigma are the basic building blocks found with the strategic leadership and vision, deployment planning, and execution phases of a deployment. They provide the proven roadmap, structure, process, performance measurement, and human systems for a successful Lean Six Sigma and other strategic initiatives. Collectively and at a minimum, the 10 Accelerators are a guaranteed insurance policy against failure with Lean Six Sigma. But for the most part, the 10 Accelerators are the practical secret of rapid deployment and rapid results, and sustainable strategic improvement.

PART III:
Next Generation Lean Six Sigma: The Intersection of Leadership, Innovation, and Enabling Technology

"It's through curiosity and looking at opportunities in new ways that we've always mapped our path at Dell. There's always an opportunity to make a difference."

Michael Dell, CEO
Dell Computers

14

Greatest Opportunities: Transactional Business Process Improvement

---

We mentioned earlier in the book that the new economy is accelerating the transformation of organizations into a complex global network of interdependent transactional enterprises. Technology is enabling this transformation faster than most organizations can assimilate it successfully. This transformation is also creating the greatest opportunities for forward-thinking organizations to improve, leapfrog competitors, and dominate global markets in the new economy. The future of improvement (see Figure 14.1) is without a doubt in the transactional enterprise and extended enterprise space. To be successful, organizations will need to become much more committed and aggressive about the core competency of strategic improvement—for the long haul. They will need to build organizations that proactively seek out and act on every improvement moment, and evolve toward a state of Improvement Excellence™: improving how they improve, or simply improving the velocity, boundaries, and magnitude of improvement.

Many of these knowledge and transactional processes and the associated wastes and inefficiencies have become institutionalized as business process norms. In fact, some functions have received their exemption from improvement because their regular duties (e.g., selling, designing, financial closing, etc.) are more important than improvement. This is a familiar and recurring version of the *separation disorder of improvement*. Organizations have focused most of their improvement initiatives in the past on their manufacturing operations. Improving yields, reducing cycle times and changeover times, reducing scrap and rework, smoothing out production schedules with pull systems, improving flow through work cells, 5S*ing* the plant, reducing maintenance costs and unplanned downtime, improving supplier quality, visual controls, and the like are valid manufacturing improvement

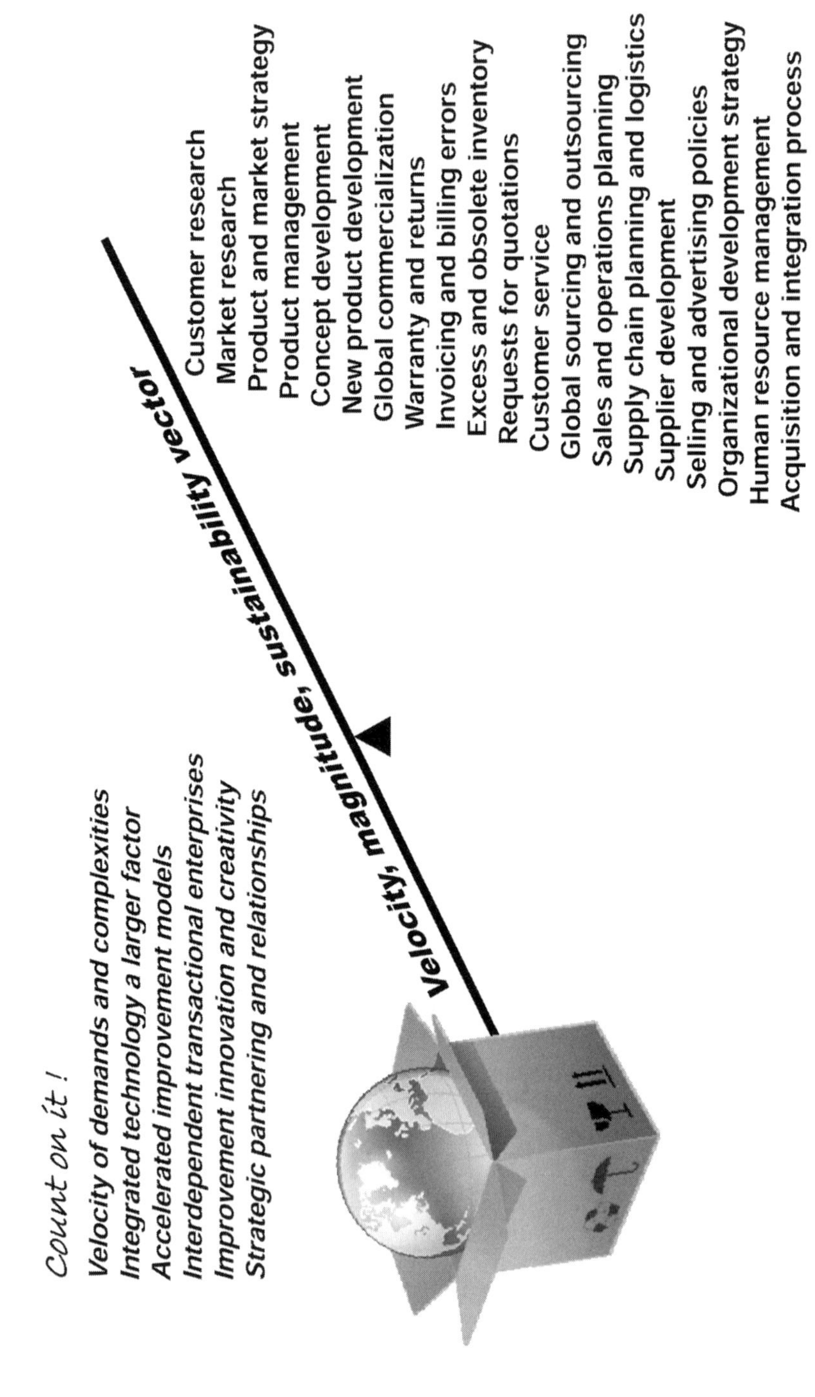

Count on it !

Velocity of demands and complexities
Integrated technology a larger factor
Accelerated improvement models
Interdependent transactional enterprises
Improvement innovation and creativity
Strategic partnering and relationships

Velocity, magnitude, sustainability vector

Customer research
Market research
Product and market strategy
Product management
Concept development
New product development
Global commercialization
Warranty and returns
Invoicing and billing errors
Excess and obsolete inventory
Requests for quotations
Customer service
Global sourcing and outsourcing
Sales and operations planning
Supply chain planning and logistics
Supplier development
Selling and advertising policies
Organizational development strategy
Human resource management
Acquisition and integration process

Figure 14.1   The future of improvement.

initiatives. For three decades, we have whipped manufacturing with the latest and greatest improvement programs with successful results, and operations executives have become better versed in improvement as a result.

Manufacturing improvement is usually a more structured and defined improvement. One can observe and touch products, physically walk through the process, and look at routine quality reports, routings, and work instructions. Transactional process improvement presents opportunity, but not without the challenge. These processes always seem to have three common versions: the way the process was designed to and should work, the way the process is documented in the ISO manual, and the way the process actually works. Value stream mapping one's way through transactional processes is often like attempting to do a book report on a book you did not read. There is usually a high level of nonstandard work content, as the book reports will vary from person to person.

The Migration to Transactional Process Improvement

A number of major events have caused this shift from manufacturing improvement to enterprise improvement:

1. The assembly content of products has shifted away from hardware and more towards software. In the 1980s for example, every minicomputer company had their own proprietary hardware with their own designs, components, suppliers, and manufacturing operations. The improvement methodologies and tools that arrived from Japan (The Toyota Production System or TPS, translated industrial engineering books on specific tools such as one piece flow, quick changeover, TQM, TPM, pull systems, kanban, etc.) were most applicable to manufacturing. As the hardware-to-software content shifted, so did the need for an improvement shift from manufacturing upstream to design and development. However, the Lean tools were not readily adaptable to areas such as software development or accounting, and many organizations ended up with several lost Lean Manufacturing people trying to force-fit their manufacturing-focused improvement techniques. Some organizations bought into activities such as 5S*ing* their offices. One organization allowed their 5S gurus to run wild in the office and ended up with everything from the contents of their file cabinets (e.g., payroll, monthly financials, executive salaries, performance reviews, time and attendance, etc.) to the paper cutter, tape dispenser, and stapler being labeled and placed in their appropriate red squares. A familiar theme throughout this book is summarized in this key question, "What is the purpose of improvement and how does this benefit the customer and other stakeholders?"
2. The hardware side of the equation has become generic. As this has happened, a mindset has developed in many organizations that anyone anywhere can build their products. Manufacturing is no longer viewed as

a necessary internal core competency, but the results of manufacturing (e.g., availability, delivery, quality, reliability, flexibility, value, etc.) are more important than ever before. In fact, product development is following this trend as hardware and software for entire products is outsourced to external contractors. Today many electronics manufacturers use the same suppliers and same components to manufacture their products. The differentiating factor in many products is the proprietary software architecture and circuitry, not the box itself. Recently, there has been a strong tendency to lessen this generic trend through innovative packaging and a new focus on the customer experience—from shopping to purchase, from opening the box to the look and feel of the product and the first few minutes of using the product. Obviously, this will not change the *genericizing of manufacturing.* For the most part, manufacturing is an afterthought in these organizations.

3. Outsourcing is fallout from the genericizing factor, and it has a tremendous impact on this shift away from local manufacturing improvement. During the past several years, outsourcing has become the latest movement to reduce operating costs, and internal manufacturing complexity and content. The primary driver of outsourcing is to establish local country presence and the incremental revenues that it represents, and to reduce manufacturing costs. There has not been due diligence when making these decisions. Organizations made significant improvements in quality, reliability, cycle time reduction, cost, flexibility, and responsiveness within U.S. manufacturing during the past three decades. Many outsourcing decisions have moved current problems or placed manufacturing back in the 1980s levels of batch-push and expedite performance. Today, many organizations are struggling with the same manufacturing issues with their offshore suppliers as they did 20 or 30 years ago in their domestic manufacturing operations. Manufacturing still matters, but it is 8000 miles away and under an external supplier's roof. In many cases, costs have only moved from the manufacturing bucket to a larger supply chain bucket. Outsourcing is generally feasible from a revenue perspective, but not always from a cost perspective. Executives are motivated by Wall Street—making sure that incremental revenues are higher than incremental costs, so the financials will show growth and earnings per share improvement. There are significant outsourcing process improvement opportunities that we will share with you later in this chapter.

4. Domestic manufacturing is just too costly, too complicated and too much work. As technology has evolved, the importance of manufacturing has diminished. Universities are turning out people well versed in science, information technology, and the Internet at a higher rate than mechanical engineers who will end up troubleshooting equipment. Besides, the offshoring mindset is at play here: "An engineer in India costs between one-third and one-half that of an engineer in the United States" or "We

can get anyone to build our products—it's not a big deal." Manufacturing is irrelevant to these organizations. What executives fail to recognize is the level of variation that is introduced by spreading and splintering things around the globe. Many executives are content building a targeted technology-driven organization focused on marketing, design, selling, and distribution. They have made a conscious decision to remain hollow when it comes to manufacturing and let one of their external suppliers worry about it. The reality is that manufacturing *is* relevant, but it is now within the control of external organizations. When hardware or software applications do not work, it is as much the organization's problem as it is the supplier's. The hidden costs of these situations are undocumented and unknown to most organizations.

5. A quality product or service provided on time, in whatever volume and mix needed by the customer, is a given in the new economy. The significant differentiation opportunities lie in total solution selling: delivering the full capabilities of the entire organization to the customer. The solutions themselves are found by building superior transactional processes such as sales and marketing, new product identification, sales and operations planning, new product development, supply chain management, customer service and support, supplier collaboration, and many other nonproduction activities.

6. The performance of transactional processes have a significant impact on the enterprise (positive or negative). When there are problems with strategic planning, sales and operations planning, new product development, or credit and collections processes, the impact on the organization is millions of dollars. Since organizations are interconnected by these interdependent transactional processes, a problem in one area produces direct problems in that immediate area and residual problems in other areas. Therefore, the opportunities for improvement are millions of dollars, with a major strategic impact on the entire organization.

As improvement professionals have become more versed in applying Lean Six Sigma beyond manufacturing and across the business, it becomes evident that the majority of root causes of manufacturing problems are created in the transactional processes. Many issues within areas such as product availability, delivery performance, quality, excess and obsolete inventory, warranty and returns, field service and repair, supplier performance, financial variances, efficiencies, overhead absorption, and many other problems are directly traceable to root causes in market research, new product concept planning, new product development, sales and operations planning, the selling process, outsourcing, and other transactional processes. In the past, it was convenient to blame manufacturing for all of the organization's problems, and that explains the focus of improvement in manufacturing for the past three decades. We beat up manufacturing with these improvement programs to reduce costs, when 80 percent or more of the cost was already locked-in back in the functional specification within the product development process. Manufacturing was far from perfect, but domestic manufacturing operations have improved significantly over the past few decades, almost to a point of diminishing returns if organizations overlook their transactional process improvement opportunities.

The good news in all of this is that organizations can improve transactional processes and significantly influence offshore manufacturing at the same time. The next decade will be interesting as China develops and their costs, quality performance, raw material availability, working conditions, lead times, flexibility, environmental problems, and political atmosphere also evolve. A few organizations have decided to relocate their manufacturing operations from China and Mexico back to the United States or some other international location. History tends to repeat itself. Maybe we will see more of this trend, but the whole outsourcing issue is a moving target that needs strategic adjustment and continuous improvement to remain profitable and in synch with global markets.

Challenges of Transactional Processes

The fusion of Lean Six Sigma combined with extensive experiences with root-cause problem solving and innovation allow organizations to view their business from a different and much healthier perspective. This is exactly what Michael Hammer and James Champy were trying to promote with their 1993 book *Reengineering the Corporation*. Conceptually, reengineering was a good idea, but it lacked a reasonable basis for just throwing out existing processes and starting over. This across-the-board thinking of *outside the box* was the wrong concept, because not everything *in the box* is bad and needs to radically change. Thinking strategically and selectively *beyond the box* is a more realistic way to think about reengineering. The Lean Six Sigma methodology and tools are enablers of both process improvement and process reengineering. This recent evolution in improvement has provided a more robust methodology (DMAIC), analytical problem solving tools, and a broader perspective of business improvement across the enterprise.

Prior to Lean Six Sigma, there were several attempts to apply manufacturing improvement tools and jargon to the office. Not surprisingly, there has been little success. The tool zealots have attempted to 5S and *lean out* the office areas, value stream map the universe, revise office layouts and information flows, simplify or eliminate redundant documents, or consolidate office supplies. But for the most part, these have been either trivial or small incremental improvements.

There exists significant opportunities by focusing on transactional processes. Transactional processes are loaded with hidden costs and inefficiencies that have negative relational impacts on other areas. An example of this is a sales force that provides incomplete information that leads to forecast errors, premium freight, stock-outs, quality issues due to expedited handling, and problems with the customer experience. Another example might be a design team that rushed an incomplete design to market to meet revenue targets, only to create supplier manufacturability problems, engineering changes, field quality problems, customer returns, and loss of market credibility. Transactional processes are extremely complex, multistage processes by nature. Since transactional processes are integrated and interdependent, an improvement in one area provides residual improvements in other areas.

The real challenge with improvement is in working one's way through the transactional maze, and defining and scoping out legitimate, data-driven transactional improvement opportunities. These are opportunities that will have a significant impact on the business and enable multiple successful executions on strategy. Chasing down these opportunities is a bit like a chess game where the distinction between cause and effect is critical. It also requires deeper leadership and expertise, key business process knowledge, and experience with industry best practices.

Information technology (IT) plays a critical role in the ability to acquire data and recreate scenarios and situational conditions so that the true root causes can be identified. The largest challenge with transactional processes is the isolation of causes and effects. For example, forecast accuracy or design reviews can be both a cause and an effect depending how the transactional opportunity is defined. It requires much more skill to structure, scope, and define transactional opportunities correctly and in an actionable manner. Even the best improvement professionals find themselves refining the objectives and scope, improvement goals, and benefits as they work their way through one of these complex transactional improvement projects.

The true story of transactional processes is not as obvious and easy to define as a scrap or cycle-time reduction project in manufacturing. Furthermore, there is a higher content of nonstandard work, regardless of what is documented in the ISO manuals. Failure to recognize the importance of leadership, key business process knowledge, and experience with industry best practices will often result in either symptomatic problem solving or boil-the-ocean problem solving. If transactional opportunities are defined ad hoc and based on opinion versus facts, the organization will waste a lot of time and resources improving the wrong areas, chasing after symptoms, and repeatedly dealing with the same issues. The appearance and perception of improvement is much different from the tangible business results of improvement. Improvement Excellence™ is the core competency that enables the latter outcome, and IT plays a major role in piecing together the puzzle of improvement.

Nearly 100 years ago, Will Rogers said, "I never met a man I didn't like." We feel just as strong when it comes to transactional process opportunities because we have never found a key business process that could not be improved significantly. Many of the common transactional process improvement opportunities that yield the greatest benefit are presented in the remaining sections of this chapter. These transactional processes are fairly common across all industries be it a high tech company, a hospital, or a financial services organization. The descriptions are not all inclusive of every improvement opportunity, but provide examples and ideas for improvement based on previous client and industry experiences.

Strategic Planning

The traditional annual strategic planning exercise has become inadequate and ineffective for many organizations. The emerging windows of opportunity and change are much shorter than the normal one- to-five-year planning horizon of strategic planning. The stagnant *update the binder* approach to strategic planning tends to be more of a financial and numbers exercise, and does not integrate the rapidly emerging challenges and opportunities of the new economy. This practice often eliminates the rigorous analysis necessary to better understand strategic opportunities, and tends to view business strategy as a discrete (annual) process instead of a continuous one.

In this economy, the annual strategic planning process becomes obsolete quickly, and most organizations are missing the formal mechanisms to keep strategic plans current and up to date. A number of organizations have modified their strategic planning horizon by applying Lean Six Sigma (e.g. Pareto analysis, value stream mapping, regression analysis, etc.) to their strategic planning process. A few organizations have shifted to a one- to three-year strategic plan with quarterly planning updates on an exception basis (e.g., the *tall pole* opportunities). Lean Six Sigma helps executives better understand the strategic levers of their business and how to best influence strategic and financial success. Strategic planning processes must become more flexible and evolving and must be guided or influenced by strategic improvement initiatives. The new economy is driving the convergence of an organization's strategic planning and annual operating plan activities.

Customer and Market Research

This involves the application of Lean Six Sigma and other data-driven analytics for ongoing processes to better understand the multiple voices of the customer. The new economy is driving the need to conduct more segmented and targeted customer analysis (e.g. size, region, sales history and trends, solution solving opportunities, etc.), real-time point-of-sale analysis, and other ongoing analytics that enable a better understanding of customers, customer segments, and their different requirements.

Organizations are using Lean Six Sigma to transition from an all-things-to-all-customers business model to a more focused and targeted customer relationship management model driven by different segments with different requirements. Several independent improvement opportunities exist in this area to develop more robust customer and market analysis processes that provide additional facts about specific data-driven requirements, competitive profiles and offerings, customers and market share, drivers of customer and market loyalty, and future business opportunities. Many organizations are inundated with customer and market research data and related information, but they do not have standardized methodologies and processes to synthesize this information and draw the right data-driven conclusions about market and new products and services opportunities.

New Product Innovation and Market Strategy

There are several high-impact transactional opportunities in this area. Organizations are challenged with defining the right new products and their associated features, functions, and other specification data. Many of these decisions are based on emotion and the gotta-have-it mindset of the sales and engineering organizations. Many are also challenged by defining new product architectures in the next three to five years with people stuck in the mindset of today's technology. In many cases, product definition and compromises are left up to interpretation by individuals downstream where it becomes incrementally costly. Other weaknesses typically include the failure to analyze and directly relate the importance of product features and functions to time-to-market impact, additional costs, quality and reliability risks, supplier capabilities, incremental market share, and updated profit-and-loss impact. Product and market strategy can benefit greatly by having a disciplined and formal fact-driven process, standardization of product definition and evaluation activities, front-loaded risk assessment, pro forma financials and modeling, and metrics for these activities.

Let's Clear Up the 3M Experience

For the past five years, nearly every product development executive has expressed their concern about Lean Six Sigma and point to 3M's bad experience of stifling innovation and revenues from new products. 3M's bad experience was not directly the fault of Lean Six Sigma; it was the naive leadership choice to deploy Lean Six Sigma everywhere, following the boilerplate GE, big bang, train-the-masses model, and demanding compliance to the methodology. As mentioned in Chapter 9, innovation is by definition a wicked problem. Blindly deploying Lean Six Sigma was the equivalent of attempting to reduce innovation to a linear, standardized, well-defined and structured five-step (DMAIC) process and a sure way to choke out innovation and new product ideas. Many have heard about the 3M experience, but there are thousands of other unpublicized examples of bad experiences and deployment choices (and bad results) with Lean Six Sigma.

Generic, across-the-board Lean Six Sigma deployments, are the least successful improvement initiatives. With innovation, strategic improvement requires leadership and practitioner judgment in terms of how to translate the ideologically qualities of Lean Six Sigma into meaningful, value-added improvements. Stated another way, the experiences of 3M and others could have been avoided through the use of creative and adaptive elements of Lean Six Sigma and other improvement approaches (e.g., voice of the market, use of innovation teams, visualization and information sharing, non-linear mapping techniques, risk and worth factor analysis, modeling, common sense, etc.). It is possible to improve the innovation process, but not with a rigid and mandated set of one-size-fits-all improvement tools. Improving innovation is best accomplished by establishing the free wheeling, open collaboration environment and culture for innovation. Organizations can benefit more from Lean Six Sigma on the execution side of innovation (i.e., how to translate new product ideas into commercialized products). The moral of this story is that in the absence of the core competency of Improvement Excellence™, Lean Six Sigma can sometimes accomplish more harm than good. The good news is that 3M is back on top of its innovation game and a benchmark new product innovation model.

Product Management

Product management involves a formal lifecycle management process for the product portfolio. Many organizations have no problem adding new products and SKU variations to their product portfolio, but it becomes a major emotional process of discontinuing old products from the portfolio. The sales organization wants anything they can possibly sell to remain in the portfolio and points out the risk of potential lost revenue. These behaviors are heavily influenced by the performance criteria of "revenue achievement." The problem with this thinking is that over time, old products generate maintenance, selling, and service costs that far exceed gross margins. A fully loaded cost analysis demonstrates that many of these products may have negative margins that subtract from total profitability. Additionally, turning the organization on its head to build and ship the trivial many, short-Pareto-pole SKUs dilutes its capabilities to nurture and grow the core business—the-tall-Pareto pole, high-potential customer, and product SKUs.

Several benchmarking studies have pointed out that over 80 percent of an organization's resources are focused on the trivial space of the Pareto analysis. Many organizations have the ability to grow by achieving superior value and service performance with their premier segment of customers and high-selling SKUs. There are always the emotional arguments such as, "What if this small customer grows" or "We can't sell X unless we have Y." There is a wealth of opportunity here by taking care of the legitimate exceptions and routinely rationalizing the entire product portfolio with facts rather than emotions. Expanding the performance criteria to gross margin contribution also drives the right sales behaviors.

One $250 million organization, in a shrinking industry, pressured their sales organization to get whatever orders they could, no matter what they had to do. The sales organization decided to promote a mass customization strategy, allowing customers to choose the color, volume, and other product features without even showing them the current product line. This seemed to make sense because once they landed new business, the company would be the sole supplier for repeat business. The sales organization also allowed customers to order products in much smaller lot sizes without any regard to the implications on their business. It was the right thing to do, right?

The reality was that the differences between customer products were so minute that it did not make a difference from a form-fit-function-features perspective

Although their *Burger King: Have it your way* strategy was unique in their industry, there were good reasons why the rest of the industry had not transitioned in this direction. At the same time, customers were demanding smaller lot quantities because they did not want to carry the inventory. This organization was set up to run large lot sizes because the equipment was large and capital intensive. So, a dilemma unfolded: the more that sales sold of their 3800 mass customized SKUs, the less capable manufacturing became at delivery. As always, the first reaction was to finger point and scream at manufacturing who was already running 24/7.

A Lean Six Sigma project was kicked off to solve the problem. The team came up with a few recommendations to reduce scrap and set-up times, but not enough to fix the problem. Next, they did a profit contribution analysis on the entire product line. The company found itself involved in many new low-volume products that they were wrapping hundred and thousand dollar bills around when they shipped. Over 90 percent of their revenues and profitability was derived from just 118 products. Worse yet, servicing these low-profit customers became a severe drain on their ability to take care of their premier customers and markets. So, the result was a continued shrinking of revenues, cancelled orders, and unhappy customers.

The team provided recommendations on how to reconfigure the business into standard and custom products and pruned several other negative-margin product offerings. The standard offerings were offered at competitive prices with smaller lot quantities. The custom products were offered at premium prices with larger lot sizes. The number of SKUs were reduced by almost 36 percent and the company became the market leader within two years. There were also residual improvements from improved forecast accuracy to higher yields and reductions in premium freight.

New Product Concept Development

This refers to the translation of an idea into a workable design concept and eventually, a solid product specification. The detracting dynamics here are the decisions that result in the continuous churning and changing of new product specifications and *feature creep* well into the development process. This causes significant hidden engineering waste and costs, delays in time to market, or huge risks in quality and reliability by pushing and expediting designs through the shrinking time horizons in the development process. These activities are often improved via many Quick Strike improvements that include standardized templates, guidelines, and information required in a product functional specification. These must be specific. Informal—"Make it like the last design" and "We can get by without that information right now"—comments are unacceptable. These informal practices cause things to fall through the cracks or force scarce engineering resources to do things over.

The goal is to freeze the specification early on in the development process to prevent feature, cost, and time creep later in the development cycle. Granted, the world is not perfect. However, when an engineering organization routinely practices drive-by engineering and adds features as the product is due to be released, there is definitely something broken upstream. Improvement requires the removal of egos and emotions, and looking at the facts about these knowledge processes.

One organization has implemented a structured new product identification process with great results. Prior to this improvement initiative, the development of new product ideas was an emotional and informal process driven by people with the most political clout in the organization. Their prior process was jokingly nicknamed "Opus I Marketing," referring to an informal process over dinner with a bottle of nice wine, scribbling and sketching new product ideas on a few napkins. This improvement initiative created a new standardized process, practices, and information templates that did not exist previously. This new process has been designed to be more disciplined and data driven, relying less on the emotions and pleas of the sales organization. It allows the larger group of new product people to evaluate the feasibility of new product ideas and proposed functions and features relative to market potential, technical feasibility, development cost, target cost, and time-to-market considerations.

This technical and business case information is carried through the development process and used to reaffirm market opportunities, hold people accountable for projected assumptions, and reprioritize projects in the development pipeline. The organization has transitioned itself from developing an endless parade of questionable SKUs to a more strategic product development organization using portfolio and product platform thinking. This transition has produced residual improvements outside the immediate area such as supplier delivery and quality performance, and less development inefficiencies.

New Product Development

This refers to the typical five-step, stage-gate product development process found in most organizations (e.g., idea or concept, functional specification and business case, product and process development, validation and test, and new product launch). Every organization claims to have a formal product development process, but the reality is that many organizations do not follow a formal and disciplined process (based on data and facts) on a daily basis. There are dozens of improvement opportunities in this lengthy and complicated set of technical business processes. Therefore, organizations should avoid trying to improve product development by defining it as a single *boil-the-ocean* project. Product development improvements must be scoped and prioritized based on total impact (e.g., Where are the top Pareto pole improvement opportunities in product development? What are the largest pain points?).

One example might be reducing the cycle time and cost of design verification, which could cost $10K to $100K per spin in some organizations. Another example might be to reduce time to market by 50 to 75 percent by eliminating nonvalue-added elapsed time, wait times, and hidden waste of resources. Yet another might be reducing the cost of engineering changes and development after product release, which adds up to millions of hidden dollars and lost or wasted engineering capacity in many development projects.

New product development is not much different from a production flow: it has specific tasks and flows, bottlenecks, resource constraints, scheduling and priority issues, quality and rework issues, measurable and hidden costs, cycle times, performance criteria, and many other similar factors. The big difference is that equipment is replaced by talented engineering and technical people. Intelligent people are less likely to follow standardized processes because they are smart enough to work around them and get things done. Often process and standardization are viewed as deterrents to creativity and innovation. The challenge with new product development is to install standardization and data-driven development that actually enables (versus stifles) more time for creativity and innovation.

A $500 million organization was experiencing many challenges in their new product development process. Products were always released late and over budget and always required significant engineering resources and time to resolve quality and manufacturability issues after product release. Their Lean Six Sigma initiative began by identifying several specific improvement projects in new product development: specification and scope creep, design for manufacturability, design validation, and post-release improvement. These were not all of the opportunities—just four high-priority opportunities out of dozens of improvements that they have made to their new product development process. Using the DMAIC methodology, the teams were able to identify root causes in these areas. For example:

- The hidden cost of specification changes amounted to millions of dollars in engineering time, material, and capital costs. The team developed a series of new product identification templates outlining the required information needed to spec a new product effectively, and saved over a million dollars and months of nonvalue-added development time. The number and magnitude of specification changes were not totally eliminated, but they were tamed to the tune of $4 million in benefits.
- Design engineers were measured on their ability to meet target unit cost for new products. This encouraged them to select less expensive through-hole components over SMT components, and other mechanical and hardware compromises. They also selected the least expensive vendors on the bet that they could develop their capabilities prior to new product release. This team documented the hidden costs of non-reproducibility in the form of missing components, shorts, blowholes, and other post-wave solder defects, misaligned holes in covers, stripping hardware, and other cost of quality items. The team recommended and implemented changes that produced over $4 million in savings.
- Another team peeled back the onion layers of design verification (DV). They quantified the hidden cost of a DV spin to be $24K to $86K depending on what was involved. They also identified that every new product

required somewhere between 1.7 and 3.9 DVs during the product development cycle. The team also identified and prioritized the root causes of DV spins, and conducted a thorough five-why analysis to get deep enough into the DV story. Surprisingly, they also documented several recurring root causes of DVs and were able to isolate root causes all the way back to specific failure categories and design engineers. Based on the number of new products released over a year, these costs quickly add up. Moreover, DVs add time to the development cycle because in effect, it is a process of doing things over because they did not work the first time. This team developed and implemented recommendations upstream in product design to reduce the number of DV spins. The benefits of this project were the elimination of over \$2.2 million in nonvalue-added development costs, and an improvement in time to market. In product development, speed is dependent on throughput and quality, just like manufacturing.

- The fourth initial team tackled the problem of engineering change notices (ECNs) after release of products to manufacturing. Most organizations have this process in place, but they have no idea how much cost and waste is involved with ECNs. The team recreated the last five new product releases as a representative sample of the process. Next, they analyzed the type and level of engineering support for various ECNs after release. These activities were grouped into categories (e.g., electrical, mechanical, vendor, etc.) and analyzed across the five product releases. The team identified specific root causes, and quantified the cost of development after release. For the five releases, these hidden costs ranged from \$24K to \$364K. Again, this is the equivalent of not having time to do things right, but finding time to do things over. Beyond the costs, the disruptions, and customer confidence, these activities take away valuable engineering time for developing new products and stretch out the development cycle—or squeeze the development cycle into the remaining time causing more ECN issues. The team developed and implemented recommendations upstream in the development process, and the amount of ECN activity after release was reduced dramatically. The benefits of this project were estimated to be over \$2.6 million per year.

The combined benefits of these four initial product development improvement teams yielded around \$13 million in benefits, at a time when they were just getting warmed up with Lean Six Sigma.

Global Commercialization

This is an afterthought with many organizations. Commercialization includes all the necessary activities that will create a smooth new product launch and a smoother post-launch evaluation. As products reach the launch phase, organizations discover that they do not have the packaging ready, or the packaging was produced with an older die cut spec, or the Asian color and corrugated specs are different than the U.S. specs, or operator manuals are not printed in all the required international languages, or one of the languages are either incomplete, misspelled, or insulting to potential customers, or the manuals are printed in all the correct internal languages but it does not fit into the box without causing packaging damage, or the software is full of bugs and not ready for release, or the service, supplies, and spare parts have not been planned and staged in distribution centers, or the mix between domestic and international power requirements is off—the list goes on and on. There are also many improvement opportunities in this area ranging from data and fact-based decision making, to prevention of these events with well-defined proactive processes. Many of these problems can be avoided by the creation of standard templates and decision matrices that are embedded in the correct spots of the development process. The cost of preventing these problems in the first place is much lower than the cost and lost customer goodwill of dealing with these problems after they are out there and visible.

Warranty and Returns

This is a complicated but significant improvement opportunity for many organizations. The way that most organizations deal with warranty and returns is to allocate financial reserves to cover the cost. Does this uncover root causes? No. Does this solve the problem? No. But this is the generally accepted financial means of dealing with this problem. Some organizations do not even view warranty and returns as a problem or improvement opportunity, but as an accepted cost of being in their business.

Another problem with warranty and returns is that these processes are weak. Most warranty data is recorded based on nonstandardized customer comments or a technician's opinion, and many warranty and return transactions are posted with a *no problem found* comment. This type of sketchy feedback to engineering does not improve much of anything. This also makes it increasingly difficult to conduct effective root-cause problem solving in this area of the business without accurate and timely data.

One method of digging to root causes is to audit trace the individual return transactions and categorize nonstandardized data into standardized root-cause categories. This can be augmented with a few phone calls to the customer to learn more about their particular customer experience and the reason for the return. The five-whys thinking is useful in projects such as these. Remember, we do not need to explain the universe. All it takes is a relevant sample that tells the story about what is going on inside the process with data and facts.

A large apparel organization became interested in Lean Six Sigma to improve financial performance and develop their people's problem-solving skills. This organization outsourced all of its manufacturing: they were more of a design, sales, and supply chain organization. Upon reviewing the financials, the returns (millions of dollars) jumped off the page. When we asked the executive team about their returns, they replied, "We just benchmarked ourselves against our competition and we're actually better than all but one company. It's the cost of being in this business."

Further discussions convinced them to open the door because most of the returns were workmanship issues (wrong SKU, wrong size, wrong color, wrong quantity, misspelled or incorrect custom embroidery, etc.). Their Lean Six Sigma initiative began with 10 out of 22 teams focused on returns problems across their entire business. Many of the root causes were attributable to simple fixes such as poorly designed web pages for Internet orders, truncation of characters on warehouse pick lists, incorrect SKU identification or stock locations, size variation between various suppliers, incorrect order entry, incorrect order fill, etc. The ten returns projects alone reduced the returns rate by more than $18 million.

Invoicing and Billing Errors

This is an area that often generates cash flow improvements. Many organizations overlook the invoicing process because the percent of billing errors are low and everything is fine. A good root-cause analysis reveals several interesting conclusions in this area—conclusions that have surfaced multiple times in different client deployments. First, there are significant waste and hidden costs associated with invoicing and billing errors that can easily be in the six-figure range. Second, the customer does not proactively call and tell an organization about an invoicing issue so they can pay their bill on time. Third, invoicing errors include both overbilling and underbilling, and customers are not proactive at telling an organization that they were undercharged. Fourth, both underbilling and overbilling require discovery and resolution on the part of the organization. Fifth, these issues create significant and snowballing cash flow problems in terms of collections and days and dollars of accounts receivable in the pipeline.

One company debated the benefits of looking at their invoicing process. The percentage of invoices with problems was low, so why should they entertain a Lean Six Sigma project in this area? A team was assigned to review the invoice process. Although the percentage of billing errors was low, they quantified the hidden cost and effort to fix billing errors to be $168K per year. They also found a few instances in their sample where customers were underbilled. Customers are not proactive in pointing this out because it produces a favorable purchase price variance (PPV) for them, which flows directly to their bottom line. Even though it is dead wrong it sets the expectation for what customers want to pay for products and services and the correction is perceived to be almost the equivalent of a price increase. The team developed and implemented many simple recommendations such as templates, crosschecks, and other basic controls to prevent billing errors. In this particular organization, billing errors have been reduced by more than 96 percent.

Excess and Obsolete Inventory

Inventory issues are usually handled similarly to warranty and returns. Rather than discovering and eliminating root causes, organizations tend to allocate reserves to cover the write-down cost of their excess or obsolete inventory. On the excess side, this practice might be paired with stock promotions and fire sales to move finished goods inventory, or possible vendor returns for raw materials. None of these practices fix the problem, because organizations go through these motions cycle after cycle. The hidden cost of these administrative motions is usually in the millions of dollars (e.g., inventory and management resource costs).

In several client situations, the root cause of excess or obsolete inventory might be pegged to continued optimistic forecasts for new products, an optimistic region's sales forecast, buyers who are under pressure to manipulate PPV, and dozens of other root causes. The data and the right analysis always tell a story, and a large amount of excess or obsolete inventory is assignable to specific root causes and can be eliminated. Successful projects in this area are able to reduce the reserve rate and significantly improve profitability.

Requests for Quotations

One of the most interesting efforts is value stream mapping the request for quotation (RFQ) process. Several common findings usually surface. It should not be a surprise that 80 to 90 percent of the elapsed time is wait-time and waste. Many organizations attempt to treat every RFQ as a unique quote and fail to use leverage from the knowledge base of previous quotes. In many situations, the confidence limit on the quote might be 60 to 70 percent despite two to four weeks of sales, applications, engineering, and financial analysis. When everything needs to be quoted, the RFQ backlog and lead-times stretch out. By the time organizations turn around the quote, the customer has placed a purchase order with a competitor.

One organization had an interesting character in their order entry organization who always complained openly about all the unnecessary RFQ activity, quotes taking too much time to turn around, and that they should be able to give a quote over the phone and ask for the order. His vision was right on the money. A team was assembled with this person as the leader. Now that he was placed in a position of more visibility and influence, he and his team were the doers of the RFQ process.

They demonstrated how to redesign the quotation process using a series of attribute and features tables. The team created an order entry matrix of product and service attributes such as material, size, color, quantity, finishes, packaging, etc. Their design was a menu-driven approach, and the goal was to generate quotes in real time for 70 to 80 percent of the RFQs. They would allow for deeper analysis on the remainder of the quotes, based on the uniqueness of the requirements.

One of the team members was an Internet GUI junkie who designed websites as a sideline. The team implemented and piloted this new RFQ application. Sure enough, when a customer called it was as simple as pick *one of these, one of these, one of these, and one of these.* Bingo! A quote and a new order in real time. For the skeptics, the team also proved with data and facts that the new instant RFQ process produced more accurate quotes than the previous analysis-paralysis approach.

Customer Service

Many best-in-class customer service organizations are beginning to resemble the floor on Wall Street. For others, it is a frustrating customer experience as calls are tossed around the organization and people become increasingly frustrated with the number of transfers, automated greetings, and inconsistent information. The key to great customer service is knowledge and talent development, access to the right information, and attention to the right details. Some of these include standardization of best practices, raising visibility and awareness of call-handling volumes, call wait time, length of calls, time to solve the customer's problem, ability to solve the customer's problem on the spot, and integration of help desk processes.

We have all experienced the frustration of talking to a customer service representative while she completely ignores the problem and begins reading ridiculous instructions (*Is the unit on and plugged in?*) from a manual. We are transferred again to another representative who proceeds to read the same diagnostics from the same manual. The hidden costs might include a return, no further purchases, and bad publicity to other potential customers. On the other hand, it is a pleasurable experience to call about a product or service problem, reach the right responsible representative or technician, and have it fixed on the spot in a few minutes.

A few years ago, I purchased a medicine cabinet and the brackets for the glass shelves were missing. I called this little Midwest company and mentioned my problem. The representative mentioned that a few other customers reported the same problem. Then she said, "The brackets are in stock, I've placed your order, and it will be packed and shipped this afternoon. You will receive the brackets by 10:30 a.m. tomorrow." The brackets arrived at 10:30 a.m. the next day via FedEx, just as she promised. Unfortunately, this seems to be the exception rather than the rule, so there are major opportunities for every organization to improve the customer experience.

Global Sourcing and Outsourcing

Executives are constantly faced with achieving goals at less cost. During the past several years, outsourcing has become the latest movement to reduce operating costs and internal manufacturing complexity and content. There has been a reluctance to further analyze outsourcing decisions because these decisions were already made, and analysis would only disrupt or slow down the transition.

Outsourcing is one of those phenomena that must be right, because everyone else is doing it. However, when one looks at the assumptions and numbers, there are gaping holes in several outsourcing decisions. The hidden costs of acquisition, ownership, and problem resolution are often much larger than the labor savings alone. The upside revenue potential of outsourcing to local markets in China, India, and other emerging markets is too enormous not to be there. However, there is a substantial opportunity to reduce costs (e.g., quality, reliability, premium freight, pipeline inventory costs, hidden administration costs, etc.) because these across-the-board outsourcing decisions are clearly not feasible and profitable at serving all markets around the globe.

Advertising and Promotions

Advertising is a high-ticket cost in many organizations, especially within consumer products companies. Many organizations do not have formal processes for identifying and developing advertising strategies, designing and running promotions, and measuring the effectiveness of these efforts. Often these activities are driven by opinions and perceived needs. Many people who work in this field are creative types who view process and measurement as foreign concepts that do not apply to their operations. Instead, things are often done without any order, out of order, with missing information, many changes, and rework swirls—all in the name of creativity. Sometimes, campaigns might be driven by other people like the vice president of sales or vice president of engineering, who may have the influence and convincing opinions about knowing what we need to promote with customers. The effectiveness of advertising and promotions is not formally measured, so organizations never know if their campaigns succeeded or met the initial objectives.

Most people do not think about the hidden costs of an ad campaign or a direct mail catalog or a failed promotional program. Often, the analysis reveals that it requires two or three times the effort to produce and execute on a particular advertising or promotional plan, which could easily generate nonvalue-adding costs in the range in the six or seven figures. Improvements in these areas often involve facilitating the creative process visually and with open collaboration and facts, but supplementing these activities with standardization of execution and gate-keeping processes, formal milestones, and measurement criteria. It is not about passing or failing, like it is for product quality. It is more about innovation followed by solid program management, objective feedback, and knowledge development. Since the advertising budget is committed, these projects are usually not about traditional cost reduction or reducing advertising budgets. Rather, these projects are about enabling organizations to accomplish more advertising with less resources, which is equal to more advertising and more effective advertising per dollar spent. Over time, improvements in this area may drive down advertising and promotion costs. The other side of these improvement initiatives is to develop formal processes to measure incremental revenues that are directly attributable to advertising and promotion efforts.

Sales and Operations Planning

This is often referred to as SOP, S&OP, or SIOP (sales, inventory, and operations planning). This key business is the turbine of the organization because the performance in this area has far-reaching implications into other areas of the organization. S&OP performance has a direct impact on inventory performance, product availability, customer satisfaction, and financial performance. The new economy is forcing organizations to rethink their traditional S&OP process and metrics such as aggregate delivery performance and forecast accuracy. In the new economy, these metrics are meaningless and unactionable. Organizations are using the Lean Six Sigma methodology to track down, Paretoize, and eliminate root causes of problems in their S&OP process. In addition, organizations are developing the capability of measuring S&OP performance by customer, product families, product groupings, sales territories and regions, time and seasonal factors, and new or existing products.

This improvement strategy in S&OP is called *segmented S&OP management*—replacing a one-size-fits-all S&OP process with a segmented S&OP process that recognizes the dynamics and attributes of different discrete groups of customers, markets, and products. The segmented S&OP process enables the management, policy deployment, and performance of these segments in different ways with different S&OP practices and policies. The goal of a segmented S&OP process is to manage the segments with appropriate planning policies, keep supply and demand synchronized realistically and with facts, and micromanage the tall poles. Segmented S&OP management provides visibility into what is going on in the strategic groupings, including elemental performance and more specific and actionable root causes.

One international organization was experiencing problems with finished goods availability and delivery performance. This organization decided that it was going to change from a make-to-stock company to an off-the-shelf supplier but failed to install the right infrastructure changes to support their strategy. Their forecast accuracy was at 24 percent, and the delivery performance was around 60 percent. The international vice president of sales and marketing explained their current dilemma with forecasting demand for so many products in Europe, the Middle East, and Asia. A team was assigned to improve delivery performance and quickly verified the metrics and poor performance. The team analyzed sales and supply chain data and found that 88 percent of revenues were sold through 14 distributors. They also learned that 85 percent of the revenue was from 50 products. They went to work implementing point-of-sale tracking capabilities with these major distributors and installed new practices to manage distributor supply and demand on a daily basis. Within months, aggregate forecast accuracy shot up to 68 percent (83% for the top 50 products) and delivery performance improved to over 93 percent.

Supply Chain Planning and Logistics

Depending on the organization, this includes sales planning and analysis, forecasting, S&OP, demand and supply planning, in-house or offshore production authorization, procurement, order administration, distribution, and offshore quality assurance. A common mistake organizations make is assigning a team to improve supply chain management. This well-intentioned initiative becomes a frustrating solve-world-hunger assignment for an improvement team.

There are literally dozens of individual improvement initiatives in the total supply chain ranging from improving forecasting accuracy to rightsizing safety stock, from removing the fluff caused by planning factors and parameters to reducing backorders and backlog, from improving a premier customer's delivery and inventory performance to reducing product and packaging damage, from rationalizing global distribution to reducing premium freight and consigned shipping strategies, just to name a few. Without even looking, the new economy has introduced improvement opportunities in global supply chains that are worth millions of dollars to most organizations.

We have worked with several organizations on their premium freight issues. Much of this is driven by noise in the planning process: expediting requirements when they are hot, but not de-expediting products when things change. In many cases, it is too late because product is in transit. For many of these projects, it is typical to find that as much as 25 to 40 percent of receipts arrive via premium freight. Many of these receipts also sit around for days or even weeks before they are placed in stock or requisitioned to the individual who ordered the material. Sometimes, premium freight is used as a security blanket, with no policies in place to monitor and control it. Many of these premium freight improvement projects end up saving their organizations millions of dollars.

Supplier Development and Management

There are a lot of improvement opportunities in the supply base. The attributes of velocity, flexibility, perfection, responsiveness, value, and flawless execution are more dependent on global supplier networks. Supplier development and management is important because suppliers represent a large cross-sectional piece of the total supply chain. The performance of the supply chain is highly dependent upon the performance of suppliers. Some benchmark studies have placed the competitive leverage due to suppliers in the total supply chain as high as 70 to 90 percent. Supplier development and management is important because there are dozens of improvement opportunities worth millions of dollars in this area. Examples of these improvement opportunities include supplier sourcing and evaluation, supplier quality and delivery improvement, collaborative and short interval S&OP, targeted cost reduction and operations improvement programs, formal information reporting and feedback processes, supplier certification and direct ship strategies, collaborative product development, supplier performance management, and supplier conferences.

Supplier development and management is a growing area of concern as organizations have shifted to their strategy of outsourcing products and services. Although the comparative labor costs appear to be attractive, there are many hidden outsourcing costs that organizations are uncovering as they develop more experience in these areas. Most organizations have an incredible opportunity to harvest millions of dollars in improvement and competitive advantage in the area of supplier development and management.

The Marketing and Selling Process

This area has been exempt from improvement initiatives because marketing and selling products and services has a higher perceived priority to some executives than that of improving how the organization markets and sells products and services. The terms *selling* and *improvement* have been commonly viewed as two distinct and conflicting business activities. In reality, organizations are capable of selling more by improving the marketing and selling process.

One of the most effective analytical approaches in sales and marketing organizations is worth factor and value analysis. Basically, this is an inventory of how these organizations spent their time and resources, instead of looking at the sales generated directly from the inventory of various activities. Not surprisingly, sales and marketing people often spend the most time and resources on customers, prospects, market opportunities, and other activities that just do not pay off. Much of this is driven by the emotion of "If we don't do this we will lose the sale."

Again, this area is an emotional roller coaster where unfortunately, emotion wins over facts (because there usually are no facts). However, when one looks at these activities and outcomes with data and facts—including the *all-in* hidden costs—the organization might have been better off and certainly more profitable if the sales associate was absent on that particular day when an order was placed. The facts demonstrate that it is not always the best use of time and resources to drive out to Timbuktu in the last few days of the month to sell a low-pole product to a one-time customer at a deep discount just to get an order.

The end of the month drives a lot of frenzied behaviors that might generate additional sales, but not always the accompanying additional profits. There are significant opportunities to improve sales and marketing efforts by realigning resources and metrics on the activities that matter the most. This also changes the focus from getting an order (any order) to landing profitable business. This analysis is also revealing in other transactional areas such as research and development, engineering and new product development, materials planning and purchasing, quality management, and finance to name a few.

Organizational Development and Human Resource Management

Most may not readily associate this area with Lean Six Sigma and strategic improvement. When things go wrong in this area, it may also impact the productivity and well-being of large sections of the organization. There are many improvement opportunities in organizational development and human resource management worth millions of dollars to the organization. Areas such as absenteeism, hiring and termination of associates, training and development, organizational planning, employee compensation and benefits, performance review processes, communication and change management, talent and career development, workplace safety, wellness initiatives, diversity planning, legal reporting and compliance, security management, and team building present major opportunities for fact-based analysis and improvement. As one can observe from this list, human resources plays both an organizational improvement role and an internal Lean Six Sigma role in deployment activities (e.g., talent selection and development, awareness and communication, change management, team effectiveness, group dynamics, conflict resolution, behavioral and cultural issues, etc.). These opportunities also include both direct and indirect benefits to the organization, both of which are quantifiable and measurable.

Global Real Estate and Space Management

This area has evolved gradually as the requirements of businesses have changed. Again, most may not associate this readily with Lean Six Sigma and strategic improvement. In most cases, the total cost of real estate and space management (including support, maintenance and repair, overhead, and utility costs) are not readily available or known. With all of the consolidations, downsizing, and outsourcing actives that have taken place recently, global real estate and space management presents new opportunities for improvement for many organizations. Since many of these costs are either hidden or unknown, quantifying these costs is usually received as a big surprise to executives. There is undoubtedly a high level of emotion with individuals in the organization regarding the pooling of workplace space, geography, proximity to amenities or other departments, furnishings, physical appearance, and perceptions of change by others. Nevertheless, there are millions of dollars in opportunity for many organizations who commit to doing the analysis and the math objectively.

Strategic Maintenance and Facilities Management

One of the largest unknowns in many organizations is unplanned maintenance or unplanned downtime. These failures seem to occur randomly, and the root causes are unknown. With a bit of creative thinking, the same issues exist in the unplanned disruptions in transactional processes. The largest reason why these failures or disruptions are unknown is due to lack of root-cause thinking and the availability of facts.

People have their opinions about why these things happen, and they typically use their intuition for improvement. Many of the preventive maintenance (PM) procedures in organizations are based more on intuition rather than on facts. This random tinkering with (physical and transactional) processes usually creates more problems and variation than it removes, and sometimes it throws processes into an unpredictable, out-of-control state. Many of these failures are extremely costly and disruptive, particularly if they represent the revenue-gating operation, or if replacement parts or servicing capabilities are not on hand. This is a challenge across all industries and all processes, whether it is a large paper machine, a line producing pharmaceutical or personal care products, a product development process or an MRI operation in a hospital. Revenue generation and customer satisfaction is a matter of keeping things up and running.

Many organizations have conducted several successful Lean Six Sigma and basic improvement initiatives in these areas. A few short case examples are:

- One team analyzed the root causes of unplanned downtime in a large plating area. A Pareto analysis was constructed based on maintenance work orders and *touch* time to repair hours. Upon reviewing the analysis, the executive sponsor and the team noticed that the low frequency repairs that were easy to fix but consumed the most elapsed time were at the bottom of their Pareto list (a lesson on using Pareto charts: sometimes, the root cause is not in the tall poles). Some of the low poles created as much as whole shifts of downtime. The team revised their analysis, isolated the vital few issues that created the most unplanned time, and began digging deeper into root causes. This was an interesting project because the root causes were part of a larger continuum: individually they can be the beginning or the end, but there were multiple connections between root causes and failure modes. The team's project was similar to putting a complex puzzle together. In the end, the team identified approximately $1.3 million in savings by reducing unplanned downtime.

- In another organization, a team began analyzing unplanned downtime for a group of screw machines. Operators ran their machines across all three shifts at their settings so there was a lack of standardized work. The team isolated the largest root cause of unplanned downtime to nonstandardized chuck changes. If the chuck was too tight, it would cause jams; if the chuck was too loose, the machines would crash causing timely and costly repairs. The real challenge was determining *how tight is tight* and *how tight is right?* Operators had a variety of answers ranging from "You can feel when it is tight enough" to "three whacks with a mallet." A common practice was wrapping a rag around a wrench and batting it with the palm of their hands. The answer through experimentation was the development of a safe torque wrench, reducing the cost of downtime by $320K per year. During this project, the team also learned that three people were out on disability leave with broken hands. This spurred several other improvement projects looking at root causes of injuries across the plant. Many of these claims were caused by similar reasons: lack of standardization and homegrown tools and methods. The company saved another $800K in disability benefits through several simple Quick Strike improvements.

- A utilities improvement team used the Lean Six Sigma methodology and tools to analyze major utility costs (e.g., electricity, fuel oil, propane, lubricants, maintenance cleaning supplies, etc.) and root causes. Within weeks they developed many basic recommendations to reduce peak electricity costs by developing a standardized equipment start-up sequence, moving selected production runs to second and third shifts, installing motion switches in less used areas of the plant and office, changing PM procedures, a consigned MRO inventory managed by the supplier, and several other simple changes. Within 90 days, the team identified over $1 million in utility savings. The team also created a visual awareness program that compared utility costs to pictures such as a Cadillac Escalade, an RV, a new home, a Hawaiian vacation for 15 people, and other comparisons with great visual impact.

- A new product organization was experiencing several unplanned disruptions at Gate 2 (product and process design) of their development process. A team conducted a simple Quick Strike project and isolated the root causes to lack of information, missing information, and changes to information up front in the product concept and definition. Digging deeper (the five whys), they learned that the right decision makers were not getting together up front, leading to many after-the-fact changes and modifications. Additionally, the process was defined well (e.g., what information is necessary to begin Gate 2) but not being followed. The team created a simple template for the Gate 1 activities, eliminated much of the engineering waste of doing things over, and reduced product development cycle time by an estimated four to eight weeks.

Financial Management

Finance is another area that most may not associate readily with Lean Six Sigma and strategic improvement. After all, finance conducts a lot of financial analysis and generates information to review and improve the business. Financial reporting and analysis is a critical business and legal requirement of all enterprises. In terms of improvement, however, there are several common problems with financial data:

- It is reported well after the path is cold, so the information is nice to know but unactionable
- It is reported in a consolidated fashion, where it reports outcomes and buries root causes

- It is sometimes inaccurate, or presented in a manner that leads people to the wrong conclusions and symptomatic actions
- It often reports the wrong or conflicting information, which leads to the wrong decisions, behaviors, actions, and results
- It leaves people conjecturing on root causes based on perceptions, opinions, or other data carefully selected to support a position

From a Lean Six Sigma perspective, finance is riddled with defects in their processes—defects caused by others in the organization outside of finance. These defects are in the form of journal entries, trial balance adjustments, and other transactions or charges that were not processed right the first time. If finance had defect-free suppliers of information, organizations could perform their monthly close process with the push of a button. It is a challenge to get finance to view these institutionalized accounting practices that have existed for 100 years as defects that create nonvalue-added work, consume time and resources to correct, and impact the entire organization when they occur. The challenge to making financial information more improvement friendly is to simplify and reduce the cycle time of reporting, report the right metrics, and expand reporting to include activity-based and hidden cost information.

A popular improvement project in finance is to reduce the monthly close cycle and other reporting cycles. It is an interesting analysis to group and *Paretoize* transactions by transaction type, root cause of transaction, cost of transaction, and time to process transaction. One will find that 80 percent of the effort, time, and cost is consumed by a small grouping of transaction types that are assignable to root causes and therefore, are correctable.

It might require a dozen valuable financial resources who act as glorified clerks, several other resources outside of finance, and several days to chase down and correct the problems. When these hidden costs are quantified, they are unbelievable! These well-paid resources could be put to better use than fixing defective transactions and analyzing the rest of the pie. The good news is that correcting 20 percent of the problem gets an organization 80 percent of the benefits. These defects are typically workmanship issues that are correctable through training, work discipline and attention to details, doing things right and complete the first time, and consequences for nonperformance. Many of these issues are caused by an attitude of "I don't have time and someone else will catch it." By the time they catch it, the cost to fix the problem has grown exponentially. Using this analysis, it is not unusual to reduce the close process from a week to days or hours.

Information Technology

Information technology is an area that often gets caught up in insatiable demands, a bombarding of questions and complaints about applications, an unending backlog of projects, the proliferation of server networks and other equipment, and large requests for additional IT expenditures. Executives complain about rising

IT expenditures, yet many costs are driven by the operating choices of key business process owners and users external to IT. The costs of IT are usually known, but the benefits of IT can sometimes be fuzzy. Some of the areas where Lean Six Sigma has generated substantial benefits has been in the areas of requirements definition and justification, IT value analysis, managing IT backlog and priorities, software development and release, user collaboration and development, IT project management, server and network uptime, and IT performance.

A major but unpopular opportunity is in analyzing IT requests for enhancements and modifications. Often users do not understand or are not aware of the full functionality, features, standard reports, etc. in their enterprise architecture. Additionally, users often attempt to create on-the-spot silo capabilities that add more waste and IT glitches than value to the organization. Since IT is a service organization, they do not have the authority to question, deny, or demand hard justification of these IT requests, so they just queue up. Many IT people are also unfamiliar with the full functionality and features of their enterprise systems. Many of these IT requests are generated because users have a particular issue with the software and do not take the time to drive to root causes. It is easier to submit an *off-the-cuff* IT request than it is to conduct true root-cause problem solving on their specific user processes. If more users used the five whys and took the time to understand why they are having problems, they would find that the corrective actions often have nothing to do with the need for another IT request. Often the problems are related to discipline, nonstandard practices and procedures, transactions without knowledge, and data integrity—issues that organizations have been struggling with since the 1970s Ollie Wight "little mrp" days.

Software development is an interesting improvement opportunity. Many of these professionals are developing software that will be integrated with hardware, but the full requirements are still in an evolving state and are unknown. It is a bit like driving to a new location without the GPS: some of the destination may be known, but it usually involves getting lost, asking for directions, and making several detours before arrival. This becomes complicated by outsourcing decisions where software development is scattered around the globe, where the variation increases proportionally with the number of people involved, regardless of development standards and practices. This often leads to software that either does not work, or software that exposes unexpected bugs and glitches some time after release. Although software development is confusing and complicated to most, the improvement of software development is more common sense than rocket science. A combination of process standardization, requirements standardization, bug and *Bugzilla* root-cause analysis, the right corrective actions, and frequent formal hardware or software integration updates goes a long way toward improving software development.

Another useful analysis in IT that was mentioned earlier is worth factor and value analysis. This is the inventory of current and proposed projects quantified by objectives, benefits, costs, time, and risks. Usually the IT group remains clogged by everything the user community is demanding of them, and lacks a formal process of routinely reviewing, reprioritizing, or cancelling IT projects. Worth factor and value analysis provides an objective method of reviewing priorities and reasoning with users, collectively deciding on priorities, and redirecting limited resources to the most critical issues. The problem with IT is similar to the catch-22 problem with engineering organizations: there is never enough time and resources to complete all the changing requirements in the pipeline, nor is it feasible to consume all of the time and hire all the resources that are necessary to complete the changing requirements in the pipeline. So what does the CIO and his or her organization do? They make the best of what they have at their disposal, manage the emotions of their user community, and continuously optimize around the operating constraints with data and facts.

Acquisition and Integration Process

This is yet another area that most may not associate readily with Lean Six Sigma and strategic improvement. A successful acquisition requires a lot more effort than analyzing financial statements, looking at customer lists, and conducting pro forma financial spreadsheet analysis. Organizations that limit themselves to this kind of thinking end up missing out on opportunities, or end up with an acquisition loaded with unanticipated problems. Many times, we are invited to participate in due diligence activities to define the current state of the business, confirm strategic fit both qualitatively and quantitatively, identify potential improvement opportunities, and develop the implementation and integration plan, which is ready to go directly after the acquisition is consummated. In addition, this additional information is critical for conducting a more robust feasibility analysis of the proposed acquisition. These acquisition decisions are not reversible for a long time, so the value of doing things right the first time is somewhere between high and off the chart.

Another improvement opportunity in this area is the development and standardization of a robust acquisition evaluation process. In many organizations, this high-risk initiative is backed up by informal ad hoc processes or a lack of processes. An acquisition without a formal evaluation process is like developing new products without a formal stage-gate process, or manufacturing products without routings. A structured and disciplined acquisition and integration process avoids millions of dollars in unexpected costs and pays for itself in the first few minutes of the acquisition.

Performance Measurement Process

Performance measurement system analysis represents a major opportunity across all transactional processes. Many organizations are unaware of the hidden costs associated with inadequate measurement systems. These may include emphasis on the wrong metrics, too many conflicting metrics, or metrics created by informal or over-specified measurement processes. The value of this information is often much less than the effort it takes to measure performance. Organizations have benefitted from several transactional measurement systems analysis projects:

- One organization that was overly conscious about product costs developed extremely detailed routings, bill-of-materials (BOMs), and tracking requirements in their ERP system. An improvement team pointed out that operators spent more time processing completion and move transactions than in building the product. The cost of assigning a part number, maintaining, cycle counting, and looking for many low C-level inventory items exceeded the value of the part. Although product costs were calculated to four decimal places, this hidden cost equated to 15 full time equivalent people employed to process and correct accounting transactions. The accountants complained about labor and material variances that were less than the hidden $450K cost of processing transactions. Routings and tracking requirements were simplified and many items in BOMs were expensed and maintained as floor stock. The accuracy of product costs and BOMs improved significantly with much less overhead costs.

- A high-tech company designed its quality system to collect very detailed information about defects and root causes. Their quality system included 84 defect codes and hundreds of secondary root cause codes. When a defect occurred, dozens of operators across all shifts were instructed to enter the correct defect and root cause code in the system. Quality engineers had the greatest of intentions, but their system incorporated too much discrimination in the assignment of defect codes. Individual operators had little consistency in repeating their own correct codes, and operators across shifts had even less consistency in reproducing the correct codes. In a sample, even the quality engineers showed little consistency in repeating and reproducing the assignment of defects to the correct defect codes. Over time, their quality data was normalized by noise, and the Pareto charts were almost flat. Therefore, it was difficult to decide where and how to improve yields. More time was spent collecting, summarizing, analyzing and presenting data than improving yields. An improvement team redesigned the quality system with less defect codes, and potential root causes were discussed in person with operators before summarizing data into potential root-cause categories. The Pareto charts began to show the tall pole problems and yields were improved significantly. The cost of scrap and rework was reduced by over $2 million annually.

- A new product development organization prided itself on getting new products released on time and at the target design cost. Many engineers were rewarded for their "over the wall" performance. An improvement team began looking in to the cost of commercialization after release (e.g., ECN activities, manufacturing rework due to design, field quality and reliability, inventory performance, lost revenue, etc.). The team demonstrated that the root cause of recurring inefficiencies was due to specific issues in the product development process. The target design cost was but one element of cost, and engineering was held accountable for design related lifecycle costs after release. The company saved millions in commercialization and post-release costs.

- Another organization created their performance war room. Two walls were covered with monthly performance charts on everything about the organization. Again, a well intentioned initiative created more confusion, emotional interpretation, debates, and finger pointing than improvement. It was difficult to differentiate causes from effects, and the data was un-actionable. The war room was replaced by a smaller set of critical, real-time, event-driven metrics in automated dashboard formats. People now had the ability to sense-interpret-decide-act-monitor (SIDAM) on a daily basis (and with real facts), and prevent potential performance issues before they occurred.

Step Up to the Transactional Improvement Challenge

The future of improvement needs to focus aggressively on the knowledge and transactional processes of the enterprise and extended enterprise. A large number of these transactional processes have developed over time, by and with different people with different requirements. The real issue around transactional process improvement is that complexity is easy to create, but making things better requires much more thought and effort. Many of these transactional processes are untouched territory and ripe for improvement with the right evolution of improvement approaches. Organizations can make dramatic improvements rapidly, and the benefits are in the millions of dollars.

The real challenge in seizing transactional opportunities rests on the ability to understand, retrofit, evolve, and apply the underpinnings of Lean Six Sigma. In the majority of cases, the fundamental blocking and tackling tools of Lean Six Sigma (e.g., basic data analysis, Pareto analysis, value stream mapping, transactional flows, cause and effect diagrams or CEDs, root-cause mapping, standardized work, process cycle time and defect analysis, etc.) are all that is required to make a large impact on transactional processes. However, it does require creativity in vision, the right problem definition, and application beyond the traditional manufacturing applications. Successful organizations have capitalized on these opportunities by looking beyond the acronyms and statistical tools of Lean Six Sigma, and have recognized and learned the inherent power of well-structured, fact-based, root-cause decision making. The idealistic aspects of Lean Six Sigma are well suited to this step-function change in scope and target. This requires the know-how of expanding the scope of Lean Six Sigma from a limited set of process improvement tools to a creative and innovative way of thinking about strategic improvement opportunities that impact the entire organization and beyond.

Any executive exposed to previous improvement initiatives might instinctively think of business improvement in terms of operations or manufacturing improvement and cost reduction, but this perspective is completely results limiting with strategic improvement in the new economy. Organizations with the most successful Lean Six Sigma deployments have learned how to improve and innovate in all areas of their businesses—their key business processes, their products and services, their target markets, and even fundamental reengineering of their business models. These organizations have significantly improved business performance while establishing cultures with an inherent inclination toward continuous improvement and innovation. For the remainder of organizations, transactional process improvement represents millions and millions of dollars in new strategic and immediate benefits.

References

Bolstorff, P. and Rosenbaum, R. 2003. *Supply Chain Excellence: A Handbook for Dramatic Improvement Using the SCOR Model.* AMACOM, New York, NY.

Cassidy, A. and Cassidy, D. 2009. *A Practical Guide to Reducing IT Costs.* J. Ross Publishing, Ft. Lauderdale.

Gordon, S. 2008. *Supplier Evaluation and Performance Excellence: A Guide to Meaningful Metrics and Successful Results.* J. Ross Publishing, Ft. Lauderdale.

Mello, S., Lasser, R., Mackey, and W., Tait, R. 2006. *Value Innovation Portfolio Management: Achieving Double-Digit Growth Through Customer Value.* J. Ross Publishing, Ft. Lauderdale.

Power, M. J., Desouza, K. C., and Bonifazi, C. 2006. *The Outsourcing Handbook: How to Implement a Successful Outsourcing Process.* Kogan Page Limited, London, UK.

Chapter 14 Take Aways

- The future of improvement is in the transactional enterprise and extended enterprise space. To be successful, organizations will need to become much more committed and aggressive about the core competency of strategic improvement—for the long haul. They will need to build organizations that proactively seek out and act on every improvement moment, and evolve toward a state of Improvement Excellence™: improving how they improve, or simply improving the velocity, boundaries, and magnitude of improvement.

- The majority of root causes of manufacturing problems are created in the transactional processes. Many issues within areas such as product availability, delivery performance, quality, excess and obsolete inventory, warranty and returns, field service and repair, supplier performance, financial variances, efficiencies, overhead absorption, and many other problems are directly traceable to root causes in market research, new product concept planning, new product development, sales and operations planning, the selling process, outsourcing, and other transactional processes.

- The real challenge with improvement is in working one's way through the transactional maze, and in defining and scoping out legitimate, data-driven transactional improvement opportunities. These are opportunities that will have a significant impact on the business and enable multiple successful executions on strategy.
- The real challenge in seizing transactional opportunities rests on the ability to understand, retrofit, evolve, and apply the underpinnings of Lean Six Sigma. In the majority of cases, the basic blocking and tackling tools of Lean Six Sigma (e.g., basic data analysis, Pareto analysis, value stream mapping, transactional flows, cause and effect diagrams or CEDs, root-cause mapping, standardized work, process cycle time and defect analysis, etc.) are all that is required to make a large impact on transactional processes. However, it does require creativity in vision and application beyond the traditional manufacturing applications.
- Organizations with the most successful Lean Six Sigma deployments have learned how to improve and innovate in all areas of their businesses—their key business processes, their products and services, their target markets, and even fundamental reengineering of their business models. For the remainder of organizations, transactional process improvement represents millions and millions of dollars in new strategic and immediate benefits.

15

The Intersection of Leadership, Improvement, and Technology

Today, global organizations are struggling with more demanding customer and shareholder expectations, lower margins, and intense competition. Businesses are redoubling their efforts to identify operational areas that can be improved, trimmed, or eliminated. There is constant pressure to ensure continuous improvement of operational performance without sacrificing customer value. As organizations become more transaction-process intensive, the shift of improvement is moving to these areas.

The chief information officer (CIO) role is one of the most challenging positions in the organization. CIOs have evolved to a role where they must be part senior executive, part improvement guru, part technology expert, and part financial value creation. This used to be a much easier role for an MIS director when most of the business content was manufacturing and the office operations were relatively small or informally managed. Much of this new CIO role has evolved from the emergence of transactional enterprises and the need to integrate the entire customer-to-supplier value stream. Although many executives might be alarmed by the costs, IT has grown to become the largest enabler of connectivity, integration, information exchange, strategic and tactical improvement, business controls, and performance management.

The intersection of leadership, improvement, and technology is about how these factors are converging to create new business opportunities. Figure 15.1 displays this convergence of competencies.

As the diagram shows, organizations need to work toward a single version of the facts. Whether it is a Fortune 500 company or the Defense Department, it is impossible to lead effectively and achieve benchmark performance with too many versions of the truth floating around within the organization. Organizations must also drive their organizations away from informal decision-making toward

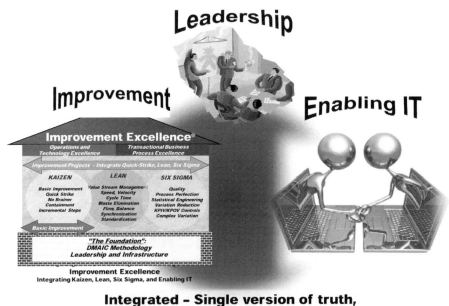

Figure 15.1   Convergence of competencies.

more structured and formalized fact-based and data-driven decision making. Despite the billions of dollars in IT investment, there are too many executives and managers leading by perception, opinion, or egos. In the future, successful organizations will embrace root-cause problem solving via enabling technology. Organizations need to bury the excuses about not having time to do root-cause problem solving because it is a proven fact (and has been proven over and over again) that it takes less time to do the right things right the first time than it does to do things wrong and then do things over. Why do executives and managers have so much trouble grasping this simple concept? Do the math and add up the hidden wastes, and it becomes a clear case to change leadership behaviors.

The new economy is driving the need for more immediate attention and more immediate response. The combination of technology and improvement is enabling organizations to build real-time, interactive supply chains where they manage by the sense-interpret-decide-act-monitor process (SIDAM). Another capability that many organizations have already embraced is real-time, event-driven metrics, walk around metrics, or good-day-bad-day metrics. The objective of these real-time performance dashboards is to communicate performance and potential issues in real time so that organizations can SIDAM in more of a prevention mode. Executive can no longer lead successfully without technology and improvement. Improvement is ineffective without strong leadership and technology to enable its success, and technology investments result in questionable value without being accompanied by a business case, business process improvement, and strong leadership. This is the future, and a great future of strategic improvement at that!

As mentioned in Chapter 14, the new economy is accelerating the transformation of organizations into a complex global network of interdependent transactional enterprises. This transformation is also creating the greatest opportunities for forward-thinking organizations to improve, leapfrog competitors, and dominate global markets in the new economy. The future of improvement is in the transactional enterprise and extended enterprise space. Since transactional processes are integrated and interdependent, an improvement in one area provides residual improvements in other areas. The real challenge with improvement is in working one's way through the transactional maze, and in defining and scoping out legitimate, data-driven transactional improvement opportunities. This process relies more heavily on information technology than it ever has before. With transactional processes, one cannot pick up a part and measure dimensional characteristics to determine defects and quality levels. The improvement expert uses the organization's integrated information architecture (e.g., SAP, Oracle, etc.) to trace the transaction trail like a detective, and constructs the story of the process. This is not your father's Lean or Six Sigma tools at work here. The challenges of harvesting these large-scale opportunities lie in an organization's ability to evolve toward a state of Improvement Excellence™: improving how they improve, or simply improving the velocity, boundaries, and magnitude of improvement.

Why IT Matters in Strategic Improvement

For years, many continuous improvement proponents pushed their ideas about Lean being in conflict with IT, or that IT was not needed as the Lean implementation unfolded. Some were even promoting the unplugging of their ERP system in favor of manual practices and visible storyboard management techniques. They supported their claims with the absence of ERP in many Far East manufacturing companies, and the manual techniques of the Toyota Production System (TPS). It sounded like a good option to management who was always questioning IT expenditures. These continuous improvement people had a static view of the world. The folks in the Far East had two things going for them: unlimited people resources and a religious practice of meticulous attention to details. Basic improvement activities such as the introduction of new products, worker ownership, acquisitions and consolidations, schedule changes, and new quality or engineering issues brought their improvements down like a sledge hammer. It was impossible to manage continuous improvement with a bunch of manual and generally misunderstood processes, and several workforce performance and reward systems that ran counter to improvement. Today, technology is a major enabler of Toyota's global success.

As the shift is occurring from the manufacturing floor to the transactional process areas, our ability to sense, observe, and touch problems diminishes greatly. With transactional issues, everyone seems to have an explanation about what is not working well, but nobody knows for sure. One cannot walk up and observe a department of customer service representatives, or accountants closing the books, or engineers having a design review and get much out of it from an improvement perspective. The level of reporting and metrics about root-cause data may not even exist: many transactional processes have evolved over time and have never been formally analyzed at any meaningful depth. The usual fix is a band-aid, another procedure, a new IT request, or some other local change that might create issues in other areas. IT is important in transactional process improvement because:

- IT drives the organization toward a single version of the facts based on the integrated enterprise architecture. It is totally inefficient to manage with a kluge of spreadsheets, and (now) via opinions and perceptions over voice and text messaging.
- IT provides the linkage between strategy and execution with standardized and customized information and feedback.
- IT provides the essence of what is needed for leadership, management, and improvement: information and data.
- IT provides structured systems, internal controls, and operating data across all transactional streams, which is necessary in analyzing root causes of transactional issues.
- IT provides the only ability to view the interactions, data flows, and transactions in suspense (defect trails) between key business processes.
- IT provides the data for the sampling plans of improvement initiatives which defines the specific data elements necessary to analyze and solve problems. IT needs to take a strong role in all improvement initiatives because it is too costly (and foolish) to collect data manually for improvement projects at the source.
- IT automates many of the manual improvement tools that people have implemented in the past such as kanban cards, schedule boards, quality issues and resolution, maintenance planning, routine analytics, and the like.
- IT is a great enabler of real-time feedback, real-time visibility into key business process performance, and all types of individual process and management performance dashboards.

To improve transactional processes in the future, improvement practitioners will need a better understanding of the technology infrastructure, data flows, and where and how to access the right improvement information. Technology and the increased focus on transactional processes are rendering obsolete the manual collection of data via mechanical check sheets.

This list is not fully exhaustive, but it is enough to build the compelling importance of IT in Lean Six Sigma, particularly in the transactional areas. The network of interdependent transactional processes, and the broader requirements of the enterprise and extended enterprise will only add to this list and increase the dependency on technology as an enabler of strategic success. Along with this evolution, organizations must learn how to integrate these larger scale IT investments in a more profit and ROI-generating manner than they have in the past. Technology is not a sunken cost to the business; it should have a positive justification and ROI like any other investment.

Disconnected Information and Technology

As a starting point, it is helpful to view information and technology separately. Today, organizations are inundated with both. As we have painfully learned from Y2K experiences, the presence of these words is extremely costly and does not guarantee success. The future of strategic improvement and business in general is in looking at and synthesizing the right information into the right actions, and in deploying the right technology to enable continued success.

IT organizations and the large software providers are constantly blamed for the extreme and growing costs of IT expenditures. This is also one of the first areas executives look to cut operating costs. During the past two years, almost 50 percent of organizations have reduced IT spending and head count. The problem with this strategy is that we are no longer building factories—we are building transactional enterprises that require infrastructure just as a manufacturing plant requires floor and office layouts, equipment, power, maintenance, and facilities management.

IT is a lot like Lean Six Sigma and improvement in general: it can either produce great results or increase overhead spending. In general, executives are slow at grasping this concept, but there is not the best of track records in deploying IT expenditures correctly, producing profitable and justifiable results. In the past, IT organizations always talked about *enabling technology*, which suggests technology to improve the business via its key business processes. Enabling technology also suggests that technology and process are inseparable. The way technology is typically introduced in organizations has not always been *enabling*—at least for some time. This is not a technology issue; it is a leadership, planning, and execution issue. IT organizations (and their executive process owners) can benefit by adopting the strategic leadership and vision, deployment planning, and execution infrastructure elements to their larger IT investments and projects.

IT is an investment that many organizations either cannot afford to make, postpone making, or invest with pessimism. Many organizations are still struggling with the leftovers of Y2K, trying to get the most out of their millions of dollars in IT investment. Most have forgotten about the root causes of these problems by now, but they can be traced back to the IT implementation. Many organizations heard stories about other astronomical IT investments, so they wanted to save money. At the time, many organizations boasted about how they implemented SAP in four months. In reality, they did not go back and fix their master data problems, they cut out expenditures for training and they decided to change processes at a later date. These were pure hardware and software sales and software module implementations, not needs and value driven business system implementations. Organizations learned the hard way that slamming in software is not the same as business improvement and sometimes has costly and long lasting consequences.

Today, most of the education is done via tribal knowledge, and many business processes still have not been reengineered and improved. Despite the millions of dollars in investment, spreadsheets are the most widely used tool for operational and financial planning activities. Despite all of this investment, Lean Six Sigma teams are forced to acquire data via manual check sheets or activity logs, and the data collection effort consumes most of the improvement project's elapsed time.

So, how can organizations expect their IT investment to produce an ROI with this level of leadership and deployment support? It is no different than training the masses on Lean Six Sigma and then moving on to more important matters.

There is an age-old problem with information technology, and traditionally it has not been the fault of the IT organization (although it is evolving in that direction). Technology is most successful when it is integrated with process improvement and enables a fact-based solution to a business problem or challenge. The problem is that process improvement and continuous improvement keeps falling out of the implementation picture. Most of this is driven by leadership's perception of saving time and money, or a plan to implement the hardware and software portion of the project first, and return to the process improvement needs at a later date. The process improvement portion is usually the first casualty and postponed indefinitely, while users blame IT for their inefficiencies. Without concurrent process reengineering or improvement, IT can often create additional and more widely spread process issues across the organization. Most have lived through the results: workarounds, firefighting, offline spreadsheets, conflicting data, hot list meetings, factory and distribution shut-downs, and many other forms of waste.

In the future, organizations must view and actually implement their IT investments as *improvement through enabling technology*. A large number of CIOs believe that they and their organizations are already acting in this manner, but they are not. They may embrace improvement through enabling technology in concept, but they do not evaluate and deploy technology in a *documented value enhancement* manner. Organizations such as IBM, Oracle, SAP, and others are providing IT consulting services, but these services are too tilted toward acquiring technology and not focused enough on improving competitiveness and financial well-being. Overlaying technology on bad processes may produce some structural benefits, but it usually automates the ability to create business problems faster. Technology may be marketed as a productivity tool, and in many cases, specific applications accomplish this objective. The added value of technology comes down to how people and organizations choose to use it. For example, Minitab statistical software is a great enabler of personal productivity, standardization of analysis, and Lean Six Sigma improvement. But the value is derived from how people use Minitab on their improvement projects and other analysis in daily work.

Quantifying the value and benefits of the larger scale integrated solutions such as ERP, CRM, and the total integrated suite of business architecture is a bit more of a challenge. Organizations have not taken the time, patience, and the efforts to plan and implement their IT investments in a value-enhancing manner. Ninety-nine percent of the problems with IT involve people and how they choose to implement technology. Only a tiny portion is due to hardware or software problems. If organizations hope to get a better ROI on their IT investments, they need to make the component of strategic process improvement a major factor in the requirements definition, evaluation, feasibility, and deployment processes.

Technology Is Evolving Quickly

On the other hand, IT is moving so quickly that organizations cannot afford to postpone these investments or they will fall behind quickly. Technology will continue to develop at speeds that will make today's digital applications look like a 1930's NCR mechanical cash register. Currently, there is a widening gap between what universities provide and what industries need—IT and technology is moving faster than our ability to educate, deploy, and improve. The latest trends include network and desktop virtualization and cloud computing, and a host of other emerging digitization capabilities.

A company's IT infrastructure has to keep pace with the evolution of this technology and growth of corporate business—or the company will lose the agility that has made it successful. The challenge becomes this: how does an organization introduce IT and process changes concurrently so the investment produces a positive ROI? Time to value is becoming a major metric for IT investments.

As we mentioned earlier, the components of strategic leadership and vision can benefit this process. It is most important to understand what issue an organization is trying to solve in their business and how an investment in IT can enable the achievement of success. What are the solutions that will best support your business strategy, and what value can be achieved? Quantifying IT decisions and the anticipated returns can be the hardest hurdle to overcome. Setting the stage for management investment approvals includes a thorough review of risk mitigation and deployment challenges and an understanding of best practices and the desired "to-be" state, as well as benchmarking business processes, both inside and outside your industry. All of these items contribute to a solid business case and return on investment, and they are necessary to achieve the consensus and resource allocation for the project.

Technology Entrapment

First, the evolution of technology is a beautiful thing. Today, most people cannot figure out how they worked 25 years ago without their laptops, e-mail, iPhones, iPods, Blackberrys, iPads and other personal devices. Back then, a pager and an executive assistant familiar with Microsoft Office was a technology blessing. The same is true in personal life with the routine presence of on-board computers and GPS in automobiles, smart toasters, networked home and automotive security systems, communicating gauge clusters in off-road construction equipment, home theaters, massaging shower stalls, and a variety of other developments. Now it is possible to view a video that continuously reports about your 16-year-old son's driving performance. Technology is beginning to manifest itself in every part of our lives, not just at work or the home office, but in religion, politics, social events, parent-teacher conferences, building new friendships, our love lives, and how we keep our secrets. Recently a teen from Brooklyn, NY received an award for the most text messaging: over 6,000 per month on average. We are in the infancy of this technology evolution as people connect and choose how they will be changed.

There is an emerging trend that causes some concern, and people hope that it is just part of the learning process. But just as we stated, technology and process must go hand in hand. Technology is an enabler of process, and it should not be confused with a replacement for process, and in particular, the process of thinking and reasoning IT and InfoTech applications are significantly impacting every day how people work in organizations. Think about a typical day at the office. People attend a meeting and are guided through a PowerPoint presentation while reading and responding to e-mails on their laptop, texting on their Blackberry, and answering their cell phone. A few attendees videoconference into the meeting and sometimes forget that others can view what they are doing. Sometimes there are groups of people in a conference room totally silent, but busy e-mailing and texting other associates. Later, as one meeting attendee takes the family out for a relaxing dinner, they find the restaurant is loaded with people conversing at their tables while communicating with other people via cell phones, e-mails, and texts. These same activities occur inside business conference rooms every day. No matter where we are these days (work, the mall, freeway, grocery store, your son's karate class, Sunday mass, etc.) we are likely to either observe others communicating, or hear a digital ring of a cell phone or alert for an email or text message. *Technology entrapment* is the use of technology in a manner that creates a perception of productivity, improvement, and accomplishment. Technology has increased the ability to multitask, which has increased the practice of multitasking. This is also promoting question-answer behaviors that are not always based on the facts. Another way of saying this is that multitasking may be replacing some level of root-cause thinking with an instant gratification game of opinions and perceptions. Numerous studies from MIT and other institutions are indicating that the more people multitask, the less effective they are on every single task, and the less effective they are overall. Multitasking provides a false sense of productivity because a lot of activities are getting accomplished, but the process promotes an intuitive, self-confident, reactionary mode of leadership and execution.

The answer is by no means to stop the evolution of technology, but to marry technology with process (once again), as it should be to produce the most successful results. When technology and process are allowed to diverge, waste and nonvalue-added effort emerges as false productivity from processes. For example, many organizations are still struggling with the basic issues of ERP such as inventory accuracy, master data accuracy, configuration management, planning parameters, sales and operations planning effectiveness, delivery performance, launching orders and expediting inside lead time, capacity overloads and backlogs, a kluge of spreadsheets, days full of informational meetings, and many other wastes. Over 25 years ago, subject matter experts like Oliver Wight, Jim Burlingame, Walter Goddard, and George Plossl were talking about the same issues at APICS conferences. With more people using technology, organizations are actually introducing the opportunity for more variation in core business processes. These are not technology issues. These issues revolve around the lack of fusion of technology and process discipline, and the choices about how to integrate and use technology as an enabler of strategic success.

Technology is creating many other changes that impact the workplace. People come to work today (but not necessarily physically) and plug into their own detached cyberspaces. Technology as it exists today has done great things, but is reducing the interpersonal and social content of work. Some claim that these relationships are no different in cyberspace, but they are for sure. For example, IBM's Westchester office was built in 1988 to house thousands of employees, and today on any given day, it is a ghost town. There are still a large number of employees, but they are working from their homes, automobiles, a customer's or vendor's site, Starbucks, or Panera Bread!

This is the new norm for IBMers, and they openly admit to the loss of interpersonal and social content of the office. Future technologies at IBM and other places are already working on improving these relationships through cyber technology, and IBM and MIT are developing simulated cyber conference capabilities where participants can digitally gain back the human interaction element of communication. Developers are forecasting the future and discussing the ability to talk and translate different languages in real time. Early signs of this evolving capability demonstrate that people will be able to meet face-to-face in cyberspace regardless of geography, language barriers, and other constraints.

Imagine six people in a cyber meeting, all talking in their native language (which is being translated in real time for all other participants), where everyone can interact with each other, share exhibits and other documents, and fully understand the conversation! There already has been initial feedback on this developing technology regarding perceptions of how people are viewed by others in cyberspace, much as it would matter if they were in the same room.

The transition to cyber technology is easy for 5 to 18 year olds who, according to recent studies, spend more than 50 hours per week in digital space. This continuation of technology not only changes the way people work, but it also changes the way people think, behave, and live. Think about the typical middle class household: the husband or wife returns home from a day of work only to find their spouse on the Internet looking for a recipe while texting a friend and the children are at the kitchen table—also on the Internet—doing their homework. Most parents make the effort to monitor and control where their children go on the Internet because it is like a large city. It has good safe neighborhoods and bad neighborhoods, or good people and bad people. Later, they all go out for ice cream, and the husband checks on the dog on his iPhone via the Web-enabled home security system. The following Saturday, the husband goes deer hunting using his handheld GPS to locate the tree stand and digital scouting cameras, and checks the memory stick for any recent sightings in the area. Life is good.

Technology always requires the balance of good and bad. In Asia, for example, there is an epidemic of teens skipping school and spending 8–24 hours in digital cafes playing cyberspace war and other violent games. They are playing these games with the seriousness of a real war, competing against other players whom they have never met, or have no idea where in the world they live. These teens have become cyber junkies—the technology has become as addictive as alcohol and drugs. Some teens have died in the café chairs from playing games so long without food and water. There are even rehabilitation clinics where some of these teens are sent to break their addiction to cyber games. Many believe that technology is modifying behaviors in younger people—encouraging them to demand and expect instant gratification. The tough work of research and analytics is being replaced by the question-answer process via the Web, texts, e-mails, or other digital media. These embedded technology norms will significantly impact how young people think and behave in the future.

Taking available technology for granted without thinking may cause the most harmful behavior changes for children. We are creating a society where people think they can do anything with the sole effort of Google, Twitter, or direct texting. Children are using technology in many cases as an *ends* rather than a *means* (or enabler) to the end. At a very minimum, it may be helpful to supplement children's use of technology with other considerations shown in Figure 15.2. Just because something shows up on a display, does not mean it is the truth or the facts. Regardless of what technology is available, people must not forget that they still need to *think* and go through the basics of listening to and synthesizing information, drawing the right conclusions from information, making the right decisions, taking the right actions with the information, and making sure that technology is working well as an enabler of whatever they are trying to accomplish.

Technology and Organizational Learning

The tough thing about technology lies in its deployment, which is not an exact science. Software applications are developed by brilliant, intelligent people but who may not actually work on a daily basis in the applications areas they design or who might overlook many TGWs (Things that can Go Wrong). It is much more difficult to quantify the total costs and benefits of IT investments because

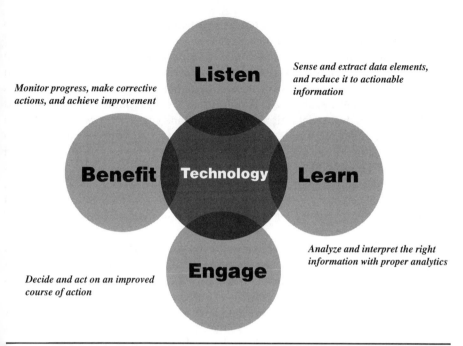

Figure 15.2   Digital thinking for children.

there are so many unknowns. There are also consequences for inaction, which are also fuzzy and unknown. Nevertheless, organizations need to stop spending money on IT expenditures based on emotion and look at the real data-driven facts. Many IT investments of the past have been rationalized by emotion and downside risk. Blindly investing in IT with questionable to no benefits is pushing organizations toward the same behaviors as Obama's emergency stimulus package spending, only on a much smaller scale.

There are no doubts that IT investments are a wicked problem as discussed in Chapter 9. IT challenges are typically characterized by significant ambiguity and uncertainty, no single correct and fixed definition of the problem, multiple views about the problem with conflicting solutions, a lack of information, different participants with different motivations, and multiple connections to other problems. Indeed, it is this *social complexity* of IT investments, not their technical complexity, that overwhelms most current problem solving and project management approaches. The need for IT investment and wicked problems in general start off as a *mess*—a complicated issue that is not clearly defined or formulated. Many of these planned improvement initiatives via enabling IT are dealing with dynamic and extremely complex problems that are difficult to define and solve. The more people with different views and objectives collaborating on a particular IT initiative, the more socially complex the initiative becomes. This is referred to as *fragmentation*. The only response to fragmentation is to create shared understanding and commitment, and team cohesion.

The nature of many IT investments is about first moving from chaos to some level of order, and then maximizing the probability of customer, market, and user community success—all while closely managing and minimizing time, costs, economic uncertainties, and risks. These factors can and should be identified and monitored through the definition, justification, and implement phases of IT expenditures. Another related area that can be improved is in the continuous monitoring and evaluation of the deployment process, rather than waiting until the organization is buried in implementation issues, time delays, and budget overrun problems. A micromanaged and microcontrolled implementation is the right best practice for wicked problems. There are plenty of opportunities for organizations to learn from their past mistakes and improve the financial performance of IT investments.

One organization in particular, has deployed technology successfully to enable a more effective and efficient new product development process. They have been at this for three years at a managed pace, learning and benefitting as they go. As one might expect, their accomplishments were not derived from rocket science. This organization has developed a detailed intranet product development application. Each product as well as the required process steps, the person responsible, the deliverable, and due dates reside in the application.

Several templates have also been developed to standardize subprocesses and deliverable expectations. When engineers do not respond with any information or updates, flags are generated as if activities have not begun yet. The traditional green-yellow-red analogy has been built into this application as well. When tasks are near completion, yellow flags are generated as a reminder and as a prompt about meeting due dates. Red flags are generated for shut-the-process-down conditions, where groups immediately caucus face-to-face or in cyberspace to make the necessary decisions and get projects back on track. At any given moment, leadership and development teams have instant visibility on the status of all development projects, resource workloads, open issues lists and corrective actions, current business case information, and pro forma financial projections if everything is executed to plan. This product development organization has a high-level individual who acts as the global master planning, scheduling and sourcing resource in a manufacturing environment.

They have also evolved the old-fashioned visual management techniques using technology and real-time performance dashboards. Their visual management process views project status, the status of activities for individual resources, and sourcing and supplier status. Rather than purchasing and force fitting a technology application on the organization, they are achieving great success by integrating leadership, technology, and business process improvement.

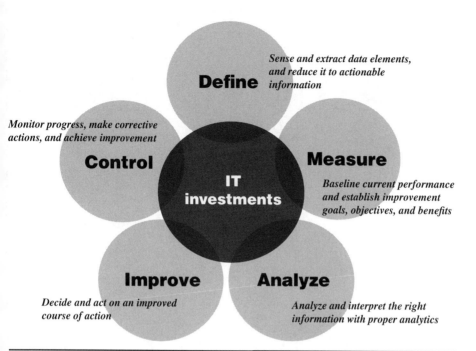

Figure 15.3   A business case study using the DMAIC methodology.

Support Technology with a Business Case

One area that needs improvement in the future is the development of better business cases for IT investments. IT investments have grown to represent as much as 3 percent or more of total revenues in many organizations. Therefore, IT performance has a high degree of leverage on financial performance. A business case is created for most improvement projects using the DMAIC methodology (see Figure 15.3). As we have mentioned numerous times, the largest advantage of DMAIC is discipline, standardization, and a common business improvement language. In this chapter, we are pointing out that IT is no different from other improvement methodologies. It should be viewed this way by executives and decision makers. Lean Six Sigma and IT are two enablers of improvement. Another powerful lesson about improvement is that the more an organization integrates the enablers, the higher the benefits of improvement. All of these enablers must be supported and driven by a business case.

Many transactional Lean Six Sigma projects have focused on this particular area by developing standardized processes, information templates, evaluation analytics, and performance metrics. Then they have piloted and followed new IT requests and investment plans through their new process with much improved results. Remember, this is not an exact science. The integration of business process improvement and discipline make this front-end IT activity more robust. This is but one of dozens of possible Lean Six Sigma projects in the IT area. What

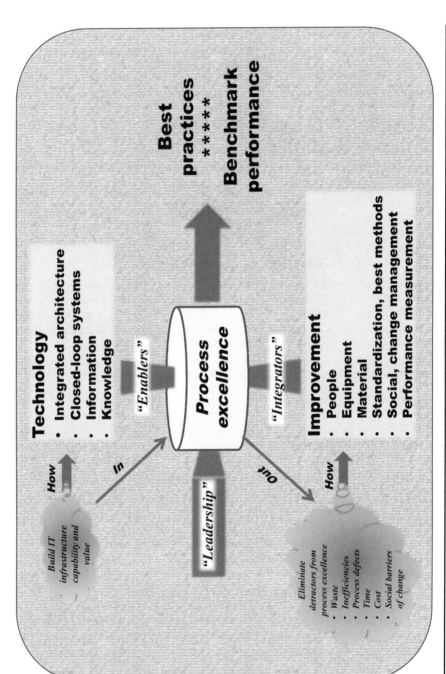

Figure 15.4 Drivers of best practices.

is meant by success was not necessarily a 250 percent ROI, but a much better understanding of the specific strategic issue, objectives, scope, a thorough cost and benefit analysis and risk assessment, resource requirements, and an agreed upon implementation approach. This may not seem like much, but this level of discipline on the front end of IT projects increases the probability of success and value enhancement significantly.

Technology Plus Improvement Equals Success

This concept has been discussed and agreed upon in concept since the introduction of minicomputers, PCs, and word processing networks. Yet the business process improvement piece keeps falling out of the equation. For vendors, the sale of servers and software applications generate revenues, and they did not want to slow down their time-to-revenue with business process improvement. This removal of business process improvement has also removed the accountability for results, leaving everyone pointing fingers at each other. From the user perspective, business process improvement would have slowed down the implementation, and the current processes were viewed to be good enough for now.

IT is no different from producing scrap on the manufacturing floor, redesigning new products via several wasteful process swirls, or replacing defective product in the field. It all comes back to that familiar adage, "We don't have time to do the right things right the first time, but we always seem to find time (and money) to do things over."

The drivers of best practices (see Figure 15.4) include this fusion of technology and improvement, which are inseparable if an organization wishes to achieve best practices and benchmark performance. If we return to the basic definition of industrial engineering in Chapter 1, it is the *integrated systems of people, money, knowledge, information, equipment, energy, material, and process.* This definition needs to be updated to include the word *technology*, because the focus of improvement is shifting from equipment, facilities, and other physical processes to digital transactional and cyber-enterprise processes. Leadership is always the engine of process excellence: executive behaviors, decisions, and action determine how technology and improvement is deployed throughout the organization. Leadership defines the limits of improvement. Leadership provides the means of defining and managing processes, and sets the capability of these processes for the organization. The performance of the organization is only as good as the processes that leadership has provided for them. This is Deming 101, Improvement 101.

Technology is the front door, the touch points, and all entry and exit points of these transactional processes. Technology provides the *enablers* of process in the form of the integrated enterprise architecture and other fully integrated applications. These are enablers because they are the means of adding in and building IT infrastructure and value, not the ends. The trouble with many technology-based deployments is that hasty and overanxious people treat technology as the ends—the quick cure all and end all to the organizations problems. Improvement provides the *integrators* of process including people, best methods, standardized procedures and policies, change management, and performance management. Improvement defines a vision for process excellence (including the integration of enabling IT), and then removes the detractors of process excellence. These may include inefficiencies, waste, process defects, time, cost, and social barriers to change.

By themselves, technology and improvement are suboptimized attempts to drive business process improvement. Technology without improvement enables people to automate bad processes and make more mistakes more quickly, thereby adding to the waste and nonvalue-added workaround activities. Improvement without technology creates a perception of improvement, but the results are merely a snapshot of a moment that lacks flexibility, responsiveness, and the continuous flow of information to reeingineer processes to accommodate ever-changing customer and market demands. For example, this is why most Lean efforts that involve manual kanbans, fixed cell designs, perfectly balanced progressive assembly stations, static work instructions, manual storyboards, and defined build rates fall apart as soon as new products are introduced, or customer replenishment requirements change.

Most antiquated, mechanically managed Lean efforts cannot be reengineered quickly enough to address ever-changing requirements evolving from the new economy. Lean, Six Sigma, and other improvement initiatives need to transform themselves into more targeted on-demand improvement activities driven by customers and markets via the IT infrastructure. It is this correct fusion and deployment of technology and improvement that drives process excellence and achieves best practices and benchmark performance. There really is no justification to implement technology and improvement in some phased sequence, eliminate improvement to save technology implementation time and costs, or implement improvement to save on IT investments. Separating technology is a *pay now, pay more later* decision. Nobody has documented the negative effects of digging out of poorly executed Y2K implementations (some organizations are still digging), but these hidden overhead costs have resulted in poor customer service, inefficient operations, multiple versions of the facts, a kluge of isolated spreadsheets—other nonvalue-added costs are in the millions for most individual organizations. The fusion of technology and improvement is the best way to optimize IT value, avoid these hidden costs, and actually achieve best practices and benchmark performance.

Like many topics in this book, it is time to return to the basics and fuse together improvement and IT. Integration of all improvement methodologies (Kaizen, Lean, Six Sigma, Theory of Constraints, etc.) and enabling technology is the roadmap of future improvement and competitiveness. When an organization chooses to integrate Lean Six Sigma and IT more often, they are able to focus on the larger transactional opportunities and will achieve larger and faster returns on their efforts. Although the recent meltdown has taken its toll on organizations, it has also changed how people and organizations will work in the future—and for the better. One should not be disappointed by all of the great improvement and technology work that has been accomplished up to this point.

Technology is raising the bar to levels that people and organizations never dreamed of—especially Improvement Excellence™—*the mastery of developing and implementing successful strategic and continuous business improvement initiatives, transforming culture, and enabling organizations to improve how they improve.* One cannot help but forecast the technology future, which might include cyber medical care, cyber automobile maintenance, new versions of cyber shopping that might include digitally trying on clothes for fit and look, individually interconnected cyber enterprises, and many other possibilities that are not that far out there.

The CIO role, as mentioned earlier, is becoming more improvement-guru focused, thus, the integration of strategic improvement and IT makes logical sense. Successful organizations will integrate strategic improvement and IT and improve the financial and value-enhancing results of their IT investments. These organizations will also accelerate their strategic improvement initiatives through the integration of IT information and data capabilities, analytics, and real-time performance dashboard capabilities. The improvement folks who are still running around peddling Lean tools and unplugging IT are the new dinosaurs of this new economy.

References

Accenture Consulting. 2010. *Accenture Technology Visions 2010*. Accenture Consulting.

Computer Economics. 2010. 2010/2011 *IT Spending and Staffing Benchmarks*. Executive summary. Computer Economics.

Dretzin, R. 2008. *Growing Up Online*. PBS Frontline documentary, http://www .pbs.org/wgbh/pages/frontline/kidsonline/

Rushkoff, D. 2009. *Digital Nation: Life on the Virtual Frontier*. PBS Frontline documentary. http://www.pbs.org/wgbh/pages/frontline/digitalnation/

Chapter 15 Take Aways

- The chief information officer role is one of the most challenging positions in the organization. CIOs have evolved to a role where they must be part senior executive, part improvement guru, part technology expert, and part financial value creation.
- The new economy is driving the need for more immediate attention and more immediate response. The combination of technology and improvement is enabling organizations to build real-time, interactive supply chains where they manage by the sense-interpret-decide-act-monitor process (SIDAM). Another capability that many organizations have already

embraced is real-time, event-driven metrics, walk-around metrics, or good-day-bad-day metrics. The objective of these real-time performance dashboards is to communicate performance and potential issues in real time so that organizations can SIDAM in more of a prevention mode.

- The future of improvement is in the transactional enterprise and extended enterprise space. Since transactional processes are integrated and interdependent, an improvement in one area provides residual improvements in other areas. The real challenge with improvement is in working one's way through the transactional maze, and in defining and scoping out legitimate, data-driven transactional improvement opportunities. This process relies heavily on information technology more than ever before. With transactional processes, one cannot pick up a part and measure dimensional characteristics to determine defects and quality levels. The improvement expert uses the organization's integrated information architecture (e.g., SAP, Oracle, etc.) to trace the transaction trail like a detective, and constructs the story of the process. This is not your father's Lean or Six Sigma tools at work here.

- IT is a lot like Lean Six Sigma and improvement in general: it can either produce great results or increase overhead spending. In general, executives are slow at grasping this concept, but there is not the best of track records in deploying IT expenditures correctly, producing profitable and justifiable results. IT organizations (and their executive process owners) can benefit by adopting the strategic leadership and vision, deployment planning, and execution infrastructure elements to their larger IT investments and projects.

- Technology is most successful when it is integrated with process improvement and enables a fact-based solution to a business problem or challenge. The problem is that process improvement and continuous improvement keeps falling out of the implementation picture. Most of this is driven by leadership's perception of saving time and money, or a plan to implement the hardware and software portion of the project first, and return to the process improvement needs at a later date. The process improvement portion is usually the first casualty and postponed indefinitely, while users blame IT for their inefficiencies.

- In the future, organizations must view and actually implement their IT investments as *improvement through enabling technology*. Many CIOs believe that they and their organizations are already acting in this manner, but they are not. They may embrace improvement through enabling technology in concept, but they do not evaluate and deploy technology in a *documented value enhancement* manner.

- *Technology entrapment* is the use of technology in a manner that creates a perception of productivity, improvement, and accomplishment. Technology has increased the ability to multitask, which has increased the practice of multitasking. This is also promoting question-answer behaviors that are not always based on the facts. Another way of saying this is that multitasking may be replacing some level of root-cause thinking with an instant gratification game of opinions and perceptions. Numerous studies from MIT and other institutions are indicating that the more people multitask, the less effective they are on every single task, and the less effective they are overall. Multitasking provides a false sense of productivity because a lot of activities are getting accomplished, but the process promotes a hip-shooting mode of leadership. The answer is by no means to stop the evolution of technology, but to marry technology with process as it should be to produce the most successful results.

- One area that needs improvement in the future is the development of better business cases for IT investments. IT investments have grown to represent as much as 3 percent or more of total revenues in many organizations. Therefore, IT performance has a high degree of leverage on financial performance. A business case is created for most improvement projects using the DMAIC methodology. IT is no different from other improvement methodologies. Lean Six Sigma and IT are two enablers of improvement. Another powerful lesson about improvement is that the more an organization integrates the enablers, the higher the benefits of improvement. All of these enablers must be supported and driven by a business case.
- Integration of improvement methodologies (Kaizen, Lean, Six Sigma, Theory of Constraints, etc.) and enabling technology is the roadmap of future improvement and competitiveness. When an organization chooses to integrate Lean Six Sigma and IT more often, they will achieve larger and faster returns on their efforts.

Guest Article Contribution

Paul Matthews leads the L.E.K. Operations Practice. He has over 25 years of experience in developing and executing operations, manufacturing, and supply chain strategies around the world for Fortune 100 companies. Prior to his current position, Paul was a partner responsible for Accenture's Supply Chain practice and vice president of supply chain management at Limited Brands.

Bring on the Basics
Paul Matthews
Senior Vice President
L.E.K. Consulting

How Can We Screw Up Something So Simple?

How complicated can it be to coordinate the planning, purchasing, production, and delivery of products to our customers? What used to be a simple sequence of events—now known as supply chain management (SCM)—has become increasingly complex.

In this article, I will outline ways that organizations can get back to basics, remembering that the fundamentals are the foundation of any successful supply chain management strategy. First, we will explore some of the history that got us to where we are today.

Requirements for the Supply Chain are Continuing to Grow

As the supply chain continues to evolve and become more complex, the requirements for successful supply chain management are becoming more rigorous. Until recently, our supply chain management vocabulary was dominated by box kicking and label licking. Now, terms such as visibility, agility, real-time, collaboration, and responsiveness are becoming commonplace. The bar for supply chain management is being raised to new levels. Customer expectations are increasing, product lifecycles are becoming shorter, and regulatory requirements are changing. Connectivity with customers and partners, which was once just nice to have, is now becoming a prerequisite for success.

Further, global economic forces are driving change with new enabling technologies and a significant increase in market volatility. Although globalization is not a new challenge to supply chain management, it is now harder than ever to ignore. China, a country of more than 1.4 billion people, is considered to be one of the best *low cost country sourcing* channels. Although the country has faced notable setbacks, its dominant position in low cost sourcing is not going away anytime soon. Leveraging value from a truly global marketplace can bring significant rewards, but only if the end-to-end supply chain is integrated and robust. As the economy continues to recover from the global recession of 2007 through 2009, mergers and acquisitions will reemerge and the definition of the end-to-end supply chain will begin to cloud.

Going forward, we will continue to face new twists to old challenges. Change in business has become inherent and it is up to business leaders to manage and adapt to their changing environment. We will be expected to quickly adapt to volatile energy prices, changes in global economic conditions, and environmental shifts. Further, we will be expected to react with transparency to both manufactured and natural catastrophes, such as the September 11th terrorist attacks and the 2010 BP Gulf of Mexico oil spill.

New Technologies and Capabilities Dominate the Supply Chain

New technologies and capabilities are beginning to dominate supply chain management. Companies are beginning to leverage sophisticated tools to transform data into intelligence. RFID, for example, has progressed from a bulky, cumbersome, and expensive chip (originally designed as an asset management tool) to an affordable micro device that facilitates inventory accuracy, traceability, and the flow of merchandise through stores. This technology allows companies to reduce shrinkage and is pivotal in allowing connectivity to the customer.

Similarly, scan-based trading that uses point-of-sale (POS) scan data to drive product replenishment, promotion, and settlement between the company and its trading partners is being used by retailers to free up capital, eliminate inventory investment, reduce labor costs, increase sales, and improve the accuracy of invoicing and payment. Advanced optimization planning software is also beginning to become commonplace in supply chain management. The software is being used by companies to support decision making, solve strategic and tactical supply chain business problems, and provide virtual connected end-to-end supply chain.

These tools serve as a representative sample of new technologies and capabilities dominating supply chain management today. They are effectively changing the landscape of supply chain management, a function that was once simplistic and technologically unsophisticated.

How the Supply Chain Role has Changed and Is Changing (People)

The role of the supply chain has evolved from a tactical cost-focused warehousing and transportation function to a seat in the executive suite advising and influencing every element of the global value chain from product development to customer intimacy. Companies have begun to create the role of chief supply chain officer (CSCO) to include supply chain management on their strategic agendas as a way to differentiate themselves from their competitors. Retail powerhouses Walmart and Sears are now led by executives with supply chain backgrounds.

Global supply chain networks are now having to ensure the efficient and effective operation of governments and corporate enterprises around the globe, heightening the focus on who in the organization is managing the supply chain and how they are addressing the complex balance required to leverage the low-cost options of global sourcing and manufacturing against the environmental impact of global distribution.

How Processes Are Evolving

Supply chain processes have also transformed over the last few decades from a discreet set of functional siloed activities to collaborative and integrated activities that often begin with the customer. The sales and operations function has hit its stride in the last few years as companies have increased their emphasis on the financial impacts of scenarios that evaluate alternative demand or supply plans. Companies that are using demand-driven supply networks leverage both technology and processes to sense and react to demand in real time across a network of customers. Suppliers attribute the dramatic financial results to its supply chain management.

The term *Lean*, which has often been associated with automotive manufacturing, is another example of how processes are evolving. The companies that have embraced the lean principles of Six Sigma and TQM have benefited from significant improvements across all elements of the supply chain and the bottom line.

As Companies are Responding, There Are Some Great Examples of Supply Chain Excellence

Several organizations have demonstrated remarkable responsiveness to the evolving requirements of supply chain management. Dell has demonstrated supply chain excellence by developing a supply chain strategy focused on reducing costs, while at the same time supporting a business strategy emphasizing customer service. In the late 1980s and early 1990s, Dell carried 20 to 25 days of inventory in a sprawling network of warehouses and call centers as its primary sales channel. However, the emergence of the Internet called for more differentiation and a fundamental change to its global supply chain. Today, Dell has no warehouses and carries no more than two hours of inventory in its factories. Virtually all of its products are made to order. Given the short product lifecycles of computer components, reducing inventory is nearly a financial imperative for computer hardware manufacturers, and in this case, results in significant cost of goods advantages for Dell.

Apple has also demonstrated superiority in supply chain management. The company has benefited from exceptional intimacy with its customers, resulting in products and services that are consistently relevant to its customers' preferences and expectations. In some instances, Apple has actually succeeded in creating relevancy by utilizing customer connectivity combined with innovative technology and creative genius. Gaining a clear understanding of customer demand and providing differentiated products to satisfy it are critical in today's economy. Like Apple, Cisco has truly embraced the need for supply chains to be more-customer driven. The company has implemented several process changes designed to achieve an external-facing customer-centric value chain organization. Internal metrics of performance such as cost, quality, delivery, and speed have been converted to customer-focused metrics such as perfect order, customer service, customer satisfaction, and gross margin.

Over the last four decades, the supply chain has made incredible strides. Today, we are able to do remarkable things that were unthinkable several years back. We are able to:

- Predict revenue per square inch in a retail store
- Have visibility into our suppliers' suppliers' suppliers' supply chain
- Trigger a payment and replenish the shelves as the product is scanned at the POS
- Track the virtual whereabouts of products in mere seconds

But for most companies, this has not come without setbacks...

We Have Demonstrated That When We Get Setbacks, We Can Recover

The vast majority of companies have not succeeded in flawless execution of supply chain excellence. Though most have hit bumps in the road during their journey, many have bounced back to become even stronger than ever before. Examples include:

- *The FoxMeyer's Lights Out Warehouse*—Implementation of its new order management and warehouse systems brought the company to a standstill due to its inability to ship product. Bankruptcy and the sale of the multi-billion dollar drug wholesaler followed in the mid-1990s.
- *The 14-month delay in opening the Denver International Airport in 1993*—Its highly automated, hugely expensive bagging system failed, costing $1 million per *day* in interest and operational expenses in addition to the $200 million expense for the system itself.
- *Hershey's Halloween Nightmare in 1999*—Startup problems and software bugs idled Hershey's order management and shipping systems, causing Hershey to miss out on a critical Halloween season. The downtime caused $150 million in lost revenue as its stock dropped more than 30 percent.

The Challenges Are Not Getting Any Easier, But Perhaps We Have Lost Sight of the Basics

After more than 30 years as a supply chain operator and consultant across several different industries and global geographies, I am seeing a phenomenon that I have labeled *bring on the basics*. To illustrate the trend, here are a few personal and professional examples of how we forget the fundamentals.

A friend recently told me a story that illustrates this point well. My friend asked his daughter to turn off the television. After multiple requests, she gave him a frustrated look and exclaimed, "But Dad, I can't find the remote."

The thought of pushing a power button on the physical television was so foreign to her that it made me begin to question—have we lost sight of the fundamentals? Have we become so reliant on technology that we no longer rely on our own common sense?

Similarly, a few years ago, a good friend of mine built a magnificent beach house on 20-foot stilts, constructed of the strongest wooden material available. The solar powered, luxury home was built using the most up-to-date technology and was built to weather the most aggressive storms and hurricanes. So much emphasis was placed on the house that no one thought of the annual chemical treatment required to prevent the pillars from rotting or corroding. If not for an off-the-cuff comment, a near catastrophe could have occurred. Again, get the foundation right first. In this case, that was literally true.

These experiences in my own personal life are similar to many of the experiences that I see as a supply chain strategy consultant. A few years ago, I was sitting in a client meeting with a company's CEO and his direct reports. The CEO asked the head of production control about the delivery status of a critical part that was expected to arrive that morning. The head of production control responded by checking his laptop for a delivery status. Two minutes later, the head of production control still had no response. He then called someone on his cell phone, and sent an e-mail from his Blackberry. Finally, he opened the conference room door and asked his assistant to find the head of shipping and ask him to call. He then told the CEO that he would have the answer shortly. At this point, the CEO was fuming. He jumped out of his seat, grabbed the head of production control, led him by the arm, and said, "Let's go take a look on the shipping dock, shall we?"

Three minutes later, the two men returned with confirmation that the part was on the dock and had in fact arrived on time. What I found most interesting was that the production control head had made four different attempts using his various modes of technology, but it never occurred to him to do the obvious, which would have produced a faster (and perhaps more accurate) answer. So, bring on the basics! Think about how often you have heard (or said) the following:

- The system is down, we cannot ship anything until the system comes back up
- The system says that we are out of stock, yet the warehouse is full of the exact SKU that is supposedly depleted
- We have terra bytes of data but no information
- I sent him three e-mails last week and have gotten no reply

Answer these questions:

- Do you e-mail or call colleagues who sit in the next office?
- When was the last time you spoke to or met a customer?
- How many times have you sat in a meeting discussing the shortage of SKU 12345, yet have no idea what SKU 12345 actually is?
- How often do you receive a spreadsheet or report and delete or throw it into the trash without opening it?
- When entering data, do you understand where it came from or where it is going—and most importantly, what it does?
- How often are you paralyzed when the system goes down?

The phenomena that I see evolving in the supply chain is not related to software, technology, demand signals, or demographics, but more fundamental issues that provide the foundational pillars of today's sustainable supply chains. History is populated with examples of great companies that have overlooked the fundamentals of supply chain management.

Polaroid, a technology company that was the brainchild of founder Edwin Land in 1943, reached revenues of over $2.4 billion at its peak. It was often regarded to be the company with the best film manufacturing plants and was credited with supply chain innovations such as its shipping decision support model that optimized its transportation costs. The company failed, however, on a basic tenant of strategy—monitoring advances of technology used in its business. By the time Polaroid discovered advances in digital technology, the Polaroid chemical technology had become obsolete. The company began to manufacture digital cameras, but it was too late in the game—other manufacturers gained market share and Polaroid was unable to compete.

In fact, the root cause of many significant company issues can be traced back to overlooking fundamental supply chain principles. In addition to Polaroid, a few other companies who were once considered to be on the leading edge in supply chain management have experienced recent troubles:

- The much publicized quality control troubles of Toyota's sticking accelerator pedal
- The different releases of the same software that cost Airbus billions in lost profit
- The quick bankruptcy of WebVan, the first online grocery delivery company, after a massive investment in automated warehouses that drained capital that could not be justified by demand

Supply Chain Challenges Are Here to Stay

So, it is clear that supply chain management is becoming increasingly complex and its challenges are here to stay. But there is also a tremendous opportunity for companies to get it right, get back to basics, and leverage supply chain management excellence to be market leaders. I think there are three key areas on which companies should focus:

1. Building a leading supply chain organization
2. Information, not data
3. Product relevancy to the customer

While companies certainly need to shorten product to cycle times and deal with globalization, if they overlook the supply chain fundamentals and forget to lick and apply the label to the box, we are not going anywhere.

The Supply Chain Organization

Today's CSCOs typically have global management experience, are strategic decision makers, and have deep cross-functional expertise. With this kind of strong leadership, there is no question that the supply chain organization has evolved from the historical box-kicking and label-licking function of years ago to both having a seat at the table in the executive suite and influencing corporate strategy.

The key now is to build the optimal organization to support that leadership. While great strides have been made to elevate this function, there is still plenty of opportunity to raise the bar even further and have this function provide a sustainable corporate advantage. In fact, a recent study highlighted that among the participating companies, only 15 percent had a CSCO or chief logistics officer, and another 62 percent had an executive or senior vice president responsible for SCM. The remaining 23 percent rely on a vice presidential level individual to control SCM functions. So there is still opportunity for growth.

There is no one organizational model for success. In fact, supply chain organization models can vary across industry and size of company. Centralized, decentralized, and center-led organizational structures each bring different attributes and relevancy. CSCOs should build his or her organization based on a clearly articulated supply chain vision and should consider matching the best structure for the organization's geographic presence, nonintegrated acquisition, and other relevant factors.

CSCOs should also align the organization with people's skills and expertise, the company culture, and the corporate strategy. It is critical to assure that the right people are in the right jobs and that teams have the right numbers and have assessed skills and backgrounds systematically before migrating to the new supply chain organization and placing names in seats.

Finally, supply chain organizations should be built around the existing culture instead of the culture that the leadership desires. Hierarchical operating models, degrees of influence and walking the talk are all critical elements that must be understood and addressed when building the organization construct. In short, all supply chain professionals need to increase their knowledge base and expand their areas of responsibility for a supply chain organization to be effective and successful.

Information, Not Data

Businesses have spent literally billions of dollars to establish data warehouses and build integrated IT infrastructures to process terra bytes of data at lightning speed. The ease and cost to collect and store data has fallen exponentially–hence businesses are amassing vast amounts of data for single transactions and are becoming increasingly reliant on the information this data is generating. So many of today's businesses are data rich—they have more raw data than ever, yet they rarely process it or convert it successfully into useful information.

In addition, businesses spend millions of dollars on integrated IT systems only to find after implementation that many functions are still using standalone Excel spreadsheets or Access databases to crunch the data. Not only have they failed to collaborate with the business to understand the information that is needed from the processed data, but they have also underestimated the user's resistance to new technology.

So, what most organizations miss is that it is not about the quantity of the data—it is about the quality of information that the data can provide. Organizations who understand this distinction will win, and those that can convert data to actionable information will:

- Build a better learning curve into the new technology rollout, and focus as much (or more) on training and organizational change needs as an organization does on technology requirements.
- Help enable collaboration between business leaders and IT, as data must be processed correctly and combined with human knowledge to create useful information.
- Improve data integrity (more data does not necessarily mean better business decisions). The old adage "garbage in and garbage out" highlights the fact that if the data is wrong, so is the information you are receiving, regardless of how much data you have, and how fast you can transact.

Product Relevancy to the Customer

It is becoming increasingly challenging to bring new and relevant products to market. Today's consumers are more sophisticated; product development time is now shorter; and competition is fiercer than ever. Few will disagree with Apple's capability to consistently churn out new and relevant products, and much has been written about its successful design-led innovation culture. But in truth, much of what makes Apple successful is sticking to fundamental product development practices.

Many companies that have invested in new product development and product lifecycle management technology and processes around a functional silo have failed to integrate or leverage enterprise-wide business processes, often resulting in irrelevant or noncompliant products.

Information is so critical in getting the right product into the market at the right time. The companies that truly get this right know that information needs to flow both ways, and they know that their supply chain organization is best qualified to know whether a particular shape or size for a product has implications beyond cost. So, a great product development process integrates the supply chain role into this two-way communication process and includes them in discussions about pipelines with stage gates and go-no-go decision points. The supply chain organization is often best positioned to suggest possible alternatives.

Getting from Here to There—Bring on the Basics!

A friend who is a CIO posed the following issue to me the other day: "How do I get the organization to understand the role technology can and should play? I feel like we are building a high-performance power train for a chassis and body that has not yet been designed. So when we finish the power train, we will then begin the modifications to integrate with the rest of the car, translating into costly interfaces and complex processes."

Once again, let's get back to basics and look at the whole value chain—physical flows, information, financial flows, systems, business structure and silos, culture—to truly understand what we are doing, instead of solving problems for something that does not yet exist. We need to go back many decades to illustrate this critical point.

One of the most complex and critical supply chain challenges was solved effectively—using not only the basics and fundamentals, but also without the aid of visibility, computer simulations, and forecasting algorithms. The result was one of the greatest examples of a demand-driven supply chain that has changed the world as we know it today!

A catastrophic event wiped out more than 50 percent of the fleet, leaving fewer than 700 in operation. Current production capabilities were below 200 units per month. All raw materials were imported (nothing domestic) and critical demand was 350 units per month (just to cover consumption.)

The tasks were to accelerate production; define and improve the supply chain; create visibility into real-time demand; plan raw materials and resources; and collaborate with suppliers and manufacturers, all in fewer than seven months. Failure was not an option.

The units in question were fighter aircraft. The event was the 1940 World War II Battle of Britain aircraft dog fight over Dunkirk (21 miles from British shores). With the help of Lord Beaverbrook, Winston Churchill, in fewer than seven months, quadrupled the Hurricane and Spitfire fighter aircraft production to nearly 500 units per month.

Even more amazing was that the modern concepts such as modularity, SKU reduction, simplification, and integration were all critical elements of the solution. Data was stored in mechanized filing system for rapid access.

Keep it simple. Bring on the basics.

Epilogue

The primary objective of *Accelerating Lean Six Sigma Results: How to Achieve Improvement Excellence™ in the New Economy* was to create a practical proven roadmap for strategic improvement that can be used by any organization in any industry. From my personal perspective, the contributors to this book include thousands of executives, their organizations, and their associates who have achieved breakthrough and sustainable success with improvement during the past few decades. Their valuable lessons and watermarks have been incorporated throughout this book. Hopefully, I have achieved my objective by providing for you proven and time-tested strategies, leadership, deployment planning, execution, enterprise and extra-enterprise integration, and measurement best practices backed by real world experiences and documented strategic and financial success. Please keep in mind that the key to Improvement Excellence™ is not achieved by blindly following the contents of this book, but in adopting and retrofitting these concepts around your own organization's strategic needs. This adaptation process is not easy or quick-and-dirty; setting a new course for strategic improvement is a core competency in itself.

Leadership is the Greatest Competitive Lever

Some of the early feedback on the manuscript of this book was that it took a tough stance on executives and their leadership and behaviors since the meltdown. First, most organizations are still emerging from the largest recession since the Great Depression. The 2007-2010 period has been a challenging time for all executives who have attempted to lead their organizations with the best of intentions. The tough work of digging out and emerging from this recession has been the largest challenge of many executives' careers. Second, many of the leadership survival behaviors were justified in the early stages of this financial crisis, but placing a freeze on improvement was not one of them. It is blatantly obvious that the only way to become more competitive, more efficient, more customer-focused, and more financially successful as a business and as an organization is to *continuously improve* the current state. Organizations should be improving before, during, and after recessions—and before, during, and after good times—and all other times between these two extremes. It is time to purge leadership comments such as, "There's no money in the budget for improvement," "The time is not quite right for improvement," "We don't have time to improve," "We had to cut back on improvement," "We know how to improve" or "Improvement is not part of my objectives." No doubt, the recent meltdown has churned out many interesting responses in leadership behaviors.

Continuing to lead organizations in the new economy with the leadership direction and behaviors of the meltdown is a sure prescription for failure. A primary purpose of this book was to provide the roadmap for successful and sustaining strategic improvement initiatives, and to raise awareness of the barriers and gaps between current conditions and where organizations need to go in the new economy. The predecessor of recognizing the need to change is awareness. Therefore, coverage of leadership observations and behaviors was never intended to be a criticism: it is a fact and a barrier to Improvement Excellence™ and certainly one that executives have the intelligence and power to overcome. More and more executives are discovering that the new economy requires new thinking, and that the strategies and behaviors that got us here will not get us where we need to go. These are the humbling leadership experiences that lead to greatness with the right choices.

In a recent keynote speaking engagement with over 300 attendees across many industries, I presented several concepts from the book including acceleration entrapment, improvement-dysfunctional organizations, improvement infrastructure, and the 10 Accelerators. When I discussed the slides relating to the characteristics of acceleration entrapment and improvement-dysfunctional organizations, I asked the audience, "How many of their organizations have the presence of these characteristics?"

Not surprisingly, 100 percent of the audience raised their hands—most of them immediately, and some after a few seconds of observing the rest of the audience's responses. The room broke into a verbal and comical rumble as people were making comments such as, "These are the biggest reasons why we can't be successful" or "Are you available to come and talk to our executives about these slides."

Their reactions and responses once again validated the existence of these common barriers to improvement, and confirmed a compelling and widespread need for the changes discussed throughout this book.

A major intention of this book has been to provide a wake-up call to expand the number of executives and their organizations that are on a positive, winning course in the new economy. It is disheartening to watch the diminishing focus on Lean Six Sigma and improvement in general because the upside potential for "improvement" is enormous for every organization. It is also disappointing to observe organizations that were once the flagship business units of their corporations continue to operate with a frenzied version of 1980s or 1990s business models and shrink toward extinction. It is important to mention here that continuous downsizing is not a viable improvement strategy. If it were the case, organizations should lay off everyone and close the doors, which makes no sense at all. Organizations stuck in this Omni slide mode (from Chapter 4) are not actively building the talent pool and capabilities to cash in on these new improvement opportunities and their continued shortsighted survival mode will have serious consequences in the new economy.

Before anything in organizations can change, there must be *recognition of the need* to change. The executive examples and case studies discussed in this book were successful because the CEO and their executive team took the time, effort, and patience to look at their organizations from more of an outside-in perspective. They recognized the need to rethink their own insanity of doing more of the same with greater urgency and effort and expecting different results, and adopt a more contemporary strategic improvement business model. The largest obstacle in organizations is creating this shared recognition of the need to change. Leadership is either the greatest competitive lever or the greatest barrier in this critical milestone. When the CEO and the executive team reach that magic point of recognizing the need to change and agree on a vision for change and commit to the never ending pursuit of change, then great things can begin to happen with strategic improvement.

Again, what may appear to be leadership criticism in this book is not that at all. The underlying purpose has been to provide knowledge and information that helps executives and their organizations to establish this shared recognition of the need to change. The early adopters of this recognition of the need to change (followed by the right choices and actions) will become the superior performers in the new economy.

Strategic improvement is the best way to sprint away from the recent meltdown. It is time to recognize that the supposed economic recovery of 2010–2012 is flat-lined at best, and that organizations must factor this reality into their business assumptions for the next few years.

Waiting for the economy to turn around is a doomed business strategy. Organizations have much more control over their competitive and economic destiny than they normally think they do. The ticket to this successful future is improvement, creativity, and innovation—now! Leading organizations have toughed it out during this recent meltdown while deploying much of the advice in this book. They have emerged from the meltdown in a healthier financial position and continue to positively influence the direction of their own recovery curves. They are also in a much stronger position to cash in on new improvement opportunities. This book has provided you with the necessary advice to recalibrate and reposition your organization for successful and sustainable strategic improvement initiatives, increased global competitiveness, and superior operational and financial performance. The decision to act on the opportunity is up to the collective leadership of your organization.

Scalable Lean Six Sigma™

Strategic improvement initiatives do not have to be structured in the big-bang, top-down, train-the-masses way, and the most successful initiatives are not. Organizations need a more simplified, less overhead intense, sustainable, high impact and high ROI approach to improvement. Scalable Lean Six Sigma™ is the accelerated improvement model that addresses the realities of the new economy, with the primary focus on breakthrough performance and sustaining improvement. Though simplified and streamlined when compared to the traditional overhead-intense approaches, it enables organizations to achieve more rapid and sustainable results. Over the years, the largest lesson learned from strategic improvement initiatives is that success has little to do with the Lean Six Sigma improvement tools themselves, it all has to do with the *process* of how Lean Six Sigma is deployed.

Strategic Leadership and Vision, Deployment Planning, and Execution: The Business Architecture of the 10 Accelerators

Strategic leadership and vision, deployment planning, and execution are the elements of the successful business architecture and foundation of Lean Six Sigma and any other strategic improvement initiative. This is the underpinning of the legitimate core competency of Improvement Excellence™—*The mastery of developing and implementing successful strategic and continuous business improvement initiatives, transforming culture, and enabling organizations to improve how they improve.* Improvement Excellence™ requires the combination of various improvement methodologies (e.g., Kaizen, Lean, Six Sigma, IT, etc.) into a uniform powerhouse initiative, and a broad scope that views and encompasses customers, all transactional and knowledge processes within the organization, and the supply chain as a translucent single enterprise model. The objective of Improvement Excellence™ is to search out, align, and pursue larger strategic breakthrough opportunities that either directly or indirectly benefit this single enterprise model.

The Future: Transactional, Multistage Process Improvement

As mentioned previously, the new economy is accelerating the transformation of organizations into a complex global network of interdependent transactional enterprises. Technology is enabling this transformation faster than most organizations can assimilate it successfully. Many organizations have focused most of their improvement initiatives in the past on their manufacturing operations. Improving yields, reducing cycle times and changeover times, reducing scrap and rework, smoothing out production schedules with pull systems, improving flow through work cells, 5S*ing* the plant, reducing maintenance costs and unplanned downtime, improving supplier quality, visual controls, and the like. While these were and still are valid improvement initiatives, the new economy offers even greater opportunities.

Over the past several years, there have been numerous attempts to apply manufacturing improvement tools and jargon to the office, and not surprisingly, there has not been much success. The tool zealots have attempted to 5S and *lean out* the office areas, revise layouts and information flows, simplify or eliminate redundant documents, or consolidate office supplies. But for the most part these have been either trivial or tiny incremental improvements. There is a simple rule of improvement: wrong problems, wrong information, and wrong improvement tools will equal wrong answer and wrong results.

Instead, think about the waste and nonvalue-adding costs associated with excess obsolete inventory, developing new products that fail in the marketplace, warranty and return costs, product development process waste and poor use of critical resources, failed sales promotions, and on and on. Chapter 14 of this book provided real world examples of transactional process improvement that yielded millions of dollars in hard savings. Creative use of the methodology and tools of Lean Six Sigma allow organizations to dive deep and conduct effective root-cause problem solving. Transactional processes are loaded with hidden costs and inefficiencies that have negative relational impacts on other areas. Transactional processes are extremely complex, multistage processes by nature. Since transactional processes are integrated and interdependent, an improvement in one area provides residual improvements in other areas. The real challenge with improvement is in working one's way through the transactional maze, and in defining and scoping out legitimate, data-driven transactional improvement opportunities. These are opportunities that will have a significant impact on the business and enable multiple successful executions on strategy. Chasing down these opportunities is a bit like a chess game, where the distinction between *cause* and *effect* is dynamic. Chasing down these opportunities also requires deeper leadership, key business process knowledge, and experience with industry best practices. Information technology plays a critical role in the ability to acquire data and recreate scenarios and situational conditions so that the true root causes can be identified. The largest challenge with transactional processes is the isolation of causes and effects. Improving transactional processes requires a much higher caliber of improvement professional with a more strategic view of the organization, deep knowledge of transactional business processes, and a working knowledge of the organization's integrated enterprise architecture.

The Intersection of Leadership, Improvement, and Technology

The rapid emergence of technology is changing the landscape of strategic improvement. Lean Six Sigma and improvement in general will continue to evolve so that it is readily applicable to current and emerging technology, which continues to replace the physical content of traditional improvement with digital organizations and cyber enterprises.

The drivers of Improvement Excellence™ include this fusion of leadership, improvement, and technology, which are inseparable if an organization wishes to achieve best practices and benchmark performance. Leadership is always the engine of process excellence: executive behaviors, decisions, and action determine how technology and improvement is deployed throughout the organization. Leadership provides the means of defining and managing processes, and sets the capability of these processes for the organization. Technology is the front door, the touch points, and all entry and exit points of these transactional processes. Technology provides the *enablers* of process in the form of the integrated enterprise architecture and other fully integrated applications. These are enablers because they are the means of adding in and building IT infrastructure and value, not the ends. Improvement provides the *integrators* of process including people, best methods, standardized procedures and policies, change management, and performance management. Improvement defines a vision for process excellence (including the integration of enabling IT), and then removes the detractors of process excellence. These may include inefficiencies, waste, process defects, time, cost, and social barriers to change. The ultimate objective is to create transparent, nimble business processes that enable people to SIDAM (sense-interpret-decide-act-monitor) in real time. The integration of leadership, technology, and improvement creates a clear enterprise that becomes capable of operating in full prevention mode. By themselves, leadership, technology, and improvement are suboptimized attempts to drive business process improvement. It is this deliberate intersection of leadership, improvement, and technology that is enabling organizations to tap into the gold mine opportunities of multistage transactional processes across the enterprise and extra-enterprise.

Conclusion

Strategic improvement is a fast moving target in the new economy. Improvement has evolved to a commodity of sorts because it exists in some shape or form in most organizations. Many executives treat Lean Six Sigma as a commodity during implementation because they shop around for the lowest cost training option and fail to recognize the most critical success factors of Improvement Excellence™: leadership, strategy, deployment, and execution (these are not commodities). There is a severe false sense of confidence in many organizations that continue to confuse the limited knowledge gained from a public workshop or DVD or the presence of a few improvement tools and storyboards with strategic improvement. It is no longer who is deploying Lean Six Sigma and who is not, because nearly every organization has some level of improvement activity going on at varying degrees of success or failure. In the new economy, the question becomes one of Improvement Excellence™—who is reinventing their business models and improving their current state at a faster rate than that of the competition.

Despite living through the largest recession since the Great Depression, there are more opportunities for improvement for organizations than ever before. The recent meltdown has neutralized many of the previous improvement efforts in organizations, and this is analogous to a short-term leveling of the playing field. Every organization has been in the same recovery boat dealing with similar issues. On the other hand, the challenges of the new economy present endless and much larger opportunities for improvement across the enterprise and extra-enterprise. Think about how annualized cost savings rates of 3 to 10 percent of revenues, plus 10 to 20 percent revenue growth would impact your organization's performance. These represent reasonable and achievable goals for most organizations that wish to remain competitive in the new economy.

Post-recession success is a controllable choice, but it requires a bold change in leadership mindset. Every executive has the potential to step up and lead their organizations to breakthroughs in improvement that were initially thought to be impossible. The front door to these new opportunities is the executive choice of regaining the power of improvement. The remaining and most critical success factors of leadership, strategy, deployment, and execution have been assembled in this book. Those who step up and make the right choices with strategic improvement will control their destinies and be the success stories in the new economy.

This book has free material available for download from the
Web Added Value™ resource center at *www.jrosspub.com*

Index